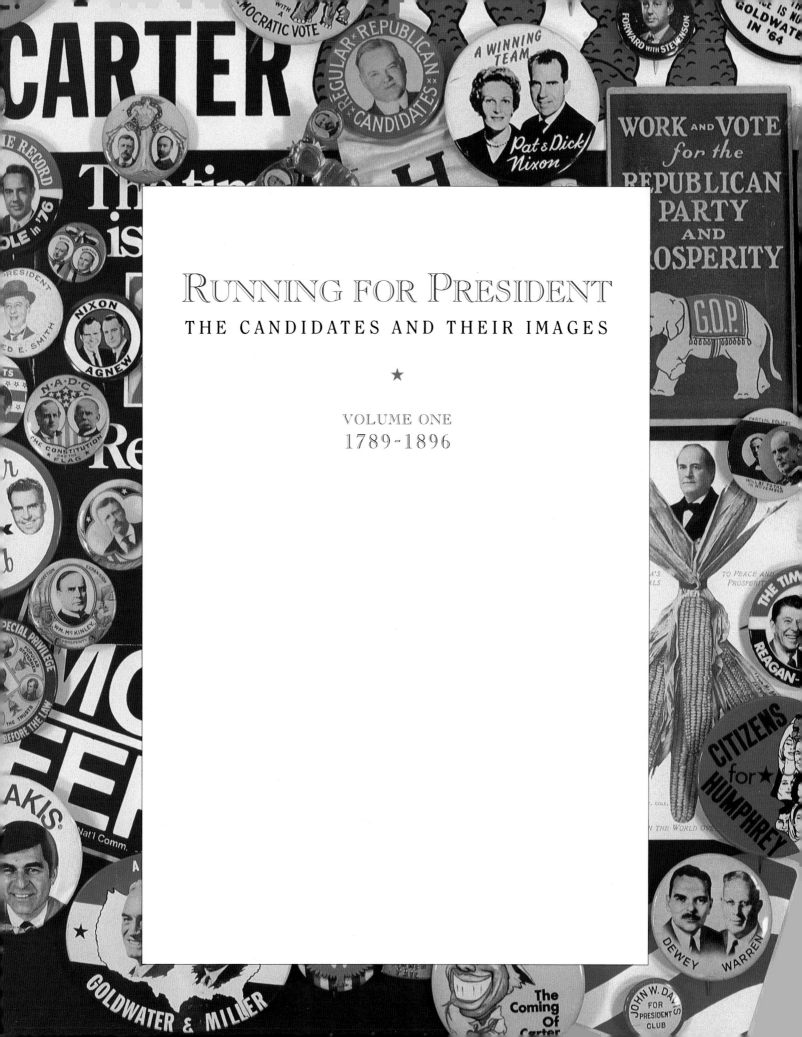

RUNNING FOR PRESIDENT

THE CANDIDATES AND THEIR IMAGES

★

VOLUME ONE
1789-1896

RUNNING FOR PRESIDENT
THE CANDIDATES AND THEIR IMAGES

★

VOLUME ONE
1789~1896

EDITOR

Arthur M. Schlesinger, jr.
Albert Schweitzer Chair in the Humanities
The City University of New York

★

ASSOCIATE EDITORS

Fred L. Israel
Department of History
The City College of New York

David J. Frent
The David J. and Janice L. Frent
Political Americana Collection

A HAROLD STEINBERG BOOK

SIMON & SCHUSTER
A Paramount Communications Company

NEW YORK   LONDON   TORONTO   SYDNEY   TOKYO   SINGAPORE

RUNNING FOR PRESIDENT was originated and prepared by Harold Steinberg and his associates. Grateful acknowledgment to: caption consultants Jonathan H. Mann and Rex Stark; the editorial assistance of Jo-Anne Elikann, Mary McCarthy Steinberg, Barbara Raynor, James Uebbing; photography of the David J. and Janice L. Frent Collection by Jim Dorn; cover photograph of the Jonathan H. Mann Collection by Fred Robertson.

Designed by Susan Lusk

Academic Reference Division
Simon & Schuster
15 Columbus Circle
New York, New York 10023

Printed in Hong Kong

printing number
1 2 3 4 5 6 7 8 9 10

Library of Congress Cataloging-in-Publication Data
     Running for president: the candidates and their images / editor Arthur M. Schlesinger, Jr.;
       associate editors Fred L. Israel, David J. Frent.
          p.   cm.
       "A Harold Steinberg book."
       Includes index.
       Contents: v. 1. 1789–1896 — v. 2. 1900–1992.
        ISBN 0-13-303371-6 (2 v. set : acid-free paper) — ISBN 0-13-303355-4
     (v. 1 : acid-free paper) — ISBN 0-13-303363-5 (v. 2 : acid-free paper).
       1. Presidents—United States—Election—History. 2. United States—Politics and
  government. I. Schlesinger, Arthur Meier, 1917– . II. Israel, Fred L. III. Frent, David J.
     E183.R96 1994
      324 .97309—dc20   93-46386
                                           CIP

The paper in this publication meets the requirements of American National Standards for Information Sciences — Permanence of Paper for Printed Library Materials ANSI Z39.48-1984.

VOLUME ONE
1789–1896

PREFACE

IN HIS PREFACE to the first edition of *History of Presidential Elections* (1884), Edward Stanwood modestly noted that his 407-page volume "professes to be little more than a record of the circumstances of such elections, and of whatever had an appreciable influence upon the result." In the ensuing 109 years abundant monographs have been written dealing with presidential elections. The Library of Congress catalog lists hundreds of titles under the entry "Presidents–U.S. Elections," and it would take a volume larger than Stanwood's just to list the scholarly articles on this subject.

In 1971, Professor Arthur M. Schlesinger, jr. edited a four-volume *History of American Presidential Elections, 1789–1968* and I served as associate editor (a fifth volume followed in 1986). Our goal then, as now, has been to provide a comprehensive history of American presidential elections written by prominent historians and political scientists. This current study is not the definitive word, such a task would be impossible. In a sense, however, we have aimed, like Stanwood, to document the circumstances and effects of such elections.

The emergence of the two-party system by the late 1830s, along with the extension of the franchise, made it necessary for candidates to convey their message directly to the voter. Until the mid twentieth century when television and the print media dictated the form, campaign artifacts, such as banners, posters, and buttons, were limited only by their makers' imaginations. But each election is a referendum whereby the nominees must demonstrate that they favor peace, prosperity, and progress while combining these and other goals with a carnival atmosphere. Our contributors, then, had two assignments: to analyze an election and to focus, wherever possible, on the diverse styles, tactics, and techniques used by presidential candidates and their parties to woo the electorate.

In organizing this project, Professor Schlesinger and I have incurred many debts of gratitude. Our first is to our contributors who graciously agreed to participate in this study. We also gratefully acknowledge the assistance of David J. and Janice L. Frent, whose outstanding collection of American campaign artifacts has been the primary source to illustrate this work. Such artifacts are ephemeral, meant for a specific use and then to be discarded. Mr. and Mrs. Frent have helped to preserve a unique aspect of Americana. It is hoped that this study will contribute to bridging the gap between the academics who write the scholarly interpretations and the collector who gathers and saves the physical relics of campaigns.

Harold Steinberg, founder and former president of Chelsea House Publishers, encouraged and reassured us, as he has for so many creative projects throughout the years. To him, Professor Schlesinger and I owe a very special thank you. Susan Lusk served as the art director and her talent, patience, and professionalism enabled us to complete this complex undertaking. The high standards which she maintained made working with her a special pleasure. In writing the captions for the illustrations, I was assisted by Jonathan Mann, a collector of political memorabilia, Rex Stark, a foremost dealer in Americana, and Mr. Frent.

We in academe depend upon publishers who convey our thoughts to the printed page. Professor Schlesinger and I are indebted to Charles E. Smith, president of the Academic Reference Division of Simon & Schuster, whose capable staff, and professional and personal guidance overcame the many obstacles presented by this complicated project.

From the inception of this project, Professor Schlesinger has been inspirational. This outstanding historian was always available for advice and assistance. His editing of each essay without missing a deadline was an impressive feat. I have known Professor Schlesinger for twenty-five years, and my admiration for this brilliant man increases each year.

Fred L. Israel
The City College of New York
December 1, 1993

THE EDITORS

ARTHUR M. SCHLESINGER, JR. holds the Albert
Schweitzer Chair in the Humanities at the Graduate Center
of The City University of New York. He is the author of more
than a dozen books including: *The Age of Jackson; The Vital
Center; The Age of Roosevelt* (3 vols.); *A Thousand Days:
John F. Kennedy in the White House; Robert Kennedy and
His Times; The Cycles of American History;* and *The Imperial
Presidency.* Professor Schlesinger served as Special Assistant to
President Kennedy (1961-63). His numerous awards include:
the Pulitzer Prize for History; the Pulitzer Prize for Biography;
two National Book Awards; the Bancroft Prize and the
American Academy of Arts and Letters Gold Medal for History.

★

FRED L. ISRAEL is the senior professor of American history
at The City College of New York. He is the author of *Nevada's
Key Pittman* and has edited *The War Diary of Breckinridge
Long* and *Major Peace Treaties of Modern History, 1648-
1975* (5 vols.). He holds the Scribe's Award from the
American Bar Association for his joint editorship of *The
Justices of the United States Supreme Court* (4 vols.). For
the past 25 years Professor Israel has compiled and edited the
Gallup Poll into annual reference volumes.

★

DAVID J. FRENT is the president of Political Americana
Auctions, Oakhurst, NJ. With his wife, Janice, he has
assembled the nation's foremost private collection of
political campaign memorabilia. Mr. Frent has designed
exhibits for corporations, the Smithsonian Institution and
the United States Information Agency. A member of the
board of directors of the American Political Items Collectors
since 1972, he was elected to its Hall of Fame for his
"outstanding contribution to preserving and studying our
political heritage."

INTRODUCTION

ARTHUR M. SCHLESINGER, JR.

AMERICA SUFFERS FROM A SORT OF INTERMITTENT FEVER—WHAT ONE MAY CALL A QUINTAN AGUE.
EVERY FOURTH YEAR THERE COME TERRIBLE SHAKINGS, PASSING INTO THE HOT FIT OF THE PRESIDENTIAL
ELECTION; THEN FOLLOWS WHAT PHYSICIANS CALL "THE INTERVAL"; THEN AGAIN THE FIT.
—JAMES BRYCE, *THE AMERICAN COMMONWEALTH* (1888)

RUNNING FOR PRESIDENT is the central rite
in the American political order. It was not always so.
Choosing the chief magistrate had been the point
of the quadrennial election from the beginning, but
it took a long while for candidates to *run* for the
highest office in the land; that is, to solicit, visibly
and actively, the support of the voters. These
volumes show through text and illustration how
those aspiring to the White House have moved on
from ascetic self-restraint to shameless self-
merchandising. This work thereby illuminates the
changing ways the American people have conceived
the role of their President. I hope it will also recall
to new generations some of the more picturesque
and endearing dimensions of American politics.

The primary force behind the revolution in
campaign attitudes and techniques was a
development unforeseen by the men who framed the
Constitution—the rise of the party system. Party
competition was not at all their original intent.
Quite the contrary: inspired at one or two removes
by Lord Bolingbroke's British tract of half a century
earlier, *The Idea of a Patriot King*, the Founding
Fathers envisaged a Patriot President, standing above
party and faction, representing the whole people,
offering the nation non-partisan leadership
virtuously dedicated to the common good.

The ideal of the Patriot President was
endangered, the Founding Fathers believed, by twin
menaces—factionalism and factionalism's ugly

offspring, the demagogue. Party competition would
only encourage unscrupulous men to appeal to
popular passion and prejudice. Alexander Hamilton
in the 71st Federalist bemoaned the plight of the
people, "beset as they continually are . . . by the
snares of the ambitious, the avaricious, the desperate,
by the artifices of men who possess their confidence
more than they deserve it, and of those who seek
to possess rather than to deserve it."

Pervading the Federalist was a theme sounded
explicitly both in the first paper and the last: the fear
that unleashing popular passions would bring on
"the military despotism of a victorious demagogue."
If the "mischiefs of faction" were, James Madison
admitted in the Tenth Federalist, "sown in the
nature of man," the object of politics was to repress
this insidious disposition, not to yield to it. "If I
could not go to heaven but with a party," said
Thomas Jefferson, "I would not go there at all."

So the Father of his Country in his Farewell
Address solemnly warned his countrymen against
"the baneful effects of the spirit of party." That
spirit, Washington conceded, was "inseparable from
our nature"; but for popular governments it was
"truly their worst enemy." The "alternate
domination of one faction over another,"
Washington said, would lead in the end to "formal
and permanent despotism." The spirit of party, "a
fire not to be quenched . . . demands a uniform
vigilance to prevent its bursting into a flame, lest,

instead of warming, it should consume."

Yet, even as Washington called on Americans to "discourage and restrain" the spirit of party, parties were beginning to crystallize around him. The eruption of partisanship in defiance of such august counsel argued that party competition might well serve functional necessities in the democratic republic.

After all, honest disagreement over policy and principle called for candid debate. And parties, it appeared, had vital roles to play in the consummation of the Constitution. The distribution of powers among three equal branches inclined the national government toward a chronic condition of stalemate. Parties offered the means of overcoming the constitutional separation of powers by coordinating the executive and legislative branches and furnishing the connective tissue essential to effective government. As national associations, moreover, parties were a force against provincialism and separatism. As instruments of compromise, they encouraged, within the parties as well as between them, the containment and mediation of national quarrels, at least until slavery broke the parties up. Henry D. Thoreau cared little enough for politics, but he saw the point: "Politics is, as it were, the gizzard of society, full of grit and gravel, and the two political parties are its two opposite halves, which grind on each other."

Furthermore, as the illustrations in these volumes so gloriously remind us, party competition was a great source of entertainment and fun—all the more important in those faraway days before the advent of baseball and football, of movies and radio and television. "To take a hand in the regulation of society and to discuss it," Alexis de Tocqueville

observed when he visited Americas in the 1830s, "is his biggest concern and, so to speak, the only pleasure an American knows. . . . Even the women frequently attend public meetings and listen to political harangues as a recreation from their household labors. Debating clubs are, to a certain extent, a substitute for theatrical entertainments."

Condemned by the Founding Fathers, unknown to the Constitution, parties nonetheless imperiously forced themselves into political life. But the party system rose from the bottom up. For half a century, the first half-dozen Presidents continued to hold themselves above party. The disappearance of the Federalist party after the War of 1812 suspended party competition. James Monroe, with no opponent at all in the election of 1820, presided proudly over the Era of Good Feelings, so called because there were no parties around to excite ill feelings. Monroe's successor, John Quincy Adams, despised electioneering and inveighed against the "fashion of peddling for popularity by travelling around the country gathering crowds together, hawking for public dinners, and spouting empty speeches." Men of the old republic believed presidential candidates should be men who already deserved the people's confidence rather than those seeking to win it. Character and virtue, not charisma and ambition, should be the grounds for choosing a President.

Adams was the last of the old school. Andrew Jackson, by beating him in the 1828 election, legitimized party politics and opened a new political era. The rationale of the new school was provided by Jackson's counsellor and successor, Martin Van Buren, the classic philosopher of the role of party in the American democracy. By the time Van Buren took his own oath of office in 1837, parties were entrenched as the instruments of American self-government. In Van Buren's words, party battles "rouse the sluggish to exertion, give increased energy to the most active intellect, excite a salutary vigilance over our public functionaries, and prevent that apathy which has proved the ruin of Republics."

Apathy may indeed have proved the ruin of republics, but rousing the sluggish to exertion proved, ironically, the ruin of Van Buren. The architect of the party system became the first casualty of the razzle-dazzle campaigning the system quickly generated. The Whigs' Tippecanoe-and-Tyler-too campaign of 1840 transmuted the democratic Van Buren into a gilded aristocrat and assured his defeat at the polls. The "peddling for popularity" John Quincy Adams had deplored now became standard for party campaigners.

But the new methods were still forbidden to the presidential candidates themselves. The feeling lingered from earlier days that stumping the country in search of votes was demagoguery beneath the dignity of the presidency. Van Buren's code permitted—indeed expected—parties to inscribe their creed in platforms and candidates to declare their principles in letters published in newspapers. Occasionally candidates—William Henry Harrison in 1840, Winfield Scott in 1852—made a speech, but party surrogates did most of the hard work.

As late as 1858, Van Buren, advising his son John, one of the great popular orators of the time, on the best way to make it to the White House, emphasized the "rule . . . that the people will never make a man President who is so importunate as to show by his life and conversation that he not only has an eye on, but is in active pursuit of the office. . . . No man who has laid himself out for it, and was

unwise enough to let the people into his secret, ever yet obtained it. Clay, Calhoun, Webster, Scott, and a host of lesser lights, should serve as a guide-post to future aspirants."

The continuing constraint on personal campaigning by candidates was reinforced by the desire of party managers to present their nominees as all things to all men. In 1835 Nicholas Biddle, the wealthy Philadelphian who had been Jackson's mortal opponent in the famous Bank War, advised the Whigs not to let General Harrison "say one single word about his principles or his creed. . . . Let him say nothing, promise nothing. Let no committee, no convention, no town meeting ever extract from him a single word about what he thinks now, or what he will do hereafter. Let the use of pen and ink be wholly forbidden as if he were a mad poet in Bedlam."

We cherish the memory of the famous debates in 1858 between Abraham Lincoln and Stephen A. Douglas. But those debates were not part of a presidential election. When the presidency was at stake two years later, Lincoln gave no campaign speeches on the issues darkly dividing the country. He even expressed doubt about party platforms— "the formal written platform system," as he called it. The candidate's character and record, Lincoln thought, should constitute his platform: "On just such platforms all our earlier and better Presidents were elected."

However, Douglas, Lincoln's leading opponent in 1860, foreshadowed the future when he broke the sound barrier and dared venture forth on thinly disguised campaign tours. Yet Douglas established no immediate precedent. Indeed, half a dozen years later Lincoln's successor, Andrew Johnson, discredited presidential stumping by his "swing around the circle" in the midterm election of 1866. "His performances in a western tour in advocacy of his own election," commented Benjamin F. Butler, who later led the fight in Congress for Johnson's impeachment, " . . . disgusted everybody." The tenth article of impeachment charged Johnson with bringing "the high office of the President of the United States into contempt, ridicule, and disgrace" by delivering "with a loud voice certain intemperate, inflammatory, and scandalous harangues . . . peculiarly indecent and unbecoming in the Chief Magistrate of the United States."

Though presidential candidates Horatio Seymour in 1868, Rutherford B. Hayes in 1876, and James A. Garfield in 1880 made occasional speeches, only Horace Greeley in 1872, James G. Blaine in 1884, and most spectacularly, William Jennings Bryan in 1896 followed Douglas's audacious example of stumping the country. Such tactics continued to provoke disapproval. Bryan, said John Hay, who had been Lincoln's private secretary and was soon to become McKinley's secretary of state, "is begging for the presidency as a tramp might beg for a pie."

Respectable opinion still preferred the "front porch" campaign, employed by Garfield, by Benjamin Harrison in 1888, and most notably by McKinley in 1896. Here candidates received and addressed numerous delegations at their own homes—a form, as the historian Gil Troy writes, of "stumping in place."

While candidates generally continued to stand on their dignity, popular campaigning in presidential elections flourished in these years, attaining new heights of participation (82 percent of eligible voters in 1876 and never once from 1860 to 1900 under 70

percent) and new wonders of pyrotechnics and ballyhoo. Parties mobilized the electorate as never before, and political iconography was never more ingenious and fantastic. "Politics, considered not as the science of government, but as the art of winning elections and securing office," wrote the keen British observer James Bryce, "has reached in the United States a development surpassing in elaborateness that of England or France as much as the methods of those countries surpass the methods of Servia or Roumania." Bryce marvelled at the "military discipline" of the parties, at "the demonstrations, the parades and receptions, the badges and brass bands and triumphal arches," at the excitement stirred by elections— and at "the disproportion that strikes a European between the merits of the presidential candidate and the blazing enthusiasm which he evokes."

Still the old taboo held back the presidential candidates themselves. Even so irrepressible a campaigner as President Theodore Roosevelt felt obliged to hold his tongue when he ran for reelection in 1904. This unwonted abstinence reminded him, he wrote in considerable frustration, of the July day in 1898 when he was "lying still under shell fire" during the Spanish-American War. "I have continually wished that I could be on the stump myself."

No such constraint inhibited TR, however, when he ran again for the presidency in 1912. Meanwhile, and for the first time, *both* candidates in 1908— Bryan again, and William Howard Taft—actively campaigned for the prize. The duties of the office, on top of the new requirements of campaigning, led Woodrow Wilson to reflect that same year, four years before he himself ran for President, "Men of ordinary physique and discretion cannot be Presidents and live, if the strain be not somehow relieved. We shall be obliged always to be picking our chief magistrates from among wise and prudent athletes,—a small class."

Theodore Roosevelt and Woodrow Wilson combined to legitimate a new conception of presidential candidates as active molders of public opinion in active pursuit of the highest office. Once in the White House, Wilson revived the custom, abandoned by Jefferson, of delivering annual state of the union addresses to Congress in person. In 1916 he became the first incumbent President to stump for his own reelection.

The activist candidate and the bully-pulpit presidency were expressions of the growing democratization of politics. New forms of communication were reconfiguring presidential campaigns. In the nineteenth century the press, far more fiercely partisan then than today, had been the main carrier of political information. In the twentieth century the spread of advertising techniques and the rise of the electronic media—radio, television, computerized public opinion polling—wrought drastic changes in the methodology of politics. In particular the electronic age diminished and now threatens to dissolve the historic role of the party.

The old system had three tiers: the politician at one end; the voter at the other; and the party in between. The party's function was to negotiate between the politician and the voters, interpreting each to the other and providing the link that held the political process together. The electronic revolution has substantially abolished the sovereignty of the party. Where once the voter turned to the local party leader to find out whom to

support, now he looks at television and makes up his own mind. Where once the politician turned to the local party leader to find out what people are thinking, he now takes a computerized poll.

The electronic era has created a new breed of professional consultants, "handlers," who by the 1980s had taken control of campaigns away from the politicians. The traditional pageantry—rallies, torchlight processions, volunteers, leaflets, billboards, bumper stickers—is now largely a thing of the past. Television replaces the party as the means of mobilizing the voter. And as the party is left to wither on the vine, the presidential candidate becomes more pivotal than ever. We shall see the rise of personalist movements, founded not on historic organizations but on compelling personalities, private fortunes, and popular frustrations. Without the stabilizing influence of parties, American politics would grow angrier, wilder, and more irresponsible.

Things have changed considerably from the austerities of the old republic. Where once voters preferred to call presumably reluctant candidates to the duties of the supreme magistracy and rejected pursuit of the office as evidence of dangerous ambition, now they expect candidates to come to them, explain their views and plead for their support. Where nonpartisan virtue had been the essence, now candidates must prove to voters that they have the requisite "fire in the belly." " 'Twud be inth'restin," said Mr. Dooley, " . . . if th' fathers iv th' counthry cud come back an' see what has happened while they've been away. In times past whin ye voted f'r prisident ye didn't vote f'r a man. Ye voted f'r a kind iv a statue that ye'd put up in ye'er own mind on a marble pidistal. Ye nivir heerd iv George Wash'nton goin' around th' countthe distributin' five cint see-gars."

We have reversed the original notion that ambition must be disguised and the office seek the man. Now the man—and soon, one must hope, the woman—seeks the office and does so without guilt or shame or inhibition. This is not necessarily a degradation of democracy. Dropping the disguise is a gain for candor, and personal avowals of convictions and policies may elevate and educate the electorate.

On the other hand, the electronic era has dismally reduced both the intellectual content of campaigns and the attention span of audiences. In the nineteenth century political speeches lasted for a couple of hours and dealt with issues in systematic and exhaustive fashion. Voters drove wagons for miles to hear Webster and Clay, Bryan and Teddy Roosevelt, and felt cheated if the famous orator did not give them their money's worth. Then radio came along and cut political addresses down first to an hour, soon to thirty minutes—still enough time to develop substantive arguments.

But television has shrunk the political talk first to fifteen minutes, now to the sound bite and the thirty-second spot. Advertising agencies today sell candidates with all the cynical contrivance they previously devoted to selling detergents and mouthwash. The result is the debasement of American politics. "The idea that you can merchandise candidates for high office like breakfast cereal," Adlai Stevenson said in 1952, "is the ultimate indignity to the democratic process."

Still Bryce's "intermittent fever" will be upon us every fourth year. We will continue to watch wise if not always prudent athletes in their sprint for the White House, enjoy the quadrennial spectacle and agonize about the outcome. "The strife of the

election," said Lincoln after his reelection in 1864, "is but human-nature practically applied to the facts. What has occurred in this case, must ever recur in similar cases. Human-nature will not change."

Lincoln, as usual, was right. Despite the transformation in political methods there remains a basic continuity in political emotions. "For a long while before the appointed time has come," Tocqueville wrote more than a century and a half ago, "the election becomes the important and, so to speak, the all-engrossing topic of discussion. Factional ardor is redoubled, and all the artificial passions which the imagination can create in a happy and peaceful land are agitated and brought to light. . . .

"As the election draws near, the activity of intrigue and the agitation of the populace increase; the citizens are divided into hostile camps, each of which assumes the name of its favorite candidate; the whole nation glows with feverish excitement; the election is the daily theme of the press, the subject of every private conversation, the end of every thought and every action, the sole interest of the present.

"It is true," Tocqueville added, "that as soon as the choice is determined, this ardor is dispelled, calm returns, and the river, which had nearly broken its banks, sinks to its usual level; but who can refrain from astonishment that such a storm should have arisen?"

The election storm in the end blows fresh and clean. With the tragic exception of 1860, the American people have invariably accepted the result and given the victor their hopes and blessings. For all its flaws and follies, democracy abides.

Let us now turn the pages and watch the gaudy parade of American presidential politics pass by in all its careless glory.

RUNNING FOR PRESIDENT

THE CANDIDATES AND THEIR IMAGES

★

1789 1792

1789: 11 STATES
1792: 15 STATES
IN THE UNION

George Washington

1789: ELECTORAL VOTE 69
1792: ELECTORAL VOTE 132

John Adams

1789: ELECTORAL VOTE 34
1792: ELECTORAL VOTE 77

George Clinton

1792: ELECTORAL VOTE 50

Other Candidates

1789: ELECTORAL VOTE 35
1792: ELECTORAL VOTE 5

REGINALD HORSMAN
is Distinguished Professor of History at the
University of Wisconsin-Milwaukee. He has
written extensively about early national
America. Among his books are *Race and
Manifest Destiny: The Origins of American
Racial Anglo-Saxonism* (1981); *The Diplomacy
of the New Republic, 1776–1815* (1985); and
*Josiah Nott of Mobile: Southerner,
Physician, and Racial Theorist* (1987).

In the first presidential election the biggest question was not who would be President but whether the newly established electoral system would work. From the time that the new Constitution was written in Philadelphia in the summer of 1787, it was seen as essential that George Washington should be the first President. In leading the Continental army to victory in the American Revolution, Washington had achieved a stature far above that of his contemporaries. He had that aura which often surrounds leaders who bring their countries to independence. Fortunately for the young republic, he had no intention of using his reputation as a means of seeking absolute or indefinite power.

At Philadelphia, in the summer of 1787, most delegates to the constitutional convention had agreed that the lack of an effective national executive had hindered the progress of the new nation, but they had been anxious to avoid the abuses and dangers of royal power. They wanted executive leadership, but they feared creating a system that would allow a demagogue to ride roughshod over the republic. The generation of politicians who shaped the new nation were educated in classical history, and they were anxious that the United States should escape the fate of republican Rome; they strove to ensure that in America the republic would be safe from imperial corruption.

There was general agreement at Philadelphia that there should be an elective presidency, but there was much argument about how this was to be accomplished. Complicating the fears of royal power were the prevailing state and regional jealousies. The small states wanted to ensure that the stronger central government being provided for in Philadelphia would not fall under the control of the states with the largest populations. The presidential election system that was finally arrived at was, like the rest of the Constitution, a compromise. At first there had been strong support for having Congress elect the President, but there was fear that such a system would result in a President controlled by the legislators who elected him. The idea of popular election was suggested, but that raised additional fears of a demagogue manipulating the general population to his own advantage, and also the objection that the general population would have no knowledge of qualified men from other states. Some were concerned that in a popular election the desires of the smaller states would be swamped by the votes of the large state populations.

The delegates had finally compromised on the system of presidential electors. It was assumed that electors would be leading men in the states they served, and that they would have the knowledge to cast intelligent votes. Even a system based on electors was controversial, however, for the idea of allotting electors to states simply on the basis of population encountered many of the same objections as a system of direct popular election. This concern had been addressed by the agreement that the num-

Political memorabilia began with the first President of the United States. Brass clothing buttons commemorated Washington's inauguration. Many appeared with the phrase "LONG LIVE THE PRESIDENT."

ber of electors from each state would equal its number of senators and representatives, thus ensuring that states as well as populations would be represented in the election of the President. The concern that most electors would simply vote for men from their own states was dealt with by providing that one of the two votes that each elector would cast would be for someone outside his own state.

As there was no assumption at Philadelphia that parties would play any part in the elections, it was arranged that the vice president would simply be the candidate with the second-highest number of votes on the single ballot; they hoped that the best man would be President, the second-best vice president. If, as seemed likely, there would be elections in which no person received an absolute majority of the electoral votes, then the House of Representatives, with each state delegation having one vote, would choose from the five highest on the list.

Although the Constitution specified that the electors would meet in their respective states to cast their votes, and then send them to the president of the Senate to be opened in the presence of the Senate and the House, the decision on when the electors would be elected and when they would cast their votes was left to Congress, and the method by which the electors were to be chosen was left to each individual state.

The Constitution had been written by September 1787, but ratification by the states was prolonged into the summer of 1788. The old Continental Congress then took action to provide for the elections under the Constitution. After some delay, it was finally agreed in mid-September 1788, that the electors would be chosen on the

first Wednesday in January, and that they would meet to vote on the first Wednesday in February. Given the difficulties in communication, and the different times at which the state legislatures convened, this gave very little time for state action.

For the most part, in deciding how the presidential electors would be chosen, the states avoided direct popular election. Only in four states—Pennsylvania, Delaware, Maryland, and Virginia—were electors chosen by popular vote. Four states simply had the state legislatures choose them, and two—Massachusetts and New Hampshire—involved both the general electorate and the state legislatures. Although New York had ratified the Constitution, that state did not participate in the first presidential election because of the inability of its upper and lower house to agree on how to proceed. North Carolina and Rhode Island did not participate in the election because they had not yet joined the Union.

The eagle-sunburst motif came from the coat buttons worn by Washington at his inauguration on April 30, 1789.

The haste with which decisions regarding the presidential election had to be taken could have created major problems in electing a President but for the general assumption that George Washington would be the first to serve. He was everyone's choice. In 1789 there was no real contest for the presidency, and no public campaign. There was, however, a degree of uncertainty, both because of Washington's refusal to make public any desire to be elected and because the President and vice president were to be chosen on a single ballot that made no distinction between the vote for President and the vote for vice president. Washington, like other statesmen of the 1790s, believed that it would be demeaning to seek office. From the summer of 1788 he was urged in private letters to serve as President, but he refused to commit himself publicly, and even in private indicated that he would be happy to continue his retirement from public life.

In these first presidential elections, candidates were not nominated in any formal sense, and there was none of the public hoopla of later elections. Individual public figures, such as Alexander Hamilton of New York, took the lead in identifying likely choices by means of private letters. When travel made it possible, they also had private conversations or small meetings, and through such means they built an informal network of influential men who could help to sway state legislators, electors, or (on occasion) general voters.

Washington never actually said he was running in 1788–1789, but Alexander Hamilton told him by letter that his service was essential: "On your acceptance of the office of President," he wrote in September

IOHN ADAMS, L.L.D.

Vice President of the United States of America

Publish'd Feb.r 15.1794 by Iohn Stockdale.

1788, "the success of the new government may materially depend." Washington made no personal moves to influence either electors or general voters, but by the fall of 1788 it was generally assumed that Washington would be the first President.

Although there were no political parties in 1788, there was concern among the sup-

Print of John Adams as vice president engraved in 1794 after a painting by John Singleton Copley.

Transfer printed ceramics originated in England in the 1780s. An early type was Liverpool creamware, a light beige soft paste pottery named for the city of its origin. This pitcher commemorates the Battle of Bunker Hill (1775) and American independence.

porters of the new Constitution that those who had opposed its ratification—the Anti-Federalists—would attempt to influence the election. They were not expected to challenge Washington, but it seemed likely that they would try to secure the vice presidency for an Anti-Federalist. Hamilton, who had taken the lead in urging Washington to serve as President, also led in trying to arrange general agreement on a vice president acceptable to those who had supported the Constitution. His personal decision, reached somewhat reluctantly, was that to counterbalance Washington (from Virginia)

the best candidate would be John Adams (from Massachusetts). Although Adams had played a key role in shaping American independence, he was not well-liked outside New England, and Hamilton was concerned at rumors that Adams was unfriendly to Washington. Some thought was given to other Massachusetts candidates, but Hamilton settled on Adams. The Anti-Federalist leaders showed less ability to manage matters than Hamilton, but some of them tried to promote the cause of George Clinton of New York for vice president. In spite of the efforts of Anti-Federalist leaders in New York and Virginia, Clinton obtained little support among the electors.

As it became obvious by the beginning of 1789 that Washington and Adams had the main support, Hamilton became concerned that the imperfect system of having the President and vice president elected on the same undifferentiated ballot could produce a fluke victory for Adams. He assumed that this might happen if all the supporters of the Constitution voted for both Washington and Adams and a few Anti-Federalists decided to omit Washington from their ballots. To counter any possibility of this, he urged that some of the electors should give their second vote to anyone other than Adams.

The haste with which the election was organized, the lack of parties, the lack of any general popular vote, and the assumption that Washington was to be President meant that there was little grass-roots interest in this first presidential election. In those states with popular voting for electors, the Federalists and Anti-Federalists organized slates of acceptable electors, but few voters went to the polls. This was very much an election managed by leading statesmen, particularly Hamilton and his friends. None of the potential candidates for President or vice president campaigned, and Washington showed a marked reluctance to acknowledge that he was in an election. Washington did not want to be President if he had to compete for it.

The counting of the votes was much delayed. Originally, the presidential inauguration was to be on March 4, 1789, but by that time neither the House nor the Senate had the quorum necessary to count the votes; not until the first week in April had enough representatives and senators assembled. The electoral choice was decisive. Four electors did not vote, but all sixty-nine who participated voted for Washington. Adams was well clear of the rest of the field with thirty-four, but his pride was hurt. Over twenty others received votes. The Anti-Federalist hopes of support for Clinton evaporated; he received only three votes. The first presidential election had demonstrated the supreme place of Washington in the minds of his countrymen, but it had also revealed defects in the electoral system. Having President and vice president on the same undifferentiated ballot was dangerous; it would become more so with the growth of political parties.

Washington's first administration saw the shaping of an effective national government, but it also brought deep divisions regarding the ways in which national security, prosperity, and growth could best be achieved. The policies of Alexander Hamilton as secretary of the treasury, and his influence on Washington, aroused opposition. This opposition coalesced around Secretary of State Thomas Jefferson and

around James Madison in the House of Representatives. By 1792 Washington still presided over a national rather than a party government, but there was an increasing division between the friends and allies of Hamilton and those who believed that he was moving Washington's administration in ways dangerous to the republic and to the individual states. There were no organized political parties, but newspapers increasingly threw their support to Hamilton or to his opponents, and the two sides tried to win adherents in Congress and in the country.

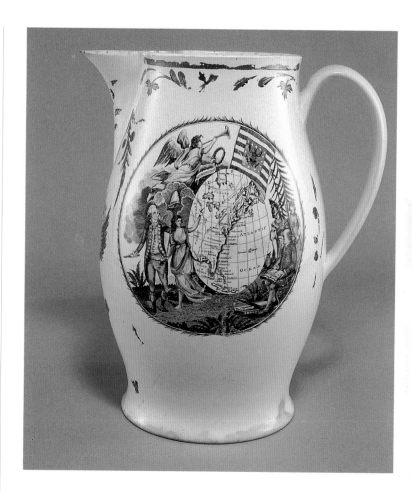

Reverse side of the Liverpool pitcher (opposite) shows George Washington and Benjamin Franklin with a map of the United States. These were made for export to the United States.

Enamel-on-copper Battersea curtain tieback depicting Washington.

Although Washington had shown greater sympathy for Hamilton's views than Jefferson and Madison ideally would have liked, they felt it essential for the well-being of the country that he should retain the presidency. This seemed likely to present difficulty, not because of lack of support for Washington, but because of his reluctance to continue in public office. In the spring of 1792 Washington demonstrated every intention of retiring, and in May asked Madison how this intention could best be conveyed to the public without any implication that he was assuming automatic reelection. The leading politicians all urged him to continue. On this matter, Hamilton and Jefferson could agree, and they suggested to Washington that, if he wished, he could perhaps retire before the end of his second term.

Throughout the summer of 1792 Washington continued to show a greater desire to retire than to be reelected, but he was persuaded by his intimates that his continued service was essential for the good of the country. As in 1788–1789, Washington in no sense ran or campaigned for the office, but by the fall of 1792 both Hamilton and Jefferson were able to assure their friends that Washington would serve if reelected.

The 1792 election involved five more states than that of 1789. This time New York participated, North Carolina and Rhode Island had entered the Union, and they had been joined by the new states of Vermont and Kentucky. In nine of the states the electors were appointed by the state legislatures. The most important state with direct popular election of the electors was Pennsylvania. As in the first election, there was no one day for the choice of presiden-

tial electors. Congress had now decided that the states could choose them anytime within thirty-four days of the first Wednesday in December.

The only competition in 1792 was for vice president. Although Adams was looked upon with little enthusiasm by Hamilton and his close allies, their decision was that he was the best candidate available. Even some of the anti-Hamiltonians were prepared to accept this, but others, as in the previous election, raised the name of George Clinton. In the summer of 1792 Clinton became the main hope of those who wished to raise some protest against the Hamiltonian tendencies of the Washington administration. For a time in the early fall it seemed possible that Aaron Burr, also from New York, might prove more acceptable to some of the New York politicians than Clinton, but this idea was resisted by Madison and other Virginia leaders. In October, it was agreed by anti-Hamilton politicians from several states, including New York and Virginia, that Clinton should be supported against Adams.

Although political leaders throughout the country acknowledged that Adams and Clinton were the leading contenders for the vice-presidency, neither man showed any inclination to campaign for the position. Adams remained at his home in Quincy, and resisted the efforts of his political friends who urged his presence in Philadelphia. The purpose of any such move would have been to influence political leaders, for there was little active public interest in the election, even in those states in which the electors were popularly elected. The turnout of voters was very low.

The electoral vote again demonstrated that Washington towered above his contemporaries in public esteem. All 132 electors who participated voted for the incumbent. There were signs, however, of growing opposition to Hamiltonianism. Adams was reelected with 77 votes, but Clinton, acknowledged as an anti-Hamilton candidate, received 50. As Adams was presumably helped by the reflected glory of Washington, this was a considerable protest vote.

In 1788–1789 and in 1792 the presidential election system was primarily the domain of an elite group of politicians who used letters and occasional small meetings to organize support behind particular candidates. Those who were supported did not become candidates in the modern sense of the term. Washington set the pattern by showing an unwillingness to compete, and by expressing frequent desires to retire. And although Hamilton, Madison, and others attempted to make sure that a vice president amenable to their views would be

Many portraits of Washington appeared on tiebacks, plaques, boxes, and other objects embellished with enamel which were imported from England through the mid-1820s.

elected, Adams and Clinton did not enter the fray in any open sense. They were content to depend on the efforts of elite politicians who could influence other important political figures in the different states. Even in the minority of states that popularly elected the presidential electors, electioneering was minimal. The contending sides shaped slates of acceptable electors, newspapers gave support to certain individuals and points of view, but there was no widespread organization and very little excitement. What was most important about the first two presidential elections was that, for all its awkwardness, the electoral system worked. The new republic had shown the world that the supreme leader of a nation could be elected, and that this could be accomplished without widespread violence or corruption. Elite political management of presidential elections began its long history in these years, but active campaigning had to await a new generation and the growth of political parties.

An example of English yard goods, circa 1785. Washington and Miss Liberty are in a chariot pulled by leopards. These fabrics were used for curtains and upholstery.

Brass buttons commemorating Washington's inauguration. The chain of thirteen links represents the original states.

Commemorative copper medal. The British Parliament altered the calendar in 1751, hence the "old-style" date of Washington's birth.

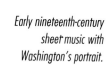

Many brass and copper buttons were struck immediately after Washington's inauguration. Above is the only one bearing a portrait of the first President.

Early nineteenth-century sheet music with Washington's portrait.

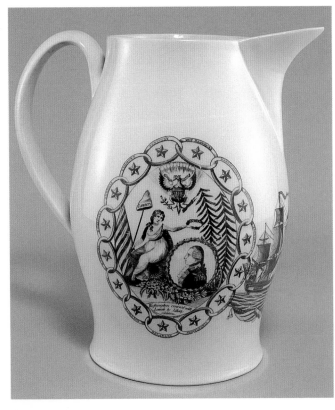

Above: Hand-painted Liverpool creamware pitcher dedicated to "the Proscribed PATRIOTS OF AMERICA" with portraits of Samuel Adams and John Hancock. Above right: Creamware jug with transfer image "Washington crowned with laurels by Liberty."

Liverpool tankard with a military portrait of Washington has stylized figures of Liberty and Justice on either side of a laudatory poem.

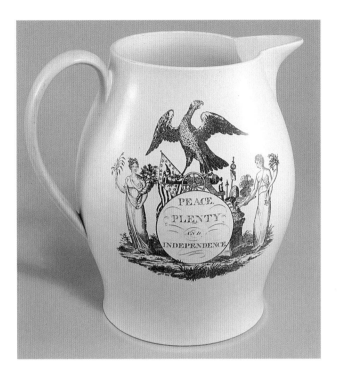

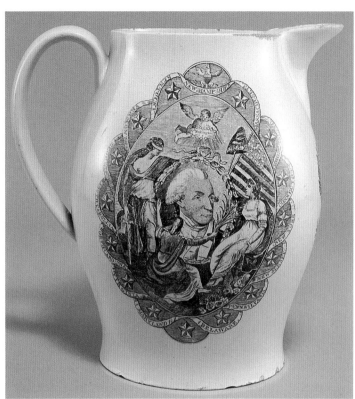

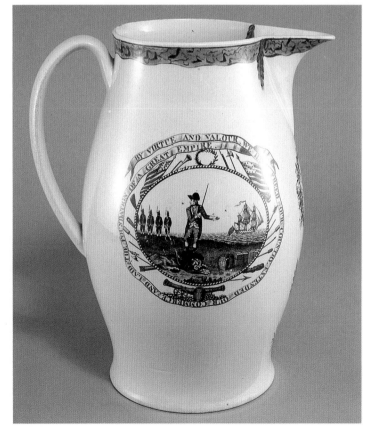

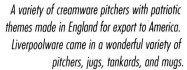

A variety of creamware pitchers with patriotic
themes made in England for export to America.
Liverpoolware came in a wonderful variety of
pitchers, jugs, tankards, and mugs.

Left: An enamel curtain tieback. Right: A burl wood snuffbox with a brass inset medallion of Washington, circa 1790–1800.

Obverse and reverse of a brass token struck during Washington's presidency.

Liverpool creamware commemorating Washington's death in 1799.

Printed textile, circa 1806, with a picture of Washington after a Gilbert Stuart painting. A paragraph from Washington's Farewell Address (1796) is on the left and a eulogy on the right.

1796

16 STATES
IN THE UNION

FEDERALIST

John Adams

ELECTORAL VOTE 71

DEMOCRATIC-REPUBLICAN

Thomas Jefferson

ELECTORAL VOTE 68

FEDERALIST

Thomas Pinckney

ELECTORAL VOTE 59

DEMOCRATIC-REPUBLICAN

Aaron Burr

ELECTORAL VOTE 30

OTHER CANDIDATES

COMBINED ELECTORAL VOTE 48

Reginald Horsman
is Distinguished Professor of History at the
University of Wisconsin-Milwaukee. He has
written extensively about early national
America. Among his books are *Race and
Manifest Destiny: The Origins of American
Racial Anglo-Saxonism* (1981); *The Diplomacy
of the New Republic, 1776–1815* (1985); and
*Josiah Nott of Mobile: Southerner,
Physician, and Racial Theorist* (1987).

Probably the most notable feature of the election of 1796 was the development of party conflict. There was still no overt campaigning, but Washington's retirement from the presidency meant that for the first time there would be competition for the office of President.

Washington's second term had been marked by bitter contention among leading members of the administration and in Congress. The divisions between the Hamiltonians and the Jeffersonians that had arisen in Washington's first term had focused on the ways in which Hamilton had broadly interpreted the constitutional powers of the federal government in pursuing national solvency and economic progress. Opponents had argued that Hamilton's elitism and pro-British attitudes threatened American republicanism. In Washington's second term, a crisis in foreign affairs had deepened existing divisions. The outbreak of widespread European war involving England and France threatened American commerce, and in 1794 brought the United States and England to the brink of war. Hamilton's belief that American prosperity depended on close ties with England led him to exert all his influence to preserve the peace. This was accomplished by the signing of Jay's Treaty in November 1794, but the opposition, led by Thomas Jefferson and James Madison, viewed the treaty as abject submission to the will of the British. It only served to increase their fears that Hamilton's pro-British policies threatened American republicanism.

In 1795 and into the spring of 1796 the evolution of the first American political parties was furthered by the debates over Jay's Treaty. These debates involved both the Senate and the House. The treaty was ratified by the Senate after a bitter fight, but treaty opponents in the House precipitated another debate by balking at voting the money necessary to carry the treaty into effect. The opposition had become generally known as the Republicans. In the mid-1790s some politicians still avoided party labels, and party organization in the country at large was often nonexistent or rudimentary, but Congress divided along Federalist or Republican lines, and Washington was now regarded as the leader of a Federalist administration, not a bipartisan government. This meant that even Washington himself was criticized in some of the newspapers that took up the cause of the opposition Republicans.

Political preparations for the presidential election of 1796 were complicated by the lack of any formal nominating procedure, and by Washington's public silence regarding his intentions. Washington had never sought the presidency, had frequently expressed his wishes for retirement, and had only reluctantly agreed to serve for a second term. He had no desire for a third term. Yet, Washington was also notoriously loathe to make public statements regarding his intentions. Even in the spring and summer of 1792 it had never been quite clear whether Washington was prepared to serve

His Excellency

JOHN ADAMS, Esq.

W. Williams pinx.   *T. B. Freeman excudit.*   *H. H. Houston Sculp.*

John Adams was the first President to live in Washington D.C. When he moved into the President's House on November 1, 1800, the building was incomplete.

or not. Throughout most of 1796 he was again publicly silent, although by May those who knew him well concluded that he did not intend to serve again as President. Throughout the summer, he delayed any public announcement.

Leading Federalist and Republican politicians had begun thinking of possible candidates in 1795, and there is little doubt that John Adams, who had served as Washington's vice president for two terms, viewed

himself as his logical successor. Adams's position was complicated because, in spite of his eminence as a revolutionary politician and diplomat, he was not well-liked, even among his fellow Federalists. His New England manner was regarded by many as cold, and his sensitivity to criticism and his suspicion of others aroused mistrust even in some quite close to him. A particular problem for Adams were the doubts long entertained by Alexander Hamilton, the intellectual leader of the developing Federalist party. By 1796 these doubts were becoming positive dislike. Moreover, Adams, like most other political leaders of the 1790s, thought it unfitting to seek the presidential office. He believed that the office should be bestowed by an admiring and grateful country, not contended for, with all the risks of rejection and personal hurt. Others now thought of Adams as a Federalist, but he wanted to believe that, like Washington, he was above the demands and arguments of the emerging parties.

The leading figure of the anti-Hamiltonian Republicans was Thomas Jefferson, and, like Adams, Jefferson thought it was unfitting to seek office. Also, far more than Adams, Jefferson had a love/hate relationship with public service. Like Washington, he often longed for the peace of his plantation, and at times during the War of Independence his colleagues in the Continental Congress had sent desperate appeals for him to return to public service at the seat of affairs. For all their political success in these tumultuous years, the Virginia statesmen of the revolutionary generation had as their ideal the amateur, not the professional politician. They idealized the senators of republican Rome, who (they supposed) selflessly served the state between sojourns at their country villas. Jefferson seemed a natural choice to those who feared Hamiltonianism in American government, but Jefferson, like Adams, wanted to be wooed. In the spring of 1795, he had tried to convince Madison that he had no intention of serving as President, and that he would not be persuaded otherwise. He said that his health was "entirely broken down," and that his early ambition had long since evaporated.

In the spring and early summer of 1796, as it became more obvious that this time Washington really meant to hold to his intention to retire, Federalist and Republican leaders began the process of identifying the men for whom they wished to generate support. As in the first two presidential elections, most of this activity was in private letters and by occasional meetings of small groups in caucus. In spite of Jefferson's reluctance to commit himself, there was general agreement among Republican leaders that he would be given their support. Republican leaders had less success in agreeing on a vice presidential possibility, and never launched any concerted drive to rally support for any one candidate.

Complicating the usual, private, elite procedure of identifying those who would be supported was the untypical approach of Aaron Burr. Burr had already risen to prominence in New York politics, had become an opponent of Alexander Hamilton, and had been suggested in 1792 as a possible vice presidential candidate. Burr's conduct foreshadowed future developments in presidential and vice presidential races as he worked assiduously to win the support of

Liverpool tankard. The angel blowing a trumpet carries a banner inscribed "ADAMS." These patriotic items were commonly displayed in homes.

leading politicians in the Northeast and in Virginia. He did not succeed in generating coordinated support for his candidacy. Republican managers worked for Jefferson, and tried to ensure that pro-Jefferson electors would be selected in the various states, but they did little for Burr.

John Adams should have been in a dominant position in 1796. He had been vice president for two terms, he had served with Washington, and because of the existing electoral system he had become vice president by running second to Washington on a single ballot, not on some separate (and inferior) vice presidential ballot. It was clear that Adams, with strong New England support and his position as vice president,

Miss Liberty, "An EMBLEM OF AMERICA," beside a monument with portraits of several early American leaders. Notice the depiction of the American Indian.

would have to be one of the two candidates that Federalist leaders would urge electors to vote for. Yet Adams was not generally liked in the South and, perhaps more important, he had less than the full backing of Hamilton at a time when he needed as much Federalist support as possible to resist the challenge of the Republicans.

In the summer of 1796 Hamilton directed his attention to securing a southerner who could balance the ticket with Adams, and also might take votes away from Jefferson in a region in which Adams was regarded as potentially weak. The eventual decision was for Thomas Pinckney of South Carolina. The Federalists were strong in that state, and Pinckney had signed a very satisfactory treaty with Spain in October 1795. By late summer it was generally un-

derstood the Federalist leaders would support Adams and Pinckney. The Republican leaders were generally agreed on Jefferson, but Burr had only selective, not general, support.

The growth of party divisions meant that public discussion of the coming election was more widespread than in 1788–1789 or in 1792, but there was still no campaigning in the modern style. Burr came closest in his efforts to seek support in the northeastern states and Virginia, but even he was not engaged in public appeals; he was occupied in trying to sway influential politicians to his cause. The two main figures involved— Adams and Jefferson—deliberately shunned any involvement. Their stance was that if the electors chose them they would serve, but they did nothing to try to influence opinion in their behalf. Thomas Pinckney, who was abroad, did not even return to the United States until after the electors were chosen.

Public discussion of the leading candidates and the different policies they represented was chiefly in the newspapers. By 1796 the press was becoming increasingly partisan, and willing to throw support to Adams or Jefferson. The Republicans also used popular resentment of Jay's Treaty to try more direct means of reaching voters. The treaty itself had led to demonstrations in the streets and broadsides attacking Adams and Federalist "subservience" to England. The Republicans were also helped by the Democratic societies that had developed in 1793 and 1794 in sympathy with France. These societies, highly suspicious of the pro-British Hamiltonian policies, generated support for Republican candidates, particularly in the towns. In general, the Republicans, because of their opposition to governmental policies, were quicker to organize on the local level than the Federalists.

Washington finally made public his decision to retire in September 17, 1796. His Farewell Address combined general advice to the American people with warnings against partisan politics which arose out of the abuse his administration had endured since 1794. But his message inaugurated a more energetic period of activity on the part of those who wished to manage the election. Most of this activity followed the familiar pattern of private letters and personal influence, but it also involved attempted foreign interference in the election by Pierre Adet, the French minister in the United States. The French government and Adet were disgusted at Jay's Treaty, which they considered a repudiation of the Franco-American alliance signed during the War of Independence. The French had flirted with diplomatic impropriety in trying to influence Congress against the treaty, and now acted still more undiplomatically in trying to ensure that Jefferson, whom they viewed as far more pro-French than Adams, should be elected to the presidency. In November, Adet publicly attacked the French policy of the Washington administration.

Sixteen states participated in the election of 1796; the additional state since 1792 was Tennessee, which entered the Union in the year of the election. Over half the states still had the state legislatures either choose the electors or play a role in that choice; six states allowed the people to choose, either on a general ticket or by districts. The only approach to general electioneering came in those states with

popular elections, particularly in Pennsylvania, the most important state providing for popular election on a general ticket. In that state both Federalists and Republicans met to arrange slates of electors supportive of their point of view, and used newspapers to publicize their candidates. But local organizations in support of individual candidates was still rudimentary.

As the electors were not bound to any particular candidates, and as their votes were not to be cast for weeks after their selection, considerable efforts were made to influence the voting after the electors were chosen. From an analysis of those who had been elected, it had become quite obvious that the vote would be very close. Jefferson was concerned that a tie, which would

Rare example of historical pottery inscribed "JOHN ADAMS, President of the United States of America."

John Adams and Thomas Jefferson both died on July 4, 1826, the fiftieth anniversary of the adoption of the Declaration of Independence. This 1826 memorial ribbon is inscribed: "Together they laboured for their country/ together they have gone to meet their reward."

from the beginning of their public life he had been the senior.

The machinations of Hamilton weakened the Federalist position in the actual voting. He had never clearly committed himself to Adams over Pinckney, and with the election obviously very close he took the position that Pinckney needed every possible vote. Ostensibly this would thwart Jefferson, but it also seemed likely that, if all the pro-Federalist electors voted for Pinckney, then Adams's weakness in the South might give the election to Pinckney rather than Adams. The New England electors decided to avert any such possibility by voting for Adams and scattering their second votes away from Pinckney. It was becoming obvious that having President and vice president on the same, undifferentiated ballot was becoming unworkable.

The final vote demonstrated that the Republicans were making major inroads against the Federalists. Adams won by a vote of seventy-one to sixty-eight over Jefferson. It was a major blow to Adams's ego. He had wanted to avoid party strife and win election by acclamation, but even the reflected glory of Washington had hardly been enough to save him from defeat. Hamilton's maneuvers had actually served to reduce rather than increase the vote for Pinckney, and had allowed the opposition candidate, Jefferson, to become vice president in what was otherwise a Federalist administration. Pinckney had fifty-nine votes, Aaron Burr thirty, and the rest of the votes were scattered among nine candidates (two were cast for Washington).

This first effort at a party election had demonstrated the degree to which both par-

throw the decision into the House of Representatives, might not even be resolved there. Showing his usual coyness about public service, Jefferson indicated to Madison that, in such a case, Madison should let it be known that Jefferson believed that Adams should have preference, because

ties were ill-formed, ill-organized, and unwilling to subordinate the politics of personalities to general party well-being. Hamilton
and his friends had never been completely
happy with Adams, and while they wanted to
defeat Jefferson and his Republicans they
would have been quite satisfied to see Adams
finish second to another Federalist. The Republicans could agree on Jefferson, but had
never really committed themselves to a second candidate. The result was that Burr received less than half of the electoral votes received by Jefferson. The major problem,
however, was in the constitutional provision
that placed both President and vice president
on the same ballot. This system simply invit-
ed attempts at political finesse with the intention of reversing the order of the two top
finishers, even if they were of the same party.
That it had even deeper potential problems
was to be shown in 1800, when greater party
cohesion in voting produced the dangerous
tie between Jefferson and Burr.

Yet, the election of 1796 was of great
importance in American history. Washington did nothing better in his career than
when he chose to give up the presidency.
History is replete with instances of successful, idolized revolutionaries unwilling to
yield power, and then subverting the very
system they had fought to establish. In
1796 the United States demonstrated that a
republic could peacefully change its elected
chief executive, and the power of Washington's reputation was such that for most of
American history two terms was regarded
as the most to which a President could as-
pire. The presidential electoral system created in 1787 was a rather clumsy procedure, but in the first elections it began to
work. The development of political parties

increased the complications, but even then
could be surmounted. Adjustments were
needed, and were to be provided after the
deadlocked election of 1800, but the United
States had shown that a republic could successfully provide for the transfer of executive power through an elective system.

*British engraving of President
John Adams, circa 1796.*

★

1800

16 STATES
IN THE UNION

DEMOCRATIC-REPUBLICAN

Thomas Jefferson

ELECTORAL VOTE 73

DEMOCRATIC-REPUBLICAN

Aaron Burr

ELECTORAL VOTE 73

FEDERALIST

John Adams

ELECTORAL VOTE 65

FEDERALIST

Charles C. Pinckney

ELECTORAL VOTE 64

FEDERALIST

John Jay

ELECTORAL VOTE 1

NOBLE E. CUNNINGHAM, JR.
is the Curators' Professor of History at
the University of Missouri, Columbia. His
recent books include *In Pursuit of Reason:
The Life of Thomas Jefferson* (1987); *The
Image of Thomas Jefferson in the Public Eye:
Portraits for the People, 1800–1809* (1981); and
*Popular Images of the American Presidency:
From Washington to Lincoln* (1991)

either John Adams nor Thomas Jefferson saw himself as "running for President" in 1800. Four years earlier, when they had stood in opposition to each other in the presidential contest to succeed Washington, neither candidate had conducted an active campaign. Jefferson then disclaimed even being a candidate, though he knew he was being "run" by others. Receiving the second-largest number of electoral votes in 1796, Jefferson became vice president, but he was never part of the Adams administration. It was generally assumed that Adams would seek reelection and that Jefferson would be the Republican presidential candidate in 1800.

In contrast to 1796, Jefferson was actively involved in the election of 1800. Indeed, he began preparing for it as early as 1798, if not earlier, though he saw himself more as working for the success of the Republican party than as seeking the presidential office. Viewing the contest as one of political principles and policy differences, he could work for a victory of the Republican party without admitting ambition for office. At the same time, the development of political parties was giving legitimacy to political campaigning that earlier had been seen as personal ambition. Thus Jefferson was, in fact, running for office.

So also was John Adams, though less visibly than Jefferson. Unlike Jefferson—regarded by all as the leader of the Republican party—President Adams was not the unchallenged head of the Federalist party. Many Federalists regarded Alexander Ha-

milton as the actual leader of the party, and for much of Adams's presidency his administration was weakened by leading members of his cabinet looking to Hamilton for direction. By 1800 the split led to Hamilton's opposing the reelection of Adams. While working for a Federalist victory in 1800, Hamilton sought to win the presidency for Charles Cotesworth Pinckney, nominally the Federalist candidate for vice president. As President, Adams enjoyed the advantages of incumbency. Having served eight years as vice president under Washington, Adams sought to maintain an image of inheritor of the mantle. Although, as the incumbent, Adams had only to stand for reelection and was less active than Jefferson in the campaign, his movements during the election year reveal a candidate running for office.

It may be argued that Jefferson began his campaign for the presidency when he secretly drafted the Kentucky Resolutions of 1798 and encouraged Madison to prepare similar resolutions for the Virginia legislature. Both Jefferson and Madison conceived their protests against the Alien and Sedition Acts in broader terms, and the Kentucky and Virginia Resolutions became the opening guns fired in the campaign of 1800. Viewing the Alien and Sedition laws—passed by a Federalist-controlled Congress and enforced by the Adams administration—as unconstitutional, Jefferson and Madison sought to build state support for overturning the acts. While no other state legislature

Mezzotint of Thomas Jefferson by David Edwin after a Rembrandt Peale portrait, circa 1800.

THE METROPOLITAN MUSEUM OF ART, MICHAEL FRIEDSAM BEQUEST, 1932. (32.56.6)

THOMAS JEFFERSON Esq.
President of the United States

endorsed the Kentucky and Virginia protests, the unpopular Federalist measures became major campaign issues in 1800. A campaign broadside issued by the state Republican Committee of New Jersey in 1800 denounced the Sedition Act "by which many citizens have been deprived of their rights, and native Americans consigned to loathsome prisons for exercising the constitutional right of public enquiry."

In private letters which were circulated among Republican activists throughout the country, Jefferson strongly affirmed his support "for freedom of the press, and against all violations of the constitution to silence by force and not by reason the complaints or criticisms, just or unjust, of our citizens against the conduct of their agents." Jefferson articulated his political views to Republican leaders throughout the country. "I am for a government rigorously frugal and simple, applying all the possible savings of the public revenue to the discharge of the national debt," he wrote, explaining his opposition to a standing army and a navy, his

support "for free commerce with all nations; political connection with none." He also emphasized his commitment to freedom of religion and other civil liberties.

Although neither political party adopted an official party platform in 1800, the Jeffersonian Republicans provided an equivalent, offering a vision of change, while Adams's supporters projected their candidate as following in the footsteps of Washington. Republicans promised not only to end the Alien and Sedition laws but also to pursue a policy of peace—at a time when an undeclared naval war against France was in progress. The Philadelphia *Aurora*, whose editor was indicted under the Sedition Act, predicted that a Federalist victory would mean war, whether Adams or Pinckney were President. "With *Jefferson* we shall have peace, therefore the friends of *peace will vote for Jefferson*—the friends of war will vote for *Adams* or for *Pinckney*."

Republican campaign literature also directed voter attention to taxes, the national debt, increased governmental expenditures, and the military expansion prompted by the threat of war with France. A Republican handbill depicted the election as deciding "whether the present system of war, debt, and encreasing taxation shall continue to be pursued, or a new line of conduct shall be adopted." One Virginia Republican urged another party stalwart to refer frequently to government expenses, arguing that instead of talking to the voters about principles Republicans ought "to bring our arguments home to their feelings. . . . Let *peace and economy* then be our constant theme." Jefferson's supporters focused more attention on unpopular Federalist measures than on

Adams personally, but charges of monarchism were still directed against him, as they had been in 1796. One Republican writer accused both Hamilton and Adams of belonging to "a monarchical party in the United States" and hoped that Americans "will never permit the chief magistrate of the union to become a *King* instead of a president."

Federalist campaign literature defended Federalist policy, linked the administrations of Washington and Adams together, and argued against change. Adams's supporters stressed the prosperous condition of the country resulting from "the sage maxims of administration established by Washington, and steadily pursued by his virtuous successor." Defending their record against mounting Republican attacks, Federalists expressed confidence that American voters would "value the blessings of good government too well to risque a change."

On the other hand, a Republican campaign leaflet employed bold print to ask the voters of New Jersey: *"Is it not high time for a CHANGE?"* Republicans painted a bleak picture: "Our agriculture is oppressed by taxation. Our manufactures are superceded by British productions. Our commerce subjected to the spoliations of foreign cruisers. . . . We are struggling under a direct tax, with heavy imposts; raising money on loan at *Eight* percent.—And our expenditures are encreasing, while our national debt is accumulating." Voters on Long Island were told that the election would determine "whether the present system of war, debt, and encreasing taxation shall continue to be pursued, or a new line of conduct shall be adopted."

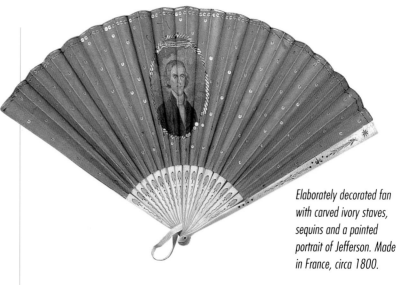

Elaborately decorated fan with carved ivory staves, sequins and a painted portrait of Jefferson. Made in France, circa 1800.

One Federalist sneered that Republicans had "a certain number of sounds, thrown into the form of regular and well connected sentences, which they can on all occasions utter with the utmost facility and volubility. In these sentences the words British Influence—Standing Army—Direct Taxes—Funding System—Expensive Navy—Commerce can support itself—Congress have too high wages—Aristocracy—and Washington's Grave Stones, are ever and anon distinctly heard." Federalists replied to Republican attacks by defending the policies of both Washington and Adams. "We forget that our government has preserved us from the two most powerful nations of the world," declared the Virginia Federalist state committee in a broadside addressed to Virginia voters.

> We forget that we have been preserved from a close alliance with either of those nations . . . and that we remain, if we will, free and independent. But the fleet, the army, taxes, all the little evils which were necessary to the attainment of these great and invaluable objects, make a strong impression, and are attributed as crimes to the government.

JEFFERSON'S MARCH.

PHILADELPHIA, Published by G. E. BLAKE, No 1 South 5th Street.

Sheet music published in Philadelphia, probably for Jefferson's 1801 inauguration.

Republican publicists extolled Jefferson as the author of the Declaration of Independence and as a statesman, "whose talents as governor of his native state, as an ambassador abroad, as legislator and secretary of state, and whose pursuits have been from first to last, to promote toleration in religion and freedom in politics." He was also lauded as "the adorer of our God; the patriot of his country; and the friend and benefactor of the whole human race." In concluding an address to the voters of New Jersey, this supporter of Jefferson pleaded:

> Let us therefore, taking the Declaration of Independence in our hands, and carrying its principles in our hearts, let us resolve to support THOMAS JEFFERSON, whose whole life has been a comment on its precepts, and an uniform pursuit of the great blessings of his country which it was first intended to establish.

On the Federalist side, Fisher Ames wrote privately that it was time for Federalists to "sound the tocsin about Jefferson" and display "the dreadful evils to be apprehended from a Jacobin President." The *Gazette of the United States* published a piece addressed to Jefferson saying: "You have been, Sir, a Governor, an Ambassador, and a Secretary of State, and had to desert each of these posts, from that weakness of nerves, want of fortitude and total imbecility of character, which have marked your whole political career, and most probably will attend you to your grave." The same Philadelphia newspaper employed bold print to warn voters that "the only question to be asked by every American, laying his hand on his heart is 'shall I continue in allegiance to GOD—AND A RELIGIOUS PRESIDENT; Or impiously declare for JEFFERSON—AND NO GOD!!!'" In a widely circulating pamphlet from which Federalist newspapers freely copied, the Reverend William Linn of New York charged that the election of Jefferson would "destroy religion, introduce immorality, and loosen all the bonds of society. . . . The voice of the nation in calling a deist to the first office must be construed into no less than rebellion against God." The editor of the *Gazette of the United States* opined that Linn's tract "convicts Mr. Jefferson of scepticism, deism, and disregard for the holy scriptures."

No issue caused Jefferson and his Republican supporters more concern than the charge that he was the enemy of religion. Jefferson's deistic views were little understood by most voters; and as an unexcelled champion of religious freedom, he saw no reason to justify or explain them. Nonetheless, he was disturbed by the Federalist invective depicting him as the enemy of Christianity. In coming to his defense, one supporter argued that "Mr. Jefferson is at least as good a Christian as Mr. Adams, and in all probability a much better one." Another champion of the Republican candidate defended Jefferson's *Notes on the State of Virginia*—the source of most of the attacks on his religious beliefs—arguing that "there is not a single passage in the Notes on Virginia, or any of Mr. Jefferson's writings, repugnant to Christianity; but on the contrary, in every respect, favourable to it."

The campaign of 1800 was not simply a contest between presidential candidates; it was an election in which the outcome was determined by numerous candidates running for state legislatures and for presidential electors. Unlike present-day elections when American voters go to the polls on a single day to vote for President, the electoral vote in 1800 was decided in different states at various times over the course of the year. In only five states were presidential electors chosen by direct popular vote. Elections for state legislators who would choose the presidential electors decided the presidential contest in most states, and in a few states the party complexion of the state legislature was not clear until after the members convened.

The election for the state legislature in New York, at the end of April 1800, was seen by both parties as nearly essential to national success. Without the New York electoral vote in 1796 Adams would not have been President, and Jefferson feared that without it a Republican victory might be impossible in 1800. Because the New

THE SMITHSONIAN INSTITUTION

York City delegation was expected to give a majority in the closely divided legislature, both parties concentrated their efforts on the city election.

With Alexander Hamilton directing the Federalist campaign and Aaron Burr managing the Republican effort, the New York City election attracted national attention. Burr's strategy was to run prominent persons for assembly seats, and he induced former Governor George Clinton and General Horatio Gates to be candidates—the names of which were not revealed until after the Federalists had announced their ticket. During the three days of balloting, both Burr and Hamilton were active at polling places. At sunset on May 1 the polls closed, and by midnight the outcome was sufficiently clear that one party worker, Matthew L. Davis, scrawled across the top of a letter to Albert Gallatin "Republicanism Triumphant." When all the votes were counted,

One of the most interesting relics of the 1800 election is this linen banner with a crude portrait of Jefferson and a ribbon with the words proclaiming "T. JEFFERSON, President of the United States of AMERICA" and "JOHN ADAMS is no MORE." Probably displayed at a Jefferson victory celebration.

Liverpool pitcher, circa 1797. The likeness of John Adams is after an engraving by H.H. Housten. The linked-states design had now been expanded to include sixteen states.

THE SMITHSONIAN INSTITUTION

the entire Republican ticket for the city had been elected, assuring the presidential electoral vote of New York to Jefferson. "To Col. Burr we are indebted for every thing," Davis told Gallatin. Burr himself wrote to Jefferson that the victory was complete and the manner of attaining it highly honorable. "On the part of the republicans there has been no indecency, no unfairness, no personal abuse," he claimed, "—on the other side, the influence and authority of office have openly perverted and prostituted and the town has been inundated with scurrility and ribaldry issuing from federal presses and circulated by federal runners."

When the news of the New York Republican triumph reached the capital at Philadelphia on Saturday morning May 3, Republican members of Congress were jubilant,

while Federalists despaired. On the evening of the same day, Federalist representatives and senators met in a party caucus and agreed to support John Adams and Charles Cotesworth Pinckney equally as presidential candidates. The ostensible explanation was to give the Federalists two chances to win the presidency, but the motivation emanated from Hamilton's scheme to elect Pinckney rather than Adams. Privately Hamilton was saying that he could no longer support Adams, even if it meant the election of Jefferson. "If we must have an enemy at the head of the Government, let it be one whom we can oppose," he wrote. His hope was that the vote of South Carolina might go to Jefferson and Pinckney, a native son. If Federalist electors elsewhere voted for Adams and Pinckney, the South

Carolinian might be elected President. Because, under the provisions of the Constitution then in force, presidential electors each cast two votes without distinguishing between President and vice president, such a strategy was viable.

A week after the Federalists held their caucus, Republican members of Congress caucused and rewarded Aaron Burr for the New York victory by nominating him as vice presidential candidate to run with Jefferson on the Republican ticket. The caucus made no formal nomination of Jefferson, whom party consensus had already recognized as the presidential candidate. While it was clearly understood that Burr was to occupy second place on the Republican ticket, presidential electors could make no such distinction in casting their electoral votes.

Success in New York gave the Republicans an initial boost, but months of competition lay ahead, and the election was recognized by party activists on both sides as very close. After Congress adjourned in May 1800, Adams made a trip to Washington to inspect the new capital, to which government offices were to move during the summer. He traveled to Washington by way of Lancaster and York, Pennsylvania, and Fredericktown, Maryland, receiving the attention accorded the President of the United States, who was also a candidate for reelection. "How is it he has taken the route . . . fifty miles out of the strait course?" queried the Republican *Aurora* of Philadelphia. The press soon reported Adams's visit to pay his respects to Mrs. Washington at Mount Vernon, where six months earlier the first President had died. On his way to Massachusetts, Adams also stopped in Balti-

Jefferson's inaugural address extended the hand of peace to his political opponents: "We are all Republicans; we are all Federalists." His statement was more hopeful than accurate.

more, and he was greeted at other places along the way home. Federalists as well as Republicans recognized the political implications of Adams's travels. "The great man has been south as far as Alexandria," wrote Fisher Ames, "making his addressers acquainted with his revolutionary merits and claiming almost in plain words at New London, office as the only reward."

Both sides increased the tempo of campaigning in newspapers, broadsides, and pamphlets as the fall of 1800 arrived with no safe prediction of the outcome. In Pennsylvania, the legislature had deadlocked over the method of choosing presidential electors, and could no longer be counted

Thomas Jefferson inaugural medal inscribed "4 MARCH 1801" and struck in 1802.

on to cast votes for any candidate. The outcome in South Carolina was also highly uncertain. The publication in October of a letter by Hamilton opposing the election of Adams created a last-minute sensation, though it may have come too late in the campaign to have influenced the result. By the end of November Jefferson had gathered sufficient information from other states to conclude that the outcome depended on South Carolina.

When it became known that Jefferson and Burr had received the electoral votes of South Carolina, the defeat of Adams and Pinckney was decided, but the election was not over. The electoral vote was Jefferson 73, Burr 73, Adams, 65, Pinckney 64, and John Jay 1. Republican party loyalty had resulted in every Republican elector voting for both Jefferson and Burr, because no clear arrangement had been made to throw a vote away from Burr. The tie now required the election be decided in the House of Representatives, where the Federalists had a majority, though neither party controlled a majority of state delegations.

The outcome was uncertain when the House began to vote on February 11. On the

first ballot, Jefferson received the votes of eight states, Burr six, and two states were divided. Nearly a week of balloting produced the same result, as Republican ranks held firm. Despite Hamilton's repeated appeals to Federalist members to vote for Jefferson in preference to Burr, no Federalist ever did so. Not until the thirty-sixth ballot on February 17 did the Federalists concede defeat, giving Jefferson the victory by abstaining or casting blank ballots.

The long, hard-fought campaign of 1800 was at an end. No previous election of an American President been so contested. Never before had the nation experienced such spirited electioneering, so much political organizing, or such wide popular interest and involvement in a political campaign. "Running for President" early had become the central drama of American political life.

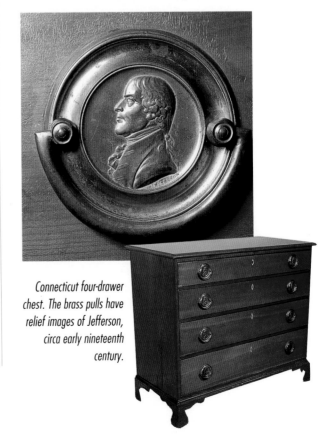

Connecticut four-drawer chest. The brass pulls have relief images of Jefferson, circa early nineteenth century.

921

AN ADDRESS,

TO THE VOTERS FOR ELECTORS OF PRESIDENT AND VICE PRESIDENT OF THE UNITED STATES, IN THE STATE OF VIRGINIA.

THE minority of the late Affembly, after an unavailing ftruggle for the ancient ufages of elections, and for your eftablifhed rights, were conftrained at laft to yield to the meafure of a General Ticket. They faw with regret, that the firft effect of this innovation would be an attempt to influence your votes; which, upon the trueft principles of republicanifm, they wifhed to remain free and unbiaffed. But the Affembly, by compelling you to vote for twenty one Electors, difperfed through every diftrict of the ftate, all of whom, except the refident in your own diftrict, muft be generally unknown to you, might fuppofe they acquired the right to enlighten, and direct your choice. Immediately there appeared what is ftyled the Republican Ticket, fanctioned by a majority of the ftate legiflature, containing great and impofing names, and calculated, in every refpect, to confine, by the weight of authority, your hitherto unlimited freedom of election.

To unite the friends of our government, it became neceffary to follow, in fome meafure, this example. But the minority have chofen for their Ticket, not thofe men, who, as leaders of a party, with vaft objects in view, have had their paffions roufed, and their tempers foured by the conflict; nor yet fuch as, enjoying the higheft ftate employments, have been accuftomed to regard the rival authorities of the union with a jealoufy, too apt to degenerate into hatred; but men, who, bearing like yourfelves only the common evils of government, and partaking only of its common advantages, are moft likely to appreciate it juftly. If this new fangled mode of election had not been adopted, you would have feen them, generally, among the candidates in your feveral diftricts.

The reafons we have to be fatisfied with our prefent government, it would be long, and we hope unneceffary, to detail. The uncorrupted feelings of every American fhould make it unneceffary; nor need he learn from foreigners the increafing profperity of our happy country, while the fevereft calamity afflicts almoft the whole of the civilized world, and has nearly ruined the faireft portion of it. To the adoption of our conftitution, to the fage maxims of adminiftration eftablifhed by the immortal WASHINGTON, and fteadily purfued by his virtuous fucceffor, may fairly be afcribed our prefent profperous fituation. The man who calmly contemplates, and can wifh to change it, may be compared to the great enemy of mankind furveying malicioufly the firft abodes of happinefs and peace.

But, an unvarying courfe of profperity, like the even tenor of health, makes no impreffion; while we betray a quick fenfibility to the flighteft misfortune or pain. We forget that our government has preferved us from two impending wars, the foundation of which was laid before its exiftance, with the two moft powerfull nations of the world, armed to the full extent of their power; and that, without any facrifice of the national intereft, or of the national honor. We forget that we have been preferved from a clofe alliance with either of thofe nations, which would have been the worft, and the moft inevitable, confequences of a war with the other; and that we remain, if we will, completely free and independent. But the fleet, the army, all the little evils which were neceffary to the attainment of thefe great and invaluable objects, make a ftrong impreffion, and are attributed as crimes to the government.

In the eager defire of change, even the meaning of language is perverted, in order to juftify it. Thus the free, peaceful, and flourifhing condition of the United Staets, under the guidance of WASHINGTON, the father of his country, is called "the calm of defpotifm." * Shall we then embark, with this writer, on "the tempeftuous fea of liberty?" † When tired of the voyage, vainly may we ftrive to regain our prefent peaceful haven. We muft endure the unceafing ftorms, and deeply drink the bloody waves, and find no refuge at laft, but in the calm of real defpotifm. Let us be content to take a leffon, on this head, from the French republic, rathar than from our own experience.

We are apt to fancy ourfelves called as citizens of the United States, to vote for the higheft officers of the government of thefe ftates. But the late Affembly has feparated us from our fellow-citizens of the union, and compels us to fpeak the voice of Virginia only. Our zeal for the Union, however increafes with ftate perfecution; and believing, as the conduct of the minority on this occafion demonftrates, that our principles are the moft purely republican; we unite thefe traits of our political character, in the ftyle of the American Republican Ticket; which by your facred regard to the conftitution, and all thofe bleffings of which it is the fource, the peace, freedom and happinefs of yourfelves, and of your pofterity, we now folicit you to fupport.

* See letter to Mazzei, afcribed to Mr. Jefferfon.   † See the fame.

The American Republican Ticket.

DISTRICTS.	ELECTORS.
New-Kent, Henrico, Charles City, James-City, York, Warwick, and Elizabeth City,	JOHN BLAIR.
Accomack, Northampton, and Princefs Anne,	JOHN WISE.
Hanover, Caroline, and Louifa,	CHARLES DABNEY.
Fluvanna, Albemarle, Amherft, and Goochland,	WILLIAM CABELL.
Madifon, Orange, Culpeper, and Spotfylvania,	JOHN JAMISON.
King and Queen, King William, Effex, Middlefex, Gloucefter, and Mathews,	CARTER BRAXTON.
Norfolk, Nanfemond, and Ifle of Wight,	JOHN NEVISON.
Suffex, Southampton, Surry, Prince George, and Greenfville,	GEORGE K. TAYLOR.
Brunfwick, Dinwiddie, and Mecklenburg,	STERLING EDMUNDS.
Amelia, Nottoway, Chefterfield, and Powhatan,	BERNARD MARKHAM.
Prince Edward, Buckingham, Cumberland, and Lunenburg,	JAMES MORTON.
Halifax, Charlotte, and Pittfylvania,	WILLIAM MORTON.
Bedford, Campbell, Franklin, Henry, and Patrick,	JOEL LEFTWICH.
Richmond, Northumberland, Lancafter, Weftmoreland, and King George,	BURDET ASHTON.
Prince William, Stafford, and Fairfax,	BAILEY WASHINGTON.
Fauquier and Loudon,	JOHN BLACKWELL.
Bath, Botetourt, Rockbridge, Greenbrier, Kanawha, and Monroe,	JAMES BRECKENRIDGE.
Hardy, Hampfhire, Pendleton, Randolph, Harriton, Monongalia, Ohio, Brooke, and Wood,	ISAAC VANMETER.
Wythe, Montgomery, Wafhington, Ruffel, Lee, Grayfon, and Tazewell,	ROBERT CROCKET.
Frederick and Berkley,	JOSEPH SWEARINGEN.
Buckingham, Augufta, and Shenandoah,	ALEXANDER St. CLAIR.

RICHMOND, 26th May, 1800.

By order of the Committee entrufted with the Ticket of the minority,

WILLIAM AUSTIN, Secretary.

124464
oo

Broadsides were widely used in 1800 for short addresses and for publicizing tickets for presidential electors, such as this address to Virginia voters issued by the Federalist state committee. Note that Federalists in Jefferson's home state labeled their party ticket "The American Republican Ticket."

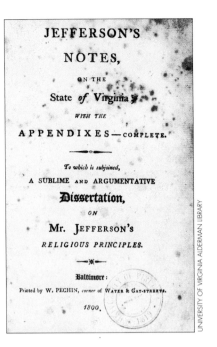

SERIOUS CONSIDERATIONS

ON THE

ELECTION

OF A

PRESIDENT:

ADDRESSED TO THE

Citizens of the United States.

TRENTON:
PRINTED BY *SHERMAN, MERSHON & THOMAS,*
M,DCCC.

1800

A

Vindication

OF THE

RELIGION

OF

Mr. JEFFERSON,

AND A

STATEMENT OF HIS SERVICES

IN THE

CAUSE

OF

Religious Liberty.

BY A FRIEND TO *REAL* RELIGION.

From Envy, Hatred and Malice, and all Uncharitableness—
Good Lord Deliver Us!
Lit. of Prot. Episc. Church.

BALTIMORE:
Printed for the Editor of the AMERICAN, *by* W. PECHIN.
PRICE—12 Cents.

JEFFERSON'S

NOTES,

ON THE

State *of* Virginia;

WITH THE

APPENDIXES—COMPLETE.

To which is subjoined,

A SUBLIME AND ARGUMENTATIVE

Dissertation,

ON

Mr. JEFFERSON'S

RELIGIOUS PRINCIPLES.

Baltimore:

Printed by W. PECHIN, corner of WATER & GAY-STREETS.

1800.

Campaign pamphlets and leaflets were numerous in 1800, and the title pages of some provide insights into the election issues. These examples illustrate the prominence of the issue of Jefferson's religion. Serious Facts was a direct Republican reply to the attack on Jefferson on religious grounds by Reverend William Linn.

SERIOUS FACTS,

OPPOSED TO

" *Serious Considerations :*"

OR, THE

VOICE *of* WARNING

TO

Religious Republicans.

ARISE—AWAKE—gird up your loins.—*Your Country is in danger !*
There shall arise false Christs and false Prophets, that (if it were
possible) they shall deceive the very Elect !

PREFACE.

I have written a very Little Book—but it contains Important Facts.—The evidence it exhibits is truly impressive. Let such circumstances be weighed with candour, and every man decide with freedom for himself. If a spirit of rational and independent inquiry is exerted, the writer will be satisfied, for his country will be saved.

There is but one path to safety, but the roads to ruin are numerous. The only security for public liberty, is the wisdom of an enlightened people ; if we surrender our rights of judgment to statesmen or to pastors, depend upon it, that sooner or later, we shall become deceived—it is to deliver the sheep unto wolves to be devoured.

Let it not be said that I have spoken irreverently of certain Clergymen—No man honours a Pious Divine with more sincerity than myself.—Those men have voluntarily entered into the forum of contention, they shall feel the wounds they shall wear the scars—they descended from the pulpit for unworthy purposes, and have justly forfeited that respect from others which they have denied to themselves.

OCTOBER, 1800.

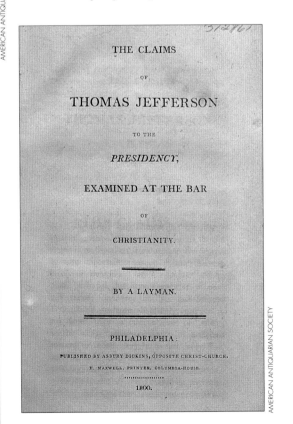

THE CLAIMS

OF

THOMAS JEFFERSON

TO THE

PRESIDENCY,

EXAMINED AT THE BAR

OF

CHRISTIANITY.

BY A LAYMAN.

PHILADELPHIA:

PUBLISHED BY ASBURY DICKINS, OPPOSITE CHRIST-CHURCH.
H. MAXWELL, PRINTER, COLUMBIA-HOUSE.

1800.

SPEECH

OF

THOMAS JEFFERSON, PRESIDENT OF THE UNITED STATES,

DELIVERED

AT HIS INSTALMENT,

MARCH 4, 1801,

AT THE CITY OF WASHINGTON.

FRIENDS, AND FELLOW-CITIZENS,

CALLED upon to undertake the duties of the first executive office of our country, I avail myself of the presence of that portion of my fellow-citizens, which is here assembled, to express my grateful thanks, for the favour with which they have been pleased to look towards me; to declare a sincere consciousness, that the task is above my talents, and that I approach it with those anxious and awful presentiments, which the greatness of the charge, and the weakness of my powers, so justly inspire. A rising nation, spread over a wide and fruitful land,...traversing all the seas with the rich productions of their industry....engaged in commerce with nations who feel power and forget right....advancing rapidly to destinies beyond the reach of mortal eye....when I contemplate these transcendent objects, and see the honour, the happiness, and the hopes of this beloved country, committed to the issue and the auspices of this day, I shrink from the contemplation, and humble myself before the magnitude of the undertaking. Utterly, indeed, should I despair, did not the presence of many, whom I here see, remind me, that, in the other high authorities, provided by our constitution, I shall find resources of wisdom, of virtue, and of zeal, on which to rely under all difficulties. To you, then, gentlemen, who are charged with the sovereign functions of legislation, and to those associated with you, I look with encouragement for that guidance and support, which may enable us to steer, with safety, the vessel in which we are all embarked, amidst the conflicting elements of a troubled world.

During the contest of opinion, through which we have past, the animation of discussions and of exertions, has sometimes worn an aspect which might impose on strangers, unused to think freely, and to write and to think: but this being now decided by the voice of the nation, announced according to the rules of the constitution, all will, of course, arrange themselves under the will of the law, and unite in common efforts, for the common good. All, too, will bear in mind this sacred principle.... that though the will of the majority is, in all cases, to prevail, that will, to be rightful, must be reasonable....that the minority possess their equal rights, which equal laws must protect, and to violate would be oppression. Let us then, fellow-citizens, unite with one heart, and one mind. Let us restore to social intercourse, that harmony and affection, without which, liberty, and even life itself, are but dreary things. And let us reflect, that, having banished from our land, that religious intolerance, under which mankind so long bled and suffered, we have yet gained little, if we countenance a political intolerance, as despotic, as wicked, and capable of as bitter and bloody persecutions.

During the throes and convulsions of the ancient world....during the agonizing spasms of infuriated man, seeking, through blood and slaughter, his long-lost liberty ....it was not wonderful that the agitation of the billows should reach even this distant and peaceful shore,....that this should be more felt and feared by some, and less by others,....and should divide opinions, as to measures of safety. But every difference of opinion is not a difference of principle. We have called by different names, brethren of the same principle, WE ARE ALL REPUBLICANS; WE ARE ALL FEDERALISTS. If there

be any among us, who would wish to dissolve this union, or to change its republican form, let them stand undisturbed, as monuments of the safety with which error of opinion may be tolerated, where reason is left free to combat it. I know, indeed, that some honest men fear that a republican government cannot be strong... that this government is not strong enough. But would the honest patriot, in the full tide of successful experiment, abandon a government which has so far kept us free and firm, on the theoretic and visionary fear, that this government, the world's best hope, may, by possibility, want energy to preserve itself?....I trust not....I believe this, on the contrary, the strongest government on earth....I believe it the only one, where every man, at the call of the law, would fly to the standard of the law, and would meet invasions of the public order as his own personal concern. Sometimes it is said, that man cannot be trusted with the government of himself. Can he then be trusted with the government of others? Or have we found angels, in the form of kings, to govern him? Let history answer this question.

Let us, then, with courage and confidence, pursue our own federal and republican principles....our attachment to union and representative government. Kindly separated, by nature and a wide ocean, from the exterminating havoc of one quarter of the globe....too high-minded to endure the degradations of the others....possessing a chosen country, with room enough for our descendents to the thousandth and thousandth generation....entertaining a due sense of our equal right to the use of our own faculties....to the acquisitions of our own industry....to honour and confidence from our fellow-citizens; resulting not from birth, but from our actions, and their sense of them....enlightened by a benign religion, professed, indeed, and practised in various forms, yet all of them inculcating honesty, truth, temperance, gratitude, and the love of man....acknowledging and adoring an over-ruling Providence, which, by all its dispensations, proves that it delights in the happiness of man here, and his greater happiness hereafter....with all these blessings, what more is necessary to make us a happy and a prosperous people?....Still one thing more, fellow-citizens, a wise and frugal government, which shall restrain men from injuring one another; shall leave them otherwise free to regulate their own pursuits of industry and improvement; and shall not take from the mouth of labor the bread it has earned. This is the sum of good government; and this is necessary to close the circle of our felicities.

About to enter, fellow-citizens, on the exercise of duties, which comprehend every thing dear and valuable to you, it is proper you should understand what I deem the essential principles of our government, and consequently those which ought to shape its administration. I will compress them within the narrowest compass they will bear, stating the general principle, but not all its limitations. Equal and exact justice to all men, of whatever state or persuasion, religious or political....peace, commerce, and honest friendship with all nations....entangling alliances with none....the support of the state governments in all their rights, as the most competent administrations for our domestic concerns, and the surest bulwarks against anti-republican tendencies....the preservation of the general

government in its whole constitutional vigor, as the sheet anchor of our peace at home, and safety abroad....a jealous care of the right of election by the people....a mild and safe corrective of abuses, which are lopped by the sword of revolution, where peaceable remedies are unprovided.... absolute acquiescence in the decisions of the majority, the vital principle of republics, from which is no appeal but to force, the vital principle and immediate parent of despotism....a well-disciplined militia, our best reliance in peace, and for the first moment of war, till regulars may relieve them....the supremacy of the civil over the military authority....economy in the public expence, that labor may be lightly burdened....the honest payment of our debts, and sacred preservation of public faith....encouragement of agriculture, and of commerce, as its handmaid....the diffusion of information, and arraignment of all abuses at the bar of the public reason....freedom of religion....freedom of the press....and freedom of person, under the protection of the habeas corpus, and trial by juries impartially selected. These principles form the bright constellation, which has gone before us, and guided our steps through an age of revolution and reformation. The wisdom of our sages, and blood of our heroes, have been devoted to their attainment. They should be the creed of our political faith....the text of civic instruction....the touchstone by which to try the services of those we trust; and should we wander from them, in moments of error or alarm, let us hasten to retrace our steps, and to regain the road which alone leads to peace, liberty, and safety.

I repair, then, fellow citizens, to the post you have assigned me. With experience enough in subordinate offices, to have seen the difficulties of this, the greatest of all, I have learned to expect, that it will rarely fall to the lot of imperfect man, to retire from this station, with the reputation, and the favor, which bring him into it. Without pretensions to that high confidence you reposed in our first and greatest revolutionary character, whose pre-eminent services had entitled him to the first place in his country's love, and destined for him the fairest page in the volume of faithful history, I ask so much confidence only, as may give firmness and effect to the legal administration of your affairs. I shall often go wrong, through defect of judgment. When right, I shall often be thought wrong, by those whose positions will not command a view of the whole ground. I ask your indulgence for my own errors, which will never be intentional; and your support against the errors of others, who may condemn what they would not, if seen in all its parts. The approbation implied by your suffrage, is a great consolation to me for the past; and my future solicitude will be, to retain the good opinion of those who have bestowed it in advance; to conciliate that of others by doing them all the good in my power, and to be instrumental to the happiness and freedom of all.

Relying, then, on the patronage of your good will, I advance with obedience to the work, ready to retire from it whenever you become sensible how much better choices it is in your power to make. And may that infinite Power, which rules the destinies of the universe, lead our councils to what is best, and give them a favorable issue, for our peace and prosperity.

THOMAS JEFFERSON.

THIRD EDITION.

PHILADELPHIA, PUBLISHED BY MATHEW CAREY.

H. MAXWELL, PRINTER.

Silk broadside of Jefferson's 1801 inaugural-address published by Matthew Carey of Philadelphia.

1804
17 STATES
IN THE UNION

DEMOCRATIC-REPUBLICAN

Thomas Jefferson

ELECTORAL VOTE 162

FEDERALIST

Charles C. Pinckney

ELECTORAL VOTE 14

NOBLE E. CUNNINGHAM, JR.
is the Curators' Professor of History at
the University of Missouri, Columbia. His
recent books include *In Pursuit of Reason:
The Life of Thomas Jefferson* (1987); *The Image
of Thomas Jefferson in the Public Eye:
Portraits for the People, 1800–1809* (1981); and
*Popular Images of the American Presidency:
From Washington to Lincoln* (1991).

An incumbent President who claimed he would rather retire to Monticello than seek election to a second term, an opposition party judged by one of the nation's leading newspapers to have no chance whatever of success—these were hardly the ingredients of a lively or hard-fought presidential election campaign. Yet neither source misrepresented the state of national politics on the eve of the presidential election of 1804. President Jefferson had no intention of conducting the active campaign he waged to defeat John Adams in 1800, and the Federalist party was so weakened by the Republican party's growing strength that party leaders seemed unable to decide which of their two candidates, Charles Cotesworth Pinckney or Rufus King, should be the presidential nominee and which the candidate for vice president. In September 1804 a letter to the editor of the Boston *Independent Chronicle* asked, "Why do the Federal party forbear to inform the public of the person they mean to support at the next Presidential election?" As late as October, a writer in the Richmond *Enquirer* insisted that an "impenetrable veil of mystery still conceals the favoured candidates" of the Federalist party.

Notwithstanding President Jefferson's professed reluctance to stand for reelection, it was widely assumed that he would be a candidate in 1804. George Washington had set the precedent of serving for two terms as President; his successor, John Adams, had sought, but failed to win, a second term in 1800. As a good politician, Jefferson did not reveal future political ambitions when he took office as President in 1801. He waited until 1804 to announce that it had been his "decided purpose" when he entered office to retire to a life of tranquillity at the end of one term. But, he said, "the unbounded calumnies of the federal party have obliged me to throw myself on the verdict of my country for trial." However sincere Jefferson may have been, it was not only his political enemies but also his political friends who influenced his decision, for in 1804 Jefferson was an immensely popular President whose reelection seemed certain. The reconciliation of parties that Jefferson had sought when he proclaimed "We are all republicans: we are all federalists" in his inaugural address in 1801 had not taken place, although the Federalist party had lost considerable ground since 1800.

Despite the fact that Jefferson appeared to be an unbeatable candidate for reelection, his Republican party had to give close attention to the campaign. At the beginning of 1804 the Twelfth Amendment—mandating separate balloting for President and vice president in the electoral college—remained unratified, requiring Republican leaders to make plans to avoid any repetition of the 1800 electoral tie vote. The Republican party in 1804 also faced the problem posed by an incumbent vice president who had lost the confidence of the President. At the time of his tie vote with Jefferson in the electoral count of 1800, Aaron Burr alienat-

An engraving of Jefferson with the Declaration of Independence. Known as a great statesman and philosopher, he founded the University of Virginia (1819) and contributed notably to the revival of classical architecture in the United States.

ed large numbers of Republicans by failing to announce that he would refuse to accept the presidency if elected by the House of Representatives. He never regained the lost Republican following. Jefferson as President refrained from taking his vice president into the confidence of the administration and made clear his lack of support by rejecting Burr's recommendations for patronage appointments in New York.

With Burr having lost support nationally, it was inevitable he would be dropped from the Republican ticket in 1804. But the situation remained delicate and embarrassing, and Republicans looked to members of Congress for direction. New Yorkers who also wished to undermine Burr's ambitions for the governorship of their state pressed for a Republican nominating caucus to act.

"The republicans here are anxiously looking to our friends at Washington for a nomination of President and Vice President," wrote Brockholst Livingston to Albert Gallatin, Jefferson's secretary of the treasury near the end of 1803. "The sooner our friends in Congress designate their candidates for their offices the better."

When the Republican congressional nominating caucus met in late February 1804, there was general agreement that Burr must be dropped from the ticket, but no consensus prevailed regarding the candidate to replace him. One hundred and eight Republican members of Congress attended the caucus on February 25, 1804, and unanimously nominated Jefferson for President. On the ballot for the vice presidential nomination, they divided their votes among six candidates, with George Clinton of New York winning the nomination with sixty-seven votes. "It is worthy of particular notice," a report in the Philadelphia *Aurora* observed, "that the name of Mr. Burr was not introduced either in the meeting, or in a single vote."

In contrast to the election of 1800, when only five of the sixteen states chose their presidential electors by popular vote, eleven of the seventeen states in 1804 employed popular election. Thus Republican state party leaders and committees had to give careful attention to organizing their campaign efforts to get out the vote in an election where a close contest would not be relied upon to draw voters to the polls. In Virginia, the Republican state committee employed the organization of county party committees directed by the general committee in Richmond which had been successfully introduced in 1800.

In June 1804, the chairman of the Virginia state Republican committee sent a circular letter to each county chairman listing the names composing the Republican ticket of presidential electors. Because voters were required to cast handwritten ballots—no printed tickets were accepted—the committee instructed that "written tickets containing the names of the Electors, should be dispersed over each County, and active and intelligent Citizens in every neighbourhood should be prevailed on to attend the election, and to bring as many of their fellow citizens as possible to give their suffrages." The state committee also recommended that newspapers be employed to publicize the names of the Republican candidates for electors and Republican principles and policies, suggesting the usefulness of emphasizing "their present state of happiness and prosperity, by contrasting it with the calamities brought upon us by the misconduct of former rulers."

Republicans also used the newspapers to get out the vote. A notice in the Fredericksburg *Virginia Express*, November 1, 1804, declared:

> We hope it will be remembered by the Democratic Republican Citizens, that every vote to be given on the 1st Monday in November for Electors of President and Vice President will count with full effect. Vote for Electors who will choose Jefferson for President and Clinton for Vice President, and by so doing you will give your aid in fixing matters for four years in safe and able hands.

On the eve of the election, an editorial in the Newark *Centinel of Freedom* made a strong appeal to New Jersey Republicans to vote, arguing that the time spent in voting was "of more importance to a farmer than the same time spent following his plow, or a mechanic at his anvil, or the merchant behind the counter." The editor also warned of suspected Federalist activities. "If our information is true, our opponents are organizing in secret, with a view of making a bold push, at a late hour, in hopes of finding republicans off guard," he cautioned, entreating New Jersey voters "to come out, do not sleep, do not slumber on the days of election. However secure we may feel ourselves, let it be remembered that we have enemies."

The absence of an active campaign by the Federalists aroused Republican fears that the Federalists were conducting a secret campaign, hoping to lull Republicans into complacency and inactivity. With the election near at hand, a Republican handbill addressed "To the Democratic Republican Electors, of the State of Pennsylvania" indicated uncertainty as to whether the enemies of Jefferson and Clinton had formed an electoral ticket. But the writer believed that they had done so and that it was "probable that they may have been encouraged secretly to form one by the idea that the democratic republicans are tired by the exertions made at the last election." He warned that "they may foolishly suppose we are divided by contests for men, or for places, so as to allow them to take the Presidents and Vice-Presidents chairs from our friends by surprise."

Tench Coxe, the author of this handbill, went on to summarize the arguments for Jefferson's reelection:

> In the administration of Jefferson the excises and direct tax have been repealed, and with them numerous offices have been abolished. . . . The Mis-

sissippi and every opportunity to trade on its banks and from its mouth have been secured to us. The Indians have been kept in peace. . . . The post-roads have been extended. Religious Liberty remains *the favourite fostered plant* in the Garden of Freedom. The militia have been nursed and rival aristocratic *"volunteers"* have been discouraged. Regular troops have been kept within proper limits by republican caution and prudence. No new treaty of *tribute* has been made with Algerine pirates. There have been no quarrels in our cabinet councils. . . . The President has no more allowance in 1804 than the President had in 1789, though our nation, over which he presides, is nearly twice as numerous. . . . Levees and other matters of parade have been abolished. The expences of our Army and Navy and Indian affairs have been made easier by procuring supplies more and more from our manufacturers. The naturalization law has been altered from the extreme term of fourteen years to a term nine years shorter, according to the time fixed in the administration of Washington.

As this summary indicates, Jefferson ran on his record in 1804, and his first term as President had been remarkably successful. He had carried out campaign promises to reduce taxes, government expenditures, and the size of the military establishment. He had reduced the ceremonial role of the President; and, in contrast to the disarray in the cabinet under his predecessor, John Adams, Jefferson had made the cabinet system work. He had also successfully met the threat posed by the Spanish closure of the port of New Orleans and the transfer of the Louisiana territory to France. His first term ended with the purchase of Louisiana from France—an accomplishment immensely

popular almost everywhere except for Federalist strongholds in New England.

The timing of the Louisiana purchase in relation to the election of 1804 could hardly have been better for Republicans. President Jefferson received the news from Paris that the treaty had been signed on July 3, 1803, just in time to be announced in the Washington *National Intelligencer* for the celebration of the Fourth of July. The transfer of the territory from France to the United States took place on December 20, 1803, just on the eve of the election year. In January, a Federalist congressman reported from Washington:

> There is a *Jubilee* proclaimed here by the Democrats. . . . There is to be such a feast, it is said, as was never known in America, on account of taking possession of *Louisiana*. There is to be dinners—suppers—ball—assemblies, dances, and I know not what. . . . The *Jubilee* is to begin here—but they expect it will run—like *wildfire*, to every dark and benighted corner of America.

As Republican newspapers called for a national festival, the *Jubilee* did spread like wildfire across the land. Jefferson's supporters seemed everywhere to be organizing celebrations. A tremendous celebration in Philadelphia on May 12 was preceded by weeks of preparation and growing anticipation. In some places disgruntled Federalists did not join in the festivities, and a few in New England even contemplated secession from the expanding Union; but they found little support for their schemes. Jefferson's first term thus ended on a note of high diplomatic success. It was a triumph that not only secured control of the Mississippi River but also doubled the territory of the United States.

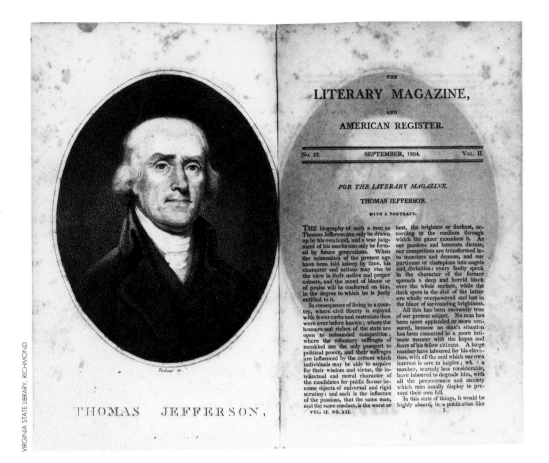

British and American magazines often included portraits of prominent people.

Jefferson called it an "empire for liberty," and only a minority of Americans withheld their applause. Republicans could not have scheduled the election at a better time. It is hardly surprising that the Federalists made so little effort to deny Jefferson a second term.

The election of 1804 lacked the vigorous debates over issues and persons carried on in private letters and public forums during the preceding presidential election. It did not produce the columns of electioneering pieces that filled the newspapers throughout the nation in 1800. Missing also were the lively controversies carried on in pamphlets and campaign leaflets in 1800. One pamphlet writer in 1804 did publish *Observations Upon Certain Passages in Mr. Jefferson's Notes on Virginia, Which Appear to Have a Tendency to Subvert Religion, and Establish a False Philosophy* (New York,

1804). Having only recently read the book, he said he "was surprised that a book which contains so much infidelity, conveyed in so insidious a manner, should have been so extensively circulated in a Christian country, for nearly twenty years, without having received a formal answer." Considering the attention focused on Jefferson's book in the election of 1800 and the replies to it that appeared in print, what is most surprising is that the controversy had escaped this author's attention. In any event, Jefferson's religion was never the issue in the campaign of 1804 that it had been in 1800. After all, Federalists predictions in 1800 that Jefferson's election would "destroy religion, introduce immorality, and loosen all the bonds of society" while pulling down the political edifice erected by Washington had not materialized.

Although Jefferson himself did not campaign for reelection in 1804, Republicans seeking election as presidential electors did so. One such candidate, Montfort Stokes, running in North Carolina, published a handbill asking voters to "take a retrospective view of the successful operations of our Government for the last four years." Though he said he did not wish to remind voters of the disagreeable scenes of the previous election, he referred to Federalists efforts in 1800 as "a weak and infuriated administration, seeking by the most corrupt and servile means to prolong its authority and perpetuate its principles." Listing "a few of the many blessings we have experienced by the wise policy of Mr. Jefferson," he wrote:

> We enjoy peace and respect abroad, happiness and tranquility at home. With many burdens lightened, and no new impositions laid we have yet been enabled . . . to diminish the public debt. . . . Without the aid of a standing army or a burthensome naval force, our commerce is less embarrassed by the depredations of foreign powers, and our frontiers less disturbed by our Indian neighbors. . . . We have no alien or sedition law. . . . By the repeal of the excise laws and other internal taxes, we have got rid of a host of revenue officers, who were fattening on the spoils of the industrious.

"It is scarcely necessary for me to add," Stokes wrote in conclusion, "that if Elected, I shall give my vote for Thomas Jefferson as President of the United States, and the vote for Vice President shall be governed by the circumstances which may occur in regard to the proposed Amendment to the Constitution of the United States." The Twelfth Amendment, to which Stokes referred, was ratified soon after his handbill was printed. Thus in 1804, for the first time, presidential electors cast separate ballots for President and vice president.

Stokes was not the only Republican to run against John Adams. New Jersey voters were told it was not necessary to recall to their recollection "the extravagant, oppressive, and unconstitutional measures of the late administration; or to direct their attention to the economical, pacific, and equitable conduct of the present. Every friend to a republican government, in form and substance, must wish to avert a recurrence of the scenes that marked Mr. Adams's administration, and to perpetuate the system practised by the administration of Mr. Jefferson."

The election returns confirmed the expected defeat of the Federalists at the polls, but it was an even bigger rout than Republicans had anticipated. Jefferson carried all but two states: Connecticut and Delaware. He also lost two of the eleven districts in Maryland but received the unanimous electoral votes of the remaining fourteen states. Jefferson's electoral vote totaled 162. Charles Cotesworth Pinckney, upon whom Federalists finally concentrated their votes, received only 14 electoral votes. Even John Adams's home state of Massachusetts was part of the Republican landslide. George Clinton and Rufus King respectively received the same number of votes for vice president as did the presidential candidate of their respective parties, and Clinton was thus elected vice president of the United States.

Thomas Jefferson did not have to campaign in 1804, but he ran for reelection on his record and won an impressive victory.

RICHMOND, June 25th, 1804.

SIR,

As the time approaches at which the election of Electors will be held in the several Counties, it will become the indispensible and sacred duty of the Corresponding Committees to use every possible exertion to advance the Republican-Ticket.....Written tickets containing the names of the Electors, should be dispersed over each County, and active and intelligent Citizens in every neighbourhood should be prevailed on to attend the election, and to bring as many of their fellow-citizens as possible to give their suffrages.....The most convenient Newspapers should be employed by each Committee, to extend the knowledge of the characters who compose our Ticket, and to recommend the principles which we advocate.

The numerous and irresistible arguments which naturally present themselves in favor of the present administration, should be urged upon the people, and they should be induced to feel and appreciate their present state of happiness and prosperity, by contrasting it with the calamities brought upon us by the misconduct of former rulers. Virginia stood foremost in the struggle for freedom and for the triumph of correct principles ; and it would be disgraceful and perfidious should she discover less zeal and less ardour than her sister States, in defence of that happy order of things which she so eminently contributed to establish. It is unnecessary for us to use any arguments to you in favor of the cause we espouse ; you are known to be the zealous advocates of republican principles, and you have signalized yourselves in the worst of times in their defence......All we have to urge is, that you will now unite with us in giving so strong and decisive an expression of the public sentiment of our republican administration, as will strengthen the well founded confidence of our friends, and prove to the world that the government of the United States is now conducted conformably with the wishes of the great body of the American people.

Your Fellow-Citizen,

PHILIP NORBORNE NICHOLAS,
Chairman of the General Committee.

Attest, JOHN H. FOUSHEE, *Secretary.*

To *John Ambler Chairman of the*
Corresponding Committee for James City County. }

REPUBLICAN TICKET.

Richard Evers Lee,	*of Norfolk Borough.*	William Ellzey,	*of Loudoun.*
John Goodrich,	*of Isle of Wight.*	William Dudley,	*of Warwick.*
Edward Pegram,	*of Dinwiddie.*	Mann Page,	*of Gloucester.*
Dr. Richard Field,	*of Brunswick.*	John Taliaferro, jr.	*of King George.*
Thomas Read,	*of Charlotte.*	Richard Brent,	*of Prince William.*
Creed Taylor,	*of Cumberland.*	Hugh Holmes,	*of Frederick.*
William H. Cabell,	*of Amherst.*	James Dailey,	*of Hampshire.*
George Penn,	*of Patrick.*	James Allen,	*of Shenandoah.*
George Wythe,	*of City of Richmond.*	Archibald Stuart,	*of Augusta.*
John Taylor,	*of Caroline.*	James M'Farlane,	*of Russell.*
Larkin Smith,	*of King & Queen.*	Gen. John Preston,	*of Montgomery.*
... Minor,	*of Spotsylvania.*	William M'Kinley,	*of Ohio.*

Broadside circular. Presidential electors were chosen by state legislatures. This item probably was distributed to the Virginia assembly.

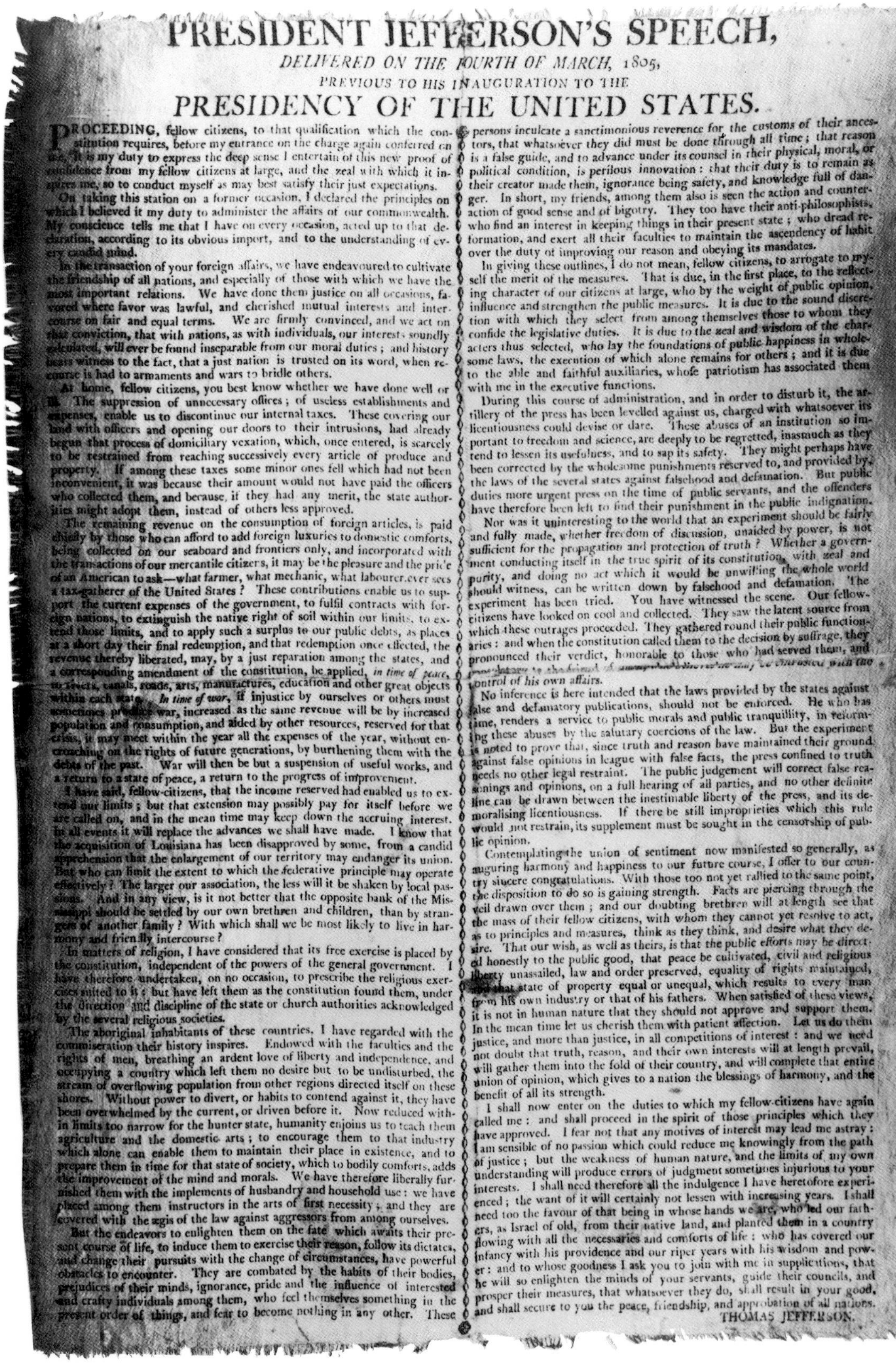

PRESIDENT JEFFERSON'S SPEECH,

DELIVERED ON THE FOURTH OF MARCH, 1805,

PREVIOUS TO HIS INAUGURATION TO THE

PRESIDENCY OF THE UNITED STATES.

PROCEEDING, fellow citizens, to that qualification which the constitution requires, before my entrance on the charge again conferred on me, it is my duty to express the deep sense I entertain of this new proof of confidence from my fellow citizens at large, and the zeal with which it inspires me, so to conduct myself as may best satisfy their just expectations.

On taking this station on a former occasion, I declared the principles on which I believed it my duty to administer the affairs of our commonwealth. My conscience tells me that I have on every occasion, acted up to that declaration, according to its obvious import, and to the understanding of every candid mind.

In the transaction of your foreign affairs, we have endeavoured to cultivate the friendship of all nations, and especially of those with which we have the most important relations. We have done them justice on all occasions, favored where favor was lawful, and cherished mutual interests and intercourse on fair and equal terms. We are firmly convinced, and we act on that conviction, that with nations, as with individuals, our interests soundly calculated, will ever be found inseparable from our moral duties; and history bears witness to the fact, that a just nation is trusted on its word, when recourse is had to armaments and wars to bridle others.

At home, fellow citizens, you best know whether we have done well or ill. The suppression of unnecessary offices; of useless establishments and expenses, enable us to discontinue our internal taxes. These covering our land with officers and opening our doors to their intrusions, had already begun that process of domiciliary vexation, which, once entered, is scarcely to be restrained from reaching successively every article of produce and property. If among these taxes some minor ones fell which had not been inconvenient, it was because their amount would not have paid the officers who collected them, and because, if they had any merit, the state authorities might adopt them, instead of others less approved.

The remaining revenue on the consumption of foreign articles, is paid chiefly by those who can afford to add foreign luxuries to domestic comforts, being collected on our seaboard and frontiers only, and incorporated with the transactions of our mercantile citizens, it may be the pleasure and the pride of an American to ask—what farmer, what mechanic, what labourer ever sees a tax-gatherer of the United States? These contributions enable us to support the current expenses of the government, to fulfil contracts with foreign nations, to extinguish the native right of soil within our limits, to extend those limits, and to apply such a surplus to our public debts, as places at a short day their final redemption, and that redemption once effected, the revenue thereby liberated, may, by a just reparation among the states, and a corresponding amendment of the constitution, be applied, *in time of peace*, to rivers, canals, roads, arts, manufactures, education and other great objects within each state. *In time of war*, if injustice by ourselves or others must sometimes produce war, increased as the same revenue will be by increased population and consumption, and aided by other resources, reserved for that crisis, it may meet within the year all the expenses of the year, without encroaching on the rights of future generations, by burthening them with the debts of the past. War will then be but a suspension of useful works, and a return to a state of peace, a return to the progress of improvement.

I have said, fellow-citizens, that the income reserved had enabled us to extend our limits; but that extension may possibly pay for itself before we are called on, and in the mean time may keep down the accruing interest. In all events it will replace the advances we shall have made. I know that the acquisition of Louisiana has been disapproved by some, from a candid apprehension that the enlargement of our territory may endanger its union. But who can limit the extent to which the federative principle may operate effectively? The larger our association, the less will it be shaken by local passions. And in any view, is it not better that the opposite bank of the Missisippi should be settled by our own brethren and children, than by strangers of another family? With which shall we be most likely to live in harmony and friendly intercourse?

In matters of religion, I have considered that its free exercise is placed by the constitution, independent of the powers of the general government. I have therefore undertaken, on no occasion, to prescribe the religious exercises suited to it; but have left them as the constitution found them, under the direction and discipline of the state or church authorities acknowledged by the several religious societies.

The aboriginal inhabitants of these countries, I have regarded with the commiseration their history inspires. Endowed with the faculties and the rights of men, breathing an ardent love of liberty and independence, and occupying a country which left them no desire but to be undisturbed, the stream of overflowing population from other regions directed itself on these shores. Without power to divert, or habits to contend against it, they have been overwhelmed by the current, or driven before it. Now reduced within limits too narrow for the hunter state, humanity enjoins us to teach them agriculture and the domestic arts; to encourage them to that industry which alone can enable them to maintain their place in existence, and to prepare them in time for that state of society, which to bodily comforts, adds the improvement of the mind and morals. We have therefore liberally furnished them with the implements of husbandry and household use: we have placed among them instructors in the arts of first necessity; and they are covered with the ægis of the law against aggressors from among ourselves.

But the endeavors to enlighten them on the fate which awaits their present course of life, to induce them to exercise their reason, follow its dictates, and change their pursuits with the change of circumstances, have powerful obstacles to encounter. They are combated by the habits of their bodies, prejudices of their minds, ignorance, pride and the influence of interested and crafty individuals among them, who feel themselves something in the present order of things, and fear to become nothing in any other. These persons inculcate a sanctimonious reverence for the customs of their ancestors, that whatsoever they did must be done through all time; that reason is a false guide, and to advance under its counsel in their physical, moral, or political condition, is perilous innovation: that their duty is to remain as their creator made them, ignorance being safety, and knowledge full of danger. In short, my friends, among them also is seen the action and counteraction of good sense and of bigotry. They too have their anti-philosophists, who find an interest in keeping things in their present state; who dread reformation, and exert all their faculties to maintain the ascendency of habit over the duty of improving our reason and obeying its mandates.

In giving these outlines, I do not mean, fellow citizens, to arrogate to myself the merit of the measures. That is due, in the first place, to the reflecting character of our citizens at large, who by the weight of public opinion, influence and strengthen the public measures. It is due to the sound discretion with which they select from among themselves those to whom they confide the legislative duties. It is due to the zeal and wisdom of the characters thus selected, who lay the foundations of public happiness in wholesome laws, the execution of which alone remains for others; and it is due to the able and faithful auxiliaries, whose patriotism has associated them with me in the executive functions.

During this course of administration, and in order to disturb it, the artillery of the press has been levelled against us, charged with whatsoever its licentiousness could devise or dare. These abuses of an institution so important to freedom and science, are deeply to be regretted, inasmuch as they tend to lessen its usefulness, and to sap its safety. They might perhaps have been corrected by the wholesome punishments reserved to, and provided by, the laws of the several states against falsehood and defamation. But public duties more urgent press on the time of public servants, and the offenders have therefore been left to find their punishment in the public indignation.

Nor was it uninteresting to the world that an experiment should be fairly and fully made, whether freedom of discussion, unaided by power, is not sufficient for the propagation and protection of truth? Whether a government conducting itself in the true spirit of its constitution, with zeal and purity, and doing no act which it would be unwilling the whole world should witness, can be written down by falsehood and defamation. The experiment has been tried. You have witnessed the scene. Our fellow-citizens have looked on cool and collected. They saw the latent source from which these outrages proceeded. They gathered round their public functionaries: and when the constitution called them to the decision by suffrage, they pronounced their verdict, honorable to those who had served them, and [illegible] *control of his own affairs.*

No inference is here intended that the laws provided by the states against false and defamatory publications, should not be enforced. He who has time, renders a service to public morals and public tranquillity, in reforming these abuses by the salutary coercions of the law. But the experiment is noted to prove that, since truth and reason have maintained their ground against false opinions in league with false facts, the press confined to truth needs no other legal restraint. The public judgement will correct false reasonings and opinions, on a full hearing of all parties, and no other definite line can be drawn between the inestimable liberty of the press, and its demoralising licentiousness. If there be still improprieties which this rule would not restrain, its supplement must be sought in the censorship of public opinion.

Contemplating the union of sentiment now manifested so generally, as auguring harmony and happiness to our future course, I offer to our country sincere congratulations. With those too not yet rallied to the same point, the disposition to do so is gaining strength. Facts are piercing through the veil drawn over them; and our doubting brethren will at length see that the mass of their fellow citizens, with whom they cannot yet resolve to act, as to principles and measures, think as they think, and desire what they desire. That our wish, as well as theirs, is that the public efforts may be directed honestly to the public good, that peace be cultivated, civil and religious liberty unassailed, law and order preserved, equality of rights maintained, and that state of property equal or unequal, which results to every man from his own industry or that of his fathers. When satisfied of these views, it is not in human nature that they should not approve and support them. In the mean time let us cherish them with patient affection. Let us do them justice, and more than justice, in all competitions of interest: and we need not doubt that truth, reason, and their own interests will at length prevail, will gather them into the fold of their country, and will complete that entire union of opinion, which gives to a nation the blessings of harmony, and the benefit of all its strength.

I shall now enter on the duties to which my fellow-citizens have again called me: and shall proceed in the spirit of those principles which they have approved. I fear not that any motives of interest may lead me astray: I am sensible of no passion which could reduce me knowingly from the path of justice; but the weakness of human nature, and the limits of my own understanding will produce errors of judgment sometimes injurious to your interests. I shall need therefore all the indulgence I have heretofore experienced; the want of it will certainly not lessen with increasing years. I shall need too the favour of that being in whose hands we are, who led our fathers, as Israel of old, from their native land, and planted them in a country flowing with all the necessaries and comforts of life: who has covered our infancy with his providence and our riper years with his wisdom and power: and to whose goodness I ask you to join with me in supplications, that he will so enlighten the minds of your servants, guide their councils, and prosper their measures, that whatsoever they do, shall result in your good, and shall secure to you the peace, friendship, and approbation of all nations.

THOMAS JEFFERSON.

AMERICAN ANTIQUARIAN SOCIETY

Silk broadside of Jefferson's 1804 inaugural address.

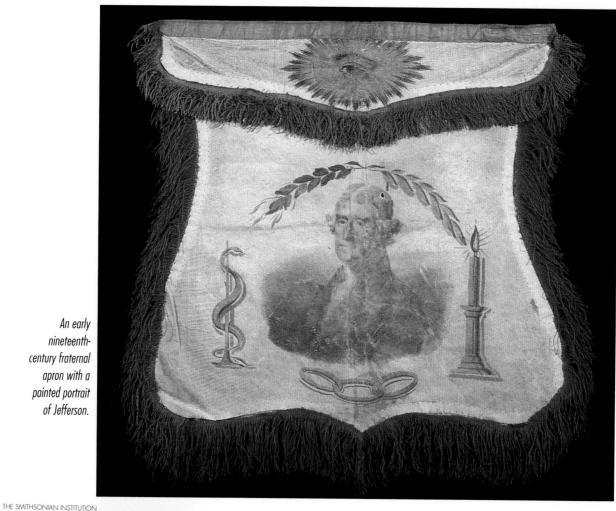

An early
nineteenth-
century fraternal
apron with a
painted portrait
of Jefferson.

Paper-mâché snuffbox with a portrait of
Jefferson probably issued after his death.

Anti-Jeffersonian
print using quotes
from Hamlet to
depict him as an
unworthy successor
to Washington.

LOOK ON THIS PICTURE,   AND ON THIS.

Commemorative pitcher, circa
1825, with a portrait of
Jefferson and scenes of the
newly completed Erie Canal.
Similar pieces bear portraits of
DeWitt Clinton, Lafayette,
and Washington.

A fine grouping of early creamware pottery.

An 1804 Massachusetts broadside protesting the choice of presidential electors.

REPUBLICAN CREED IN
1804.

MASSACHUSETTS' LEGISLATURE.

COMMONWEALTH OF MASSACHUSETTS.......In SENATE, June 14, 1804.

The undersigned Members of the Senate protest against the Resolve this day passed, for the choice of Electors of President and Vice President of the United States on the part of this Commonwealth by a GENERAL TICKET *for the following reasons:*

1st. Because it is a departure from the practice of this Commonwealth in all former instances of the choice of electors; in which, so far as the people have had any agency, they have always voted by *districts.*

2d. Because it is a deviation from the system of election established by law in the analagous case of choosing Representatives in Congress by *districts;* a system introduced with great deliberation, and sanctioned by fair experiment.

3d. Because it is inconsistent with the constitutional principle of electing Senators and Representatives in our State Legislature by *districts.*

4th. Because it is an innovation upon the general and immemorial custom of the people of this Commonwealth, who have inherited from their ancestors the usage and habit of voting for their public officers, by *districts,* of convenient extent, in all cases where more than one are to be elected by their suffrages, to the same office or trust. The election of a Governor and Lieutenant Governor by a general ticket is founded upon absolute necessity, there being but one person to be elected for the whole Commonwealth, to each of those offices. It is, therefore, neither an exception from the general rule, nor an example applicable to elections in which no such necessity exists. Besides, those two state offices are not only single, but also permanent, and are filled by annual elections; for which a few prominent characters residing any where in the State, are, from year to year, generally for a long time, held up to public contemplation as candidates; by which means the people at large have a reasonable opportunity to form a judgment of their qualifications and pretensions: whereas there are *nineteen electors* to be now chosen, to perform one important duty only, without any such probationary introduction, or any further continuance in office. The embarrassment of the people will be rendered still greater, by their being confined to vote for one Elector in each district throughout the Commonwealth, instead of being left at liberty to vote for a part only, or for their general ticket, the candidates best known most and approved by them, in whatever counties they may happen to reside.

5th. Because from the peculiar situation and circumstances of this Commonwealth extending from the State of New York to the province of New Brunswick, a distance of more than five hundred miles, separated by the interjacency of another state, comprehending three original colonies, and two independent judiciary districts, and containing eighteen counties, above four hundred towns, and more than half a million of inhabitants, the qualified voters in one extreme, have not, and cannot have, such knowledge of the principles and characters of the candidates in the other extreme of the Commonwealth, as to be able to act understandingly in making their own choice. They must, therefore, either omit to act, and thus lose their elective rights, or act upon the judgment of others, and merely adopt a list presented to them under the form of a nomination. The result of such a process, however dignified with the name of an election by the people at large, will in reality be nothing more than an appointment made for them by a few individuals.

6th. Because it is incompatible with the true spirit of our representative system of government; as, under the existing circumstances of the Commonwealth, its operation will be to deprive a large proportion of the citizens thereof of the *benefit* of a fair exercise of their constitutional right of suffrage.

7th. Because we believe the public sentiment, which ought to be duly respected by Legislators, in order to give general satisfaction, is in favour of a choice by *districts,* in preference to a *general ticket.*

8th. Because in the present political state of things, the object of a *general ticket* must be to place all our electoral suffrages in the hands of one political party, to the entire exclusion of an opposing party, nearly equal in numbers. Its inevitable tendency will therefore be to stimulate these parties to opposite electioneering exertions, and to increase their mutual jealousies, prejudices and passions, without any probable effect upon the result of the approaching national election.

9th. Because it appears to us, as is avowed by some of its principle advocates in the Legislature, to be a measure of *State opposition* to the present administration of the Federal Government; an administration possessing, and in our opinion highly meriting, the confidence, affection and support of a great and increasing majority of the nation. Such an unreasonable and unavailing *opposition* to the republican system of measures adopted by the constituted authorities of the union, and sanctioned by the deliberate sense of the American people, in addition to its intrinsic impropriety, is calculated to injure the respectability of this Commonwealth, to incur the reciprocal opposition of other States, to diminish our weight and influence in the national councils, to weaken both the general and state governments, and endanger an eventual dissolution of the Federal Union.

For these reasons we move that this our protest may be entered on the journal of the Senate.

JOHN BACON,	WILLIAM HULL,
ISAAC COFFIN,	BARNABAS BIDWELL,
JONATHAN MAYNARD,	JOHN WOODMAN,
JOHN ELLIS, Jun.	JOHN HOWE,
JOSIAH DEAN,	JOHN CHANDLER,
AARON HILL,	JOSEPH BARTLETT,
WILLIAM HILDRETH,	NATHANIEL MORTON, Jun.

PROTEST OF THE HOUSE.

We, whose names are hereto subscribed, Members of the House of Representatives, do protest against and think it proper and necessary to assign to our Constituents and the rest of the good people of this Commonwealth, the reasons which influenced our Votes, against the Resolve, which prescribes the mode of appointing the Electors of President and Vice President of the United States, by a 'General Ticket.' And for giving our votes in favour of the People in each of the seventeen Districts established for the choice of Representatives to Congress; having also the right to choose one Elector in each District, and the remaining two Electors to be chosen at large by the whole People, and request leave to have the same entered on the journals of the House.—We are opposed to the GENERAL TICKET, *for the whole number of Electors—*

1st. Because it defeats the first principles of the Elective Franchise, which is, that the elector should know and be acquainted with the character and sentiments of the candidate for whom he votes, which in a Territory, so extensive as that of Massachusetts, and where the candidates are to reside at a distance so remote from each other, we consider impossible.

2d. Because it is repugnant to the habits and usage of the people of this Commonwealth, who, ever since the adoption of their present constitution, and from the earliest period of their history as a People, have never been accustomed to an Election by a General Ticket of the whole People, where more than one officer of the same rank and kind were to be chosen.

3d. Because this mode is calculated to open the door to intrigue and imposition on the People.

4th. Because this mode of Election is fallacious in the face of it. It locates one elector in each of the seventeen Districts on the principle that such District is to be represented in the Electoral College; whereas unless the majority of such District be, of the same political sentiments with the majority of the Commonwealth, there will be selected from among them a candidate in opposition to their sentiments and wishes.

5th. Because the advocates of this novel mode of appointing the Electors openly avowed their intention to be, to oppose with the whole strength of the State, the re-election of the present chief magistrate of the Union.

6th. Because this mode will deprive one party of their due weight in the appointment of the first magistrate of the Union, who is the common President of the national sovereignty of the whole people; entitled to representation in sections of equal numbers, as well as of the state sovereignties, entitled to a representation of two Electors in the Electoral College of each State.

7th. Because in a State like Massachusetts, where political parties are nearly balanced, this mode must necessarily produce great political heat and asperity in the public mind, and has a tendency to subvert that harmony and tranquility so essential to the happiness of society.—We are in favour of voting by seventeen distinct Districts—

1st. Because a choice in this mode is, in our opinion, more fair, more consonant to the spirit of the constitution, less subject to the excitement of party heat, and agreeable to the wishes of the people of Massachusetts.

2d. Because the people of this State have been accustomed, ever since the adoption of their constitution, to choose the Senators of our own State, and Representatives to Congress by Districts, and they have never yet found any inconveniencies resulting from that mode, or even complained against it.

PEREZ MORTON,	ALBERT SMITH,
WILLIAM CLEAVELAND,	J. STEBBINS,
JOHN HATHORNE,	NATHAN WILLIS,
JOHN SOUTHWICK,	STEPHEN MONROE,
THOMAS HARRIS,	SAMUEL JONES,
DAVID GOODWIN,	THOMAS BROWN,
SAMUEL FLAGG,	ISRAEL WASHBURN,
TIMOTHY CHILDS,	JOSEPH WOOD,
THOMAS ALLEN, Jun.	JOSEPH HEATH,
SAMUEL H. WHEELER,	RICHARD F. CURTIS,
ADONIJAH BIDWELL,	EZEKIEL TOLMAN,
WALTER McFARLAND,	THOMAS FILLEBRON,
ASA WILLIAMS,	SAMUEL ELWELL,
WILLIAM MOODY,	ZECHARIAH PEIRSON,
JOSEPH MORRELL,	JACOB REEVES,
ABRAHAM HOWLAND,	ISAAC HASTINGS,
ABIEL MITCHELL,	JONATHAN CARVER,
JOHN DILLINGHAM,	EBENEZER FISHER,
JONATHAN RICHARDSON,	OZIAS EBENCH,
JOSEPH CHANDLER,	LEVI HUBBARD,
EDMUND CUSHING,	WILLIAM WHITTEMORE, Jun.
MICAJAH COFFIN,	JONATHAN OAKES,
MARTIN KINSLEY,	DAVID TUCKER,
WILLIAM BREWTEN,	JONATHAN SMITH, Jun.
THOMAS PARK,	THOMAS KITTRIDGE,
CHRISTOPHER MASON,	AARON HOBART,
JOHN SMITH,	JOHN FARLEY,
ALEXANDER McINTIRE,	MOSES CARLTON, Jun.
SAMUEL HOAR,	JOHN PIKET, Jun.
MARK ADAMS,	TIMOTHY FREEMAN,
DANIEL MASON,	CHARLES HAYDEN,
JOHN TINKHAM,	JOHN SELMAN,
SAMUEL MERRILL,	HOLDER SLOCUM,
JOSEPH BEMIS,	NATHAN B. MARTIN,
JOHN FREEMAN,	JONATHAN WEBSTER,
JOHN DRAKE, Jun.	DANIEL SNOW,
JONES GODFREY,	WILLIAM SIMONDS,
NATHAN FISHER,	EBENEZER NORTON,
JOHN LORING,	WILLIAM WORTH,
JOSEPH ADAMS,	SIMON DEARBORN, Jun.
ASA KINGSBURY,	BENJAMIN BRIDGE,
JEREMIAH WARDWELL,	CROWEL HATCH,
WILLIAM ROUNSEVILLE,	PAUL BLAKE,
FREDERICK DROWN,	SETH SPRAGUE,
MOSES RICHARDSON,	EBENEZER GRAVES,
ELNATHAN SHERWIN,	OLIVER CHAPIN,
EBENEZER BROADBROOKS,	MEDAD ALEXANDER,
DAVID NYE,	WILLIAM ADAMS,
J. WILLINGTON,	TIMOTHY WALKER,
AMOS HOLBROOK,	JONAS BROOKS.

17 STATES
IN THE UNION

DEMOCRATIC-REPUBLICAN
James Madison
ELECTORAL VOTE 122

FEDERALIST
Charles C. Pinckney
ELECTORAL VOTE 47

DEMOCRATIC-REPUBLICAN
George Clinton
ELECTORAL VOTE 6

ROBERT A. RUTLAND
is professor emeritus of history at the
University of Virginia. He was editor-in-chief of
The Papers of James Madison (1960–), and
editor of *The Papers of George Mason*:
1725–1795 (1970) in three volumes.

In one sense, the 1808 presidential campaign was over before it started. James Madison's election was never in serious trouble, despite a noisy campaign that was all sound and fury but no substance. The Federalists belatedly picked a candidate, lacked a basic strategy, and left the field open for two Republican rivals (George Clinton and James Monroe) who were equally inept. Indeed, it is almost fair to say Madison won by default.

The stage had been set fourteen years earlier, when Thomas Jefferson had told Madison that he hoped to see his friend move from Congress "to a more splendid and a more efficacious post. There I should rejoice to see you; I hope I may say, I shall rejoice to see you." Then Jefferson himself became President, and as his second term entered its last year, speculation on his successor was muffled by the circumstances. During his two terms, Jefferson's right arm was Madison, his secretary of state. Albert Gallatin, the secretary of the treasury was his left. Madison was the President's closest confidant, chief adviser in the critical area of foreign affairs, and a fellow Virginian whose friendship extended back to Revolutionary days in the Continental Congress. Gallatin was caught in a factional dispute in his home state of Pennsylvania, however, and apparently was never given serious consideration as a possible candidate.

In 1800 Republicans had begun the practice of using a congressional caucus to nominate candidates. In 1804, with Jefferson up for reelection, Republican congressmen simply went through the motions. Late in 1807 the rumor circulating through Washington boarding houses was that Madison was Jefferson's choice, and only the formalities needed to be observed. Early in January, Thomas Ritchie, the arch-Republican editor of the *Richmond Enquirer* told readers that only a presidential nod was needed to begin the process. As he wrote, Senator Stephen R. Bradley of Vermont was probably listening to Jefferson's instructions (in all likelihood, Virginians William Branch Giles and Wilson Cary Nicholas were also consulted). On January 19, 1808, Bradley published a call for a caucus and sent it to all members of Congress, Federalists as well as Republicans. The irascible John Randolph of Roanoke, Jeffersonian loyalist-turned-enemy, immediately branded the proceedings spurious and kept his small following of party irregulars (popularly known as "Quids") away from the meeting. This left the Randolph faction free to cry "foul," but the overwhelming vote for Madison (he received eighty-three votes to three each for Vice President George Clinton and James Monroe) made Randolph's venom less potent.

The campaign thus launched was to be one of the first presidential contests with only one genuine candidate. Randolph and the "Quids" soon issued a manifesto, condemning the caucus as a usurpation of the constitutional process, and the wily Randolph obtained Monroe's tacit approval for

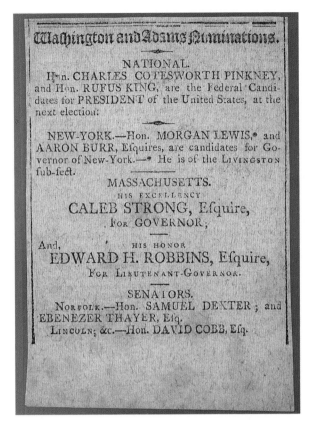

Washington and Adams Nominations.

NATIONAL.
Hon. CHARLES COTESWORTH PINKNEY,
and Hon. RUFUS KING, are the Federal Candidates for PRESIDENT of the United States, at the
next election.

NEW-YORK.—Hon. MORGAN LEWIS,* and
AARON BURR, Efquires, are candidates for Governor of New-York.—* He is of the LIVINGSTON
fub-fect.

MASSACHUSETTS.
HIS EXCELLENCY
CALEB STRONG, Efquire,
FOR GOVERNOR;

And, HIS HONOR
EDWARD H. ROBBINS, Efquire,
FOR LIEUTENANT-GOVERNOR.

SENATORS.
NORFOLK.—Hon. SAMUEL DEXTER; and
EBENEZER THAYER, Efq.
LINCOLN; &c.—Hon. DAVID COBB, Efq.

Newspaper endorsement for Charles Pinckney and the Federalist ticket. Note the misspelling of his name.

mounting a drive for the presidency. But Monroe's candidacy floundered from the outset, and only the obstreperous conduct of the New York congressional delegation kept the decrepit Clinton's hopes alive.

Madison, on the other hand, had the whole force of the Republican party behind his nomination. This meant little in terms of a cohesive national organization, but it gave Madison the backing of the regular majority in Congress, which meant that the legislatures (where most of the electoral votes were decided) were fairly secure. Equally important, Madison's nomination was hailed by the Republican newspapers with sufficient enthusiasm to make the pretensions of any other candidate seem either

disloyal or hopeless. In fact, the campaign of 1808 simply enlarged the earlier practice of making the press the primary battleground for the election—a practice that dominated the nation's political life until the advent of television.

Madison had no choice in the matter, for Washington's precedent of ignoring the whole election process had been observed by all candidates thereafter as a matter of proper decorum. Campaigning by public appearances, speeches, or any overt gestures would have offended Washington's memory!

During 1808 the tempo of journalistic infighting reflected the rapid growth of newspapers in the young nation. In the decade 1790–1800 newspapers in the United States doubled in number to nearly two hundred, but in the next eight years another one hundred newspapers came into being. No one was more acutely aware of this expansion than Samuel Harrison Smith, editor-publisher of the Washington *National Intelligencer,* the powerful journalistic voice of the Jefferson administration that reached subscribers in all seventeen states and the several territories. Not far behind, in terms of influence, was the Philadelphia *Aurora* edited by the wheelhorse of Pennsylvania politics, William Duane. Ritchie, from his base in Richmond, commanded respect in southern circles, and with his *Enquirer* as part of the Republican newspaper trinity, the opposition was always on the defensive.

At the time, of course, enough dissension existed in the Republican ranks to make it appear that a genuine contest over the presidency was under way. Clinton's friend in New York City, William Cheetham, unfurled the banner of dissent in his *Ameri-*

can Citizen and appeared to keep Clinton's dismal chances alive. The sixty-nine-year-old vice president had the ambition of a West Point graduate but a frail body and his mental powers were suspect. Still, Clinton had control of his state's party apparatus, including the lucrative printing contracts that kept newspapers financially healthy.

The Federalist party had no national newspaper to compete with the Philadelphia-Washington-Richmond trio, and as the campaign progressed an increase in anti-Madison criticism in pro-Federalist newspapers was attributed to Cheetham's supposedly Republican journal. This in itself became an embarrassment to party loyalists, who published a manifesto declaring that Cheetham's apostasy justified reading him out of Republican ranks. Cheetham remained defiant (since his printing contract was secure), but Tunis Wortman, an able writer who lacked conviction as well as cash, abruptly did an about-face and returned his *New York Public Advertiser* to Madison's camp after rescue from financial woes by party regulars.

Such fireworks as existed were supplied in the spring and summer of 1808 by supporters of Clinton or Monroe with access to newspaper columns. Their makeshift strategy was to impugn the caucus system as an unconstitutional way to nominate a President. The pro-Federalist Boston *Columbian Centinel* denounced the "Imperial decrees" of "King Stephen I" with a sarcastic column wherein the Vermont senator commanded "all our loving subjects" to accept the caucus result unquestioningly. "It is our further pleasure that all the provisions of a certain worm-eaten instrument, called the *Constitution of the United States*,

which relates to the election of a President and Vice President, [shall] be declared null and void." The pro-Monroe *Virginia Argus* published a screed written by Monroe's future son-in-law denouncing the caucus nomination as skulduggery and "hidden intrigue" fashioned by Madison's followers; but the Albany *Register* distanced itself from Clinton after the state legislature adjourned without any action on the caucus recommendations. "We disapprove of the decision of the CAUCUS at Washington," the *Register* announced, "but if that decision cannot be counteracted, without . . . ruinous schism in the republican interest of the Union, we shall be for acquiescing in it."

Duane's reaction to the caucus could not have overjoyed Madison, for the *Aurora* editor admitted he was not an enthusiastic Madison supporter. But, Duane told readers, the Republican party was created by and for majority rule, and "I am willing to sink my *personal predilection* in the voice of the greatest number." Cheetham's friends in New York held a mass meeting in his office for "Old School Republicans," who proceeded to declare "Mr. Madison is *not fit* to be President" and then nominated Clinton for the office.

Federalists observed these partisan antics with high glee, but still had no candidate themselves. For months Federalist editors had badgered the opposition; and although they complained about the Embargo Act (which kept American shipping out of international commerce, and cut off supplies from Europe), the caucus system, and Jefferson's anti-British policies, they still had no candidate of their own. Then in September at a rump meeting of Federalist congressmen and senators in New York, "a number of respectable gentlemen" chose Charles Cotesworth Pinckney for their presidential nominee and gave Senator Rufus King the second spot. It was a caucus even more exclusive than the one Bradley called, but that fact was glossed over as the Federalist kingpins tried to accentuate the difference in the two tickets. The Federalist candidates' "affections are wholly centered on their native country. . . . They are governed by those great and salutary principles . . . illustrated in the administration of WASHINGTON, and bequeathed by him as a sacred legacy to his country," the *Commercial Advertiser* proclaimed in late October.

The Federalists late start neither hurt nor helped them. They had no platform and no program except the implied promise to call off the Embargo, avoid a war with England, and revive commerce even if it meant war with France. From their Massachusetts strongholds mass meetings had poured forth a stream of well-publicized petitions to Jefferson, beseeching the President to suspend the Embargo. The *Columbian Centinel* insisted that the Embargo in a year's time had cost American trade valued at fifty million dollars, "or double the amount of 'our national debt'. . . . We must consider the Embargo as intended to aid that Great Republican, *Bonaparte*; that friend of neutrals, Napoleon . . . against lordly, monarchical England." At New Bedford, Federalists prepared a petition that called the Embargo a "millstone on the neck" of American sailors, farmers, and merchants. By implication, Madison was as pleased with the Embargo as Jefferson and as President would make the Embargo a permanent fixture so "that after a few years

the people would be in the habit of using domestic manufactures and be content to live without commerce."

Republicans squirmed as the Federalists linked Madison to Jefferson's coattails by reminding voters that both were Virginians and slaveholders. How could such men know or care about shipping, trading, or the economic lifeblood of New England? "Are we a commercial people, and do we submit without a murmur or complaint to the *Tarapin* [sic] *Policy* of Virginia?" asked the Providence *Gazette*. Most Federalist newspapers tried to contrast the northern interests with "the slave-holding states [that] are un-commercial—their planters are too proud to labour, and they hold commerce in contempt." A week later the *Gazette* reminded readers that the Pinckney-King ticket was the "Washington and Anti-Embargo ticket," and Rhode Island voters were in that small band that voted directly for a presidential slate. (Virginia, Kentucky, Maryland, and North Carolina were the other states with direct voting on presidential electors; elsewhere electors were chosen by the state legislatures.) America's woes, the *Commercial Advertiser* charged, "originated in that jealous Virginia spirit, which pines at the prosperity and opulence of the North" and wreaks havoc on "the commerce of the Union" like a "pestilent flock of insects."

Madison probably was more worried about the Hessian flies bothering his wheat crop than about the Federalist critics. He spent most of the summer at Montpelier, a silent candidate but an interested reader of the newspapers that carried the brunt of the fight. When Federalists claimed that Madison had wrecked a British peace mission attempting to settle the *Chesapeake* dispute, Madison's friends published his stern formal messages to the English envoy to refute charges of Anglophobic bullheadedness. Madison's enemies in Congress tried to make hay in the summer with a charge that Madison had truckled under to France, favored a two-million dollar bribe to Napoleon, and allowed the French emperor to determine American foreign policy. Perhaps even worse was the assertion in the *New York Register* by Edmund Genet, a French revolutionary turned New Yorker, that Jefferson and Madison were French sycophants because they had been made French citizens by the bloodthirsty National Assembly in 1793. Now the truth was out, Genet charged, and these Francophiles wanted the "maritime states humbled and impoverished, [while] Virginia, resting on the arm of slavery," would dominate the Union.

Madison chose to ignore the charges—which were half-true—since he had accepted honorary French citizenship as a gesture of friendship toward a fellow-revolutionary. Washington and Hamilton had also been named, but they chose silence for their answer in 1793 and in 1808 Madison was the only survivor. "French Citizens at the head of an American Government," cried the pro-Clinton *Commercial Advertiser* in mock horror, declaring that Jefferson and his minion Madison were "inexorably bound to the skirts of Napoleon." Clinton, by implication, was the only honest alternative to such rascality.

Clinton's role in the campaign, however, became an embarrassment. He decided to be coy and allow his name to go before

Liverpool jug with a purported likeness of James Madison.

the New York legislature as a bona fide presidential candidate. That prompted dark hints that the old man was secretly in league with the Essex Junto, an influential but informal New England branch of the ultra-Federalist party desperate to defeat any proponent of the Embargo. Madison had long suspected such an alliance. Weeks before his nomination he told William Pinkney "the Essex party in Massachusetts are strongly suspected of plotting disunion. . . . Such is the hatred of that faction to this administration and its devotion to England as to account for the most desperate plans." Now a rumor circulated in Republican newspapers that Clinton's nephew, DeWitt Clinton, tried to make a deal with the New Englanders but none ever emerged. Meanwhile,

Clinton refused to disavow efforts to make him into a serious contender.

So did Monroe, despite mounting evidence that his candidacy was a Randolphian trick that was turning into a farce. Monroe brushed aside pleas from Virginians who knew how the political winds blew. "For the public good and your future prospects," a trusted friend begged, "put a stop to the contest." Instead, Monroe stubbornly clung to his phantom campaign. "Attacks on me will do no harm, & silent contempt is the best answer to them." Jefferson tried to soften the blow with a gentle hint that Monroe ought to bow out, but his letter only provoked Monroe into a request that the President's kind words be made public. When even his closest advisers had surrendered, Monroe still thought he had a chance. "If the [New England] federalists cannot elect their own man," he confided, "it is believed that they

wo[ul]d prefer me to Mr. Madison. . . . If Massachusetts supports me, the Eastern States generally will probably join her." Late in October the *Aurora* printed an incredible report from Virginia that Monroe's supporters claimed 95 electoral votes to 37 for Madison, with 24 in doubt. After this ludicrous gesture, the Monroe skyrocket fizzled.

There were no public bonfires, no rallies on the village common, or none of the campaign bombast awaiting for Monroe, and precious little for Pinckney and Clinton. Early returns in Vermont boosted Federalist hopes when they won a legislative skirmish that gave Pinckney seven electoral votes. "Election returns indicate that FEDERAL TRUTH has triumphed over *Lying* Democracy," a partisan newspaper pealed. The Federalist trend continued in New England, but in New York Clinton's hold weakened and he

Montpelier, Virginia, the Seat of the late James Madison. Engraving by J.F.E. Prudhomme after John G. Chapman.

Congrefs OF THE *United States,*
begun and held at the City of New-York, on
Wednesday the Fourth of March, one thousand seven hundred and eighty nine.

THE Conventions of a number of the States, having at the time of their adopting the Constitution, expressed a desire, in order to prevent misconstruction or abuse of its powers, that further declaratory and restrictive clauses should be added: And as extending the ground of public confidence in the Government, will best ensure the beneficent ends of its institution.

RESOLVED by the Senate and House of Representatives of the United States of America, in Congress assembled, two thirds of both Houses concurring, that the following Articles be proposed to the Legislatures of the several States, as amendments to the Constitution of the United States, all, or any of which Articles, when ratified by three fourths of the said Legislatures, to be valid to all intents and purposes, as part of the said Constitution; viz.

ARTICLES in addition to, and amendment of the Constitution of the United States of America, proposed by Congress, and ratified by the Legislatures of the several States, pursuant to the fifth Article of the original Constitution.

Article the first. ...

Article the second. ...

Article the third. ...

Article the fourth. ...

Article the fifth. ...

Article the sixth. ...

Article the seventh. ...

Article the eighth. ...

Article the ninth. ...

Article the tenth. ...

Article the eleventh. ...

Article the twelfth. ...

ATTEST,

Frederick Augustus Muhlenberg, Speaker of the House of Representatives
John Adams, Vice-President of the United States, and President of the Senate.

John Beckley, Clerk of the House of Representatives
Sam. A. Otis, Secretary of the Senate

James Madison synthesized state ratifying convention demands for a bill of rights into twelve amendments. Until 1992, two were never ratified; the other ten are the original Bill of Rights. At left is a facsimile of the federal government's official copy.

took only six of nineteen votes. The slow grinding of the New York legislative process provided the only tension as state reports from the South and West—from late September onward—pointed toward a complete Madison victory. Pennsylvania provided the needed surge after a threatened Republican split was healed in time to give Madison twenty solid votes when the electoral college met in early December. A week earlier, the *National Intelligencer* hailed Madison's victory as soon as the required eighty-eight votes were tabulated from the returns. Thereafter, the slow reports provided only an anticlimax.

Madison received a personal testimonial from his home territory when Virginia voters gave him a landslide victory with 14,655 votes to 3,408 for Monroe and a handful for Pinckney. New England went solidly for the Federalist candidates, but from New York south and westward the Madison-Clinton ticket won by thumping majorities. The final tally gave Madison 122 electoral votes, Pinckney 47, and Clinton 6. Monroe received not a single vote for President but had three token vice presidential votes. Clinton was reelected vice president with 113 votes.

As his partisans across the nation celebrated with informal parades and other Republicans shouted toasts to the President-elect or watched an impromptu "illumination," the object of their esteem went to his State Department desk on the day following his election and conducted his routine business, apparently too business-like to acknowledge the fact that voters had fulfilled Jefferson's 1794 prophecy.

★

1812

18 STATES
IN THE UNION

DEMOCRATIC-REPUBLICAN

James Madison

ELECTORAL VOTE 128

FEDERALIST

DeWitt Clinton

ELECTORAL VOTE 89

NORMAN K. RISJORD

is a professor of history at the University of
Wisconsin-Madison. His scholarly works
include *The Old Republicans: Southern
Conservatism in the Age of Jefferson* (1965) and
Chesapeake Politics, 1780–1800 (1978).
He has also written several popular works in the
field of early American history, among them
*Representative Americans: The Revolutionary
Generation* (1980); *Representative Americans:
The Colonists* (1981); and *Jefferson's
America, 1760–1815* (1991).

America declared war on Great Britain in June 1812, and five months later it held a presidential election to determine the future of the incumbent, James Madison. The election itself would turn on the question of war or peace, but the campaign, which began at the beginning of the year, initially involved a more mundane issue. Northern Republicans had fretted about Virginia's control of the presidency and southern domination of Congress since Jefferson's second term. For eight years this anti-Virginia sentiment had pinned its hopes on the vice president, George Clinton of New York. By 1812, however, age and ill-health dimmed Clinton's chances of mounting a challenge to Madison (Clinton died on April 20, 1812). In the early weeks of 1812 anti-Madison feeling within the Republican party focused on the vice president's nephew, DeWitt Clinton, who was both lieutenant governor of New York and mayor of New York City.

Since 1796 caucuses of the members of each party in Congress had chosen presidential candidates, and it was assumed that this method would be used again in 1812. However, in the first days of the year Congress was knotted in debate over war preparations, and it was uncertain if or when a caucus would be summoned. Hoping to forestall a Clintonian rebellion, Republicans in the Virginia assembly caucused in February and nominated a slate of twenty-five electoral candidates pledged to Madison. They had used the same tactic in un-dermining the Monroe candidacy four years before, and for the moment it seemed to work again. On March 7 the Republican caucus in Pennsylvania endorsed the Madison nomination and published a slate of loyal electors. Clinton hoped to receive the support of the New York assembly later that month, but his plans were frustrated when Governor Daniel D. Tompkins, a Madison loyalist, sent the legislature home because of a bribery scandal. By the time the New York legislature reassembled in late May the caucus of Republican members of Congress had already met.

The congressional caucus met in the Senate chamber on the evening of May 18. Madison was the unanimous choice of the eighty-two senators and representatives present. Uncertainty over the vice presidential selection necessitated a second meeting, however, where Elbridge Gerry of Massachusetts was chosen as Madison's running mate. Elected governor of Massachusetts only a month earlier, Gerry was expected to draw some New England votes. At the same time, at age sixty-seven, he was too old to threaten the Virginia succession in 1816. At this second caucus ten more Republicans declared for Madison, giving him the support of more than two-thirds of the congressional party.

At the end of May the New York assembly reassembled and voted in caucus to nominate DeWitt Clinton, although the move left the Republican party in New York badly divided. The Federalists were unenthusiastic

Medal of DeWitt Clinton who served as mayor of New York City 1803–1806; 1809; 1812–1815, and as governor of New York 1817–1821 and again from 1825 until his death in 1828.

about Clinton, but they came to view him as their only chance of returning to power, even if fusion with Clintonian Republicans meant only partial power. Federalist agents met with the lieutenant governor in July and received some encouragement. Clinton hinted that he was contemplating a complete break with the administration, even to the extent of making Federalist appointments and relying on the Federalists for advice. It was agreed on both sides, however, that the impending alliance had to be kept secret. Federalists were planning a "peace convention" for September, and they wanted to attract as much dissident Republican support as possible.

The convention, whose membership was carefully tailored by the Federalists, met in New York City on September 15, 1812. To avoid damaging Clinton's prospects among Republicans in the middle states, it did not formally endorse the lieutenant governor; it merely recommended that Federalists throughout the country exert themselves to secure presidential electors who would bring about a change. The further advantage to Federalists of this strategy was that, if the Clinton ticket happened to win an electoral majority, they could drop Clinton and bring forth a Federalist candidate in the electoral college. The ruse fooled no one; newspapers and the public identified Clinton as the Federalist candidate. Clinton, however, could not win without Republican support, and this dictated his campaign strategy.

The concept of public campaigning was as yet unborn. Voters would have regarded as unseemly a candidate who openly courted their votes. Politicians and voters alike were governed by the classical maxim that an officeholder was summoned by public need, and he accepted office only from a sense of public duty. Presidential elections in particular did not lend themselves to public campaigning because voters had little say in the outcome. In nine of the eighteen states presidential electors were still chosen by state legislatures, and these were elected months and sometimes years before the presidential campaign began. Even in states where electors were chosen by popular ballot, the personal stature of the elector was often as important as the popularity of the candidate to whom he was pledged. In Quincy, Massachusetts, old John Adams, disgusted with his party's antiwar stance, placed himself on the ballot as a Madison elector. It was a noble gesture, but in this particular case had no effect. Aware of these conditions, presidential candidates made only a few formal utterances during the campaign, and left mudslinging to their followers.

A committee of New York Clintonians assumed the direction of Clinton's campaign. On August 17 it issued an "Address to the People of the United States" which functioned, for practical purposes, as Clinton's platform.

The cleverly devised document skirted the war issue and sought broad popular appeal in the North and West. Denouncing the caucus system as "hostile to the spirit of the federal constitution," the Address suggested that nomination by caucus placed the election process in the hands of a "junto of Congressmen," instead of the people. Moreover, because the nomination was performed in secret by a small minority, it was subject to possible foreign influence, an insinuation tailored to the longstanding Federalist accusation that Madison was a tool of France.

Noting that Virginians had controlled the presidency for twenty out of the twenty-four years since the Constitution was adopted, the Address exploited northern jealousy of Virginia. Arguing that Virginia's dominance had arrayed agricultural and commercial states against each other, the Address contended that only a candidate from a middle state, such as New York, could hold the Union together. It also pointed out that New York's western frontier was likely to bear the brunt of the fighting, and that only a New Yorker, such as Clinton, could understand the needs of the West and conduct the war effectively. Without denouncing the war in principle, the Address accused Madison of having rushed into the conflict without sufficient preparation. Clinton, in contrast, offered new leadership—"from his energy we anticipate vigor in war and a determined character in the relations of peace."

Since Clinton was not beholden to any foreign power, argued the authors of the Address, he would be able to negotiate an honorable peace that would benefit the nation's commercial interests and restore national unity.

Silk memorial ribbon for DeWitt Clinton, 1828. Clinton was chiefly responsible for the successful completion of the Erie Canal (1825).

Although this document provided grist for Clintonian appeals throughout the country, it did not unify the campaign. In order to have a chance, Clinton had to win votes in both New England and the states to the south of New York, and the profound differences between those two constituencies forced him into a deadly inconsistency. New Englanders hailed him as the missionary of a speedy peace. Under the title "Madison and War! or Clinton and Peace," one amateur poet devoted twelve rhapsodic stanzas to "the base wretch . . . who is for WAR," and him "who lifts his righteous hand and swears, This base, outrageous WAR shall cease."

In the states south of New York, where the war was popular, Clinton's agents portrayed him as a man who would prosecute the war until every American objective was attained. The strategy met little success. A Philadelphian reported to Madison that

This blue Staffordshire plate commemorates the opening of the Erie Canal (1825). The canal, extending from Albany to Buffalo, linked the Hudson River with Lake Erie.

"The current elections," he remarked casually to Jefferson in mid-October, "bring the popularity of the war or of the administration, or both, to the *experimentum crucis*."

Madison injected himself into the campaign on only two occasions. In July he sent a letter to a nominating convention organized by New Jersey Republicans. His message defended the war in general terms and promised an honorable peace. Praising New Jersey's role in the Revolution, he ended the letter with the implied hope that the state would exhibit equal patriotism in the present emergency. Although it was hardly a stirring appeal, the message was widely circulated in the Republican press.

Madison's other foray into the campaign was a letter addressed to the South Carolina assembly in September. Replying to the assembly's address of August 28 in support of the war, Madison acknowledged its "Fidelity to the national rights and sensibility to the national character. It is a war worthy of such a determination," he continued. "Having its origin neither in ambition or in vain glory, and for its object neither an interest of the Government distinct from that of the People, nor an interest of part of the people in opposition to the welfare of the whole." Implying that the Clintonian opposition was hampering his conduct of the war and efforts toward peace, the President informed South Carolina that if its loyalty and patriotism were emulated by other states it would help speed "the blessings of a just and Honourable peace." As with his message to New Jersey, this was more a reasoned defense of the war than a plea for reelection, but it mattered little. It was directed at the most bellicose of states and one firmly in the administration camp.

thinking men in that city viewed "with a distrustful eye the man who is supported by a party" with internally opposite principles and policy.

In the face of such tactics it was probably to Madison's benefit that he adhered strictly to the principle of aloofness. Charles Jared Ingersoll, son of Clinton's running mate, Philadelphia Federalist Jared Ingersoll, recorded long after the election "on high authority, that while a candidate for the presidency, no one, however intimate, ever heard him [Madison] open his lips or say one word on the subject." Elbridge Gerry followed the same policy. To a friend who urged him to take a more active role in the campaign Gerry replied: "I cannot alter the method which brought me to high political office and make a direct appeal to the voters." Madison, in fact, seemed to regard himself as a disinterested observer.

Because of the reticence of both presidential candidates, the campaign was fought principally in the newspapers. Control of the press was thus crucial. In New York a member of the Livingston clan reported that Clinton's handling of political patronage made it possible "to purchase and maintain party writers and presses in almost every county of the state." Public funds, he continued, enabled two Clintonian papers in New York City to "poison the public mind in the remotest parts of the state," while the Madison forces had "but one poor rickety print . . . whose miserable columns are scarcely seen beyond the limits of the city."

To extend their influence the Clintonians established two new journals outside of New York, the *Pilot* in Boston and a *Whig Chronicle* in Philadelphia. Clinton's chief New York organ, the *Columbian,* helped obtain subscriptions for both of the new papers. The *Pilot* was under the same editorial direction as the Boston *Yankee,* a Republican weekly which in September suddenly switched its support from Madison and lost its ardor for the war. Caustic comments in the Madison papers about these births and rebaptisms aroused the *Columbian*'s indignation. They could charge the editor of the *Yankee* with apostasy if they wished, fumed the *Columbian,* but to insinuate that the editor had "sold himself for gold, and changed his politics, is not less absurd than indecorous and unjust." Unjust though the accusations may have been, both the *Pilot* and the *Whig Chronicle* disappeared after the election.

Most contributors to newspapers did so under a pseudonym. Anonymity allowed the writers to plunge to new depths of scurrility.

Pewter-rimmed commemorative medallion with a glass-covered engraved portrait of Clinton.

Typical of the broadsides of the day was a pamphlet entitled "Republican Crisis, An Exposition of the Political Jesuitism of James Madison. By an Observant Citizen of the District of Columbia." The writer attributed the "abyss into which we have been drawn" to the "imbecile policy and pernicious councils" of the Madison administration. He claimed that Madison's foreign policy had been one of "jesuitical tergiversation, of futile experiments, and pusillanimous subterfuges." Clinton, by contrast, was noted for his "attachment to the interests of commerce, agriculture, and internal improvements," most notably a canal connecting Lake Erie with the Hudson River. "In this awful crisis," concluded the pamphleteer, "the finger of heaven points to DeWitt Clinton, as the saviour of his country, under the good providence of the Most High."

Madison not only remained aloof from such spleen; he refused even to take steps to further his own cause. General William Hull's surrender of Detroit in August was a severe blow to the administration's electoral chances. Clintonian agents laden with pamphlets were swarming through the

HONOR TO THE DEAD.
August 25, 1836.

LIBERTY

JAMES MADISON.
EX-PRESIDENT OF THE UNITED STATES.
Born 17th March, 1750.
Died 28th June, 1836.

Madison silk memorial ribbon (1836). He was the last survivimg signer of the Constitution.

Pennsylvania mountains, reported a resident of Carlisle, blaming the administration for the loss of Hull's army and for general want of energy. Much of the country blamed the disaster on Secretary of War William Eustis, a Massachusetts physician who was widely known as an inept administrator. Despite numerous calls from within his party for Eustis's dismissal, Madison refused to replace him (though he did so after the election).

Balloting began on Friday, October 30 in Pennsylvania, and it went on for several weeks, as each state had set its own election day. Several days before the Pennsylvanians went to the polls, Madison received important dispatches from Jonathan Russell, his charge d'affairs in London. The dispatches detailed Russell's talks with the British government during the summer after the United States learned that the orders in council had been revoked. The dispatches revealed an American readiness for peace, which was dashed by the British government's intransigent refusal to stop impressment of American seamen in the Royal Navy. At the same time, Secretary of State James Monroe was conducting armistice negotiations, albeit with negative prospects, through Admiral Borlase Warren, British fleet commander at Halifax. If released prior to the election this information would have been powerful campaign material. Madison, however, held the documents until Congress opened and he delivered his annual message on November 4. By that time all the states, except Maryland, the Carolinas, and Ohio, had voted. Had the dispatches been published in time, Elbridge Gerry wrote to the President, they would almost certainly have influenced election results in Massachusetts. Industrious Republicans did manage to print and circulate several thousand copies of the dispatches in South Carolina, where, according to one Madisonian, they gave "most completely the lie to the base and unprincipled insinuations" of the Federalists and enemy agents.

In the end, Republican party discipline probably counted for more than the campaign strategy of either side. Clinton carried Federalist New England, except for Vermont, as well as New York and New Jersey, two states that had long been evenly divided between the parties. In addition, he picked up scattered electoral votes in Delaware and Maryland, two states that also had a history of Federalist sympathy. Madison won everything else in a sprawling but contiguous block from Pennsylvania to Georgia, and Ohio to Louisiana. The electoral count, when it was tallied on December 3, was: Madison 128, Clinton 89. The republic thus completed its first wartime election in relative tranquility.

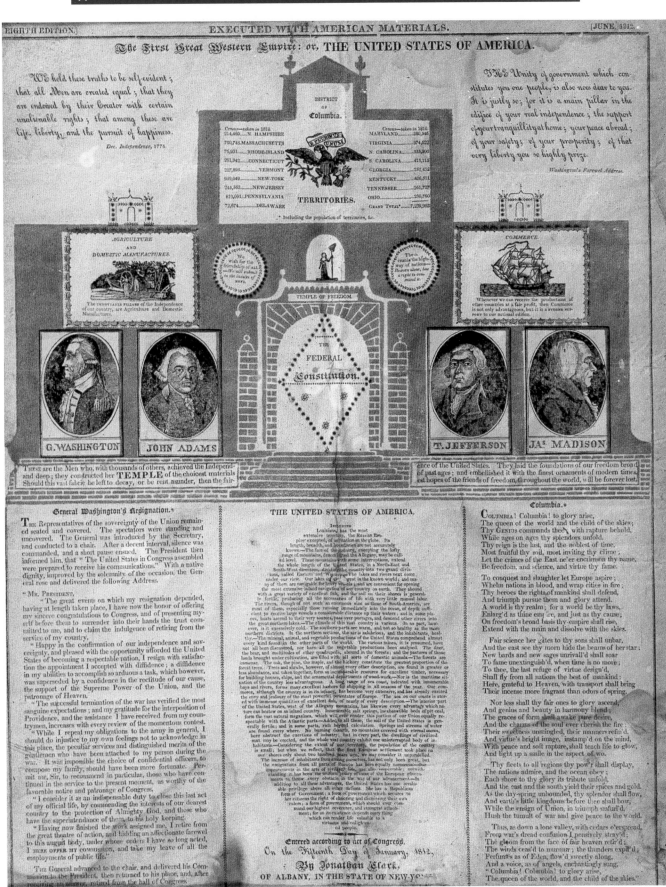

An elaborately engraved print published in 1812.

★

1816
1820

1816: 19 STATES
1820: 24 STATES
IN THE UNION

DEMOCRATIC-REPUBLICAN

James Monroe

1816: ELECTORAL VOTE 183
1820: ELECTORAL VOTE 231

FEDERALIST

Rufus King

1816: ELECTORAL VOTE 34

INDEPENDENT REPUBLICAN

John Quincy Adams

1820: ELECTORAL VOTE 1

KENNETH CMIEL
teaches history at the University of Iowa.
He is author of *Democratic Eloquence:
The Fight Over Popular Speech in Nineteenth-
Century America* (1990).

The campaigns of 1816 and 1820 have left almost no visual record. This is not surprising, for many would say there *were* no campaigns in those years. The Federalist party was falling apart. In 1816 it did not run a national campaign. In 1820 it had no candidate at all. The election of James Monroe as the fifth President of the United States was the result of private negotiations among Republican politicians in the first months of 1816. His reelection four years later was a foregone conclusion.

In 1816, Monroe's chief obstacle was not the disintegrating Federalist party, nor jealous fellow Republicans. Monroe's main enemy was the system of choosing Presidents itself. One problem was Virginia's domination of the presidency, the so-called "Virginia Dynasty." Another was the increasing distrust of the caucus system, the practice of having members of Congress choose the party's nominee. And there was also increasing dissatisfaction with the ways that states chose members of the electoral college. In nine states, electors were still picked by the state legislature instead of by the voters.

Nothing was heard more commonly in political circles than dissatisfaction with the way Presidents were chosen. Mahlan Dickerson, a future senator from New Jersey, was typical, noting in 1819 that the presidential election "is probably the rock upon which our liberties are to be wrecked." According to the New York Congressman Jabez D. Hammond, "the power of the States to choose, or direct the manner of choosing Electors for the President, is a rotten, a gangrenous part of our Constitution, which if not removed will infect and poison the body politic." Monroe became President in 1816 because he was able to get this "rotten" system to work one more time. He was reelected four years later because no one yet imagined an alternative.

James Monroe had wanted to be President for some time. A protégé of Thomas Jefferson, Monroe had been a diplomat, senator, and governor, as well as secretary of war and secretary of state. A solid figure, uninspiring to many, Monroe nevertheless was a more than capable administrator. In 1816, he was sure his time had come.

Yet Monroe had to be careful. Not every Republican trusted him. Eight years before he had unsuccessfully challenged James Madison for the Republican nomination. A number of prominent Virginia Republicans had never forgiven him. And while Monroe had to soothe the feelings of those Virginia Republicans, he also had to try *not* to look like "the Virginia candidate." Virginians had held the office of the presidency for all but four years since 1789; by 1816 significant opposition was appearing to the "Virginia Dynasty." Monroe was thus in the unenviable position of having to shore up his support from Virginians at the same time he tried *not* to look like that state's candidate.

This was not quite as hard as we might think. In 1816 there was no public campaign for President. The Republican nomination

This child's mug measures only 2 1/2" high and is printed in bright blue on white creamware. Most early ceramics misspelled Monroe's name.

would result from private negotiations among state party leaders and members of Congress. In 1816 the party's nominee, as since 1796, would be chosen by a caucus of Republican congressmen and senators.

The character of contemporary communication also helped Monroe. It was conducive to private campaigning. There were no telegraphs, radios, televisions, or satellite hookups to speed information. As important, the public glare of deeply partisan politics was also missing. This campaign was a game of factions rather than of full-blown political parties. It was not until later in the 1820s that local partisan newspapers would play a significant role in presidential elections. While the number of papers was steadily expanding, the press had not yet taken the quantum leap that would come after the middle 1820s. In 1816, the *National Intelligencer* was the single most important Republican paper, its stories reprinted by dozens of party papers across the nation. And in 1816, the *Intelligencer* clearly supported James Monroe.

The "campaign" might be said to have begun in the spring of 1815 when Monroe and his son-in-law George Hay began to cultivate fellow Virginia Republicans. Monroe had reason to be concerned. Important Republicans like Spencer Roane and Thomas Ritchie still harbored grudges based on Monroe's failed challenge to Madison eight years before. Hay devoted considerable effort to mending fences for his father-in-law. When the Virginia delegation to Congress caucused, it decided to support Monroe. Yet it was done somewhat surreptitiously, by selecting electors favorable to Monroe without publicly naming him their candidate. All the Virginians were aware of the country's increasing resentment of the state's lock on the presidency.

The most organized opposition came from New York. This was no surprise. The commercial expansion of the state, and particularly New York City, was rearranging the weight of the nation. In 1790 Virginia had been the most populous state; in 1820, it was New York. In the past, Virginia Republicans had picked a New Yorker as vice president. By 1816, however, this bone was not enough. All sorts of New York Republicans wanted their governor, Daniel D. Tompkins, to be the Republican nominee.

Tompkins was not the only potential challenger. William H. Crawford of Georgia was another. Only forty-four years old, he was well known in Washington, having served as a senator, secretary of the treasury, secretary of war, and minister to France. Crawford was a big, handsome, jovial man, enormously popular among Washington Republicans. Since it was Congressional Republicans who would choose the nominee, this made Crawford a very attractive candidate.

But both Tompkins and Crawford had their problems. While the choice of most New York Republicans, the largest and most organized opponents of Monroe, Tompkins was an unknown elsewhere; he lacked the national reputation necessary to secure the nomination. And while William Crawford was well known in the capital, he was a most reluctant candidate. It was Crawford supporters, rather than Crawford himself, who pushed his candidacy.

The machinations heated up in the first months of 1816. By January, Republican politicians of all factions were trying to scope out how the congressional caucus would vote. Martin Van Buren, already a force in New York politics, spent a few days in Washington looking over the situation. He studiously sidestepped queries about whom the New York delegation might support. Back in New York, Van Buren kept in touch with the situation via trusted correspondents. By the middle of January, he was convinced that Tompkins had no chance of winning the nomination.

The key New York friends of Crawford, however, were some of Van Buren's most bitter local enemies. Consequently, Van Buren continued to lobby for Tompkins, even though he knew it probably would mean the nomination of Monroe.

Meanwhile, Crawford was getting cold feet. By the middle of January rumors were circulating that he did not want to challenge Monroe. On February 1, Senator William W. Bibb, a trusted friend of Crawford and his public spokesman, announced in the *National Intelligencer* that Crawford had no desire to run for the Republican

Another example of a child's creamware mug.

nomination. A relatively young man, Crawford was convinced he could become President at a later date. And since he was unsure that he would beat Monroe, he didn't want to alienate other Republicans.

Crawford's reluctance, however, did not stop his supporters. Throughout February, Republican politicians continued to canvass for Crawford, one good sign of how widespread was the distaste for another Virginia President. Rumors continued to circulate that Crawford really wanted the nomination, that his demurrals were insincere. State politicians, especially in New York, continued to hope for a Crawford candidacy.

In such a climate, Monroe supporters by no means felt sure of themselves. "Every day thins the ranks of Mr. Monroe's friends," one Georgia observer noted. Some friends of Monroe got so worried that they argued in the first week of February that he should skip the congressional caucus altogether. Instead, they suggested, he could easily become the nominee by relying on individual state caucuses made up of Republican state legislators. In a memo he wrote to himself sometime in February, Monroe expressed a similar point of view.

The fears were not groundless. They were based on real opposition to Monroe's candidacy—especially in the capital. Monroe himself was not the problem; it was the Virginia dynasty that was under attack. On February 14, New York Republicans met in Albany and voted that the state's congressmen should back Tompkins in the caucus. The next week, New York's congressional Republicans met twice but could not reach a firm decision to back anyone. In late February a group of congressmen representing every state except Virginia met to figure out how to stop Monroe.

The "stop-Monroe" movement was basically a Washington affair. Outside New York, little evidence exists of any state-level efforts to oppose the Virginian. In the last days of February and the first days of March, Pennsylvania and Rhode Island Republicans met to publicly endorse Monroe .

Reverse side of a clothing button showing the shank. The claim "EXTRA STRONG" was made by the manufacturer and does not refer to Monroe.

On March 10, an anonymous call for a party caucus to take place two days later was posted in the House of Representatives. This was a move by the Crawford forces to preempt the nomination. The Monroe faction stayed away; only 58 of 141 Republican congressmen attended the meeting. The consensus was that such that a small group could not make any nomination. Instead they scheduled a more official caucus for March 16.

No one was sure of the outcome. Monroe pondered the possibility of having his supporters skip the second caucus and go to the state legislatures for the nomination. At the same time, Senators Bibb and Tait of Georgia were spreading the word that Crawford would not oppose Monroe. The *National Intelligencer* reported Crawford's disinclination to be President, probably a plant by Monroe supporters. At the caucus the next day, Henry Clay, fearing a Crawford victory, moved to block any nomination. John Taylor, senator from Virginia, made a motion denouncing the whole caucus system. Both failed. And when the vote for the nomination came, Monroe proved victorious. The margin was small—65 Monroe votes to 54 for Crawford—but it was enough. Daniel Tompkins became the vice presidential candidate.

The Federalists did not field a national candidate in 1816. Rufus King was the party's choice, but a number of states never bothered to put up a slate of electors. Originally from Massachusetts, King moved to New York where an advantageous marriage pushed him into the highest ranks of society. Respected by many, he was loved by few, suffering from what one historian has called "an austere haughtiness."

King's run for the presidency was lackadaisical to say the least. Little in his correspondence even suggests he was a candidate. Especially after his losing battle for the governorship of New York in April, King was resigned. "I presume that the failure [to become governor] will, as I think it should, discourage the Federalists from maintaining a fruitless struggle," King wrote. "Federalists of our age must be content to live with the past."

King's attitude was symptomatic of the whole Federalist effort. There was no Federalist caucus in Washington, nor any agreement in Federalist newspapers about who should run for President. Indeed, there was some confusion about whether any Federalist should be a candidate.

Part of the problem was organizational. Federalists did not communicate the way Republicans did. While they had organized state parties in earlier years, they had never developed extensive interstate networks, even informal ones such as the Republicans had. There remained Federalists (at least a few) all over the nation, but they tended not to talk to each other. There was no effort to coordinate efforts across state lines, none of that rich political gossip that traveled through Republican circles at this time.

Beyond the Republican nomination, there was no real campaign in 1816. Federalist newspapers repeated stories of Monroe's failures in the Washington administration, now twenty years past. Republican papers offered glowing recountings of Monroe's life and accomplishments. On November 5, King noted in a letter that practically nobody was thinking about the election at all. For "so certain" was the outcome "that no pains are taken to excite the community

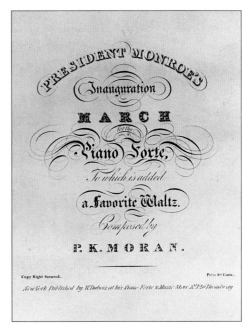

Sheet music written for Monroe's first inauguration, March 4, 1817.

on the subject. It is quite worthy of remark, that in no preceding election, has there been such a calm respecting it."

States could select their representatives to the electoral college in three ways. Seven states had a system similar to ours—voters casting ballots for a slate of candidates committed to either Monroe or King. In three states voters in each district elected their own representatives to the electoral college. This had the advantage of appearing more democratic but the disadvantage of splitting the state's vote. In nine states there was no popular election. The state legislature chose the electors. (It was only from this last group that King received any votes.) The final tally was 183 votes for Monroe and 34 for King.

In 1820 there was no campaign. It was clear that Monroe would be renominated. It was clear no Federalist would oppose him. Even the Panic of 1819 did not bring out any

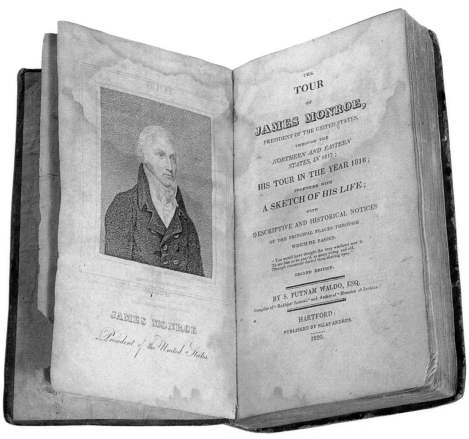

1820 biography of Monroe detailing the President's 1818 tour of the northern and eastern states.

opposition to Monroe. It was the last time in United States history that an economic downturn did not at least raise serious electoral difficulties for an incumbent President.

There was so little contention that even the caucus proved unnecessary. A congressional caucus was announced but attendance was sparse. Madison was not formally nominated there. In fact, he was never formally nominated at all. In December, he received every electoral vote save one. William Plumer, a cranky New Hampshire Federalist, cast his ballot for John Quincy Adams. Monroe became the only President outside of George Washington to run unopposed.

In this moment of relative quiescence the phrase "era of good feelings" was coined. But the term is a misnomer. As early as 1817 Monroe saw politicians jockeying for position, trying to place themselves so as to become the next President. By the end of 1821 there were four candidates for President. A year later there were eight. The politics of faction continued to be played with ferocity. By 1824, openly partisan politics reemerged; and the system used since the end of the 1790s, that which relied extensively on private party negotiations, nomination by caucus, and limited popular campaigning, was gone forever.

Some of the 1816 campaign sounds like what we might expect from contemporary politicians—the forging of secret alliances, the cold calculation of where critical votes would fall, and the deft use of rumor to further an agenda. Such tactics are familiar. But in 1816 the surrounding context of this sort of behavior was obviously vastly different. There weren't two credible candidates. There wasn't any popular campaign. (These were the last presidential elections that kept no record of the popular vote.) Most important, there was none of the institutionalized apparatus for a popular campaign that would develop in the next decade and a half. There were no party conventions or vibrant partisan press. There were no mass torchlight parades or popular campaign slogans. And no one was yet talking about such things. In 1816 and 1820, popular politics were not yet imagined.

The old system was rotting, that much was clear. Even Monroe disliked the caucus. In 1816 his own operatives had tried to stop the caucus nomination. This was, of course, a moment of panic, a recoil from the fear that Crawford might grab the party's banner. But Monroe genuinely felt (with some good reason) that popular sentiment was in his corner. He later stated that he did not think the caucus reflected public opinion.

Within a decade, the notion that the caucus subverted "public opinion" would be critical to the emergence of new ways of electing Presidents. In 1824, William Crawford found himself attacked for his support of the caucus. The caucus, so it was claimed, was a way for politicians to manage the election. Instead, it was argued, the people should manage the politicians. It was not that anyone expected the private maneuvering of party politicians to end, but a complicating factor was added—the need to actively sway huge groups of voters. The congressional nominating caucus that Monroe used with trepidation in 1816 disappeared in the 1820s for a new style of electioneering, one rooted in the ideological commitment to the popular election of the President.

James Monroe died on July 4, 1831. His remains were removed from New York City to Richmond, Virginia, in 1858.

1824

24 STATES
IN THE UNION

John Quincy Adams

ELECTORAL VOTE 84, POPULAR VOTE 30.5%

Andrew Jackson

ELECTORAL VOTE 99, POPULAR VOTE 43.9%

William H. Crawford

ELECTORAL VOTE 41, POPULAR VOTE 13.1%

Henry Clay

ELECTORAL VOTE 37, POPULAR VOTE 13.2%

MELBA PORTER HAY,
former editor of *The Papers of Henry Clay*,
is currently manager of the Research
and Publications Division of the
Kentucky Historical Society.

The presidential election of 1824 was unique in many ways. It marked the end of the one-party "Era of Good Feelings" and the beginning of a modern two-party structure. It had an unusually large number of serious contenders, and it was the last election in which the congressional caucus was used as a nominating device. A number of new techniques such as state nominating conventions, mass meetings, and public opinion polls came into widespread use. There was more popular participation, and newspapers played a greater role than ever before.

Reelection of James Monroe in 1820 produced a horde of aspirants all jockeying for the succession. By 1824 approximately seventeen candidates had been reduced to five—Secretary of the Treasury William H. Crawford of Georgia, Secretary of War John C. Calhoun of South Carolina, Secretary of State John Quincy Adams of Massachusetts, Speaker of the House Henry Clay of Kentucky, and U.S. Senator Andrew Jackson of Tennessee. Since no one was expected to receive a majority of electoral votes, it appeared the President would be chosen by the House of Representatives from the top three.

The 1824 election has often been viewed as a contest between personalities, each backed by a group of admirers. This, however, overlooks the importance of developing sectional interests and the issues with which each candidate was identified. The South, opposed to a protective tariff and internal improvements, favored states' rights as a shield for slavery. New England, only beginning to shift from a commercial to a manufacturing center, still tended to oppose the tariff and was determined to end Virginia's hold on the presidency. The West, supporting both the tariff and internal improvements, had areas of strong antislavery sentiment and was also opposed to Virginia's domination. The campaign took place primarily in the press and in the speeches of presidential electors in instances where they were chosen by the people and in debates in state legislatures where electors were chosen by the legislature. Although still publicly following the dictum that it was improper to electioneer for the presidency, virtually every candidate directed his own campaign through extensive correspondence. In addition, the candidate or his "friends" would supply newspapers with ammunition to use against his opponents.

For a long time the front-runner appeared to be William H. Crawford, who had stepped aside in 1816 in exchange for an unofficial promise that he would receive the Republican congressional caucus nomination at the end of Monroe's administration. Regarded as leader of the states' rights faction of the Republican party, Crawford was strong only in the South—particularly in Georgia, Virginia, and North Carolina—and in New York where Martin Van Buren's Albany Regency gave him a base. His partisans portrayed him as a man whose native genius

ADAMS MEETING.

THE Citizens of Newburyport and Vicinity, friendly to the Election of JOHN QUINCY ADAMS to the Presidency, and who prefer him to any other Candidate, are requested to meet at the Town-Hall, THIS EVENING, at half past 6 o'clock, to adopt such measures as may be thought necessary to secure for him a full vote at the approaching election.

☞ It is expected that there will be a general attendance of the Citizens thus disposed, without respect to party distinctions.

ARTHUR GILMAN,
JOHN COFFIN,
BENJ. G. SWEETSER,　} COMMITTEE.
GREENE SANBORN,
NATHAN FOLLANSBEE,
ROBERT B. WILLIAMS,

Newburyport, October 30th, 1824.

1824 meeting announcement for supporters of John Quincy Adams.

had raised him to greatness. They lauded his refusal to oppose Monroe in 1816, they praised him as a champion of economy, simplicity, and peace, and they emphasized his hostility to the tariff and internal improvements. The support of such influential newspapers as the Washington *National Intelligencer* and the Richmond *Enquirer* gave him an apparent advantage, because newspapers were the most important instruments in molding public opinion.

By the summer of 1822, warfare raged between Crawford supporters and the partisans of John C. Calhoun. Heated newspaper exchanges occurred between the Washington *Gazette*, a Crawford paper edited by Jonathan Elliot, and the Washington *Republican*, a Calhoun paper edited by Thomas L. McKenney. A nationalist who favored a protective tariff, internal improve-

ments, and a national bank, the young secretary of war was strong in Pennsylvania and his home state of South Carolina. Ironically, these two states differed in their attitudes toward internal improvements and the tariff. Calhoun's supporters pointed to their favorite's high intellect and his efficiency in reforming the War Department, and they were vociferous in attacking the congressional caucus form of nomination.

Secretary of State John Quincy Adams, the least personable of all the candidates, was probably next in strength to Crawford at the beginning of 1824. Describing himself as a "reserved, cold, austere" man, Adams stood on his record of diplomatic achievement and remained aloof from the campaign. Affirming that the presidency should go to the best man by the unbiased choice of the people, he refused either to state his position on the issues or to allow his letters to be published. In some areas such as Ohio, where his antislavery views might have attracted sympathy, he lost votes because of his refusal to endorse the tariff and internal improvements, even though he favored both. The New York *American* exhorted northerners to support him in order to curb the slave states, while his opponents called him a Federalist, an aristocrat, and a friend of England. Although his aloofness seemed to confirm some of these charges, he could count on his native New England and had a considerable following in New York.

Speaker of the House Henry Clay, noted for his nationalistic American System and for his championing of western interests, believed he would carry the six states of Kentucky, Louisiana, Illinois, Indiana, Ohio, and Missouri and could thereby be one of the three candidates to go before the

House of Representatives. He had won the Speakership in 1823 by a vote of 139 to 42 and felt election was assured if his name went before the House. His close identification with western interests injured his prospects elsewhere, and his role in the Missouri Compromise as well his ownership of slaves probably cost him substantial support in areas which were for the tariff but against slavery. Since as speaker he could not hide his political views as could the candidates who were in the cabinet, he never hesitated to use his great oratorical skills in House debate. Many of his significant speeches, such as those on the tariff of 1824, were widely published in newspapers. He was confident that this would help the American people see the value of the American System and cause them to reward him with their support.

The surprise candidate of 1824 was Andrew Jackson, the hero of the Battle of New Orleans. Although his personal popularity was great, his military career and his reputation for violence, rash judgment, and violation of civil liberties were thought by many to make him unfit for the presidency. His candidacy emerged in 1822 when the John Overton faction, which was really for Henry Clay, engineered his nomination for President by the Tennessee legislature in order to gain their own advantage in state politics. They were totally unprepared for the outpouring of enthusiasm for his candidacy that swept the country. Unable to control the flood they had unleashed, many of them eventually joined the opposition, but devoted Jackson friends such as John Eaton and William B. Lewis directed his campaign with great effectiveness. They presented

Jackson as a son of the American Revolution, a second George Washington, a true man of the people. A great military hero and an incorruptible man, Jackson would redeem the national government from years of intrigue and misrule by the politicians. And the Hero played his part well. When the Tennessee legislature sent him to the U.S. Senate in 1823, he conducted himself with a great show of courtesy and good manners, taking care to conciliate as many of his old enemies as possible.

In a campaign which relied heavily on the written word, one of the most skillful bits of political writing was the Nashville *Gazette*'s "Political Horse Racing and Presidential Contest," which appeared in 1823 and was subsequently copied in various pa-

Engraving showing Andrew Jackson victorious over his many detractors. In 1815, a federal judge fined Jackson $1,000 for declaring martial law during the Battle of New Orleans. In 1844, however, the House of Representatives voted to return the money— with 6% interest.

Brass token from the 1824 election. These tokens or medalets were among the first mass-produced campaign souvenirs.

pers. The horses were given the names of the candidates, and after running through all the states, the Crawford won. The Nashville *Whig* spoofed the "Woodbee" family, which included John Q., Henry, and John C. Two of the best campaign pamphlets were "Southron" and "South-Carolinian." The former disagreed with some of Crawford's positions but endorsed him as one who would pay the national debt and reduce taxes, while the latter presented fifteen objections to Crawford and endorsed Jackson. Even though the Richmond *Enquirer* was for Crawford, Thomas Ritchie published anti-Crawford material written under a pseudonym by Winfield Scott. Mahlon Dickerson of New Jersey wrote an anti-Calhoun pamphlet, "Economy, Mister Calhoun," and Monroe's son-in-law George

Hay published anti-Crawford material. Many papers printed articles that displayed more passion than sense, and cartoons often favored terrible puns such as, "How is Clay now?" "Oh dirt cheap."

One of the prime targets for political cartoonists and satirists became "King Caucus." Jackson despised Crawford, and his forces led in opposing the treasury secretary's expected congressional caucus nomination. Others who opposed Crawford—such as Samuel Ingham, a supporter of Calhoun from Pennsylvania, and Hezekiah Niles of *Niles's Register*—joined the attack. Although Jefferson, Madison, and Monroe had been nominated by congressional caucus, the caucus system was increasingly considered undemocratic, especially since there was only one party. A convention in Maryland in September 1823 instructed that state's representatives not to participate in such a nomination, and the following month, the Tennessee legislature also went on record against the caucus. Despite growing anti-caucus sentiment, Van Buren and other Crawford supporters continued to press for a caucus nomination. On February 7, 1824, a notice in the Washington *National Intelligencer*, signed by eleven Crawford men, summoned congressmen to meet on February 14 to select a candidate. In the same issue another notice, signed by twenty-four congressmen from fifteen states, declared a caucus "inexpedient" and stated that 181 of 261 members of Congress felt this way. With only sixty-six attending, the caucus nominated Crawford for President and, in an effort to attract Pennsylvania votes, Albert Gallatin for vice president. Gallatin proved to be an unpopular running-mate; moreover, as a native of Switzerland, he was ineligible for the presidency. He finally withdrew in October. On March 13 *Niles's Register* termed the caucus the most unpopular political measure ever taken in the United States and insisted the *"mere fact"* of such a nomination destroyed Crawford's chances.

A larger factor working against Crawford's election, however, was the illness that had struck him in September 1823. Either a stroke or the effect of medication and bleeding left him nearly blind, partially paralyzed, and with a serious speech impairment. Although he improved somewhat in the spring of 1824, he soon suffered a relapse and was unable to attend cabinet meetings until after the election. His opponents made much of the fact that treasury documents were apparently signed with a facsimile of his signature.

Even Crawford's ill health did not stop his opponents from criticizing his conduct of the Treasury Department. This all came to a head in 1824 in the so-called "A.B. Plot." In 1823 the Washington *Republican*, a Calhoun paper, had published letters signed "A.B.," alleging that Crawford had mismanaged public funds and suppressed information concerning relations between the treasury and certain western banks. In the spring of 1824, after Monroe appointed Illinois Senator Ninian Edwards as minister to Mexico, Crawford submitted a report that questioned Edwards's veracity in earlier testimony. Edwards then admitted he was "A.B." and charged Crawford with specific violations of the law. The House committee that investigated the matter exonerated Crawford, apparently believing that some unusual practices had been necessary in order to prevent greater hardship in the

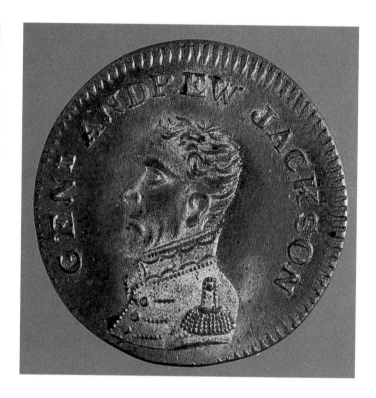

West during the panic of 1819. Adams and Calhoun followers felt Edwards's charges were justified and approved their publication, but the episode backfired against Edwards, whose national career was ruined.

The "A.B. Plot" was only one example of the intrigues carried on in Washington. As early as 1822, Adams had been informed that someone had gone through State Department accounts in the hope of finding something to use against him. In the same year, the "duplicate letter" controversy arose between Adams and Jonathan Russell over a letter Russell had written to then-Secretary of State James Monroe while he and Adams were serving as two of the U.S. negotiators for the Treaty of Ghent. When the original could not be found in the State Department files, Russell provided a "dupli-

With most Jackson material, his army career and the Battle of New Orleans are prominent themes. Jackson in military regalia appears on this brass token from the 1824 campaign.

United States large copper cent counterstamped with Adams's name. During the nineteenth century, merchants and politicians used coins and currency for free advertising. This practice was later outlawed.

cate." Monroe subsequently found the original in his own papers, but passages in the copy, more detailed than in the original, accused Adams of attempting to give the British the right to navigate the Mississippi River in exchange for U.S. fishing rights in the Atlantic. Adams believed the duplicate letter was an attempt to discredit him in the West, and he blamed Henry Clay, another negotiator at Ghent, although he knew the Calhoun men were participating in the attack. Adams then wrote a scathing letter to Congress demolishing Russell's charges and attacking Clay for demonstrating sectionalism at Ghent. Newspaper editor and future Jacksonian Amos Kendall defended Clay in a series in the Frankfort *Argus of Western America*. These articles were later released as a pamphlet which became a major Clay campaign document.

As for Calhoun, he suffered criticisms of his management of the War Department. The Crawford men dubbed him the "Army candidate" and charged he would impose direct taxes in order to strengthen the nation's defenses. A key part of Calhoun's strategy against Crawford was to try to wrest North Carolina from him, and by late 1823 Calhoun had half of the newspapers in that state on his side, including the powerful Salisbury *Western Carolinian*. Yet Charles Fisher, his skillful campaign manager there, was unable to prevent a state legislative caucus from drawing up a Crawford electoral ticket in December. By then the Adams and Jackson campaigns were beginning to get organized, which allowed the three Crawford challengers to join together and place the odium of the caucus nomination on the treasury secretary. Meanwhile, a secret committee planned a Calhoun ticket.

Aware that a separate Jackson ticket would assure a Crawford victory in North Carolina, Fisher urged William Polk, the Jackson leader in the state, to join in a People's ticket that would support Jackson if it appeared Calhoun could not succeed. The Hero's appeal to the common man soon enabled his followers to capture the People's ticket and shift the election in North Carolina to a contest between Crawford and Jackson. The blow that finally crushed Calhoun's chances both in North Carolina and elsewhere was his loss to Jackson of the Pennsylvania nomination on March 4, 1824. When the Harrisburg convention went on to nominate Calhoun for vice president, he pulled out of the presidential contest and declared for the second office.

Another candidate losing ground to the Jackson boom was Henry Clay. He hoped to be nominated first by Ohio, where his American System was very popular, but the Ohio legislature refused in December 1822, so Missouri, where his campaign was managed by Thomas Hart Benton, became the first state to nominate him. Kentucky and then Ohio followed suit. Fueled by popular meetings, the Jackson movement grew rapidly in parts of Ohio, especially after Jackson announced that he was for a "judicious tariff." Charles Hammond skillfully directed Clay's campaign in Ohio with letters to the newspapers, while the Adams men, using the slogan "John Quincy Adams/ Who can write,/ Andrew Jackson/ Who can fight," attempted to get Jackson to run for vice president with their candidate. Throughout the contest Clay's campaign was beset by rumors of his withdrawal or of a coalition with Crawford. In an effort to quash these rumors, a circular, published in the Washington *National Intelligencer* on June 16, announced that Clay's friends would "*adhere* to him steadily to the end" and, if he failed to reach the House, would hold the balance of power and determine the result. A signed pledge at a Clay meeting in Columbus in July 1824 promised that Clay electors would vote for Clay alone. Yet, even in the closing days of the campaign, Jackson forces in the Cincinnati area circulated handbills declaring that Clay had withdrawn and gone over to Jackson. The work of a vigilance committee created to try to counteract these false reports ultimately helped Clay carry Ohio.

Clay's chances were not so good in other vital states. In early 1824 it appeared that the Indiana legislature was for him, but the Jackson movement soon swept the state, and left Clay running second. In Illi-

Paper-mâché snuffbox. The paper transfer portrait was sealed with several coats of lacquer.

nois, Jackson won two electoral votes and Adams one. Missouri and Kentucky remained firmly in the Clay column, but Louisiana, where electors were chosen by the legislature, ended up giving Jackson three and Adams two electoral votes after several mishaps. Clay had hoped to take New York or Pennsylvania, but even Josiah S. Johnston, his campaign manager in that area, admitted in September 1824 that the cause lacked direction and management. Nevertheless, late in the campaign Johnston was able to persuade the Philadelphia *Aurora* and the New York *Patriot* to come out for the Kentuckian, giving him for the first time major eastern papers that could be distributed to other parts of the country. In an attempt to win New York, Clay forces nominated Nathan Sanford, the state's chancellor, for vice president. Rumors of withdrawal, lack of national press support until too late in the campaign, and, most of all, the unexpected growth in the Jackson campaign stole enough of Clay's strength to keep him from being one of the three candidates presented to the House.

As 1824 progressed, Adams and Jackson became the front runners. Campaign biographies of both men were published, with Jackson's, written by John Eaton, becoming perhaps the most important document of the campaign. This work helped turn the conservative planter and slaveholder into the idol of the common man. Jackson benefited from the U.S. visit of the Marquis de Lafayette, who revived memories of the Revolution. One public letter, signed "E.P.," appeared in the Washington *National Intelligencer*, appealing to Adams, Clay, and Calhoun to withdraw in favor of Jackson, "the only surviving hero of the Revolution . . . the second Washington." One broadside claimed that Jackson's "history is . . . the record of his country's glory." He also benefited from new techniques used during the campaign—straw votes at militia musters, grand jury meetings, and on steamboats, and popular meetings called to endorse candidates. In Wilmington, Delaware, a book was left open for recording voters' preference. Toward the end of May, the register stood 150 for Jackson, 97 for Adams, 4 for Clay, and 2 for Crawford. A circuit court grand jury in Maryland gave Jackson double the votes it gave Adams, his nearest opponent. At a public sale in Orange County, North Carolina, 97 of those attending favored Jackson, 3 Adams, 2 Crawford, and 1 Clay. But it was the militia musterings, held in virtually every com-

munity, where the cry of "Old Hickory" brought forth the greatest enthusiasm. These unofficial votes helped create a bandwagon effect which was difficult to counter. Jesse Benton attempted to do so in his widely distributed pamphlet, *An Address on the Presidential Question*. This bitter attack recalled the violent acts of Jackson's career and warned of the dangers involved in elevating to the presidency a military chieftain with little respect for the law or the Constitution. Yet nothing seemed able to stop the Jackson surge.

As the race moved into the final phase, all eyes turned to New York. One of six states in which the legislature still chose presidential electors, New York with thirty-six electoral votes was pivotal. Van Buren and the Albany Regency continued to push for Crawford, despite his persisting illness. However, the Regency's unpopularity led to the formation of a People's party favoring Adams but promising Clay enough electoral votes to make him one of the top three. After much wheeling and dealing, twenty-five Adams electors were apparently chosen, with seven for Clay and four for Crawford. If this had held, Clay would have tied Crawford for third place in the electoral college, but when the New York electors met in December, they cast only four for Clay, with twenty-six going to Adams, five to Crawford, and one to Jackson.

Jackson now had a total of ninety-nine electoral votes, Adams eighty-four, Crawford forty-one, and Clay thirty-seven. Focus then centered on Clay, who while not one of the top three, could determine the outcome. Friends of each candidate courted him. Clay ruled Crawford out of the picture because of his health, and he had long felt

Probably a trinket or sewing box with a hand-colored lithographed portrait under glass. This unusual item measures but 3 1/4" by 5" and is 2" high.

the election of the "military chieftain" Jackson would be a catastrophe. By the last week in January it was known that Clay favored Adams, whose policies generally agreed with his own.

Rumors abounded that Clay and Adams had made a "bargain," and as the House vote approached, intrigue followed intrigue. James Buchanan of Pennsylvania approached Jackson with a proposal that Jackson agree to make Clay secretary of state in exchange for Clay's support in the House. Jackson, who indignantly refused, always believed the proposition came from Clay, though it did not. Robert P. Letcher of Kentucky sought promises from Adams that Clay would be given a cabinet post. Adams and Clay eventually met and were apparently mutually satisfied with each other. When Clay led the Kentucky delegation in voting for Adams despite legislative instructions in favor of Jackson, then was

offered and accepted the office of secretary of state, Jacksonians immediately cried, "corrupt bargain."

On February 11, 1825, election day in the House, each state had one vote, to be determined by a majority of the state's congressional delegation. The votes of Delaware, Illinois, Mississippi, and Missouri were decided by a single delegate. Again, New York's vote was crucial, and its delegation was evenly split between Adams and Crawford supporters. Van Buren wanted to keep it that way and prevent Adams's election on the first ballot. If he succeeded, he hoped then to step in and get the vote for Crawford. Stephen Van Rensselaer, Van Buren claimed, had promised his vote to Crawford, but after talking with Clay and Daniel Webster (and also seeking divine guidance, so some said), he cast a vote that gave New York and the election to John Quincy Adams. The campaign for 1828 had begun.

Pressed cardboard thread box
with an inside portrait of Adams.
The pincushion on the lid reads
"BE FIRM FOR ADAMS."

Rare John Quincy Adams 1825 inaugural
medal struck in both silver and pewter.

Reverse painting on glass of General Andrew Jackson. In 1824, Jackson became the first presidential candidate to win a plurality of votes but failed to win a majority of the electoral votes.

Gen: Andrew Jakson.

Battersea enamel pillbox. The portrait is not of Jackson but of the Marquis de Lafayette. Dating from the War of 1812 this is not a campaign item.

English copper lustre pitchers inscribed with the slogan
"General Jackson/The Hero of New Orleans."

Transfer printed 3½" cup plate by Enoch
Wood with a civilian portrait of Jackson.
Extremely rare in ceramic, the cup plate
held the handleless cup of the early
nineteenth century while the diner sipped
coffee or tea from the saucer into which
the hot beverage was poured to cool.

French textile, circa 1827. These fabrics were roller-printed from copper engravings. A similar pattern was issued later for Jackson's inauguration and includes his portrait.

★

1828
24 STATES
IN THE UNION

DEMOCRAT

Andrew Jackson

ELECTORAL VOTE 178, POPULAR VOTE 56%

NATIONAL REPUBLICAN

John Quincy Adams

ELECTORAL VOTE 83, POPULAR VOTE 44%

ROBERT V. REMINI
is the author of a three-volume biography of
Andrew Jackson: *Andrew Jackson and the Course
of American Empire, 1767–1821* (1977); *Andrew
Jackson and the Course of American Freedom,
1822–1832* (1981); and *Andrew Jackson and the
Course of American Democracy, 1833–1845*
(1984). He is also the author of *Henry Clay:
Statesman for the Union* (1991).

During the presidential election of 1828, a new style of political campaigning emerged, one that has since become very typical of American elections. The smear and slander tactics, the hoopla and nonsense to attract voter interest initiated by the newly organized Democratic party and its opposition, the National Republican party, constitute only one aspect of the innovations of 1828. The type of presidential candidate—military heroes, for example, rather than experienced and proven statesmen—and the organizational style developed to conduct their campaigns helped form many of the modern methods by which present-day political parties go about nominating and electing the nation's chief executive.

The previous election had been a four-way contest with each candidate running without a party label. All four—John Quincy Adams of Massachusetts, Henry Clay of Kentucky, Andrew Jackson of Tennessee, and William H. Crawford of Georgia—claimed membership in and loyalty to the old Republican party of Thomas Jefferson and James Madison. None received a majority of electoral votes required by the Constitution and so the election went to the House of Representatives where John Quincy Adams, with the help of Henry Clay, was chosen the sixth President of the United States. Andrew Jackson, who had a plurality of popular and electoral votes in the election and seemed to be the favored choice, charged Adams and Clay with a "corrupt

bargain" to defeat the will of the people. "There was *cheating*, and *corruption*," stormed Jackson, "and *bribery* too." None of these charges was ever proved but the cry of a "corrupt bargain" between the "coalition" of Adams and Clay became the central issue of the 1828 campaign when Adams ran for a second term as candidate of what became known as the National Republican party. Jackson ran against him as candidate of the Democratic-Republican, or simply the Democratic, party.

Many of the leaders of this revitalized two-party system—Democrats such as Martin Van Buren, John C. Calhoun, Thomas Hart Benton, and National Republicans such as Henry Clay and Daniel Webster—were skillful leaders and politicians. They placed great emphasis on the value of the party system to perpetuate republican principles and maintain stability in government; they espoused party discipline; they organized correspondence committees, local political clubs, and statewide conventions; and they arranged parades, barbecues, tree plantings, street rallies, and all manner of hoopla to control and direct the great masses of voters recently enfranchised by the liberalization of several state constitutions throughout the 1820s, especially after the last election.

Organized support for General Jackson began in the winter of 1826–27 with an agreement between Calhoun and Van Buren to bring together their respective constituencies, namely "the planters of the South

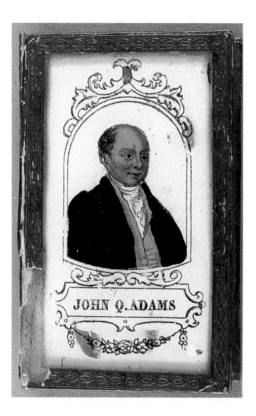

Pressed-paper box with Adams's portrait reverse-painted on a glass insert. This was a commemorative piece, made after his death in 1848.

JOHN Q. ADAMS

and plain Republicans of the North," and thereby provide what Van Buren called "the substantial reorganization of the old Republican party." Following this initial meeting a series of congressional conferences were reportedly held in which "schemes [were] devised, questions debated & the minority was ruled by the majority." They agreed to commence their labors to elect Jackson on July 4, 1827, "in every part of the Union at once." In Nashville, Tennessee, Jackson's hometown, a Central Committee was formed "for the purpose of corresponding with other Jackson committees in the different sections of the country." And so began the elaborate task of structuring a national organization of committees at every political level and in all the states to defeat John Quincy Adams

and replace him in the White House with Andrew Jackson.

Attuned to the mood and aspirations of the greatest number of Americans, the Democrats showed uncommon political shrewdness and wisdom by supporting a candidate who was a national hero of unparalleled popularity rather than simply a well-known politician. Andrew Jackson's tremendous victory over the British at New Orleans during the War of 1812 won the admiration, respect, and devotion of the American people as no one had ever done before, not even George Washington. "The *Hurra Boys*," remarked one National Republican, "were for Jackson . . . and all the noisy *Turbulent Boisterous* Politicians are with him and to my regret they constitute a powerful host." The Hurra Boys appropriated Jackson's nickname, "Old Hickory," which gave the party a usable symbol for campaign purposes. Local Democratic organizations were called "Hickory Clubs." Hickory trees were planted during rallies; hats sported hickory leaves; and hickory walking canes, brooms, and buttons with hickory symbols were introduced by the party as a means of designating political preference. The raising of a hickory pole was quite common throughout the campaign of 1828. They appeared "in every village," reported one man, on steeples, on signposts, "as well as upon the corners of many city streets. . . . Many of these poles were standing as late as 1845, rotten momentoes [sic] of the delirium of 1828."

"Planting hickory trees!" snorted one outraged opposition newspaper. "Odds nuts and drumsticks! What have hickory trees to do with republicanism and the great contest?"

In addition to the hickory symbol the Democrats also employed Jackson's likeness on a wide variety of material objects, such as ceramic plates, snuff boxes, pitchers, badges, bandanas, and ladies' hair combs. Once in a while the "corrupt bargain" might be mentioned on these items but most of them usually referred to the Battle of New Orleans or Jackson's participation as a messenger boy during the American Revolution. They all had the happy effort of linking indelibly in the public mind Old Hickory's name with the nation's glorious past.

Organized barbecues were another means of exciting voter interest. Said one leader, obviously referring to National Republicans: "Those who fear to grease their fingers with a barbecued pig, or twist their mouths away at whisky grog, or start at the fame of a 'military chieftain' [as Jackson was sneeringly referred to by Henry Clay and other National Republicans] or are deafened by the thunder of the canon [sic], may stay away."

One such "Grand Barbecue" was held in Baltimore to commemorate the successful defense of the city against British attack during the War of 1812, but it soon became a rally for Jackson. "I am told by a gentleman who is employed to erect the fixtures," Jackson was informed, "that three Bullocks are to be roasted, and each man is to wear a Hickory Leaf in his hat by way of designation." The festivities commenced with the firing of a cannon, followed by a parade of seven hundred marshals, after which there were speeches, the singing of several songs in praise of Old Hickory, and then the splendid repast of barbecued bullock provided by the Democratic organizers presided over by Roger B. Taney.

On one occasion Jackson himself took part in these demonstrations, although it was considered grossly improper for a candidate to participate actively in his own campaign. "You *must*, I say, you *must* visit us next autumn in person," wrote an Ohio organizer to the general. But Jackson graciously declined, as he did many other such invitations. However, he did accept the request of the Louisiana Central Committee to attend ceremonies in New Orleans on January 8, 1828, to mark the thirteenth anniversary of his victory over the British in 1815. Presumably it was a national celebration, not a political rally, so Jackson accepted.

But, in fact, it did turn out to be a political rally of extravagant proportions. It was "like a Dream," recorded one man. "The World has never witnessed so glorious, so wonderful a Celebration—never has *Gratitude & Patriotism* so happily united,

Pewter medal. Many of these tokens had holes punched or drilled through the top enabling them to be worn on a chain or ribbon.

As popular voting increased, new artifacts were introduced to promote candidates, images, and slogans. Pewter medalets remained popular until the 1896 election.

son, "the soldier boy of the Revolution," stepped forward and "saved" the nation from possible destruction.

The delight to which the public responded to this new brand of electioneering encouraged party leaders to devise a wide range of entertainments, such as songs, marches, funny stories, poems, puns, and cartoons. For the Democrats the songs and marches naturally focused on the Battle of New Orleans. Probably the most popular song was "The Hunters of Kentucky" with verses by Samuel Woodworth and adapted by Noah M. Ludlow to a melody from the comic opera *Love Laughs at Locksmiths*. The song invariably had the effect of rousing an audience to near-hysterical shouts of praise for Old Hickory and the men who fought with him. Two lively stanzas of this song, which included mention of the defeated British commander, Sir Michael Pakenham, went as follows:

so beautifully blended—& it will form a bright page in American history." When the Hero of New Orleans arrived by steamboat in the crescent city a huge crowd, numbering in the thousands, had been waiting anxiously for him at the levee beside the Mississippi River. When they finally spotted him aboard his steamboat they started screaming in unison, "Huzza! Huzza! Huzza!" as artillery "thundered from the land and the water." There followed welcoming speeches, a parade through the French quarter and a splendid dinner in the evening. For four days the celebration continued, and at every opportunity the glorious battle of January 8 was recounted in French and English, all of which was duly reported in the Democratic newspapers throughout the country. The American people were thus reminded that in their hour of greatest peril General Jack-

> You've heard, I s'pose, of New Orleans,
> 'Tis famed for youth and beauty,
> They've girls of every hue, it seems,
> From snowy white to sooty,
> Now Pakenham had made his brags,
> If he that day was lucky,
> He'd have those girls and cotton bags
> In spite of Old Kentucky. . . .
>
> But Jackson he was wide awake,
> And was not scared at trifles,
> For well he knew Kentucky's boys,
> With their death-dealing rifles,
> He led them down to cypress swamp,
> The ground was low and mucky,
> There stood John Bull in martial pomp,
> And here stood Old Kentucky.
>
> Oh! Kentucky, the hunters of Kentucky!
> Oh! Kentucky, the hunters of Kentucky!

Other songs and marches included "Hickory Wood," "The Battle of New Orleans," and the "General Jackson March" and these were sung and marched to at street rallies, local meetings and conventions, and in taverns and hotels around the country.

The jokes and puns were uniformly terrible but they apparently served a purpose. Some samples include the following:

"Hurray for *Jackson*," cried one man.
"Hurrah for the Devil," responded a National Republican.
"Very well," replied the Democrat. "You stick to your candidate, and I'll stick to mine."

Question: "Why is Adams on ticklish grounds?"
Answer: "Because he stands on slippery Clay."

One "funny" story that made the newspaper rounds accused the National Republicans of acting like the Frenchman who boasted that King Louis had spoken to him.

"What did the King say to you?" asked an envious friend.
"He told me to get out of his way," replied the delighted Frenchman.

In their campaign propaganda Democrats regularly depicted Adams as the candidate of the aristocracy who strolled through the White House like a king and recklessly spent the people's taxes on the trappings of royalty. "We disapprove," cried the Democratic press, "the kingly pomp and splendour that is displayed by the present incumbent." As proof evidence was advanced to show that $25,000 of public funds had been used to equip the White House with gambling furniture, including billiard table, cues, balls, backgammon

board, dice, and a set of expensive chessmen made of ivory. Clearly, such mindless nonsense about cues and balls and chessmen was meant to demonstrate that the Democratic party, in the name of the American people, was engaged in a struggle against privilege and wealth. "The Aristocracy and the Democracy of the country are arrayed against each other," declared one Jacksonian.

Secretary of State Henry Clay, noted for his American System to encourage the development of domestic manufactures and industry, was also denounced for his extravagant tastes. He reputedly used English

Silk memorial ribbon. After leaving the presidency, Adams was elected to Congress (1831–48). He opposed the "gag rule," which forbid discussion or action in the House on antislavery petitions until its defeat (1844). In 1848 he died at the age of eighty.

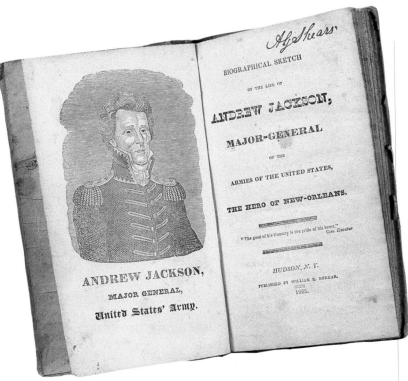

1828 Andrew Jackson biography glorifying his military achievements.

Newspapers played a vital role in propagating and advertising much of the foolishness and hoopla. Early in the campaign Democratic congressmen decided to establish "a chain of newspaper posts, from the New England States to Louisiana, and branching off through Lexington to the Western States." They recognized that a hard-hitting, vigorous press was essential for party success. "We have at considerable expense," wrote one Democrat, "established another newspaper in the northern part of New Hampshire. We have organized our fences in every quarter and have begun & shall continue without ceasing to pour into every doubtful region all kinds of useful information." The best of these Democratic journals included the Washington, D.C. *United States Telegraph*, the Richmond *Enquirer*, the Albany *Argus*, the Kentucky *Argus of Western America*, the Boston *Statesman*, the New York *Courier, Inquirer,* and *Evening Post*, and the Charleston *Mercury*. It was estimated that six hundred newspapers operated in this election, fifty of them dailies, a hundred and fifty semiweeklies, and four hundred weeklies.

writing paper in his department! "O fie, Mr. Clay—*English* paper, *English* wax, *English* pen-knives, is this your *American System."*

Ethnic and religious bigotry also raised an ugly head in this election. In cities where it might generate votes, Democratic newspapers reminded their readers that Jackson was "the son of honest Irish parents. . . . That natural interest which all true hearted Irishmen feel in the fame of one who has so much genuine Irish blood in his veins, had drawn down upon the heads of that devoted people, the denunciations of the partisans of Messrs. Adams & Clay." "Mr. Adams," on the other hand, hated the Irish and "denounced the Roman Catholics as bigots, worshippers of images, and declared that they did not read their bibles." Worse, he was secretly working to "unite CHURCH AND STATE after the manner of the English monarch."

Some newspapers stooped to gutter tactics and made libelous charges of explicit sexual misconduct by one or the other candidate. For example, John Quincy Adams was accused of pimping for the czar of Russia! A brief campaign biography of Jackson published by Isaac Hill, the Democratic organizer of New Hampshire, stated that Adams, when minister to Russia, procured an American girl for the czar. Actually, the girl in question was Martha Godfrey, Mrs. Adams's maid and nurse to young Charles Francis Adams. She wrote letters back home repeating the gossip of the Russian

court and including mention of the czar's love affairs. One letter was intercepted and shown to the czar who expressed a wish to see the girl. As it developed, when Charles Francis Adams was presented to the czarina's sister he was accompanied by his nurse. Then, during the presentation, the czar suddenly appeared and spent several minutes talking with the child and the gossipy Martha. John Quincy Adams recorded in his diary that Martha's letter had afforded the czar "some amusement. . . . It was from this trivial incident that this base imputation has been trumped up," he added.

Trumped up or not, the Democrats made excellent political use of it. Adams was mocked as a "pimp" whose fabulous success as a diplomat had at last been explained. "The Pimp of the Coalition" was one of the titles conferred on him by Democrats. Adams was also accused of premarital sex with his wife.

The organization of the National Republican campaign fell mainly to Clay, Webster, and other leaders in Congress and the states. But their organizing efforts palled along side those of the Democrats. A meeting of the friends of the Adams administration for the purpose of forming a new party convened in Boston. They were urged to forget the "old political landmarks." Theirs would be a new party but one rooted in the broad tenets of republicanism. Personal factions must end. No longer should the Republican party be divided among four or more candidates, as had happened in 1824, each claiming to represent the identical party. Said Clay: "It appears to me to be important that we should, on all occasions, inculcate the incontestable truth that *now* there are but two parties in the Union."

The obverse and reverse of an 1828 medal. "ADVOCATE OF THE AMERICAN SYSTEM"!! Indeed a strange slogan for Andrew Jackson. Nevertheless, in the 1828 campaign, he was acclaimed as a frontier hero, a symbol of the common man, and a supporter of the "American System."

Like the Democrats, National Republican leaders emphasized the importance of a vigorous and hard-hitting press, and by and large Adams was well served. In Washington the *National Intelligencer* and the *National Journal* provided excellent support. Elsewhere in the country they were echoed by the New York *American*, the Cincinnati *Gazette*, the Virginia *Constitutional Whig*, *Niles Weekly Register* of Baltimore, the Massachusetts *Journal*, the Kentucky *Reporter*, the Illinois *Gazette*, and the Missouri *Republican*, among others.

Several of these sheets turned out powerful editorials, and a few stooped to a new low level of mudslinging, one rarely equaled in American history. The unusual, not to say strange, circumstances of Jackson's marriage to Rachel Donelson Robards received extended notice. The worst paper was the Cincinnati *Gazette*, edited by Charles Hammond with financial support from the National Republican party through the good offices of Henry Clay. On March 23, 1827, Hammond let fly his first fistful of filth. "In the summer of 1790," he wrote, "Gen. Jackson prevailed upon the wife of Lewis Roberts [Robards] of Mercer county, Kentucky, to desert her husband, and live with himself, in the character of a wife." Under normal circumstances such sexual impropriety would have annihilated Jackson's candidacy. But the Nashville Central Committee responded with documentary evidence that branded the story a complete distortion and fabrication. Jackson and Rachel, the Central Committee contended in a published report, believed that Robards had obtained a divorce and so they married in Natchez, only to learn later that no divorce had been granted. When the divorce

was finally granted in 1793 Jackson and Rachel remarried. Naturally, nothing was said about the Kentucky court that found Rachel guilty of desertion and adultery with another man. Hammond responded to the argument of the Central Committee by asking: "Ought a convicted adulteress and her paramour husband to be placed in the highest offices of this free and christian land?"

The charge devastated both Jackson and Rachel. Shortly after the election Rachel died of a heart attack, brought on, claimed her husband and friends, by lies and slander generated during the campaign.

And it got even worse. In one of the most vicious and unconscionable editorials ever to appear in an American newspaper, Hammond intensified his assault against the Old Hero:

> General Jackson's mother was a COMMON PROSTITUTE, brought to this country by the British soldiers! She afterwards married a MULATTO MAN, with whom she had several children, of which number General JACKSON IS ONE!!!

Jackson's reputation as a duelist and gunfighter and an all around ruffian was also given considerable notice in the opposition press. Hammond provided a list of fourteen "juvenile indiscretions" attributed to Jackson between the ages of twenty-three and sixty, involving public brawls, gunfights, duels, stabbing and other acts of mayhem which supposedly documented the general's *"intemperate life and character."* Surely such a man, argued Hammond, was singularly "unfit for the highest civil appointment within the gift of my country."

Hammond's journalistic assaults on Jackson's character were aided by John

Binns, editor of the Philadelphia *Democratic Press*, who conceived the so-called "Coffin Hand Bill." This leaflet, entitled "Some Account of Some of the Bloody Deeds of GENERAL JACKSON," described how six militiamen were put to death during the Creek War because they tried to return home at the conclusion of their enlistment. The handbill was bordered in black with six black coffins drawn under the names of the six militiamen. In one corner of the handbill Jackson is seen running his sword cane through the back of a man in the act of picking up a stone to defend himself. A grand jury acquitted the general of wrongdoing in this incident when he pleaded self-defense. "Gentle reader," said the handbill, "it is for you to say, whether this man, who carries a sword cane, and is willing to run it through the body of any one who may presume to stand in his way, is a fit person to be our President."

Other accusations included gambling, cockfighting, drinking, swearing, slave-trading, and participating in the Burr Conspiracy. Jackson did in fact build boats for Aaron Burr but swore he never believed or knew that there was a conspiracy to dismember the Union.

And his executions of two British citizens, Robert Ambrister and Alexander Arbuthnot, during the First Seminole War when he seized Florida from the Spanish, was denounced as a lawless act that nearly triggered a war with England.

Jackson won the election of 1828 despite these distorted and frequently manufactured stories of impropriety. He won because the American people loved and trusted him and because the Democratic

Pewter goblet with the inscription "JACKSON'S BIRTHPLACE," which was Waxhaw, South Carolina (March 15, 1767). The log cabin identified Jackson with the common man.

party proved to be better organized and run by superior politicians. His inauguration on March 4, 1829, resulted in a popular explosion of joy and happiness that almost wrecked the White House. And although the election inaugurated party management of a mass electorate and produced some of the grossest and most disgusting campaigning in American history, it also marked the beginning of practices whose aim and purpose was to directly involve the American people in the election of their chief executive.

★

American Statesman Extra.

INDEAPENDENT,   UNPLEDGED,

NATIONAL REPUBLICAN

Electoral Ticket.

Rev. THOMAS BALDWIN, D. D.   } *Electors at large.*
Hon. WILLIAM BAYLIES.

Hon. WM. WALKER, *Berkshire District.*
Gen. SAMUEL PORTER, *Franklin.*
Dr. TIMOTHY HORTON, *Hampden.*
Hon. SOLOMON STRONG, *Worcester North.*
Dr. DANIEL THURBER, *Worcester South.*
Hon. EDMUND FOSTER, *Middlesex.*
DAVID HOW, Esq. *Essex North.*

WILLIAM SUTTON, Esq. *Essex South.*
Hon. SAMUEL HUBBARD, *Suffolk.*
Hon. BENJAMIN REYNOLDS, *Norfolk.*
Hon. JOHN M. WILLIAMS, *Bristol.*
BENJAMIN HOBART, Esq. *Plymouth.*
NYMPHAS MARSTON, Esq. *Barnstable.*

To the Independent Electors of Massachusetts.

THE undersigned, chosen as a Central Committee for the State, at a meeting of the citizens of Boston, and in pursuance of the request of the Convention in Berkshire, for the purpose of communicating with the people in the various districts of the Commonwealth, relative to a nomination of unpledged candidates as electors of President and Vice President, were instructed by their constituents to publish, in their behalf, an address to you. The time approaches, fellow citizens, when an election of the highest importance under the government of the United States must take place; and the part you are to act is not only of consequence to you, but to the reputation of the state, and to the interests of the community. A majority of your representatives, at the last session of the Legislature, passed a law, that the electors of President in Massachusetts should be chosen by a general ticket; and a portion of those representatives soon after met in Caucus, and designated the candidates to be voted for for that high and responsible trust. We did suppose the past history of this Commonwealth would have saved us from so daring an encroachment upon our rights. Your sentiments could not have been mistaken by them, for in 1804, at a period when the excited passions of men urged them to the extreme bounds of propriety and good faith, you solemnly proclaimed the measure to be destitute of principle, and an usurpation on your rights. The opposition you then made to this odious law is one of the noblest acts recorded on your political annals, as it proves that neither the ardour of excited passions, nor the discipline of party, could seduce you from an adherance to principle, or a regard for justice. The act was adopted by the party which the majority of the people then supported, but the stern integrity of the people themselves rejected the measure of their representatives, and sacrificed the ascendancy of party to the preservation of justice. There was something in the conduct of many federalists on that occasion worthy at once of our respect and imitation. They were told, as the noble Aristides told the people of Athens, that the measure would be beneficial to them, but would not be just; and like the illustrious Athenians, they replied, "we seek justice before our interests." The protest of a republican minority was nobly sustained by many federalists as well as by the republican party; and the attempt to build up a party ascendancy, by trampling on the rights of a minority, was put down, in part, by those for whose benefit it was intended.

After so deliberate an expression of the will of the people, it is not without surprise, fellow citizens, that we have recently beheld another Legislature emboldened to the repetition of a similar attempt; and if any thing could add to the astonishment which is excited when the wishes of the people are disregarded their representatives, it would be that the party which now renews the attempt, is that which entered its protest against it in 1804. In addition to the protest of the minority of the Senate, one hundred and one members of the House of Representatives, made a solemn remonstrance against the general electoral law, with a request that it might be permanently entered on the records of the House; and among others the following were the reasons which they assigned.

1. "It defeats the *first principle* of the *elective franchise.*"
2. "It is *repugnant to the habits and usages* of the people of this Commonwealth."
3. "It is calculated to open the door to *intrigue, and imposition on the people.*"
4. "It is fallacious on the face of it, appearing to give an elector to each district, while it may secure one in direct opposition to the majority of its voters."
5. "It will deprive one party of their due weight, in the appointment of the *first magistrate of the union.*"

Such, fellow citizens, were the sentiments of the republican members of the Legislature in 1804:—will it not challenge human credulity to believe, that it is the *republican Legislature* of 1824, by whom a measure which they thus characterised when a minority, is now adopted and defended? Is it they "*who have consented to defeat the first principle of the elective franchise,*" "*to adopt a course repugnant to the habits and usages of the people,*" "*to open the door to intrigue and imposition,*" and "*to deprive the party,*" now in the minority, "*of their due weight in the appointment of the first magistrate of the union*"? Is it the *republican party* who practice in power the principles they condemned when out of it; who will oppress the minority who, when they themselves were oppressed, magnanimously interfered in their protection, and sacrificed their own interests in defence of republican rights. Will republican citizens manifest less regard for principle now than federal citizens did in 1804, and show that while their representatives can follow an example they have condemned, the people will not imitate a virtue they admired.

But great as is the outrage of the general ticket law on the usages and feelings of the people of this state, it sinks into insignificance compared with the high-handed measures which followed it. Not content with taking from the people in the districts their ancient right of choosing their own electors, the usurpation was followed up by an act for which the party efforts of this state afford no precedent. A part of the republican members of the Legislature met in caucus, and dictated the candidates for whom the people should vote. But not satisfied with taking from districts the right of election, they endeavoured to defeat even the humble privilege of *nominating their candidates*; and, as if it were even too great a concession to the people, that they should be oppressed by their own representatives, a *junto* of *five* men was created, with power to *change the candidates* if they thought proper, whom the people should be at *liberty to support.* We can follow this train of usurpation, fellow citizens, no farther, without feelings to which we find it difficult for language to give expression. The occasion has shown with what facility men can pass from injury to insult, and add a mockery of the constitution to an outrage on the people. Four of the five members of the junto thus set up by the Legislature, to guide the people in the choice of electors, were men prohibited by the national constitution from choosing a President. The second article, first section of the constitution of the United States, provides, that "no senator, representative, or person holding an office of trust or profit under the United States, shall be appointed an elector;" and yet two of the five composing the junto, were representatives in Congress, to wit, Messrs. Crowninshield and Fuller; and two others held offices of "trust and profit" under the United States, Mr. Dearborn, the Collector of Boston, and Mr. Hill, the Postmaster.

If the principles proclaimed by the republican party in 1804, and sanctioned by the people, were right, it was wrong to deprive the districts of the right of choosing their electors, and oppression and injustice to take from the minority in the state "its due weight in the appointment of the first magistrate of the union." No power remained with the people to repeal the law, but there was one right remaining of which no usurpation could deprive them. It was still competent to the people to give or withhold their sanction to the injustice, and to nominate the candidates for whom they would vote. Attempts have indeed been made to awe them into submission, but force and violence have not yet destroyed the last vestige of the elective franchise which is protected by our constitution and laws. To nominate such electors in each district as would express the sentiments of the people, of whatever party they might be, was the only alternative which the law had left open, and we are happy to have it in our power to announce to you that this right has been exercised. The ticket thus made up is composed as the republican protest in 1804, contended it should be, of both political parties, allowing both to the majority and the minority, "their due weight in the appointment of the chief magistrate of the union." The men thus offered for your support are entitled to your confidence, and have generally heretofore received it, for the most important trusts in your power to confer; and the principle which has governed the people in the selection of them, has been, it is believed, invariably, a regard to the political sentiments of the majority in the district for which they were nominated.

We have been compelled to recommend for your support a candidate for the district of Barnstable, without having for the recommendation the previous sanction of the electors of that district, at some public meeting; but the time for the election is so near that much solicitude has been manifested from all parts of the commonwealth, for the immediate publication of the ticket, and the undersigned have not felt at liberty to delay it any longer. In recommending the gentleman for that district, however, we have been guided by such information from the voters in that quarter, as to leave us no reason to doubt that it will meet their cordial approbation and support.

In concluding the remarks which we have felt bound to submit to you, we regret the necessity of adverting to a subject which cannot have failed to excite in your minds, the same sentiments of regret and surprise which it has occasioned to this committee. To say that the unwillingness manifested, at so late a moment after their nomination, by Governors Eustis and Brooks, to stand as candidates, was *unexpected* and extraordinary, is but to express, we believe, the sentiments of all fair and intelligent men. It imposed on this committee, from the impracticability of holding, in each district of the state, an additional meeting of the people, the responsible duty of recommending others in their place. In the discharge of this duty we have communicated with the committees chosen by the people for their several districts, and we feel confident in the assertion, that the names which have been substituted, will, to say the least, be equally acceptable to the people and as auspicious to our success.

The ticket thus offered to you, we hazard nothing in saying, is entitled to as strong a support as any which has been submitted to the people of this commonwealth; and if information from all quarters of the state, and from the most respectable sources, is entitled to credit, we feel authorized to anticipate for it, with due exertion, a decided success.

LEONARD M. PARKER,
EBENEZER SEAVER,
HENRY ORNE,
DAVID HENSHAW,   } *Central Committee of the State.*
WILLIAM INGALLS,
SAMUEL BILLINGS,
BARNEY SMITH,

1829 political broadside published by a Massachusetts newspaper.

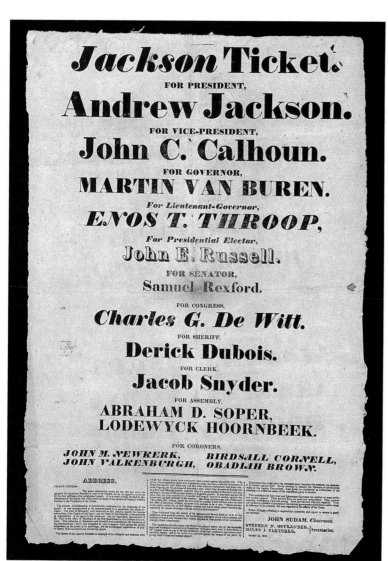

1828 political broadside and a grouping of rare Jackson medals, including a Jackson brass clothing button.

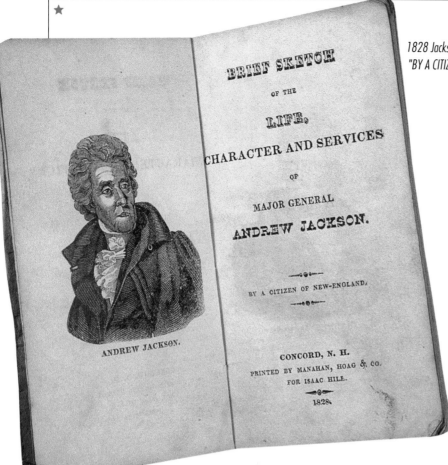

1828 Jackson campaign biography
"BY A CITIZEN OF NEW ENGLAND."

Jackson medal depicting the Battle of New Orleans.

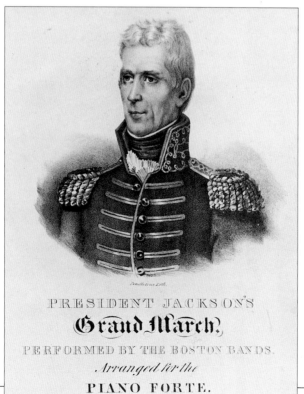

*The earliest campaign music dates from 1800. With the 1828
campaign, elaborate candidate portraits decorated the sheet music.*

Some Account of some of the Bloody Deeds of
GEN. JACKSON.

Jacob Webb.   David Morrow.   John Harris.   Henry Lewis.   David Hunt.   Edward Lindsey.

A brief account of the Execution of the Six Militia Men.

As we may soon expect to have the *official documents* in relation to the SIX MILITIA MEN, arrested, tried, and put to death, under the orders of General Andrew Jackson, this may not be an improper time to give to the public some of the particulars of their execution, as we have them from "AN EYE WITNESS," who appeals to Col. Russell, for the truth of every word he relates.

Harris was a Baptist preacher, with a large family. He had hired as a substitute for three months. This was the case with most of them. They were ignorant men, but obstinate in what they believed right, and what they had been told by their officers was right. They were all sure they could not be kept beyond three months, and they gave up their muskets, and had provisions dealt out to them, from the public stores, before they left the camp. This confirmed their convictions that they were right, and doing what was lawful.

Col. Russell commanded at the execution. The Militia men were brought to the place in a large wagon. The military dispositions being made, Col. Russell rode up to the wagon and ordered the men to descend. Harris was the only one who betrayed feminine weakness. The awfulness of the occasion; his wife and nine children; the parting with his son; and the fear of a quickly approaching ignominious death! quite overcome him, and he sunk in unmanly grief. No feeling of military pride could brace him up.

Col. Russell, doubtless, felt as a man, but he felt also for the pride of the army, and desired to animate the men with fortitude. "You are about to die," said he, "by the sentence of a Court Martial—die like men; *like soldiers.* You have been brave in the "field—you have fought well—do no "discredit to your country, or dishonor to the army, or yourselves, "by any unmanly fears. Meet your "fate with courage."

Harris attempted to make some apology for his conduct, but while he spoke, he wept bitterly. The fear of death, the idea that he should never again behold his wife and little ones, and his son weeping near him, had taken such entire possession of his mind that it was impossible he should rally.

Lewis, the gallant Lewis, said in a clear and manly tone, "Colonel, I "have served my country well. I "love it dearly, and would, if I could, "serve it longer and better. I have "fought bravely—*you know* I have, and "HERE I have a right to say so

"MYSELF. I would not wish to die in "this way"—here his voice faltered, "and he passed the back of his right "hand over his eyes—" I did not expect it. But, I am now as firm as I "have been in battle, and you shall see "that I will die as becomes a soldier; "you know I am a brave man." "Yes, Lewis," said the Colonel, "you "have always behaved like a brave "man." Other sentences were uttered, other declarations were made, and words of comfort spoken, but they were lost on me: my attention, says an Eye Witness, being chiefly directed to Lewis.

Six coffins were ranged as directed, and on each of them knelt one of our condemned American Militia Men. Such a sight was never seen before! I trust to God it never will be seen again! Six soldiers were detailed and drawn up to fire at each man. What an awful duty! Their white caps were drawn over the faces of the unhappy men. Harris evidently trembled, and I could almost persuade myself that the heart of Lewis was enlarged, and that his bosom rose with manly courage to meet death. The fatal word was given and they all fell.

As we approached the scene of blood and carnage, Lewis gave signs of life; the rest were all dead—he crawled upon his coffin. After the lapse of a few minutes, he said—I give

his very words: "Colonel!"—the Colonel was close to him—"Colonel, I "am not killed, but I am sadly cut "and mangled." His body was now examined, and it was found that but four balls had wounded him. "Colonel, said he, "did I behave well?" "Yes, Lewis," said the Colonel in the kindest tone of voice, "like a man."— "Well, sir," said he, "here I not "atoned for this offence? *Shall I yet* "live?" The Colonel was much agitated, and gave orders that the Surgeon should, if possible, preserve his life. They did all that skill and humanity could do: it was all of no avail. Poor Lewis expressed a great desire to live. "I am not," said he at one time, "that I fear death, but I would repent "me of some sins, and I desire to live "yet a little longer in the world." He suffered inconceivable agony from his wounds and died on the fourth day.

Many a soldier has wept over his grave. He was a brave man and much beloved. He suffered twenty deaths. I have seen the dog in the chase each other down his forehead with pain and anguish. There was much sensibility and sympathy throughout the camp. I would not have, unjustly and unnecessarily, signed this death warrant for all the wealth of all the Indies. The soldiers detailed to shoot Lewis had, from strong feelings of sympathy, or mis-

taken humanity, failed to shoot him—but four balls had entered his body.

"An Eye Witness" appeals to Col. Russell, who he thinks now lives in Alabama, for the perfect truth of this sketch. He does not fear but the Colonel will keenly recollect and faithfully depict the horrors of the day on which six Americans were shot to death under his command—but not by his orders.

The order bears date the very day after General Jackson returned in triumph to New Orleans, and the day before he joyfully went, under triumphal arches, to the temple of the living God; where, says the historian, "they crowned their adored General with laurels." The order for the execution of these six unhappy men bears date January 22, 1815. His crown of laurels had not yet withered when blood, the life's blood of his countrymen, of his fellow soldiers, flowed plentifully by his order. May that order and its consequences, sink deep into the hearts of the American people, and steel them against him who had no flesh in his obdurate heart; who did not feel for Man; in the midst of Joy and Revelry, almost in the immediate presence of his Creator, who issued the fatal order to put his fellow creatures to death, and to make their wives and children, widows and orphans.

MOURNFUL TRAGEDY;

Or, the death of Jacob Webb, David Morrow, John Harris, Henry Lewis, David Hunt and Edward Lindsey—six militia men—who were condemned to die, the sentence approved by Major General Jackson, and by his order the whole six shot.

O! did you hear that plaintive cry
Borne on the southern breeze?
Saw you John Harris earnest pray
For mercy, on his knees?

Low to the earth he bent, and pray'd
For pardon from his chief;
But to his earnest prayer for life
No answer, no relief.

"Spare me," he said, "I mean no wrong,
"My heart was always true;
"First for my country's cause it beat,
"And next, great Chief, for you."

"We thought our time of service out—
"To clasp her only son,
"We meant to violate no law,
"Nor wish'd to shun the foe.

"Our officers declar'd that we
"Had but three months to stay!
"We serv'd those three months faithfully
"Up to the latest day.

"No one suspects intended wrong;
"The judgment only err'd:
"In such a case, O noble Chief,
"Let mercy's voice be heard.

"At home an aged mother waits
"To clasp her only son;
"A wife, and little children—this arm
"Alone depend upon.

"Cut me not off from these dear ties:
"So soon from life's young bloom:
"O 'tis a dreadful thing to die,
"And moulder in the tomb!

"Sure mercy is a noble gem
"On every Chieftain's brow;
"More sparkling than a diadem—
"O exercise it now."

'Twas all in vain, John Harris' pray't,
"To clasp her son's relief!
Hard as the flint was Jackson's heart;
He would not grant relief.

He order'd Harris out to die,
And five poor fellows more!
"And mangled men, in prise of life,
To welter in their gore!

Methinks I hear the muffled drum,
And see the solemn move;
Lo here these men—how sad their looks!
Farewell to life and love!

See six black coffins rang'd along—
six soldiers to each grave!
Webb, Lindsey, Harris, Lewis, Hunt,
And Morris knell'd and pray'd.

They kneel'd, & pray'd, & the'd of BORY,
And all Redear delights—
The deadly tubes are levell'd now—
The scene my soul affrights!

Sure he will spare! Sure Jackson yet
Will all reprieve but one—
O hark! these shricks! that cry of death!
The dreadful deed is done!

All six militia men were shot!
And O it seems to me
A dreadful deed—a bloody act
Of needless cruelty.

Do not be startled, gentle reader, at the picture before you. It is all true and every body ought to know it. Gen. Jackson having made an assault upon Samuel Jackson, in the streets of Nashville, and the latter not being disposed to stand still and be beaten, stooped down for a stone to defend himself—While in the act of doing so, Gen. Jackson drew the sword

The reader is reminded that it was on the 21st day of January, 1815, that General Jackson returned to the city of New Orleans from the battle ground. The British had abandoned the enterprise and retired. The General was received with the strongest demonstrations of joy and gratitude. It was on that very day, January 21, that he issued the order for the execution of the six militia-men. The 23d was appointed a day of general thanksgiving, when the General was provided with a wreath of laurel by the hands of the Bishop. On the 28th of the same month an order was issued for the execution of twelve soldiers, condemned by a Court Martial at Nashville. All to be executed within four days after the promulgation of the order!!

"Extract from the General order, dated 'Adjutant General's Office, New Orleans, January 28th, 1815, Head Quarters, 7th Military District, on the proceedings of the General Court Martial, held at Nashville on the 19th of October, 1814, and continued by adjournment till the 28th of November, 1814.'"

"'Was also tried the following-named men, soldiers of the army of the United States, severally charged with 'desertion,' viz.: Richard Wall, of 3d Rifle Regiment; Jacob Perregrin, of said Regiment; both of Capt. Willey Martin's company; John Jones, of the 24th Regiment of Infantry; William Myers, of Capt. Humphrey's company of Artillery; Jacob King, of Capt. Reed's company, said corps; Benjamin Harris, of the 44th Infantry; John Young, of the 39th Infantry; Nathaniel Chester, of the corps of Artillery; Drury Puckett, of the 24th Infantry; Wyat Grantt, of the 39th Infantry; Joseph Mackelroy, of the 24th Infantry; and James McBride, 3d Rifle Regiment; to which charge they severally pleaded Not Guilty, except Jacob King, who pleaded Guilty. The Court, after the examination of testimony on each of the cases, and deliberation had thereon, pronounce on each and every one of them 'Death by shooting.' The Major General approves the sentence passed on the above named soldiers of the Army of the United States, and orders the same to be carried into full effect in four days after the promulgation of this order, at the post where they may be, under the direction of the senior officer present."

Another was to have been executed at the same time. He was a young man, who had deserted one month before his time had expired. General Jackson doomed him to die with the others. He was saved by a writ of habeas corpus from Judge M'Nairy, who fell under Jackson's displeasure for snatching this one victim from his blood stained hands. If Jackson's army had been at hand, no doubt M'Nairy would have shared the fate of Judge Hall and Judge Fromentin. Capital punishments in an army, are designed for example as well as for punishment; but in this case it was a transaction of horror to peaceful citizens: no army was there to witness the bloody tragedy. He has ever been a man of "blood and carnage."

There can be no doubt that every one of these men were executed. There was no power to save them after the promulgation of this order. Thus we see that Gen. Jackson, within the space of one week, in the midst of exultations and rejoicings, ordered eighteen of his fellow men to be put to death!!! Is there any instance on record, in any history of modern warfare, that equals this for barbarity? The time, the circumstances, the numbers. And can it be that this barbarian shall be elevated to the chief magistracy of a free, a generous, and a merciful nation?

On the 27th day of March, 1814, General Jackson had found at an Indian village, at the head of the Tallapoosa, about 4000 Indians, with their *squaws and children,* "running about among their huts." The following is an account of the sanguinary massacre which took place—It is Gen. Jackson's own, and therefore must be received as sufficient evidence against himself. He says:—"DETERMINING TO EXTERMINATE them, I detached Gen. Coffee with the mounted men and nearly the whole of the Indian force, early in the morning of yesterday, to cross the river about two miles below the encampment, that none of them should escape by attempting to cross the river." The result he then details:—"*Five hundred and fifty-seven were left dead on the Peninsula, and a great number of them were killed by the horsemen attempting to cross the river. It is BELIEVED THAT NO MORE THAN TEN ESCAPED.* WE CONTINUED to DESTROY *many of them who had concealed themselves under the banks of the river, until we were prevented by the night.* THIS MORNING WE KILLED 16 WHICH HAD BEEN CONCEALED."

We ask you to pause and reflect that the above tragic narration of cold blooded and merciless cruelty, is taken from an official communication, made by General Andrew Jackson.

The General, after sleeping (with what composure, we cannot say) through the night ensuing the tragedy we speak of, awoke in the morning surrounded by the corpses of "five hundred and seventy" fellow creatures, to whom, by way of worthy afterpiece, sixteen others to be dragged from their concealments, and put to death in cold blood. We cannot boast of more than common sensibility, but we must think that to witness such an act, would make ours a little cold also. What are the general's words?—these: "this morning we killed sixteen which had been concealed!"—and the man who acts and speaks thus; who has half as much blood upon his conscience, as he has upon his hands—he, forsooth, is to be called the poor and like of Washington, the happy warrior———!" When every man at arms could wish to be.

But it is time to have done with the unpleasant subject. We will observe in addition to the details already given, that the village was burnt, and several women and children killed. In conclusion, we ask our fellow citizens, whether Gen. Jackson though he has contributed largely to the military reputation of our country, has not done enough to disqualify him, in the eyes of the people as virtuous as they are free, for the office he seeks at their hands.

 Gen. Jackson, detailing his progress among the Indians, in the course of which, men, WOMEN and CHILDREN, were indiscriminately "exterminated," their towns burnt, and their country laid waste, with the utmost complacency and *sang froid,* says, in his letter dated, "Camp before St. Marks, April 9, 1818—"Captain McEver having hoisted English colours on board of his boats, Francis the *Prophet,* Hoccmochtemucko, and two others, were decoyed on board! *These have been hung to-day!*" Reader, mark the perfect indifference with which Gen. Jackson shoots, hangs or sticks his fellow beings, with or without trial; and the more than callous, aye, even exulting composure, with which he details his horrid and bloody deeds! If the Indians, according to the customs of their nation, put to death a prisoner, all the feelings of our nature rise into indignation against them. With what feelings then should we contemplate the *decoying* & the cold-blooded murder of prisoners, by a civilized man, in the face of the laws and customs of his country.

Poor JOHN WOODS; he was a generous hearted, noble fellow as ever lived, who had volunteered in the service of his country. He was on guard one day at Fort Strother—the officer of the guard had permitted him to go to his tent, and snatch a hasty breakfast; whilst disposing of his scanty meal, seated on the ground beside his skillet, an unstart little officer, who was not Woods's equal at home, ordered him to pick up and carry off some bones that lay scattered about the place—Woods refused, and the little officer attempted to compel him. In this instant, Gen. Jackson, having heard the dispute, came out of his tent, and without knowing any thing of the merits of the case, repeatedly vociferated—"*Shoot the damn'd rascal—Shoot the damn'd rascal.*" For this offence, the unfortunate, the gallant Woods, was tried, condemned and shot. Before his trial, Gen. Jackson used this language to the court-martial; "*By the immortal God! if you find him guilty I will not pardon him!*" And he kept his promise; though he did offer a pardon provided he would enlist in the regular service—Thus perished so noble a fellow as ever lived, for as trifling an offence as ever took the life of man!!!

FRANKLIN, Tenn. September 10, 1818.

A difference which had been for some months brewing between Gen. Jackson and myself, produced on Saturday, 4th inst. in the town of Nashville, the most outrageous affray ever witnessed in a civilized country. In commanding the affair to my friends and fellow citizens, I limit myself to the statement of a few leading facts, the truth of which I am ready to establish by judicial proofs.

1. That myself and my brother, Jesse Benton, arriving in Nashville on the morning of the affray, and knowing of Gen. Jackson's threats, went and took lodgings in a different house from the one in which he staid, on purpose to avoid him.

2. That the Gen. and some of his friends came to the house where we had put up and commenced the attack by leveling a pistol at me, when I had no weapon drawn, and advancing upon me at a quick pace without giving me time to draw one.

3. That seeing this, my brother fired upon Gen. Jackson, when he had got within eight or ten feet of me.

4. That four other pistols were fired in quick succession; one by Gen. Jackson at me; two by me at the Gen.; and one by Col. Coffee at me. In the course of this firing, Gen. Jackson was brought to the ground; but received no hurt.

5. That daggers were then drawn. Col. Coffee and Mr. Alexander Donaldson made it me, and gave me five slight wounds. Capt. Hammond and Mr. Stokeley Hays engaged my brother, who, being still weak from the effects of a severe wound he had lately received in a duel, was not able to resist two men. They got him down; and while Capt. Hammond beat him on the head to make him lie still, Mr. Hays

attempted to stab him, and wounded him in both arms, as he lay on his back parrying the thrusts with his naked hands. From this situation a generous hearted citizen of Nashville, Mr. Sumner, relieved him. Before he came to the ground, my brother clapped a pistol to the breast of Mr. Hays to blow him through, but it missed fire.

6. My own and my brother's pistols carried two balls each; for it was our intention, if driven to arms to have no child's play. The pistols fired at me were so near that the blaze of the muzzle of one of them burnt the sleeve of my coat, and the other, aimed at my head at a little more than arm's length from me.

7 Capt. Carroll was to have taken part in the affray, but was absent by the permission of Gen. Jackson, as he has proved by the General's certificate; a certificate which reflects I know not whether less honour upon the General or upon the Captain.

8 That this attack was made upon me in the house where the Judge of the District, Mr. Searcy, had his lodgings! Nor has the civil authority yet taken cognizance of this horrible outrage.

These facts are sufficient to fix the public opinion. For my own part, I think it scandalous that such things should take place at any time; but particularly so at the present moment, when the public service requires the aid of all its citizens. As for the name of *courage,* God forbid that I should ever attempt to gain it by becoming a bully. Those who know me, know full well that I would give a thousand times more for the reputation of Croghan in defending his post, than I would for the reputation of all the duellists and gladiators that ever appeared upon the face of the earth.

THOMAS HART BENTON, Lieut. Col. Thirty-Ninth Infantry
And now a member of the Senate of the United States.

Jackson's controversial life inspired harsh negative campaigning. Several broadsides took issue with Jackson's "noble" military record. Many held "Old Hickory" accountable for excessive executions during the Creek War (1813–14). This is one of several broadsides featuring coffins.

French textile, circa 1829. Roller-print bearing likenesses of all the Presidents.
The frigate "Constitution," made famous during the War of 1812, appears on the right.

Hand-painted
French porcelain
bowl with a
portrait of John
Quincy Adams.

Jackson whiskey flask with a
portrait of Washington on the
reverse. There are twelve
different flasks picturing
Andrew Jackson.

Pewter-rimmed medallions with lithographed portraits under glass.

Hexagonal Adams thread box.

★

1832
24 STATES
IN THE UNION

DEMOCRAT
Andrew Jackson
ELECTORAL VOTE 219, POPULAR VOTE 55%

NATIONAL REPUBLICAN
Henry Clay
ELECTORAL VOTE 49, POPULAR VOTE 37%

ANTI-MASONIC
William Wirt
ELECTORAL VOTE 7, POPULAR VOTE 8%

NATIONAL REPUBLICAN
John Floyd
ELECTORAL VOTE 11, POPULAR VOTE 2%

ROBERT V. REMINI
is the author of a three-volume biography of
Andrew Jackson: *Andrew Jackson and the Course
of American Empire, 1767–1821* (1977); *Andrew
Jackson and the Course of American Freedom,
1822–1832* (1981); and *Andrew Jackson and the
Course of American Democracy, 1833–1845*
(1984). He is also the author of *Henry Clay:
Statesman for the Union* (1991).

Important innovations in American political history were provided by the presidential election of 1832: It was the first election in which the candidates were nominated by their respective parties at national conventions; and it also marked the emergence of the first third party in American history, the Anti-Masonic party.

The disappearance and presumed murder of William Morgan in Batavia, New York, in 1826, allegedly at the hands of Masons, provoked intense antagonisms against members of this secret society and finally produced a new political party. The Anti-Masonic agitation began in upstate New York and quickly spread into Pennsylvania, Vermont, and other sections of New England and parts of the Midwest. Such astute politicians as Thurlow Weed, William H. Seward, Thaddeus Stevens, John C. Spencer, Samuel A. Foot, and Henry Dana Ward provided strong leadership for the fledgling party and summoned a meeting in Baltimore of delegates from the several states on September 26, 1831, to nominate their presidential candidate.

Represented at this first national nominating convention were the states of New Hampshire, Maine, Massachusetts, Rhode Island, Connecticut, Vermont, New York, New Jersey, Pennsylvania, Ohio, Maryland, Delaware, and Indiana—with New York, Pennsylvania, and Massachusetts dominating the proceedings of the convention by virtue of the size of their delegations. Chief Justice John Marshall and former Attorney General William Wirt attended by invitation and watched the proceedings from their seats next to the presiding officer. At the last moment the leaders decided to nominate Wirt for the presidency, despite his former membership in the Masonic order, because he was a man of national reputation and prestige and had readily agreed to have his name offered to the convention.

There were no nominating speeches at this convention, and on the first ballot Wirt received 108 votes to one for Richard Rush, with two blanks. Wirt's nomination was then made unanimous, after which Amos Ellmaker of Pennsylvania was named the vice presidential running mate.

In his letter of acceptance, Wirt demonstrated extraordinary insensitivity to the passionate antipathy that the delegates felt toward Masons by stating that freemasonry had been "designed for the promotion of good feeling among its members, and for the pecuniary relief of their indigent brethren." Although appalled by Morgan's apparent murder, he refused to believe that this heinous crime reflected on all Masons. After all, some notable Americans had been Masons, including George Washington.

The delegates listened stony-faced to this incredible letter and several expressed their desire to replace Wirt with someone more ardent in his hostility to freemasonry. But it was too late to make a change and the Anti-Masonic party was forced to campaign with a candidate whose commitment to the cause they strongly doubted.

However, the platform adopted by the delegates made the party's position very clear. Freemasonry, it said, is "infamous beyond all parallel in human annals. Its principles are vicious, murderous, treasonable; and so far as they prevail fatally hostile to those of our government." Therefore, Masons must be driven from public office, for the "evils of freemasonry operate upon the moral and political condition of the nation, and can be removed only by moral and political means."

The nominations of the two other parties went quite differently. For the past four years the friends and supporters of the National Republican party knew who they wanted for their presidential candidate. None would suffice except Henry Clay of Kentucky, former Speaker of the House of Representatives and secretary of state under President John Quincy Adams. Clay himself desperately wanted the nomination and the party obliged him at their first national convention held in Baltimore on December 12, 1831. One hundred and fifty-five delegates represented eighteen states. Peter R. Livingston nominated Clay and the delegates unanimously gave their approval. No other name was placed in nomination. The following day John Sergeant of Pennsylvania was named as Clay's vice presidential running mate.

In his letter of acceptance Clay swore fidelity to the Union, the Constitution, the principles of public liberty, "and to those great measures of national policy which have made us a people, prosperous, respected, and powerful."

Several months later, on May 7, 1832, a National Republican Convention of some three hundred young men, dubbed "Clay's Infant-School," met in Washington, D.C., and confirmed Clay's candidacy. Some 316 delegates attended but what made this convention unique was the sudden appearance of the candidate himself to accept the nomination and express the "deep and grateful sense which I entertain for the distinguished proofs which you have . . . given to me of your esteem and confidence." When he ended his speech of acceptance, Clay went around the room and shook the hand of each delegate to thank him for his support.

The convention of the Democratic party did not nominate a President. There was no need. No one remotely considered replacing Andrew Jackson. The delegates therefore met in Baltimore on May 21, 1832, to select Jackson's running mate. Since the President had already indicated his choice, the delegates were reduced to endorsing his decision. A total of 334 participants, representing every state but Missouri, overwhelmingly agreed on Martin Van Buren as vice presidential candidate.

It was a cut-and-dried convention. There were no great speeches, no statement of principles, no exaltation of what Jackson had accomplished in his first term in office. Such an exercise seemed pointless. The delegates knew they had a candidate of incomparable popularity and an organization to support him that neither the Anti-Masons nor National Republicans could match. Before they concluded their business, however, the delegates declared that they "concurred" in the many nominations Jackson had already received from numerous state legislatures and conventions.

The well-organized Democrats immediately set up committees to distribute political literature, raise money, and correspond with party members around the country. These committees became operational quite early in the campaign and functioned at every level: state, county, and local. A central committee of sorts, located in Washington, with Amos Kendall, the fourth auditor of the Treasury Department serving as national party chairman, attempted to coordinate the activities of the various state committees. Kendall demanded intensive organization from local politicians, and he called for the founding of newspapers. "You must try by an efficient organization and rousing the patriotic enthusiasm of the people," he wrote one party leader, "to counteract the power of money." "Have you an organization in your state?" he asked another. "Whether you have or not . . . send me a list of names of Jackson men good and true in every township of the state . . . to whom our friends may send political information. I beg you to do this *instantly*." Kendall also prodded local leaders to make Jackson's reform program the focus of their campaign.

At the outset of his administration President Jackson announced his intention of carrying out a program of "reform, retrenchment and economy," by which he meant the elimination of corruption in the operation of the government through the removal of those who had betrayed the public trust, the reduction of government operating costs, especially personnel, and the scaling back of congressional appropriations for internal improvements in order to pay off the national debt.

The "No BANK" slogan refers to Jackson's opposition to rechartering the Second Bank of the United States. The origin of this 1832 silk ribbon is something of a mystery because Congressman Joel Barlow Sutherland. was an avid supporter of the bank which was headquartered in his district.

Jackson brass token dated 1833.

Part of his reform also involved changes in the operation of the Second Bank of the United States, a quasi-public institution chartered by the government and charged with collecting and disbursing government funds. Jackson believed the bank had abused its privileges and meddled in political affairs, thus endangering individual liberty. In July 1832, he therefore vetoed a bill to recharter the bank for another twenty years, thus providing the National Republicans with an issue they believed would offset his popularity and assure his defeat. The president of the bank, Nicholas Biddle, circulated Jackson's veto message during the campaign in the mistaken belief that the American people needed the bank, appreciated its worth, would reject Jackson's arguments for refusing to extend its charter, and vote for Henry Clay in the fall election.

In the ensuing campaign the Democrats tended to make the bank and Nicholas Biddle the main focus of their attack rather than Clay or Wirt. Jackson's mouthpiece, the Washington *Globe*, expertly edited by Francis P. Blair, kept up a steady drumbeat of criticism of the bank and its supporters.

The "Golden vaults of the Mammoth bank," pronounced the *Globe*, had been opened wide to encourage bribery and corruption. "Let the cry be heard across the land. Down with bribery—down with corruption—down with the Bank. . . . Let committees be appointed in every township to prosecute every Bank agent who offers a bribe."

"The Bank," warned Senator William L. Marcy of New York, "is in the field and I cannot but fear the effect of 50 or 100 thousand dollars expended in conducting the election in such a city as New York." A New Hampshire man echoed the warning: "The Bank is scattering its thousands here to affect us." Out West the cry was the same: "I fear the Bank *influence* more than anything else. I have no doubt that the Bank managers will expend a large sum of money." Said another: "If the Bank, a mere monied corporation, can influence and change the results of our election at pleasure, nothing remains of our boasted freedom except *the skin of the immolated victim.*"

Blair and Kendall issued *Extra Globes* designed to "throw this paper into every neighborhood of the United States." The paper was "sent in bundles by the Administration and its officers, into every town where a Jackson man can be found to distribute them," reported the Maine *Advocate*, an opposition journal. "Letters are written and *franked* by the different officers at Washington, and sent out in all directions, soliciting 'names and money,' and it is avowed to be their intention to introduce them into every house in the State, if possible. . . . At what former period have we seen the government officers, and even the President himself . . . writing electioneering letters, and circulating papers filled with political trash and the vilest falsehoods."

"The Jackson cause," trumpeted the Democratic press, "is the cause of democracy and the people, against a corrupt and abandoned aristocracy."

The National Republicans newspapers countered by accusing Jackson of tyranny and despotism. This became the thrust of the attack by Clay and his party. "The spirit of Jacksonianism," they chorused, "is JACOBINISM. . . . Its Alpha is ANARCHY and its Omega DESPOTISM. It addresses itself to the worst passions of the least informed portion of the People." By his many vetoes, and especially the bank veto, Jackson had annulled two houses of Congress, the Supreme Court, and the Constitution of the United States. The "Constitution is gone!"cried the Washington *National Intelligencer.* "It is a dead letter, and the will of a DICTATOR is the Supreme Law."

In all their publications the National Republicans claimed a wide variety of failures and tragic mistakes by President Jackson: rotation of office, which they dubbed a "spoils system" after William L. Marcy declared on the Senate floor that "to the victor belong the spoils of the enemy"; the removal of the southern tribes of Indians to places west of the Mississippi River; the contempt shown the Supreme Court by vetoing legislation already deemed constitutional by the high court; the fact that he had vetoed more bills than all previous Presidents put together; his veto of needed internal improvements such as the Maysville Road which would extend the National Road in Kentucky; his confused position on the tariff; his determined effort to destroy a financial institution that provided the nation with sound currency and

Pewter medal of Henry Clay.

credit; and, perhaps most heinous of all, his presumption in choosing his probable successor for the presidency, the "Little Magician," Martin Van Buren, by making him his running mate. "He has proved false to his promises, to his country, to his friends, to everything but his own wretched ambition," declared one opposition pamphlet. But, "fellow-citizens," the pamphlet went on, there was still time to repair the damage this tyrant has imposed, still time to restore republican purity and simplicity to American institutions. It can be done if the electorate will throw the Democratic rascals out of office and replace them with National Republicans. "One more opportunity—*perhaps the last*—is yet afforded us," declared an Ohio newspaper, "of strangling the monster of despotism before it shall have attained its full growth, and checking the full tide of corruption before it shall have become too strong to be resisted. The power still remains in our hands. Let us so use it as men who are to render an account to our God, to our country, to the world—and all will be well."

Perhaps more effective in attracting voter support than political pamphlets were the cartoons published by the National Republican press. Indeed, political cartooning came of age in this election. Democrats also issued cartoons but those directed against Jackson tended to demonstrate greater skill and imagination than those directed against Clay because the President was a more colorful and exciting figure and made an easy and inviting target.

Many cartoons related to the Jackson-Van Buren relationship and either made dark references to Van Buren's "magical" hold over Jackson or condemned his dexterity in advancing his own presidential ambitions.

One showed Jackson being crowned by Van Buren and receiving a scepter from a devil. Another showed the President and his wrecking crew attired as burglars, aiming a large battering ram against the front doors of the national bank. A third showed a flying red devil with strings attached to his fingers, feet and tail and jiggling the strings to make spoils men tied at the other end of the strings jump and bounce like puppets. And one well known cartoon portrayed Jackson and Clay as jockeys in a horse race to the White House with Clay leading Jackson by a length or more. Perhaps one of the best cartoons related to the mass resignation of Jackson's first cabinet on account of the furor generated by the refusal of the wives of several officials to receive the "notorious" Peggy Eaton, wife of the secretary of war. The cartoon showed Jackson sprawled in a collapsing chair with four rats scurrying for cover. Each rat has the face of one of the members of Jackson's cabinet. Some two thousand copies of this

cartoon were sold in Philadelphia on a single day!

But the one cartoon to achieve historical distinction was entitled "King Andrew the First." It depicted Jackson as a monarch, dressed in full regal attire, complete with ermine robe and crown. In his one hand he holds a rolled document labeled "veto," in the other he holds his scepter. He stands on a torn copy of the Constitution. Along the four sides of the picture are written the words: "Born to Command" on top; "King Andrew the First" at the bottom; "of veto memory" to the left; and "had I been consulted" to the right.

Both the Democrats and National Republicans followed the practice of the 1828 campaign in organizing parades, barbecues, street rallies, and other forms of popular entertainment to generate enthusiasm for their respective candidates. Editorials and cartoons were grand in many ways, said one commentator, "but a hickory pole, a taking cry, a transparency, a burst of sky rockets and Roman candles (alas! that it should be so!) have a potency over a large third of our voters that printed eloquence can not exert."

One of the best parades in New York City was sponsored by the local Democratic organization. Michel Chevalier, a Frenchman who was touring the United States at this time and witnessed this parade, described it in detail. He could hardly believe that it stretched more than a mile:

> The Democrats marched in good order, to the glare of torches; the banners were more numerous than I had ever seen them in any religious festival; all were in transparency, on account of the

Miniature painting of Jackson in formal military dress by Ralph E. W. Earl.

1833 silk ribbon with a portrait of Andrew Jackson.

were mingled with emblems in all designs and colors. Among these figures an eagle, not a painting, but a real live eagle, tied by the legs, surrounded by a wreath of leaves, and hoisted upon a pole, after the manner of the Roman standards. The imperial bird was carried by a stout sailor, more pleased than was ever any city magistrate permitted to hold one of the strings of the canopy in a Catholic ceremony. From further than the eye could reach, came marching on the Democrats. I was struck with the resemblance of their air to the train that escorts the viaticum in Mexico or Puebla. The American standard-bearers were as grave as the Mexican Indians who bore the sacred candles. The Democratic procession, also like the Catholic procession, had its halting places; it stopped before the homes of the Jackson men to fill the air with cheers, and halted at the doors of the leaders of the Opposition, to give three, six or nine groans.

National Republicans also held parades and rallies some of which reportedly drew ten thousand participants. "We looked around," reported one newspaper editor, "and we saw the mariner and the merchants, the storekeeper and the mechanic, the manufacturer and the day laborer—all glowing and gratified at the eloquence of the orators." This particular rally proved to be a "glorious one for our cause," remarked one delighted National Republican. "It reanimated our friends, added warmth to their patriotism—and has given fresh ardour to their exertions."

darkness. On some were inscribed the names of the democratic societies or sections: *Democratic young men of the ninth or eleventh ward*; others bore imprecations against the Bank of the United States; *Nick Biddle* and *Old Nick* were figured largely. Then came portraits of General Jackson afoot and on horseback; there was one in the uniform of a general and another in the person of the Tennessee farmer, with the famous hickory cane in his hand. Those of Washington and Jefferson, surrounded with Democratic mottoes,

Barbecues, like parades, sky rockets and Roman candles, always captured the interest and fancy of the electorate. If we tell Democrats we have great strength in state legislatures, scolded a National Republican, *"they reply by swallowing a pig."* If we show them our gains in the Senate, *"they reply by devouring a turkey."* If we point to our two-thirds majority in the House of Representatives, *"they reply by pouring off a pint of whiskey or apple-toddy.* There is no withstanding such arguments. We give it up."

Indeed, political leaders seemed to sense most acutely that hickory poles, Roman candles and barbecued pork found greater favor with the electorate than serious talk about banks, tariffs, and internal improvements. Better to shout against aristocracy and privilege and in favor of democracy and equality of opportunity than worry voters about paper money or the national debt. Better to cheer Old Hickory or Harry of the West; better to denounce Masons or Czar Nick.

The Anti-Masons proved very adept at personalizing their attacks since both Jackson and Clay were Masons. Jackson was labeled "a grand king" of the order involved in an "aristocratic conspiracy" against the people, while Clay was accused of regularly attending the secret meetings of "Lodges, Chapters &c." Jackson admitted membership but claimed he had not attended "the great Lodge of Tennessee," where he once served as "Royal Arch Mason," in several years; and he had not attended the "Chapter" in nearly twenty-five years. Clay also admitted membership in the Masonic order and refused to repudiate his membership. "I am myself a Mason," he wrote to his New York manager, "and although not a bright one nor a regular attendant of the Lodge, I respect the craft, and its members generally."

Because, over the years, Clay had advanced the idea of an "American System" to speed the nation's economic growth, the National Republicans issued medals identifying their candidate as the advocate of internal improvements and the champion of a republicanism that encouraged the development of industry and agriculture. They also distributed flasks, Clay busts, and glass saucers on which to rest hot coffee or teacups. Clay's various nicknames, such as "Harry of the West," "Prince Hal," and "the Great Compromiser" were decorated on some of these materials.

Not wanting to be outdone, the Democrats produced flags, ribbons, and other trinkets depicting Jackson as the friend of democracy and the enemy of privilege and aristocracy. "Democracy and No Bank," ran one such banner, "Equal Rights to All Legal Voters."

The hoopla and ballyhoo ended at the polls and Jackson again won a thumping victory, taking 55 percent of the popular vote while Clay received 37 percent and Wirt 8 percent. In the electoral college Jackson won a majority of 219 votes, Clay 49, and Wirt 7. Quite obviously the electorate trusted and admired Andrew Jackson and if he directed the destruction of the national bank then so be it. They would go right along with him.

"Who but General Jackson would have the courage to veto . . . the Bank," asked one Democrat, ". . . and who but General Jackson could have withstood the overwhelming influence of that corrupt Aristocracy?" Said the defeated William Wirt: "My opinion is that he may be President for life if he chooses."

1836

26 STATES
IN THE UNION

DEMOCRAT

Martin Van Buren

ELECTORAL VOTE 170, POPULAR VOTE 50.9%

WHIG

William H. Harrison

ELECTORAL VOTE 73

Hugh L. White

ELECTORAL VOTE 26

Daniel Webster

ELECTORAL VOTE 14

W. P. Mangum

ELECTORAL VOTE 11

WHIG CUMULATIVE POPULAR VOTE 49.1%

Daniel Feller
is associate professor of history at the
University of New Mexico and the author of
The Public Lands in Jacksonian Politics (1984).

In 1836, the presidential campaign took shape as a kind of laboratory experiment of the effectiveness of the emerging political parties. For the reigning Democrats, it tested whether Andrew Jackson, the party's founding demigod, could bequeath his mandate to an unpopular successor. For the anti-Jacksonians, now beginning to be called Whigs, the question was whether their diverse elements could coalesce to wage a national campaign at all.

The Democrats held a commanding lead in organization. Throughout his two presidential terms Andrew Jackson worked to shape the diffuse coalition that had swept him into the presidency in 1828 into a disciplined, unified national party devoted (in a favorite phrase of the time) to "measures not men." His counselor and confidant in this enterprise was Martin Van Buren, whose New York state political machine, the "Albany Regency," furnished a working model for Jackson's national Democracy. Serving Jackson initially as secretary of state, Van Buren quickly gained the Hero's confidence; before his first year as president was out, Jackson already looked to Van Buren as his successor. Van Buren's elevation to vice president in 1832 made him the public heir-apparent.

Yet superior cohesiveness and an obvious candidate were mixed blessings. Jackson's own campaigns had established the democratic principle that presidential candidacies must come, or at least must appear to come, directly from the people. The old procedure of nomination by a congressional caucus had been thoroughly discredited. Its successor, the national convention, was a new device, first employed in 1832. To Jackson, the perfect instrument for ascertaining "the choice of the great body of republicans" was a national assemblage of "delegates fresh from the people." But the very concert necessary to stage a convention exposed it to charges of management and executive dictation. These suspicions would acquire special force if the outcome of the convention seemed to thwart the popular will.

Such was sure to be the case if the Democrats nominated Van Buren, the least-loved national politician of his day. Southerners thought him anti-Southern and westerners anti-Western; Pennsylvanians resented him for furthering the ascendancy of rival New York. Van Buren's Albany Regency exemplified a type of machine politics that most voters abhorred, and his own behind-the-scenes role in the Jackson administration made it easy for Jacksonians disgruntled over the Hero's policies to keep the faith by blaming Van Buren as the malign counselor, the evil influence behind the throne. In the public eye Van Buren was no chivalric Hero, no bold and clear-eyed statesman. He was not, as John C. Calhoun said in the Senate, "of the race of the lion or the tiger; he belonged to a lower order—the fox; and it would be in vain to expect that he could command the respect or acquire the confidence of those who had so little admiration for the qualities by which he was distinguished."

In 1832 only the Democrats' enthusiasm for Old Hickory and dislike of Henry Clay had forestalled a rebellion against Van Buren's nomination as vice president. His seemingly predetermined elevation to the presidency, precisely because it did seem predetermined, evoked widespread dissatisfaction. The question of the campaign, simply put, was what advantage the opposition could make of it.

The first revolt against the inevitability of Van Buren came from within Democratic ranks. Its figurehead was Richard Mentor Johnson, a Kentucky congressman of outspoken convictions and limited intellect whose chief claim to fame was his service on the Canadian front in the War of 1812, where, at the Battle of the Thames, he purportedly fired the shot that killed the Indian leader Tecumseh. Until recently no one would have considered this lucky hit a qualification for high office, but Jackson's 1824 and 1828 campaigns had validated battlefield exploits as a presidential selling point. Johnson's supporters, mainly westerners, suited him up in Old Hickory's ill-fitting garb and peddled him as another warrior hero. Already by 1833 Johnson handbills were circulating in the West. There soon followed the customary campaign biography, an engraving of the Thames battle, an unsingable anthem ("The Warrior Sage") and a five-act play *Tecumseh, or the Battle of the Thames*, in which Johnson muses that "ere yon glorious sun, which now on Alleghany's mist-encircled brow stands tiptoe, shall see itself reflected from the West-

ern lakes, the day is lost or won," then buckles on his armor and charges into battle crying "Mount, mount we now our snorting steeds!" Voters of less Shakespearean taste got the message through a pithy popular rhyme: "Rumpsey, Dumpsey, Colonel Johnson killed Tecumseh."

The Van Burenites deftly coopted the Johnson movement by taking him up for the vice presidency. But in moving to secure their western wing they further weakened their southern flank. Johnson had two daughters by a mulatto mistress, and his attempt to bring them into society made him "affirmatively odious" in southern eyes, as Tennessean John Catron, later a Supreme Court justice, told Jackson in March 1835. Besides, Catron went on, Johnson "wants capacity, a fact generally known, and universally admitted. . . . I pray you to assure our friends that the humblest of us do not believe that a lucky random shot, even if it did hit Tecumseh, qualifies a man for Vice President."

Revulsion against Van Buren ran deepest in Jackson's own lair, Tennessee. There rebellion was sparked by quondam Jackson men led by John Bell, who had opened a party breach by defeating the administration candidate, fellow Tennessean James K. Polk, for Speaker of the U.S. House of Representatives in June of 1834. Six months later eleven Tennessee congressmen, including Bell and David Crockett, caucused and announced their choice for President: Hugh Lawson White, senator from Tennessee and another former Jackson intimate now distancing himself from the President.

The White men claimed the status of original Jacksonians and spurned the Whig label. But the backing they received from antiadministration men, and their refusal to pledge support for the nominee of the upcoming national convention (which they believed rigged for Van Buren) tagged them as oppositionists in Jackson's eyes. Jackson saw it all as a plot to divide the party and smuggle in Henry Clay. But despite Jacksonian wrath, White's candidacy caught on quickly in Tennessee and in surrounding plantation states.

On May 20, 1835, the Democrats convened at Baltimore. Though more than six hundred men attended, the convention was hardly representative. Maryland, Virginia, and New Jersey contributed over half the delegates. Three states were unrepresented and four others nearly so; a Tennessean who happened to be in town was drafted to cast his state's fifteen votes for Van Buren. To no one's surprise the convention nominated Van Buren unanimously and Johnson over southern protests.

Led by Andrew Jackson, regular Democrats applauded the selection of Van Buren by "an assembly fresh from the people, the true representation of their unbiased wishes, the faithful echo of their opinions." Others saw it differently—as a charade of democracy, an orchestrated conclave of officeholders and office-seekers, tools of the executive, slavishly ratifying the royal succession. "What a humbug!" sneered Duff Green's *United States Telegraph.* "Management, management, management!" cried the *Baltimore Patriot.*

The convention's address to the people reflected the party's unease with its nominees. Filling ten columns of tiny print in the Washington *Globe*, it mentioned Van Buren and Johnson once near the end,

Pewter medallions for Van Buren and Harrison. Four campaign medalets were issued for Van Buren, and but one for Harrison.

Pewter medal with slogan "EQUAL & FULL PROTECTION TO AMERICAN INDUSTRY." The protective tariff was favored by emerging northern industrialists and the Whig candidates.

while naming Jackson eighteen times, Jefferson eleven, Madison nine, Monroe six, and Washington four. The address defended the convention as the only mode of guaranteeing party unity and victory, begged Democrats to put aside "personal animosities or personal preferences" and accept Van Buren as "a lesser evil," and practically apologized for nominating him.

The Baltimore proceedings drove the White men into open opposition. Still disclaiming Whiggery, White in October accepted a formal nomination from the Tennessee legislature. The legislators went on to denounce the Baltimore convention for showing "the same violation of the spirit of the constitution, the same tendency to a usurpation of the rights and powers of the people in the election of president, the

same spirit of intrigue, the same liability in the members to be corrupted and influenced in their course by the promise and expectation of office" as the old congressional caucus.

Meanwhile an avowed Whig had entered the lists: Daniel Webster, the unanimous choice of a convention of Massachusetts Whig legislators held in January 1835. This nomination, intended like all the others to look spontaneous, was actually the product of furious behind-the-scenes lobbying by Webster and his coadjutors. By coming out first, Webster hoped to head off possible Whig contenders John McLean and Henry Clay. But Webster's candidacy attracted few converts outside of New England.

Farther west, some anti-Jacksonians looked first to McLean, an Ohioan with a carefully cultivated reputation for nonpartisan public service. He had served Monroe and Quincy Adams as postmaster general before Jackson elevated him to the Supreme Court. Under a reserved exterior, McLean nursed acute presidential ambitions. But he was as colorless as he was competent; his perennially whispered candidacy inspired little objection and even less enthusiasm. While sitting on the Court, McLean dared not openly promote his own cause; he could only wait for public acclamation. When his candidacy failed even to sweep Ohio, McLean withdrew.

Clay too chose to sit out the campaign, though he believed he could come closer than any other Whig to beating Van Buren. Unlike his Senate collaborators Webster and Calhoun, Clay had feet firmly planted in both northern and southern anti-Jackson camps. While northern "National Republicans" who had run him in 1832 still looked to him as their champion, Clay had recently mended fences with fellow southerners by placating South Carolina in the Compromise of 1833. On the other side, the independent Anti-Masonic party, whose votes were crucial to hopes of Whig success in the Northeast, would have none of Clay, and he still bore the taint of defeat from the pasting Jackson gave him in the last campaign. After two failed tries at the presidency Clay was overexposed. The one man who might have forged a national candidacy out of the abundant but discordant elements of anti-Van Burenism was dismissed as a loser, even by himself.

The eclipse of McLean and Clay was sealed by the sudden emergence of a new western contender, yet another claimant to Old Hickory's martial legacy. As late as mid-1834 William Henry Harrison, former territorial governor, general, and Ohio congressman and senator, had no idea of being a candidate for anything. His only ambition, as he explained to a friend in December 1833, was to go hunting and trapping with his old Indian companions, it being too late in life to repair his finances by taking up the law, medicine, or hotel-keeping.

Harrison's candidacy erupted unexpectedly out of Richard M. Johnson's. Borrowing the old Jackson technique of appropriating patriotic exultation over military success to campaign purposes, Johnson partisans in 1834 staged commemorations of the Battle of the Thames, in which they subtly elevated Johnson from slayer of Tecumseh to mastermind of victory and, by implication, commander of the army. An

invitation to one of these celebrations brought a public rebuke from Harrison, the real commander, putting Johnson politely but firmly in his place. The proud old soldier's defense of his laurels triggered an idea that apparently struck everyone at once: Why not run Harrison himself? An editor in Chillicothe, Ohio, caught the allure of it: "Hurrah for Harrison! There's euphony in that; and you must have euphony in any popular cry. The very fact that the name ends in *on*, is of great importance. The popular men have had such names. There was Washington, Jefferson, Madison and Jackson. Why not Harrison? It is just the right name." The next issue of the *Scioto Gazette* carried "For President, in 1836, General William Henry Harrison" emblazoned on its masthead.

Medal inscribed "VAN BUREN & DEMOCRACY."

Van Buren brass token.

Alone of the men contending for the presidency, Harrison inspired real popular enthusiasm. The surprised general reported in January 1835, that "in relation to the *candidacy* (a newly coined word, I believe), it progresses here & else where astonishingly." Soon engravings of Harrison's victory over the Indians at Tippecanoe in 1811 were rolling off the presses, and in November a big commemorative celebration was held on the battlefield. In the Northwest, where local feeling still outweighed partisanship, Jackson men came over to Harrison in droves. Webster's operatives tried to shunt Harrison off to the vice presidency, but he spurned their overtures and with good reason: he was the stronger man. Late in 1835, Whig and Anti-Masonic conventions in Pennsylvania and Maryland endorsed his candidacy, followed soon by New York, Delaware, New Jersey, and even Vermont. Webster was left stranded in Massachusetts.

By the opening of the election year, then, three opposition candidates were in the field. Each secure in his own base, none would withdraw (Webster offered, but was deterred by Massachusetts Whigs), and it was obviously pointless to divide the anti-Van Buren vote by invading each other's territory. A combined ticket was out of the question. No candidate's following was clearly deliverable to any other, and alliance would invite the same charge of manipulation that all three were now mouthing against the Van Burenites. White would not even admit to being a Whig, and Harrison's candidacy, though embraced by Whigs, was initially a nonpartisan one having, in his own words, "nothing to do with the parties as heretofore existing." With full concert impossible, the opposition fell back upon trying to defeat Van Buren by carrying enough states to throw the election into the House of Representatives—not as preferred strategy, but as the only hope left.

This was too much for former President John Quincy Adams, who thought it better to lose with convictions than win without them. "The remarkable character of this election is, that all the candidates are at most third-rate men. . . . The opposition . . . have been driven in mere desperation to set up men of straw . . . and they have taken up Hugh Lawson White and William Henry Harrison, as the Israelites set up a calf, and as the Egyptians worshipped oxen and monkeys." Adams saw the presidency becoming the plaything of corrupt and raucous electioneering factions "without one ounce of honest principle to choose between them."

The reproach of debasing the presidency by taking up Harrison has stuck to the Whigs ever since, though Democrats with Richard M. Johnson on their ticket were in no position to point fingers. To be fair, on his record William Henry Harrison in 1836 held a better claim to the mantle of a statesman, if not of a Hero, than Andrew Jackson in 1828. That he was a true man of the people, the people themselves were now showing. Whigs sensitive to the charge of cynicism defended themselves by pointing to the original cynicism of the Democrats, who had ballyhooed Jackson into the White House while burying substantive political debate under an onslaught of demagoguery. Democrats habitually branded every foe of their party as an enemy of the people, an agent of sinister anti-republican forces. Many who voiced these accusations, including Andrew Jackson, believed exactly what they said, but to Whigs the perennial Democratic war-cry of "the people" against "the aristocracy" was noxious, hypocritical cant. Skewering Van Buren with his own party's rhetoric was a prospect Whigs relished.

So the first objective in each camp was to seize the high ground for its candidate as the man of the people against the politicians. The entire campaign was thus framed within a paradox. Candidacies had to appear spontaneous, unorganized, and effortless, yet only careful planning could produce the desired effects. A circular strategy ensued: the best way to make a candidate popular was to show that he already was. To send this message, partisans staged open public meetings, at which the crowds, always described as "numerous and respectable," adopted resolutions commending the candidate to their fellow citizens. Published in friendly newspapers, the proceedings of dozens of such meetings around the country could create an impression of massive popular support.

Behind these ostensibly spontaneous expressions of public opinion lay a great deal of surreptitious organizing. Partisan enthusiasts formed corresponding committees, drew up resolutions for approval, raised money for publicity, and disseminated pamphlets and pictures and broadsides. Campaign newspapers sprang up, subsidized and distributed by the party faithful. All of this activity, if not exactly secret, was made to appear locally initiated. Direction by state central committees and personal agents of the candidates was both effective and carefully concealed.

The candidates avoided campaigning too openly. A tradition stretching back to George Washington said that the office must seek the man. Popular resentment of grasping politicians imposed a reticent, even furtive posture upon men who feared revealing their unfitness for the presidency by daring to show an interest in it. All carefully disclaimed any personal initiative in their candidacies. Van Buren accepted the Baltimore nomination asserting that "I have neither solicited the aid nor sought the support of any man in reference to the high office for which I have been nominated." White, accepting nomination by the Tennessee legislature, denied that "at any moment of my life I have ever wished to be president of the United States." Harrison remarked: "I did not bring myself forward; my friends did not bring me forward—I was brought out by the Spontaneous Will of the People."

Friends of the candidates employed two devices to keep them before the public while avoiding any appearance of volition on their part. The first was the public letter. In April 1836 a Kentucky congressman, Sherrod Williams, asked Harrison, White, and Van

Buren for their policy views on transportation, land, banking, and finance. The replies, published in the press and widely circulated in pamphlet form, served in lieu of the latter-day campaign platform or position paper. Queries from sympathizers also gave candidates an opening to clarify their opinions and repel misrepresentations. Van Buren used public letters to denounce abolitionism, Harrison to defend his military and congressional record, and White to answer Jacksonian accusations of betrayal.

The second way to present a candidate was to invite him to a political dinner where, as guest of honor, he was toasted and called on to speak. Proceedings of the dinner were then published in friendly newspapers. Going from dinner to dinner, a candidate could travel the campaign trail and expound his views without appearing to obtrude himself upon the public, since his attendance was always by request. White hit the dinner circuit in Tennessee, and Harrison in Ohio and Indiana. An eastern trip, ostensibly on business, also gave Harrison a pretext to meet crowds in Baltimore, Philadelphia, and New York. Van Buren, whose reputation for unseemly ambition required him to tread most cautiously, stayed close to home and declined public appearances, while Jackson campaigned for him on a summertime swing down to Tennessee.

In many states campaign enthusiasm slackened once the failure to combine nationally against Van Buren became apparent. Van Buren himself was too circumspect, and the opposition too fragmented, to sustain much excitement. The multiplicity of candidates strengthened the Democrats by fortifying their warnings that Van Buren's defeat would throw the decision into the House of Representatives, where intrigue and management would prevail as they had in 1824. Since no one else could win a majority of electoral votes, the alternatives were Van Buren by popular choice or no popular choice at all. Fear of subserving a Harrison victory in the House especially undercut support for White among uncertain southern Jacksonians.

Voting began in Ohio and Pennsylvania on November 4, and concluded in Rhode Island three weeks later. Van Buren won a surprisingly narrow victory, with a bare majority of the popular vote and 170 electoral votes to the opposition's 124. White took Tennessee and Georgia, Webster held Massachusetts, and South Carolina (where the legislature still chose presidential electors) voted for Senator Willie P. Mangum of North Carolina. Harrison carried seven states from Vermont to Kentucky; a shift of 2,200 votes would have given him Pennsylvania and thrown the election into the House.

Despite defeat, Whigs were encouraged. Harrison, gratified at his showing and eager to try again, believed that "our friends had the Victory in their power but believing that the influence of Genl. Jackson & the application of the spoils could not be resisted they would not make the effort." The lesson Whigs learned from 1836 was that with Jackson gone the Democrats could be beat, but that it would take a national campaign to win a national election. For Democrats, the message was that against a strong opponent, even superior organization could not guarantee victory with an unpopular man at the head of the ticket. Party and personality—in the future, winning the presidency would require both.

Text of Martin Van Buren's 1837 inaugural address printed on silk.

26 STATES
IN THE UNION

WHIG

William H. Harrison

ELECTORAL VOTE 234, POPULAR VOTE 52.8%

DEMOCRAT

Martin Van Buren

ELECTORAL VOTE 60, POPULAR VOTE 46.8%

LIBERTY

James G. Birney

ELECTORAL VOTE 0, POPULAR VOTE 0.3%

SEAN WILENTZ
is a professor of history at Princeton University.
His books include *Chants Democratic:
New York City & the Rise of the American
Working Class, 1788–1850* (1984).

The 1840 election brought the Whig party's famous Log Cabin campaign—and the start of a new era in presidential politics. Reversing their conservative prejudices against democratic electioneering, the Whigs greeted the voters with unabashed hoopla, empty emotionalism, and liberal draughts of alcohol—and elevated their nondescript candidate, General William Henry Harrison, to the White House. The result shook Americans all along the political spectrum. To the mainstream Whig press, suddenly, it was morning again in America. ("After a long and dreary night of misrule," one Memphis editor rejoiced, Whigs could finally see "the streaks of returning day.") The Jacksonian Democrats, nonplussed, judged the contest a tragedy. ("We have taught them how to conquer us," moaned the *Democratic Review.*) In Charleston, the slaveholders of the South Carolina legislature formally voted to condemn the election as "corrupt and indecent . . . an insult upon the dignity of free men." A political world away, the antislavery ex-President, John Quincy Adams, feared he was witnessing "a revolution in the habits and manners of the people." Even Henry Clay, the Whig stalwart, privately regretted that his party had seen fit to appeal to "the feelings and passions of our Country men, rather than to their reason."

Historians, more amused than shocked by the Whigs' tactics, agree on the importance of the Log Cabin campaign—"a landmark," one scholar writes, "in the carnival-ization of American elective politics." Yet beneath the razzle-dazzle, the proceedings held substantive implications about democracy, ideology, and the nation's future.

From the start, the election posed difficulties for both major parties. The Democratic incumbent, Martin Van Buren, had never commanded the personal following of his predecessor and patron, Andrew Jackson. Saddled, weeks after his inauguration, with deep economic depression, he entered the 1840 contest stigmatized as President Van Ruin, unsure of the loyalty of major forces within his own party. Yet the Whigs also suffered from their own bitter divisions: Henry Clay fully expected to win the nomination, but he was under challenge by Harrison and by another general, Winfield Scott; in the Northeast, a potentially vital sliver of the antislavery Whig vote was increasingly alienated from the party. Above all, no matter who they ran, the Whigs had yet to prove that they could mount an effective, unified presidential campaign.

Enter a new sort of Whig political genius, best exemplified by Thurlow Weed of New York. Cigar-smoking, warmhearted, and supremely cynical, Weed held deeply conservative views, but he was the farthest thing from a punctilious Whig patrician. Having risen from a career as a tramp journeyman printer through the Anti-Masonic party to head the most powerful Whig state organization in the country, Weed had learn-

Miniature hand-colored engraving under glass in a brass brooch showing Harrison's alleged humble birthplace. For the 1840 campaign, the Whigs adopted the log cabin as one of their symbols.

ed the futility of addressing the expansive new electorate as conservatives normally had done, with a lofty rhetoric of classical virtue. Whiggery would triumph, he realized, only if Whigs presented themselves as plain-spoken champions of the people—and cast the *Democrats* as the aristocratic party. At the same time, he knew, Whigs would have to bury their differences, abandon squeamishness about party competition, and build the kind of disciplined national apparatus that had served Jackson and Van Buren so brilliantly. As a sign that the party meant business, Weed and others arranged for a national Whig convention to meet in Harrisburg, Pennsylvania, late in 1839 to sort out the nominations. Thereafter, along with other state leaders of roughly similar backgrounds—Thaddeus Stevens of Pennsylvania, Thomas Corwin of Ohio—Weed democratized both the imagery and the machinery of American conservative politics as never before.

The instrument for this little revolution would be the ambitious old soldier, Harrison—a man ideally suited to such purposes. Harrison had won enduring national fame nearly thirty years earlier in his victory over Chief Tecumseh and the Shawnees at the Battle of Tippecanoe. He had proved an able vote-getter as one of three opposition candidates in the 1836 presidential election. Most important, although he was generally supportive of Clay's nationalist programs, he had served without distinction in the House and Senate (and with ineptitude as Jackson's minister to Colombia), and thus lacked the kind of well-established record or strong views that might have upset party unity. Above all, Harrison was "available" (that is, electable)—far more so, as the unsentimental Weed and others saw things, than the slaveholder and outspoken opponent of Jackson's "Bank War," Henry Clay.

With consummate skill—and a few dirty tricks—Weed and Stevens engineered Clay's defeat at the Harrisburg convention, and joined forces behind Harrison (Stevens's original choice). Eager to appease Clay's outraged supporters, they settled on John Tyler of Virginia as the vice presidential candidate. And once Clay had swallowed his pride and announced his support, the unified campaign ensconced an Executive Whig Committee in two rooms at the Washington city hall—which quickly became the national party's nerve center. Whig congressmen, making generous use of franking privileges and loyal government workers, turned the impromptu headquarters into a fountain of propaganda. By pooling their mailing lists, the congressmen were then able to send reams of Whig material directly to where it would do the most good. Down the chain of command, the Whig state committees, county committees, town committees, and the all-important local Tippecanoe clubs geared up to oversee stump speaking, campaign festivities, patronage matters, and the crucial details about getting Whig voters to the polls. Out at Harrison's home in North Bend, Ohio, the national campaign supplied the general with his own personal committee—to shield him from troublesome correspondence, prepare whatever public remarks he might have to make, and otherwise ensure that he said or did nothing that might offend anybody.

The campaign theme necessary to drive this new machine came as a gift from the Democrats. In the aftermath of the decisive Harrisburg Whig convention, a Baltimore Van Burenite paper wisecracked that Harrison would happily retire from the contest so long as he was granted a barrel of hard cider and a pension—enough to allow him to "sit the remainder of his days in his log cabin." Democratic editors reprinted the joke, an opening shot in the year's campaign against "Old Granny," the worn-out hack. Several days later, in a mansion on the banks of the Susquehanna River, the banker Thomas Elder sipped some rare wine with his guest, the Whig editor Richard Elliott. The two men discussed what to make of the Democratic attacks and they came to an inspired conclusion. Before long, the entire campaign had picked up the refrain that the Whigs were, as charged, the party of hard cider and log cabins (not of Madeira and mansions)—the party that would vindicate homely, manly American virtues against the slurs of effete, out-of-touch, self-professed democrats like Martin Van Ruin.

Turning William Henry Harrison into a plebeian folk hero was a feat in itself. The

Enameled glass brooch with an intaglio portrait of Van Buren.

college-educated scion of an old and important Virginia family, Harrison could not claim the authentic populist origins of his opponent (the son of a plain country tavernkeeper from Kinderhook, New York). After settling in Ohio, Harrison had indeed lived briefly in a log cabin, but he had quickly remodeled the place into a stately residence. (Campaign workers hastily made a temporary restoration for public viewing.) Still, the log cabin image nicely symbolized Harrison's reputation as an Indian fighter and war hero, with a western base—which in turn evoked associations with the popular champion, Jackson. It also drew attention to Van Buren's perfumed, polished, impeccably-tailored style, which the President had mastered the hard way as he climbed the social and political ladder. By hammering home the log cabin and hard cider theme, Thurlow Weed and the new-style Whigs would ridicule a genuinely self-made Democrat as a class traitor, while puffing the down-home virtues of a born aristocrat all dressed up in homespun. (It took a century and a half before Americans would again see this trick performed on quite this scale, in the country-and-western metamorphosis of George Herbert Walker Bush.)

Handed their message, the Whigs and their supporters pitched it into every cranny of American life. Whig campaigners never entirely abandoned their traditional policy emphases on banks and tariffs, and on how increased wealth for the fortunate few would eventually trickle down to the hard-working many. But in giving such arguments a populist spin, they relied more on symbolism than on high-minded persuasion. Log cabins sprouted up all over, in every imaginable form, as cheap trinkets, parade floats—and, in hundreds of towns and cities, as actual edifices, surrounded by barrels of hard cider to treat all who cared to enter. Engravers and lithographers churned

A Harrison pewter medallion.

out endless streams of decorative vignettes and cartoons featuring Harrison as patriot-general, as farmer-citizen, as champion boxer. Medallions of bronze and copper turned up like newly-minted pennies, with the log cabin on one side, Harrison on the other, and the motto, "He leaves the plough to save the country." Porcelain makers supplied campaign mugs and pitchers and platters of every grade to help voters eat, drink, and be merry in the unending presence of the Log Cabin campaign.

No item was too small or too ordinary to avoid the Whigs' imprint. At the height of the campaign, the historian Robert Gray Gunderson recounts, a man might spend his entire day immersed in Harrison paraphernalia:

> Upon rising in the morning, a loyal Whig could shave with "Tippecanoe Shaving Soap" or "Log-Cabin Emollient," don a "Harrison and Tyler necktie," stuff a "beautiful pongee handkerchief with the American flag and a likeness of Gen. Harrison" into his pocket, and pin a huge Harrison badge on a suit with "handsome log-cabin buttons." Thus attired . . . [he] might plant his garden on the advice of the *Harrison Almanac*, regale his friends with stories from the book of *Log-Cabin Anecdotes*, write his Loco-Foco Congressman an indignant letter on "beautiful Harrison letter paper" with facts from the *Tippecanoe Text-Book*. . . . That evening, [he] had the choice of attending a Harrison song rally at the local log cabin, or of pocketing his miniature log-cabin flask of "Old Cabin Whiskey" and attending a Harrison Hoe-Down to dance the "Tippecanoe Quick Step."

One of these souvenir items actually wound up permanently enriching the American vocabulary—for the popularity of the

"Old Cabin Whiskey" (distributed freely along the Erie Canal) brought fame to its makers, the E.C. Booz Distillery of Philadelphia. Thus the birth of "booze."

This cavalcade of Whig gewgaws and bric-a-brac—a latter-day antiquarian's delight—bespoke a new departure in electioneering, beyond anything imagined by earlier purveyors of political mementos and insignias. The Whigs and their enterprising supporters tapped into what was, in 1840, a new and burgeoning American commercial culture, then infused it with politics—and as far as possible blurred the differences between the two. At the very moment that mass-produced pianos and sheet music were entering American parlors as markers of middle-class respectability, the Whigs came rushing after with their "Tippecanoe Song Sheets" and "Log Cabin Cotillions." Minstrel shows—a city-born entertainment that had swept the country in the 1830s—now featured players decked out in coonskin, performing pro-Whig skits. Glee clubs, urban and rural, sang the Whigs' praises, as did popular itinerant singers, among them the great Titus of Toledo. Most important, the Whigs established a string of partisan penny newspapers to amuse, instruct, and flatter the voters. (The most successful of these sheets, *The Log Cabin* of New York City, proved a career-making coup for its editor, Thurlow Weed's protégé Horace Greeley.)

The Whigs also took to the political stump as never before. The younger Whig pols included ex-farmers and mechanics, whose abilities at turning folksy quips mightily reinforced the Whigs' populist appeal. They all seemed to have nicknames;

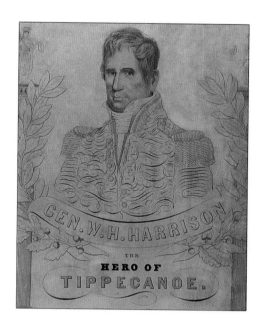

Harrison campaign print of a pen and ink drawing.

among the more talented were John W. Bear ("the Buckeye Blacksmith"), Tom Corwin ("the Wagon Boy"), F. W. Kellogg ("the whole-souled Tippecanoe mechanic"), Henry Wilson ("the Natick Cobbler"), Elihu Burritt ("the Learned Blacksmith")—and, in Illinois, "Honest" Abe Lincoln ("the Rail-splitter"). More refined national figures, with little affinity for this kind of campaigning, also did their part. Henry Clay, who knew his limits, retained his public dignity but managed to tell the voters with a straight face that they had to choose "between the log cabin and the palace, between hard cider and champagne." The austere, godlike Daniel Webster got more into the swing of things, dropping his renowned classical cadences in favor of a more conversational, down-home delivery. (Although he carefully tailored his speeches to match his audiences' prejudices, Webster generally proclaimed himself a fearless democrat—indeed, a Jeffersonian Democrat—and threatened to clobber any man

Enameled glass brooch with the log cabin and cider barrel motif.

ably the first campaign speech ever delivered by an American presidential candidate.

Harrison proved a capable canvasser, delivering some twenty-three speeches, each one more theatrical and equivocal than the last. He shamelessly milked his martial glory, timing his speeches to coincide with anniversaries of his military victories, and always making sure to have some local old vet from the War of 1812 totter up on the stage beside him. In mid-speech, he would suddenly stop and ostentatiously take several swigs from a barrel plainly marked "Hard Cider," throwing the audience into an uproar. As to substance, his speeches took unterrified stances against monarchy in government and all unnecessary uses of the executive veto, and pledged he would serve for only one term. Occasionally, a few lines about actual issues slipped in, almost all of them contradictory. ("I am in favor of paper money," the general proclaimed in one speech, adding straightaway, "I am not a Bank man.") His speaking style was bland, at times stumbling, but none of that really mattered: Harrison showed his gray head to the people, said nothing dangerous, and played wonderfully to the crowd.

Above all, Harrison helped to pull those crowds—the stamping masses of voters who, as much as anything, became the mainstay of the Log Cabin campaign. Since the birth of the republic, political groups had experimented in the use of public parades and festivities, both on nonpartisan civic occasions and in elections—transforming what, before the Revolution, had been ordinary people's traditional role as

who dared deny it.) Not to be outdone, the erudite South Carolina editor and ex-congressman Hugh Swinton Legaré—as close to a principled aristocrat as could be found in American politics—dressed up in rough clothes and a coonskin cap and conducted a "slangwhanging expedition" through five states. ("Instead of expatiating upon Sparta and Lycurgus," the chief Democratic paper reported, "the eloquent H.S. Legaré discourses right sturdily about 'gammon,' and 'scare crow,' and 'scape goat'.")

Even the candidate made a historic breakthrough on the hustings. The original Whig strategy was to deny Harrison the use of pen and paper; Weed and company gave no thought to directing his public appearances, since it was still thought vulgar for a presidential nominee actually to campaign on his own behalf. Yet once the Democratic press began attacking Harrison as "General Mum," a senile codger encaged by his handlers, Harrison was willing to break with tradition. He began on June 6, with an unscheduled speech on the steps of the National Hotel in Perrysburg, Ohio—prob-

"the mob" or "the people out-of-doors" into an authentic democratic display. It took the Whigs in 1840 finally to perfect the craft. Enormous contingents of pro-Harrison marchers rallied with torchlights behind their designated banners—"The Eleventh Ward Young Man's Whig Club," "Boot and Shoemakers for Old Tip," and so on—and then set off, one after the other, along the designated route. (Labor insignias and names were a special favorite of Whig organizers, ever eager to link their cause to the workingman's.) In Cleveland, an industrious band of Whigs banged together an immense tin ball, which they then pushed through towns and hamlets to a Whig convention at the state capital, Columbus, well over a hundred miles away, cheered and sung to by the faithful:

> As rolls the ball,
> Van's reign does fall,
> And he may look
> To Kinderhook.

After arriving in Columbus, the Clevelanders met up with another, even larger ball, covered in cowhide, which had been sent on a wagon by the Whigs of Muskingum County. Similar rollings occurred around the country.*

The reported turnouts for these events were enormous, even by the Democrats' undercounts. In a major campaign innovation, the Whig planners made sure participation was not restricted to men. Women had made only infrequent political appearances prior to 1840, usually on behalf of radical, egalitarian causes—from free love to abolitionism. But the Log Cabin Whigs mobilized women supporters by the tens of thousands—parading not as feminists but exemplars of the blossoming, sentimental cult of domesticity, who looked to General Harrison as their worthy protector. Here and there, women actually gave speeches; more typically, Whig advance men gathered the ladies together, supplied them with Harrison handkerchiefs for waving at appropriate moments, and included them conspicuously in the ceremonies. Obviously, there was no women's vote to be won— but wives and daughters could certainly exercise domestic moral suasion. (The advent of Whig womanhood did verge at times on illogic, especially when the decorous ladies praised "Hard Cider" Harrison as a temperance man. But even here, Whig strategists handled the apparent contradictions, releasing testimonials to the effect that the party's log cabins coaxed men away from taverns and hard liquor, toward more temperate pursuits.)

The Democrats, slow to awaken to this political earthquake, never mounted an effective counterattack. At first, they discounted the Log Cabin mania as a bit of condescending mummery, which the people, in their infinite wisdom, would resent and reject. "The Log Cabin hard cider and coon humbuggery is doing us a great ser-

---

*The ball was mocking reference to the boastful remarks of Senator Thomas Hart Benton, made in 1837, when the Senate officially expunged its censure of President Jackson passed three years earlier: "Solitary and alone, I set this ball in motion." As one Whig chorus ran:

> This Democratic ball
> Set rolling first by Benton
> Is on another track
> From that it first was sent on.

The first sizable ball rollings kicked off state Whig meetings which convened on Washington's birthday.

Gilt brass clothing button with Martin Van Buren's name around the shank on the reverse side.

vice," Andrew Jackson wrote early on in the campaign from retirement at the Hermitage, "and none more so than in Tennessee." (In the end, Jackson's own district would break five to one for Harrison.) Only well into the game did the Democrats realize the Whigs were galvanizing a wholly new set of voters—men who had not bothered to vote in the past, either out of inexperience or indifference, but who now felt for some reason that they had a cause. Untested at this sort of mammoth political spectacle—in the past, they had relied more on printed appeals and party discipline to get out the vote—the Democrats were slow to respond in kind. Instead, following plans laid down by Van Buren's campaign chief, Amos Kendall, they issued familiar declarations about hard money, monster banks, and the rights of labor mingled with personal attacks on Harrison—which only worsened their situation as Harrison grew into an overnight sensation.

The Democratic vice presidential nominee, Harrison's former army subordinate, Colonel Richard Mentor Johnson, did manage a vigorous stump campaign, similar in tone to the Whigs'. "Rumpsey Dumpsey/ Colonel Johnson Killed Tecumseh" went his backers' chant, a reminder that it was Johnson, and not Harrison, who claimed credit for actually butchering the Shawnee

chief at the battle of the Thames. But Johnson's performances cut against his party's grain—and Johnson himself was open to scurrilous ridicule in large parts of the country, as a man who lived openly with a mistress of partial African descent. The only truly inspired bit of Democratic campaigning came when a New York newspaper started referring to Van Buren as O.K. (for "Old Kinderhook"), adding yet another indispensable term to the American lexicon. But while the Democratic faithful scrawled O.K. on meeting halls and taverns, around the corner marched the Log Cabin multitudes, gathering strength as the campaign wore on and the state-by-state voting commenced. The Maine elections, held in September, brought a narrow Whig victory— and with it the most famous chorus of the campaign:

> And have you heard the news from Maine
> And what old Maine can do
> She went hell-bent for Governor Kent,
> And Tippecanoe and Tyler too,
> And Tippecanoe and Tyler too.

So went the nation. When the final results were in, Harrison had gained 234 electoral votes to Van Buren's 60.

The election was Thurlow Weed and company's masterpiece. With energy, imagination, and all the luck they could ask for, Weed and his new-style Whig friends had turned the Whig party into an effective national vote gathering organization—that is, into a true *party* in the modern sense. The Whigs, as the editor Elliott observed, had "gone down to the people"—and won. In doing so they helped increase the popular turnout by more than 54 percent over that in 1836, reaching one of the highest levels of participation by the eligible presidential electorate in all of American history. But at what cost? As Elliott himself freely admitted years later, "principle and reason" flew out the window of the Log Cabin campaign, replaced by appeals to "passion and prejudice"—for "all we wanted was to carry the election." Ever since, the campaign has stood as a textbook case in demagoguery and manipulation, with ample lessons for later unscrupulous candidates and campaign managers. To some historians, it is one of the finest examples of the basic hollowness of our electoral political culture.

But the 1840 election suggested other things as well. First, it firmly committed American conservatism to pursuing office as a popular party—placing American politics on populist-democratic grounds that still made many conservatives extremely nervous in 1840, as both a denial of conviction and an ultimately self-defeating strategy. Second, despite the Whigs' extraordinary efforts, the returns were not nearly as lopsided as the electoral count implied. The popular vote was far closer, with 52.8 percent going to Harrison and 46.8 percent to Van Buren—a decisive victory, but no landslide. (Van Buren actually *increased* his vote total by nearly 50 percent over what he had received in 1836; a shift of about 8,000 votes in the right states would have made him the winner.) Considering that he was linked directly to the worst economic depression in the nation's history to that time (and considering what has happened to later incumbent candidates and parties under similar circumstances), Van Buren ran better than might have been expected—which may say some-

thing about the limits of hard cider politics, even in hard times.

Finally, another, much smaller, often unnoticed feature of the 1840 election indicated that the Log Cabin campaign had hardly drained American politics of all principle and reason. In April, the antislavery splinter party that some Whigs had feared came to life as the Liberty party with the Kentucky ex-slaveholder James G. Birney as its presidential nominee. The party fared dismally in the conventional sense, winning only seven thousand votes (0.3 percent of the total), with the bulk in just two states, New York and Massachusetts. Still, the election established an important toehold for the antislavery forces. Four years later, the Liberty party again polled a tiny percentage—but drew enough votes away from Henry Clay in New York to help throw the election to James K. Polk. Four years after that, the more broadly-based Free Soil party, using some of the same campaign methods pioneered in 1840, would make a far more impressive sectional showing—with none other than Martin Van Buren as its presidential nominee. All along, antislavery politicians, increasingly well versed in the latest techniques of stump speaking and getting out the vote, were winning key congressional seats, fixing the slavery issue squarely at the center of national political debates despite the best efforts of Whig and Democratic leaders to keep it out. This, too, was part of the political legacy of 1840. It would eventually contribute to the coming of the Civil War—and with that to a democratic revolution far more profound than anything anybody could have possibly imagined amid the torchlit furies of the Log Cabin campaign.

Cotton bandanna with the log cabin, plow, and cider barrel. Harrison, the Ohio farmer, welcoming a disabled veteran while another person draws hard cider.

1840 flag banner. This is the earliest use of a candidate's portrait using the flag design.

An equestrian portrait of William Henry Harrison surrounded by scenes depicting his earlier life.

Campaign print for Martin Van Buren and Richard Johnson.

"Columbian Star" Staffordshire china with the log cabin motif designed by John Ridgeway. The pattern was so popular, it remained in production a generation after the 1840 election.

Harrison copper lustre pitcher.

Teapot with log cabin motif designed by British potter, William Adams.

Harrison cup and saucer designed by William Adams.

Pewter coffee pot with log cabin motif.

Rare Harrison water pitcher produced by a New Jersey potter.

Glass cup plates manufactured by the
Sandwich Glass Company.

Right: Harrison cup and saucer.
Below: Glass doorknob with an
encased cameo bust of Harrison.

A variety of Harrison log cabin motif brooches. Exquisitely fashioned, these items were usually imported from France.

Pewter mug with medalic portrait of Harrison.

A BEAUTIFUL GOBLET OF
WHITE-HOUSE CHAMPAGNE.

AN UGLY MUG OF
LOG CABIN HARD CIDER.

FIRST WARD
SPRING-GARDEN.

THOUGHT OF THE PEOPLE

THE SECOND SOBER — IS ALWAYS RIGHT.

VAN BUREN, JOHNSON.

WE, PLEDGE OURSELVES TO A FIRM, ACTIVE
AND UN-COMPROMISING OPPOSITION TO ALL
ALIEN AND **SEDITION GAG LAW** AND
BLACK COCKADE CANDIDATES,
ALTHOUGH DISGUISED BY THE
NAME OF WHIG,

1840.

TO COMMEMORATE
THE
BATTLE OF YORKTOWN,
October 19th, 1781.

IN HONOR
Of the Founders and Defenders of
AMERICAN
INDEPENDENCE.

*Silk ribbons with historical themes. "BLACK
COCKADE" on the item above is a derisive
reference to black hat ribbons worn by
Federalists and is an example of the Democrats'
portrayal of the Whigs as latter-day elitists.*

*Anti-Van Buren mechanical "metamorphic" card which
changes from "A BEAUTIFUL GOBLET OF WHITE
HOUSE CHAMPAGNE" to "AN UGLY MUG OF LOG
CABIN HARD CIDER." Drawn by David Johnston.*

*Van Buren medal
designed by F. Smith.*

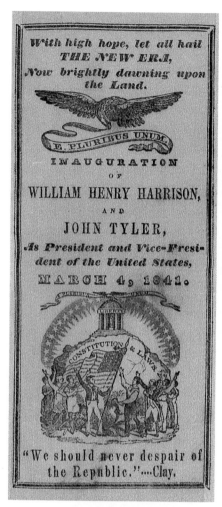

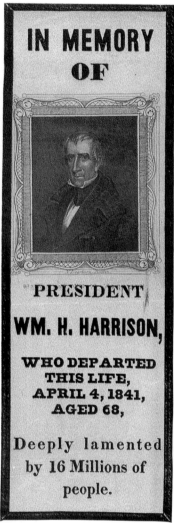

Silk ribbons. The Tyler piece on the right was issued after Harrison's death (April 4, 1841).

Harrison inauguration medal. Harrison's North Bend, Ohio, home appears beneath the horse. The reverse side shows the Capitol building.

★

1844

26 STATES
IN THE UNION

DEMOCRAT

James K. Polk

ELECTORAL VOTE 170, POPULAR VOTE 49.6%

WHIG

Henry Clay

ELECTORAL VOTE 105, POPULAR VOTE 48.1%

LIBERTY

James G. Birney

ELECTORAL VOTE 0, POPULAR VOTE 2.3%

ROBERT V. REMINI

is the author of a three-volume biography of
Andrew Jackson: *Andrew Jackson and the Course
of American Empire, 1767–1821* (1977); *Andrew
Jackson and the Course of American Freedom,
1822–1832* (1981); and *Andrew Jackson and the
Course of American Democracy, 1833–1845*
(1984). He is also the author of *Henry Clay:
Statesman for the Union* (1991).

As the presidential election of 1844 approached, the Whigs fully expected to repeat the great triumph of their Log Cabin campaign of 1840 by using the same techniques they had perfected since first introduced in 1828: parades, barbecues, street rallies, songs, slogans, and other forms of ballyhoo to capture popular interest and support. And what made their desire for another electoral triumph more intense was the fact that they had been "cheated" of their 1840 victory when President William Henry Harrison died within a month of his inauguration and Vice President John Tyler, a former Democrat, states' righter, and strict constructionist, assumed the presidency and vetoed all their efforts to enact the Whig program into law.

Moreover, the Whigs had as their presidential candidate this time an undisputed statesman and charismatic leader: Henry Clay of Kentucky, or, as he was frequently called, "Harry of the West," or "Prince Hal," or the "Great Compromiser." The mistake of nominating "Tippecanoe and Tyler, Too," in 1839, rather than a dedicated, loyal and healthy Whig, like Clay, convinced Whigs as early as 1841 that "Harry of the West" must head their ticket in 1844.

To add to Whig anticipation, the Democrats were expected to nominate a former President, Martin Van Buren, known as the "Little Magician," even though he seemed thoroughly discredited on account of the economic depression that had begun in 1837 during his administration. Everything point-

ed to a complete and total victory for the Whigs in 1844. They could hardly wait.

Clay himself prepared for the coming triumph by resigning his seat in the Senate and returning home to encourage the party faithful to efforts surpassing those of 1840. A collection of Clay's speeches was published along with admiring campaign biographies by Epes Sargent, Daniel Mallory, and Calvin Colton. "Clay Clubs" were formed and the president of one of them, John S. Littel, published a collection of campaign songs entitled, *The Clay Minstrel, or National Songster*. Throughout the campaign the party provided a variety of songs to fit every occasion. "Yankee Doodle" was thus appropriated in the songbook:

> Our noble Harry is the man
> The Nation most delights in;
> To place him first is now the plan;—
> For this we're all uniting!
> For farmer Clay then boys hurrah,
> And proudly here proclaim him
> The great, the good, the valiant Hal
> And SHOUT WHENE'RE YE NAME HIM!

It was a happy beginning. Soon Clay clubs commissioned musical marches, portraits, lithographs, and busts of the great statesman. Clay himself got deeper into the campaign by deciding, against the advice of many friends and supporters and even before he had been officially nominated, to take a campaign swing during the winter months of 1843–1844 through the Southeast: Georgia, North and South Carolina, and Virginia. Since he was a magnificent

Pewter-rim medallion with lithographed portrait under glass of Henry Clay.

orator and would undoubtedly receive requests to speak wherever he went, he hoped the trip might go a long way toward locking up the South for him.

Clay pretended that he was making the trip for reasons of health and also to fulfill prior commitments to visit these states. In no way did he wish the electorate to get the erroneous idea that he was campaigning for office since that practice by presidential candidates was still frowned upon in the 1840s. Nevertheless, he did manage to give speeches in nearly every town and city he visited. Mostly he talked about his American System and how it would restore prosperity and advance the nation's economic development. He urged the enactment of another national bank, a higher tariff, and internal improvements. But as he soon discovered, the American people had grown tired of these old and familiar issues. The spirit of "manifest destiny" animated their thinking, and they wanted to know where Clay stood on the question of the annexation of Texas and Oregon.

The Oregon country, roughly stretching from the Rocky Mountains to the Pacific Ocean between 42nd parallel to 54º 40', was jointly occupied by the United States and Great Britain under an agreement reached in 1818. Texas, on the other hand, had recently gained its independence from Mexico and was now an independent republic. The United States had recognized its independence but had resisted many calls from Texans and Americans for annexation. President Tyler hoped to bring Texas into the Union before he left office. Negotiations to bring it about diplomatically had already begun when suddenly, without warning, both Clay and Van Buren published letters in Washington newspapers on April 27, 1844, expressing their opposition to immediate annexation.

A few days later, on May 1, 1844, the Whig party held their national nominating convention in Baltimore. Despite Clay's letter on annexation, it nominated him for President and Theodore Frelinghuysen of New Jersey for vice president. A former senator, Frelinghuysen was active in Protestant religious activities and societies. His nomination was expected to add "moral weight" to the ticket. The party platform said nothing about Texas.

Van Buren was not so fortunate as Clay. The Democrats dumped him when they convened in Baltimore on May 27. Ex-President Andrew Jackson had declared against the "Magician" because of his opposition to annexation, as did many southerners (especially those committed to expansionism and manifest destiny). On the ninth ballot the delegates finally united behind James K. Polk, a former Speaker of the House of Representatives and governor of Tennessee. As his running mate they chose George M. Dallas of Pennsylvania. They then adopted a party platform that endorsed the Jackson reform program and called for the "reoccupation of Oregon and the reannexation of Texas at the earliest possible period."

"Who is James K. Polk?" asked many bewildered Americans. "Young Hickory," answered the Democrats, and cut from the same strong tree as Old Hickory. But overconfident Whigs scorned and ridiculed Polk's credentials. "Who is the opponent of Henry Clay?" sneered a former Mississippi congressman. Why nothing more than "a blighted burr that has fallen from the mane of the warhorse of the Hermitage." Polk was subsequently labeled a "dark horse," the first dark horse in American presidential history. "This nomination," declared one Whig newspaper, "may be considered as the dying gasp, the last breath of life, of the 'Democratic' party."

Throughout the contest the two parties seemed determined to emulate the tactics they had employed in earlier victories—the 1840 campaign for the Whigs; the 1828 and 1832 campaigns for the Democrats. Mudslinging began almost immediately. And Clay took the brunt of it. He was described in one handbill as "that notorious *Sabbathbreaker, Profane Swearer, Gambler, Common Drunkard, Perjurer, Duelist, Thief, Robber, Adulterer, Man-stealer, Slave-holder, and Murderer!*" Clay's "moral fitness for the presidency" was further questioned on account of the "corrupt bargain" he and John Quincy Adams had allegedly concluded in 1825 by which Adams was lifted to the presidency over Andrew Jackson. Moreover,

"the history of Mr. Clay's debaucheries and midnight revelries in Washington is too shocking, too disgusting to appear in public print," declared one outraged pamphlet.

Henry Clay was also accused of cynically switching sides on issues to solicit votes, such as his opposition to the Bank of the United States in 1811 and his fervent support of the institution in 1832. Democrats also claimed that he advocated free trade to southerners and protective duties to northerners. They even rhymed their accusation:

Orator Clay had two tones in his voice:
   The one squeaking thus and the other down so,
And mighty convenient he found them both—
   The squeak at the top and the guttural below.

Orator Clay looked up to the North;
   "I'm for a Tariff Protective," said he;
But he turned to the South with his other tone,
   "A Tariff for revenue only 'twill be!"

Orator Clay to the North, with a squeak:
   "I'm for a Bank, for a National Bank!"
Orator Clay to his friends at the South:
   "I confess my opinions are not very rank!"

Pewter-rim medallion with lithographed portrait of James K. Polk. Vice presidential candidate, George M. Dallas, appears on reverse side.

Portrait of the Liberty candidate, James G. Birney.

JAMES G. BIRNEY,
Eleventh President of the United States.

Abolitionists added their contempt for the Whig candidate in their literature and public rallies. Although both Polk and Clay were slaveholders, abolitionists reserved their most vicious attacks for Clay because he was on record as opposing slavery and yet would not free his slaves nor advocate immediate emancipation. Besides, Polk was Clay's intellectual "inferior," and as far as they were concerned his election would do less harm to their cause. Abolitionists supported James G. Birney of Michigan for President on the ticket of the Liberty party.

For their part the Whigs sought to convince the electorate that Polk lacked intellectual acumen and other presidential qualities of leadership. His grandfather's loyalties during the Revolutionary War were questioned. Polk himself was accused of branding his initials on the shoulders of his slaves. Compared to Clay, the Whigs said, he was distinctly third-rate in ability and talent—a mediocrity, pure and simple. Twice defeated as governor of his own state, a foe of protectionism whose election would mean wholesale unemployment in manufacturing, a pliant tool of southern disunionists pledged to the immediate annexation of Texas even if it meant war with Mexico, Polk would bring unmitigated disaster to the country. "He is destitute of the commanding talent—the stern political integrity—the high moral fitness—the Union should possess at this time," argued Whig propaganda, "and . . . having no hold upon the confidence or affections of his countrymen at home, and no talent to command respect for us abroad, he is not the man for the times or for the Union."

Polk cleverly nullified some of this propaganda by writing a letter to John K. Kane of Philadelphia in which he denied hostility to protectionism. Conscious that past opposition to the tariff could cost him the important vote of Pennsylvania and other manufacturing states, he swore in this letter that he had "sanctioned" such duties as would "afford reasonable" protection for home industry. He only opposed, he declared, "a tariff for protection *merely* and not for revenue."

Pennsylvania Democrats applauded the Kane letter and promised to deliver the state in the fall election. Jackson's ward and nephew, Andrew Jackson Donelson, laughingly told Polk that "your letter to Kane will kill Clay." It did indeed. "Nothing," roared the outraged Clay, "has surprised me so much as the attempt now making in Pennsylvania to represent Mr. Polk as the friend and myself as the foe of Protection. If it should succeed I shall distrust the power of the press and of truth." The Whig press echoed his resentment and dismissed the Democratic candidate as a willing tool of the radical Locofoco movement of New York: "Mr. Polk is a loco, out and out, of the free trade school. He is for Free Trade and every other Loco abomination; and against every Whig principle and measure."

Unfortunately, many mistaken Whigs also thought they could injure Polk and help Clay by identifying themselves with the nativist movement that had begun to emerge in the 1840s. They circulated stories that Clay favored stricter immigration and naturalization laws, hoping it would exploit the rising anti-foreign and anti-Catholic resentment provoked by the sharp increase in the numbers of German and Irish immigrants entering the country. But the strategy backfired and sent thousands of Irish and German Americans in the large cities, especially in New York, trooping into the Democratic party. Nor did the career of Theodore Frelinghuysen, the Whig vice presidential candidate, help. His involvement with evangelical Protestants deeply offended Catholics who were "goaded almost to madness by what they consider a concerted attack upon their religious liberty & their political rights."

Through an intermediary Clay approached Archbishop John Hughes of New York in an effort to limit the damage inflicted by pro-Clay nativists. But it soon became obvious that most Catholics regarded the Whig party as hostile to their presence and a

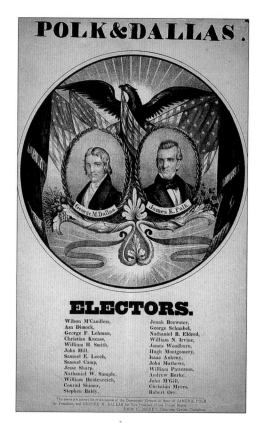

Election broadside for Polk and Dallas.

threat to their liberty and safety. "The Catholics are with us," rejoiced one Democrat in a letter to Polk, "& the other side will keep them so, no fear of that." When the Reverend Martin John Spalding, the future Archbishop of Baltimore and a Kentuckian who greatly admired Henry Clay, announced his decision to vote for the Great Compromiser but not Frelinghuysen, he was told that he could not vote for one without the other. Replied Spalding: "Then I shall not vote for Mr. Clay."

Since he was so adept at compromise, Clay tried to appease both sides of the nativist issue by declaring in a confidential letter to the editor of the New York *Courier and Enquirer*—the "sense" of which he

Henry Clay paper-mâché snuffbox. The 1844 campaign was Clay's third unsuccessful attempt to become President. His supporters felt him so deserving, they coined the slogan "Justice to Henry Clay."

wished conveyed to his friends and supporters—that "every pulsation of my heart is American and nothing but American. . . . I am in favor of American industry, American institutions, American order, American liberty. Whilst I entertain all these feelings and sentiment, I wish our Country, forever, to remain a sacred asylum for all unfortunate and oppressed men whether from religious or political causes."

But Clay's attempted appeasement was only seen as another example of the way he straddled issues to enhance political advantage. And as though to prove the truth of this charge he then went on to commit a colossal blunder that virtually destroyed his candidacy. In a published letter to the editor of the Tuscaloosa *Monitor,* he declared that he "personally" had no objection to the annexation of Texas provided it did not threaten the existing Union of states. This letter shocked both northerners and southerners who immediately presumed that he had switched his position in order to win support from annexationists. "Mr. Clay's letter has caused much depression, & some consternation, among his friends," sighed one man. It was, said another, "Mr. Clay's

political death-warrant." To make matters worse, Clay then wrote a second Alabama letter in which he said that if elected President he would be glad to see the annexation of Texas but "without dishonor—without war, with the common consent of the Union, and upon just and fair terms."

That about finished him off. The Democrats could hardly conceal their delight. Henry Clay a statesman? Hardly. He waffles on issues; he straddles wherever he can; he wants it both ways. Again, the Democrats rhymed their mockery:

> He wires in and wires out,
> And leaves the people still in doubt,
> Whether the snake that made the track
> Was going South, or coming back.

To add to his discredit in antislavery circles, Clay got into a controversy with a distant cousin, Cassius M. Clay, an ardent Kentucky abolitionist. In a letter to the *New York Tribune* Cassius Clay assured the nation that his cousin was no emancipationist, "but I believe his feelings are with the cause." The real issue, he went on, was *"Polk, slavery, and Texas"* versus *"Clay, Union and liberty."*

Henry Clay immediately repudiated cousin Cassius in the Lexington *Observer and Kentucky Reporter.* Cassius Clay had written his letter, Clay said, without my knowledge, or any consultation or authority from me. So far as Cassius attempts "TO INTERPRET MY FEELINGS, HE HAS ENTIRELY MISCONCEIVED THEM." Antislavery Whigs despaired. Clay "is as rotten as a stagnant fish pond, on the subject of Slavery & always has been," wrote one former congressman. "Confound him and all his compromises from first to last."

While Clay seemed thoroughly engaged in self-destruction, Polk proved he had a sharp eye and keen mind for political strategy. In addition to defusing resentment on the tariff question, he also announced at the very start of the campaign his decision not to seek a second term. This pledge had the happy effect of pulling a divided party together by encouraging defeated rivals, such as Van Buren, John C. Calhoun, Lewis Cass, and others, to support him in the hope of assuming party leadership in 1848. Polk made excellent use of Jackson by inducing him to restate publicly his belief in the "corrupt bargain." Old Hickory was also instrumental in talking Tyler out of running for a second term as an independent—an exercise that might well have split the South. On August 10, Tyler publicly announced he would not run.

With the contest now reduced essentially to Young Hickory and the Great Compromiser—Birney was discounted as a serious candidate, although it was recognized that he could inflict serious damage to Clay's candidacy in several northern states—the two parties anticipated a campaign of frolic, fun, and nonsense reminiscent of the Log Cabin campaign four years before. Songs, marches, quicksteps, caricatures, hats, buttons, canes, snuffboxes, cigar cases, shaving mugs, banners, and campaign ribbons and rosettes made their required appearance. In addition, musical entertainment in the form of fancy balls became fashionable. William Henry Harrison had been sung into the presidency, laughed Philip Hone, a wealthy New York Whig, and "if Mr. Clay should succeed it will be effected in some degree by dancing."

This 1844 Clay ribbon is considered the first political ribbon to be printed in color.

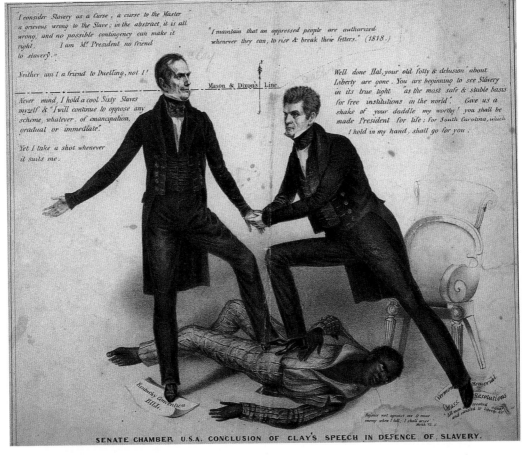

An anti-Clay caricature print contending that Clay had contradictory positions on slavery.

None of the songs of this campaign matched the popularity of "Tippecanoe and Tyler, Too," perhaps because neither candidate could offer a military victory as part of their career credentials, but the Whigs supplied numerous lyrics to be sung to the tunes of "The Star Spangled Banner," "Rosin the Bow," and "Royal Charlie." One workingman's song included these lines:

The Laboring Men that want more work,
And higher wages too,
Will help to put in Henry Clay
With better times in view.
They'll saw and chop, and grub and dig,
And shovel, and shovel away,
And shovel, shovel, shovel, shovel,
And vote for Henry Clay!

To the tune of "Auld Lang Syne" the Whigs sang:

Leave vain regrets for error past
Nor cast the ship away,

But nail your colors to the mast
And strike for Harry Clay.
And strike for Harry Clay, my boys,
And strike for Harry Clay,
And nail your colors to the mast
And strike for Harry Clay!

or they sang the following to the tune of "Ole Dan Tucker" and used the symbol of the "coon" (raccoon) which had been identified with the party since 1840 and with Clay himself:

The moon was shining silver bright,
The stars with glory crowned the night,
High on a limb that "same old coon,"
Was singing to himself this tune:—
Get out of the way, you're all unlucky,
Clear the tracks for old Kentucky.

The Clay banners identified the candidate as the friend of agriculture and manufactures. "The Farmer of Ashland," read one; "Champion of the American System," read another. Such ribbons and tokens as "Henry Clay and a Protective Tariff" or "A National Currency, Revenue and Protection" were regularly displayed in northern manufacturing states.

But Whig enthusiasm flagged during the campaign, probably on account of Clay's many political gaffes. No flags and bunting decorated the "towns, cities and boat-landings," reported one man. The campaign lacked "excitement, zeal, or clamor for Clay, neither on the water nor on the land." The "attempt to get up something like the log cabin *fooleries* has thus far failed."

Democrats tended to eschew floats, banners, and transparencies and other fooleries in favor of devices advertising Polk's firm commitment to the annexation of Texas and Oregon, an issue which steadily captured interest and excitement as the campaign progressed. "Oregon, Texas, and Democracy" proclaimed one ribbon. Another declared: "Texas and No Bank."

An interesting sidelight was the fact that a great many women expressed their support for Henry Clay. "The ladies were all '*Clay men*,'" declared Nathan Sargent, even though their husbands, brothers, and fathers preferred Polk. Hendrick B. Wright who presided at the Democratic National Convention in Baltimore discovered that his wife had organized a group of women to prepare Clay banners, flags, and badges. "Though my husband is a *Polk* man," said Mrs. Wright, "I am a *Clay* man; in fact, the ladies are all Clay men. The Whigs are to have a great gathering . . . and we ladies, several of us the wives of Polk men, are preparing banners and badges for the occasion." In fact she offered one "of our most

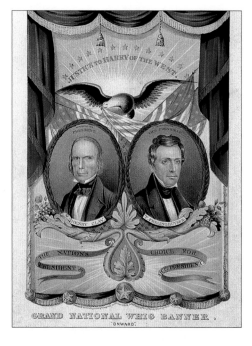

Multicolored N. Currier print. Similar Grand National Banner prints were issued between 1844 and 1876.

beautiful Clay rosettes" to a dumbfounded Democrat. "You ought to delight to follow so noble a chief as Henry Clay," she lectured. And an English lady visiting the United States was told by a group of women that she could not return home without visiting the "Sage of Ashland." "You never heard such a voice," they cried, "you never knew such a man in England as our Mr. Clay."

Unfortunately for him, little of this did Clay any good. For the third and last time in his career the Great Compromiser, the Star of the West, Prince Hal went down to ignominious defeat. In the popular vote Polk polled 1,337,243, Clay 1,299,062, and Birney 62,300. A mere 38,181 votes separated the two front-runners. In the electoral college Polk received 170 votes to Clay's 105.

"James K. Polk, the pigmy in intellect . . . the mere politician," wailed one Whig newspaper, "is elevated to the highest office in the gift of the American people." Worse, said a disgruntled Whig, Polk's election means the annexation of Texas, and Texas ultimately means secession and civil war.

Painted glass portrait of a youthful Clay on a split-column mantle clock.

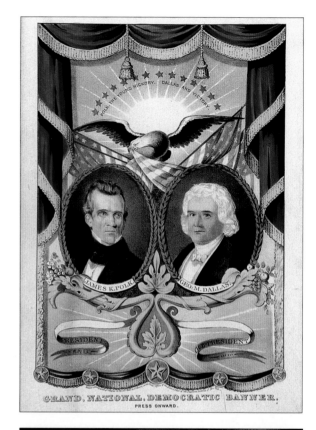

Grand National Banner prints. The Polk is by N. Currier and the Clay print by Kellogg, both noted lithographers.

Henry Clay cotton flag banners. The raccoon became the Whig symbol. The Democratic emblem was the rooster.

Rare Polk cotton flag banner. The extra star symbolizes Polk's support for the admission of Texas to the Union.

Henry Clay Sandwich Company glass cup plates.

PRESIDENTE DE LOS ESTADOS UNIDAS

JAMES K. POLK.

Polk commemorative china. Plate made in France.
The teacup is hand-painted Paris porcelain.

Henry Clay Sandwich Company
glass cup plate in rare cobalt blue.

Berlin needlepoint based on
the John Neagle portrait
which hangs in the Capitol.

Clay cotton bandanna. Campaign
slogans appear in the corners.

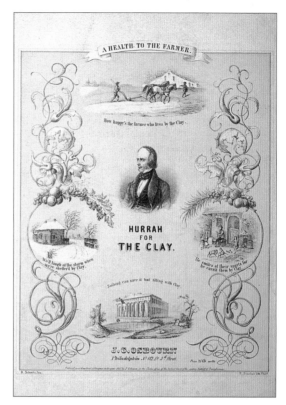

Examples of Henry Clay campaign sheet music.

Henry Clay snuffbox. Use of the snuffbox for political campaigns reached its peak in the 1840s.

Brass brooch pins with miniature portraits of Henry Clay.

Heavy glass paperweight with intaglio bust of Clay.

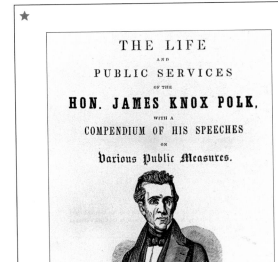

Pewter-rim Polk medallion.

Various pieces of
campaign literature.

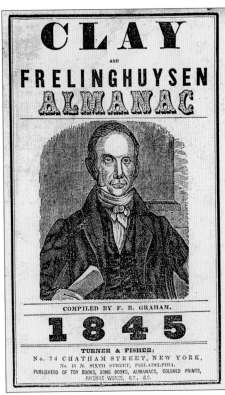

The Clay almanac, actually printed in 1844,
is typical of political almanacs which
included regional information, campaign
issues, and candidate biographies.

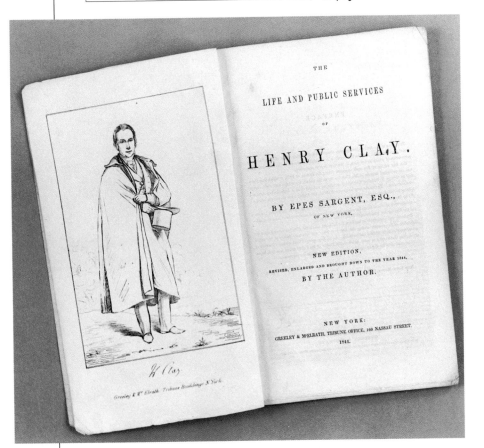

Henry Clay medallion depicting the protectionist campaign theme to benefit American industry and shipping.

Brass shell Polk medallion and a pewter Polk medal.

Henry Clay sheet music and song book.

An outstanding pair of snuffboxes.

Clay silk ribbon. Clay is flanked by figures representing agriculture (left) and science (right). Vignettes illustrate his support for shipping, commerce, and farming. The dog, bottom, holds a scroll inscribed "Fidelity."

A selection of silk ribbons from the 1844 campaign. These ribbons delineated issues of the day. The Native American or Know-Nothing movement, active from the 1830s to 1860, opposed foreign and Catholic church influence in American life.

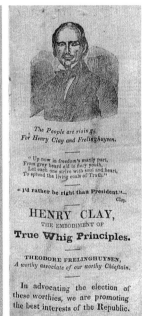

★

1848

30 STATES
IN THE UNION

WHIG

Zachary Taylor

ELECTORAL VOTE 163, POPULAR VOTE 47.4%

DEMOCRAT

Lewis Cass

ELECTORAL VOTE 127, POPULAR VOTE 42.5%

FREE SOIL

Martin Van Buren

ELECTORAL VOTE 0, POPULAR VOTE 10.1%

GIL TROY

is the author of *See How They Ran:*
The Changing Role of the Presidential Candidate
(1991). He is professor of history at McGill University.

A n 1848 lithograph pictures Major General Zachary Taylor, the Whig presidential nominee, sitting atop a mound of skulls, all victims of the Mexican War. This crude attack on Taylor's primary presidential qualification proved an apt metaphor for the 1848 campaign. Having acquired California, New Mexico, and the Rio Grande boundary, Americans were sitting on top of the world. These new territories, however, helped stir all kinds of sectional ghosts.

Throughout the 1840s, as America fulfilled its "manifest destiny," the country was haunted by slavery. Northerners who accepted southern slavery as the price of the Union vowed to keep the new territories free. Congressman David Wilmot of Pennsylvania proposed an amendment to an appropriations bill banning slavery from the new territories. "Free Soilers" in the North championed this Wilmot Proviso, while southerners denounced such "Yankee" infringements.

Both the Whig and the Democratic parties had a difficult time appeasing the warring sections. But at the same time, despite internal divisions, party loyalty remained strong. In the two decades since the Jacksonian revolution, parties had become an accepted part of the American political furniture. There is only "one broad paramount issue" in American politics, the *Democratic Review* declared in 1844: "Which of the two great leading parties shall be placed in power?" The campaign of 1848, therefore, featuring the Democrat Lewis Cass, the Whig Zachary Taylor, and the Free Soiler Martin Van Buren, was a three-way battle as the two great forces in mid-nineteenth century American politics—sectional allegiance and party loyalty—collided.

I ronically, the central figure in this battle, General Zachary Taylor, had dubious ties to both his party and his home region. A career soldier, Taylor had never even voted for President. When his Mexican War heroics made him the leading presidential candidate, Taylor laughed: "Such an idea never entered my head, nor is it likely to enter the head of any sane person." Similarly, although he owned a plantation with almost three hundred slaves in Louisiana, he never openly advocated slavery. Northerners dismissed him as a slaveholder, while southerners suspected his silence.

Nevertheless, in an era when wags noted that a potential President's most important ability was his "availability," Taylor was a formidable candidate. His popularity and his silence made him acceptable to either of the two national parties. His nonpartisanship appealed to a republic where many still distrusted the party system. "If I ever occupy the White House it must be by the spontaneous move of the people," Taylor insisted. He would only enter the presidency "untrammeled" by pledges and free to be "a President of the nation and not a party."

Taylor's pose harked back to the days of another soldier-farmer, George Washington. In keeping with the Framers' republi-

Daguerrotype portrait of General Zachary Taylor. Daguerrotypes were first used for political purposes in the 1848 campaign.

can sensibilities, Washington had done nothing to advance his candidacy. Candidates were supposed to *stand* for the presidency, they did not *run*. Especially once nominated, candidates retired to their farms and awaited the people's call in dignified silence. Passivity demonstrated the candidate's virtue. The presidency was neither to be solicited nor declined. Taylor echoed: "I ask no favor, and shrink from no responsibility."

The rise of political parties during the first half of the nineteenth century at once strengthened and undermined this republican taboo on campaigning. Both Democrats and Whigs feared that active nominees threatened party success—glib candidates might upset fragile electoral coalitions. In 1844, Henry Clay's letters about the annexation of Texas alienated voters on both sides of the issue. After Clay's defeat, party managers added expediency to the traditional demands of propriety inhibiting candidates. But at the same time, the democratic tidal wave sweeping America and the growing intensity of partisanship made apolitical candidates unacceptable. Why should party members dedicate themselves to electing a President who would be "untrammeled" by pledges to them or devotion to their ideals?

From his military camp near Monterey, Taylor waded into these murky waters. In reply to letters asking him about the presidency, Taylor inched toward affiliation with the Whigs—while still professing nonpartisanship. Taylor repeated that he had never been "mixed up with political matters." But, if he had voted in the "last presidential election, it would have been for Mr. Clay."

Taylor's letters alienated Whig regulars. Correspondence of any kind could be suicidal but these protestations of nonpartisanship were insulting. "We *cannot*, with any decency, support Taylor," wrote Horace Greeley of the whiggish *New York Tribune*. Senator Daniel Webster of Massachusetts, himself an aspirant for the Whig nomination, blanched at the thought of "a swearing, fighting frontier colonel" for President. Henry Clay sighed: "I wish I could slay a Mexican."

Still, the people pushed for Taylor. Typical of the popular manifestations of support was the Buena Vista Festival, held at Philadelphia on February 22, 1848. This "Great Whig Demonstration" celebrated Washington's birthday and Taylor's candidacy. Hundreds of Whigs mobbed the lower saloon of the Museum building on Ninth Street, below Chestnut. The saloon was festooned with red-white-and-blue bunting, state banners, and draped signs emblazoned with various mottoes. "GENERAL TAYLOR NEVER SURRENDERS" testified to the candidate's military—and political—fortitude. "WE ARE FOR THE UNION AS IT

IS, AND FOR THE UNION AS THE WILL OF ALL THE STATES, LEGITIMATELY EXPRESSED, MAY HEREAFTER MAKE IT," reflected the Whigs' desire to avoid the sectional imbroglio. And "IN MASSES RESOLVE AT THE BALLOT-BOX TO ACT," affirmed the people's power. Even amid this multicolored display, a full-length portrait of "the Hero of Buena Vista" dominated. Speeches and testimonials from prominent Whigs characterized "ZACHARY TAYLOR AS AN UNDOUBTED WHIG" and as "THE MAN OF THE PEOPLE." The men assembled then toasted Washington's birthday, Taylor, Clay, Major General Winfield Scott, the Whig national convention, the army and the navy of the United States, the Whigs of the Union, a protective tariff, the volunteers of Pennsylvania, Washington and Taylor, and, finally, for good measure, "Woman—The guardian of infancy—the companion of manhood—the solace of age; from the cradle to the grave, the ministering angel of humanity."

Celebrating party, patriotism, Taylor's heroism, and the raucous masculinity of American politics, such festivals enlivened the campaign. Soon Taylor advanced his own cause by embracing the Whig party more fully. In a letter to his son-in-law, Captain John Allison, on April 22, 1848, Taylor refused to make pledges and continued to ignore political "details." Still, he announced, "I AM A WHIG, *but not an ultra Whig*," distancing himself from "party domination." Taylor then closed the subject. "I trust I will not be again called on to make further explanations," he said.

Taylor's "Allison letter" helped quiet the Whig debate between availability and loyalty, between expedience and virtue. Taylor's

nonpolitical pose now seemed calculating. This inversion of the traditional etiquette reflected the changing mores and continuing confusion in presidential politics.

Meanwhile, the Democrats squabbled about the extension of slavery. On the fourth ballot, a divided convention nominated Lewis Cass. Leader of the botched invasion of Canada during the War of 1812, governor of the Michigan territory for eighteen years, secretary of war and minister to France under Andrew Jackson, and a senator from Michigan since 1845, Cass was a party loyalist. In December of 1847 he had published his "Nicholson Letter," suggesting that the settlers in each territory decide the slavery question for themselves. "Popular sovereignty" positioned Cass as a compromise candidate between the warring northern and southern factions. His opponents disparaged Cass as a "doughface," a northern man with southern principles, but he was the best the Democrats could muster.

The cost of compromise was great. Former President Martin Van Buren and his New York "Barnburners"—so named because they seemed willing to burn down the barn simply to clear out some rats—seceded from the party. Within weeks, Van Buren was running as the nominee of a renegade party uniting disgruntled Democrats, antislavery "Conscience Whigs," and refugees from the Liberty party of 1844. Embracing the Wilmot Proviso, the Free Soilers challenged fundamental notions of party loyalty. Rather than uniting disparate factions around a party ideal, they built a coalition on one explosive issue. This one-note Free Soil party vowed to prevent slavery from polluting one more "foot of freedom's sacred soil."

Lacking even the rudimentary organizational structures the other two parties enjoyed, the Free Soilers relied on "stumpers," individual orators who fanned out across the nation. While all parties used surrogates for their passive candidates, Free Soil stumpers were particularly zealous. "I frequently spoke as often as three times a day and generally from two to three hours at each meeting," one orator, George Julian, recalled. "I spoke at crossroads, in barns, in pork houses, in saw-mills, in any place in which a few or many people would hear me." Julian and others were threatened with mob violence and "subjected to a torrent of billingsgate which rivalled the fish market." They took comfort in "having truth on their side."

The Free Soil revolt all but doomed the Democratic effort. Once nominated, Cass had resigned his Senate seat, hoping to withdraw from politics for the duration of the campaign. In his letter of May 30, accepting the nomination, Cass embraced the Democratic platform, as well as "the principles and compromises of the constitution." In keeping with the republican tradition of silence, Cass stood by his public record of forty years. "This letter," Cass declared, "closes my profession of political faith."

Cass did, however, consent to be serenaded by the people on his way home—and would take a number of side trips in the Midwest during the fall. These ritualized greetings of prominent visitors harked back to ancient times but were particularly elaborate in a young, vast country searching for a tradition and for heroes. The day he heard that Van Buren had agreed to run on the Free Soil ticket, Cass arrived in Syracuse on the way to his Detroit home. Sixteen-year-old Andrew Dickson White took to the streets with thousands of his townsmen. White saw Cass "welcomed by a great procession of Democrats, and marched under a broiling sun, through dusty streets to the City Hall, where he was forced to listen and reply to fulsome speeches prophesying his election, which he and all present knew to be impossible." White would long remember "the picture of this old, sad man marching through the streets, listening gloomily to the speeches, forced to appear confident of victory, yet evidently disheartened and disgusted."

Still, the Democrats and Cass tried their best. Most northern Democrats agreed with the *New Brunswick Times* that "it is true that Gen. Cass does not advocate the Wilmot Proviso, but he is a democrat. On every cardinal point of the democratic creed he is known to be right, and we have no wish to introduce other issues in this election." For the first time, partisan editors compiled a "Democratic Textbook," a compendium of articles and resolutions praising the nominee and his party. In the ensuing decades, the campaign textbook would become each party's bible for the duration of the contest.

Furthermore, the Democratic National Committee (DNC) was formed to coordinate the various state committees. Although by 1840 both parties held national conventions, they lacked permanent structures. The conventions were periodic and had no fixed principle of representation. In 1844 the Democrats had created a temporary "central committee" in Washington to promote James Knox Polk's election. Legislation in 1845 established a uniform date for the selection of presidential electors in each state, forcing simultaneous campaigns and creating the need for a permanent coordinating body. Benjamin Hallett proposed the establishment of an electoral committee and was then drafted to serve as chairman. The DNC included one member from each state and was active only during congressional and presidential campaigns. Whigs continued to rely on ad hoc campaign committees and committees of correspondence. Only after the Republican party established its own national committee in 1856 would the DNC have a permanent rival.

When the Whig convention nominated Taylor on June 7 in Philadelphia—without any party platform—some Whigs bolted. "Self-respect, the consistency of my character, and my true fame require that I should take no active or partisan agency in the ensuing contest," Henry Clay moped. "The Whig party has been overthrown by a mere personal party." Some Whig papers ignored the convention and endorsed Clay. William Henry Seward of New York refused to stump for Taylor because "what would be effectual when said I should be unwilling and ashamed to read."

In keeping with the quaint fictions of the Republican taboo, the convention designated a notification committee to draft a letter informing the "unsuspecting" nominee of his good fortune. The gentleman would then accept the nomination in a letter affirming his party loyalty and articulating his positions, if he so desired. Whig leaders now worried when no acceptance letter from their candidate appeared. Unfortunately, Taylor's notification letter lacked sufficient postage and ended up in the Dead Letter Office—a fitting place, Democrats joked, for

Carte de visite of Lewis Cass, circa 1861.

both the missive and the nomination itself.

By July 15, Taylor had paid the $7.30 postage due, retrieved the letter, and accepted the nomination. He confessed to friends that he kept his acceptance letter "very brief." Having learned to be "as cautious as possible," still ambivalent about running, and sensitive to the proprieties, Taylor chose to "enter quietly on my duty." He would assuage Whig concerns in private, while avoiding public statements. On the rare occasions when he ventured from his plantation after the nomination, Taylor "gave politics a wide berth," the *New Orleans Weekly Delta* noted.

Still, Taylor wrote the occasional letter and continued to pose as the candidate of "the whole nation." When renegade South Carolina Democrats nominated him, Taylor reaffirmed his commitment to the Whig party but said he would have accepted the nomination of any party, including the Democrats. While Whigs fumed, Democrats attacked Taylor for trying to be all things to all men and for ignoring the people. In a cartoon entitled "Questioning a Candidate," office seekers quizzed Taylor on the issues. The reclining general dismissed them, saying: "Do you think I sit here to answer your bothering questions? You'll find out what I think when I'm President, & then it will be my part to command & yours to obey."

Taylor the Democrats charged, was the candidate of "no avowed principle," a General "Mum" standing by his uniform and his horse, Old Whitey. Taylor was "two-faced," seducing abolitionists and slaveholders with his silences, his contradictions, and his evasions. "Ask a Taylor man if he is in favor of a U.S. Bank," the *Detroit Free Press* sneered, "The reply is Buena Vista." Ask if he expects "to get the votes of the old tired Whigs, who have for years contended for principles," and the reply is: "Old Whitey."

Frustrated with their own candidate, Whigs responded by attacking Cass. With different campaign biographies circulated in the North and in the South, Cass, Whigs claimed, was the true two-faced candidate. Cass was also an expansionist, a demagogue, a land speculator, and a chiseler, having overcharged the government $64,865.46 for expenses over the years. Whigs even scoffed at Cass's war exploits. If the Democrats ever "take me up as their candidate for the presidency, I protest they shall not make fun of me, as they have of General Cass, by attempting to write me into a military hero," the one-term Whig congressman, Abraham Lincoln, quipped. After months of attacks, one Whig punned:

> And he who still for Cass can be:
> He is a Cass without the C.

Partisans plunged into the contest, singing, parading, and distributing hundreds of campaign badges and ribbons throughout the country. A Cass ribbon proclaimed: "Principles Not Men!" while a Van Buren badge pronounced: "Our Country Forever! No More Extension of Slavery." A popular Taylor banner pictured the general in military regalia, surrounded in each corner by the name of a different Mexican War battlefield: Palo Alto, Resaca De La Palma, Buena Vista, Monterey.

Once again, despite Whig and Democratic desires to "make the contest an era of good feelings," to fight "on the legitimate grounds of facts, principles, . . . fair discussion and truthful publications," the campaign degenerated into a name-calling contest. Deterioration was unavoidable in a nation where politics was a popular pastime and where the Democrats and Whigs were evenly matched. In 1848 it seemed that every vote counted and that everyone had to be mobilized. The ritualized calls for substance and fairness reflected the still-powerful legacy of the Founders' republicanism; the intense and vulgar contest highlighted the democratic revolution that was transforming America.

Political parties, Taylor learned, were central to this revolution. Bowing to pressure, he made one more appeal to Whig regulars. Taylor's second "Allison letter" of September fourth reaffirmed that he was "A Whig—decided but not ultra in my opinions." Caught by contradictory mores which demanded party loyalty while disdaining party politics, Taylor deemed his position in keeping with "good Whig doctrine." He was "not a party candidate, nor am I in that straightened and sectarian sense which would prevent my being the president of the whole people, in case of my election." Once again, Taylor declared the matter closed.

The second Allison letter allowed thousands of Whigs to return to the party fold. William Henry Seward even took to the stump, spending so much time away from home that his wife Frances spurned dresses and hats as peace offerings. In the end, at least some prominent antislavery Whigs supported Taylor, while most of the prominent antislavery Democrats spurned Cass and voted for Van Buren.

Although the enthusiasm in 1848 never quite reached the heights of 1840 and 1844, 72.7 percent of the electorate swarmed to the polls on Election Day. The newly formed Associated Press invested over $1,000 in reporting by telegraph that General Taylor had been defeated and that James Knox Polk had been reelected—a mistake that took three days to correct.

In fact, the Free Soil party had played the role of spoiler. Taylor received 1,360,967 popular votes, Cass received 1,222,342, and Van Buren's Free Soil party 291,263. The electoral vote tally was 163 for Taylor, 127 for Cass. Van Buren received no electoral votes, but his 120,510 votes in New York swung New York's 36 electoral votes, and the election, to Taylor.

To Whig managers like Thurlow Weed, the election results "vindicated the wisdom of General Taylor's nomination." But to others, Whig principles had been shipwrecked on the shoals of availability. The 1848 election "demoralized" Whigs and undermined the faith of "the masses" in the party, Horace Greeley concluded. It was, he

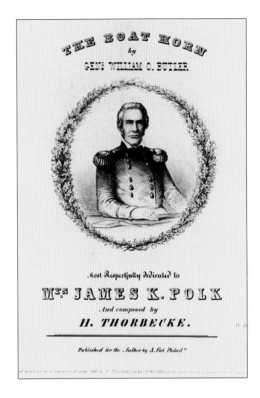

Sheet music written by Democratic vice presidential candidate William Butler and dedicated to Mrs. Polk.

believed, a Pyrrhic victory: Whigs were "at once triumphant and undone."

Ironically, this Whig party sellout marked a triumph for the idea of party, and the power of party loyalty. Most Whigs, forced to choose between principles and party loyalty, voted with their parties. Those who voted their consciences and bolted the parties were vilified.

While the 1848 election affirmed the power of party loyalty, underlying questions festered. How could the needs of the North and the South be reconciled in one Union? How could American politics balance party loyalty and individual principle, active candidates, and presidential dignity? The Civil War would help answer the first question. The second set of questions continues to bedevil us today.

Campaign poster with tiny images of soldiers on top of the letters in scenes from the Mexican War. On each letter there are forts, tents, and battle scenes.

Paper-mâché Zachary Taylor cigar case painted with a colorful Mexican War scene.

Stone-lithographed print of General Taylor, published in 1846, featuring his 1848 campaign slogan "ROUGH AND READY."

Grand National Banner prints from the 1848 campaign. Printed as a continuing series, these lithographs featured a standard design of draping, eagles, scrolls, and flags. The Van Buren print, above, is from his last campaign as a candidate of the Free Soil party.

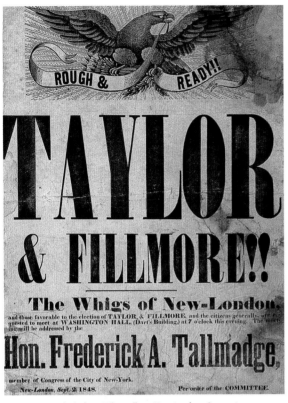

Broadside for a Whig rally in New London, Connecticut.

One of many classic mechanical caricature cards designed by David Johnston. This card mocks the LOCOFOCO, a Democratic party faction. When the tab is pulled, the smile becomes a frown. "HURRAH FOR CASS" changes to "WHAT! OLD ZACK ELECTED!"

Embossed tin tray of General Taylor with the slogan "OUR COUNTRY RIGHT OR WRONG."

FOR PRESIDENT
ZACHARY TAYLOR,
OF LOUISIANA.

FOR VICE PRESIDENT,
MILLARD FILLMORE,
OF NEW YORK.

"I shall continue to devote all my energies to the public good, looking for my reward to the consciousness of pure motives, and to the final verdict of impartial history."—*Z. Taylor.*

FOR PRESIDENT,
LEWIS CASS,
OF MICHIGAN.

FOR VICE PRESIDENT,
WILLIAM O. BUTLER,
OF KENTUCKY.

"If we are not struck with judicial blindness, we shall cling to this Constitution as the mariner clings to the last plank, when night and the tempest close around him."—*Lewis Cass.*

FREE SOIL, AND FREEDOM OF THE PUBLIC LANDS TO ACTUAL SETTLERS

Published by Edwd P. Whailes, cor. Broadway & Courtlandt st. N.Y.

Trio of silk ribbons for the three 1848 candidates. Most Lewis Cass material is rare.

Snuffbox with a General Taylor portrait.

Miniature painting on
porcelain of General Taylor.
His campaign was based on his
military record with almost no
mention of political issues.

Embossed brass shell
medallion of Van Buren.

Pewter medals and multicolored pewter-
rim medallions from the 1848 campaign.

Campaign cigar box with 1848 candidates on the label.

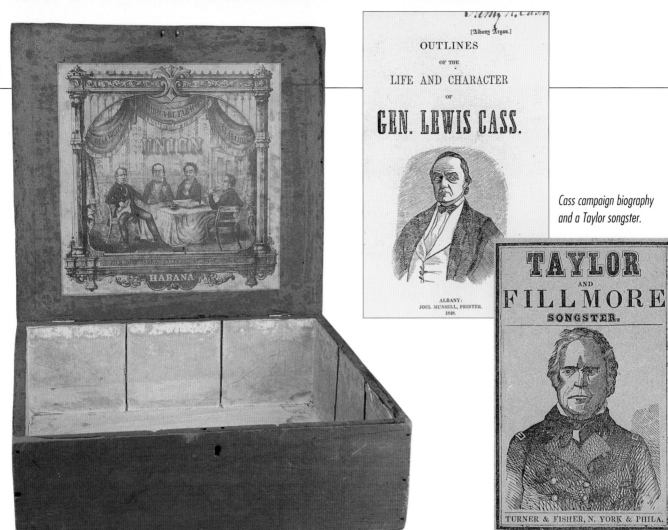

Cass campaign biography and a Taylor songster.

Gilt-stamped, velvet-covered case with a miniature reverse painting on glass of General Taylor.

General Taylor cigar case.

General Taylor porcelain mug.

Extremely rare Staffordshire-type pitcher inscribed
"GENERAL Z. TAYLOR/Born Nov. 24th, 1784
ELECTED PRESIDENT OF AMERICA 1848."

A Taylor whiskey flask. These usually are
found in aqua, other colors being rare.

Needlework depicting General Taylor.

The ribbon design was used for the 1849 inaugural and reissued as a memorial piece by adding the top and bottom inscriptions.

Carved shell cameo of Taylor.

1848 cotton bandanna. Legend reads: "Gen. Z. Taylor/ROUGH and READY."

1852
31 STATES
IN THE UNION

DEMOCRAT

Franklin Pierce

ELECTORAL VOTE 254, POPULAR VOTE 50.9%

WHIG

Winfield Scott

ELECTORAL VOTE 42, POPULAR VOTE 44.1%

FREE SOIL

John P. Hale

ELECTORAL VOTE 0, POPULAR VOTE 5%

Joel H. Silbey

is the President White Professor of History at
Cornell University. He has written, most recently,
The American Political Nation, 1838-1893 (1991).

By the time of the campaign pitting Franklin Pierce against Winfield Scott in 1852, the experienced managers of the two major political parties had perfected the mechanisms, content, and tone of electoral warfare. Since the late 1830s they had developed and refined popular techniques of articulation, presentation, and mobilization. Campaigning called for thorough organization designed to bring voters to the polls. Managers had learned from experience that they could generally count on party loyalty. But voters still had to be stimulated and cajoled to demonstrate their commitment on election day. As one Whig newspaper put it in August, "victory is not to be accomplished without exertion; . . . a vote for Winfield Scott . . . cannot be obtained without labor—untiring, systematic persevering labor."

Little was left to chance. The campaign went through several stages, beginning with nominations at the national conventions and culminating in the busy activities of party workers on election day. Each stage in this sequence made a specific contribution to each party's defined needs and goals. The conventions in June produced not only candidates but also platforms elaborating the policies on which each party would run as well as forwarding the structure that managed the campaign. From bottom to top the key was "the most direct, systematic and effectual" organization at every level, everywhere possible. As one campaign newspaper demanded:

Arouse, then, democrats! organize! act! Let every school district in the state have its vigilance committee, let that committee canvass every vote, learn the names of the wavering, stimulate the inactive. And pour a flood of democratic truths into the fortresses of the doubting.

After the conventions, Whig and Democratic leaders established nationwide organizations, built anew for each election. Organizations were triangular in shape, beginning at the base with the broad range of the party's adherents and climbing to the apex of national committees in Washington. Below them, state committees located in each state capital ran the nuts and bolts of the campaign. The same pattern was repeated at every level downward: town, district, county and congressional committees issued calls, arranged meetings, and structured the whole.

These organizations were developed and run by the handful of activists in each locality. Such elites always understood that their targets were the inactive majority. Therefore, parties stressed activities calling for constant, intense, public participation. The centerpiece was the public rally held by each party at every level of society. State and local committees sent speakers throughout the state while national committees organized more prominent speakers to cross state lines. Ratification meetings immediately after the national and state conventions featured the acceptances, with un-

Pierce silk ribbon.

bounded enthusiasm, of candidates and platforms; they were followed by speeches, debates and rallies at congressional district and county levels. Volunteer organizations like the Democrats' Hickory Clubs, organized parades around Hickory Poles or behind mementoes of America's recent triumph in Mexico. All this had a military cast. The "minute men of party" marched and sang, responding to the command of "the sergeants and corporals" who led them.

Rallies were exuberant social affairs involving the entire partisan community of a locality, white male voters and wives and children, bound together across the social and gender spectrum. Food was served, partisan materials distributed, cheers and spontaneous outburst constantly pushed. The highlight was a speech by some local notable or visitor to the open-air assembly. Most stump speaking was done by surrogates for the presidential candidates. So Senator Stephen A. Douglas spoke in a dozen states before going on the circuit for the Democrats in his home state of Illinois.

Mass meetings were not the only means used by the parties in getting their message out. Staunchly partisan newspapers played central roles in informing and mobilizing the electorate. Each party had its flagship paper usually located in Washington (such as the Democrats' Washington *Daily Union)* or in another large city (as, for example, the Whig's *New York Tribune).* Each state capital also had its own party newspapers—the Richmond *Whig*, the Indianapolis *State Sentinel*, the *Albany Evening Journal.* Newspaper editors such as the Whigs' Horace Greeley and Thurlow Weed, and the Democrats' John W. Forney and Edmund Burke, were important members of the party leadership. Their editorials set the tone for the local leadership and editors to pick up and repeat. In addition, editors, under party direction, published pamphlets circulated in the hundreds by Whig postmasters and by party workers. These pamphlets, some written in German, reported meetings, choice speeches, useful editorials, the lives and outlooks of the candidates, and other materials to be read by or to the faithful. Local party newspapers were constantly calling for more documents, suggesting their utility and importance. Campaign papers were set up in state capitals, and local party leaders and adherents were urged to distribute copies through meetings, party reading rooms, and face-to-face contacts. Editors and party workers compiled almanacs of useful information and compilations of speeches as guides and as lodestars for the faithful. Campaign biographies appeared, distinguished in 1852 by Pierce's life as told by his Bowdoin College classmate Nathaniel Hawthorne.

Incessant, organized, purposive activity was the hallmark of politics in 1852. The carnival air of the rallies, the boisterous children rushing about, the hangers-on off to the side, even the heckling by opponents, did not conceal the effectiveness of communication and mobilization. Campaigns stoked memories, emphasized differences, pointed with alarm. As one editor put it, the campaign was "a means of indoctrinating those who are not with us with the pure principles of our political faith; of strengthening the wavering, if we have any such, and of anchoring forever those who are already firm." Whatever internal divisions plagued party leaders, the campaigns were designed to bring people together and usually did so.

All this took money and, although far from perfect, the parties had developed regular means of fundraising. Leading adherents in every locality were expected to contribute substantially. Each congressional district was assigned a financial quota to be sent to the national committees. Each state and local committee made and imposed its assessments and often received from officeholders a portion of their salaries.

The role of the presidential candidates was also regularized by custom. They were

Bronzed plaque of General Scott.

not supposed to campaign directly. They did receive delegations at their homes to whom they addressed a few words. Occasionally they wrote strategic letters to some corner of the nation. Franklin Pierce followed convention, stayed at home, made a few local statements and waited. Winfield Scott, on the other hand, as the underdog, broke with convention by traveling on an alleged inspection tour in his role as general-in-chief of the United States army. This trip took him to several western states—all to the disgust and shock of the Democrats offended by this disregard of accepted proprieties.

The machinery of electoral mobilization was running well throughout the months of party combat. But campaigning for President (and governorships and congressional seats also up) involved much more than organization. At the center of the campaign was language—a political language of content, not cant, although framed often in extreme and hyperbolic ways. Party leaders realized that organization served one purpose—of getting a message out, of providing means of reacting to pictures of themselves and their opponents drawn by words. The message was the campaign, and that message had to benefit a particular party while, at the same time, aligning itself with American proprieties and values.

Much thought went into determining what to say. A very great deal was considered to be at stake. Simon Cameron of Pennsylvania was not entirely engaging in hyperbole when he argued that "upon the success of the democratic party . . . must depend, in the end, the very existence of our liberties." This election was "second in importance to none we have had." It was "a battle more important in its results than that of Trafalgar." But, since hoopla and hyperbole alone could not maintain interest, voters had to see the relation to their own concerns. Each party, therefore, honed a central message, a combination of strategy and ideology, and particular ways of presenting it. For the Whigs, the electoral arithmetic was not promising. Although presidential elections had been close since the mid-thirties, the Whigs had won only when the country was in economic crisis, as in 1840, or when the Democrats were badly split, as in 1848, and when, as in both cases, the Whigs nominated someone from outside their normal party ranks. In short, they had reason to believe that the Democrats had some national advantage electorally. So it was not surprising that the Democrats stressed party loyalty in their message, while the Whigs denounced blind loyalty and called on voters not to act like "branded sheep," and to vote on behalf of nation, not of party.

The Democrats' nomination of the comparatively unknown politician, Pierce, as their latest "Young Hickory," on a plat-form sought to remind everyone that he stood in direct descent from Andrew Jackson. As a volunteer general in the Mexican War, he was also seen as a match for his Whig opponent as a fighting man. The Whigs, in their turn, had nominated General Scott, rather than a party wheelhorse such as Millard Fillmore, because, as one editor pointed out, Scott, "the hero of a hundred battles," was "stronger than the party" and would bring the Whigs extra votes. But this strategy did not "sacrifice . . . the principle of party fidelity." Scott was also a good and devoted Whig who would push Whig principles and help Whig candidates for other offices.

In discussing the issues, the rhetorical structure was the same for each party. Each sought to align itself firmly with existing consensual values, that is to establish legitimacy before the electorate, and then do one's best to denigrate and delegitimize the other side. Such consensual language resonated directly with the existing political culture.

First among these was the dark question of each party's illegitimate ancestry. "Keep it before the people," a Democratic editor wrote, "that the leading, the most prominent Whigs of the Union are in feeling and sentiment the 'lineal descendants' of the old FEDERAL PARTY, of Hartford Convention memory, which was opposed to the War of 1812." Not true, the *American Whig Review* replied, the Democratic name was "ingeniously assumed by the old Federalists when the majority of them passed over to the party of General Jackson." Clearly, the federalism of the pre-1815 era was redolent of defeat, despair and treason.

The second consensual theme involved the honesty and commitment of each party.

NO GO AND GOING WITH A RUSH.

Published by J. Childs, 84, Nassau S⁰ N.York

1852 caricature print. Pierce races ahead on a Democratic horse while Scott is stalled on a jackass. Scott is aided by William Seward and the Native Americans while the Whig donkey is prodded from behind by blacks with pitchforks.

The American political culture still contained elements of an earlier antipartyism, or at least of that part of it which suggested that parties too often were deceptive and manipulative of the people's will. "Self interest inspires" the Democratic party, "circumstances govern it, and artifice is its main helper," was a Whig editor's summary. He was quickly countered by the Democrats' response that "the great distinction between the two political organizations . . . is that the Democratic party is based and conducted upon principle, and the Whig party upon expediency." Such familiar, delegitimizing, charges were constantly repeated.

The final consensual articulation was more specific to present day concerns. The conflict over slavery extension still shadowed American politics with the recent uproar over the territories and the active presence of the remnants of 1848's Free Soil Party behind their 1852 candidate, John P. Hale. Both major parties used the same formula—that the compromise measures of 1850 settled all outstanding matters. There were, they suggested, more important issues to discuss. Some thrust and counter-thrusts did emerge over which party was more faithful to the Compromise of 1850 and more devoted in the commitment to move beyond sectional issues. "While the country had been quarreling about sectional issues," the New York Democrat and former Free Soiler, John Dix, complained, "selfish men, and more selfish associations have been depredating upon the public treasure."

Cartoon of a boxing match between Scott and Pierce. Chapultepec refers to the fortress captured by General Scott during the Mexican War (1846–48).

GRAND FIGHT FOR THE CHAMPIONS BELT BETWEEN GRANITE PIERCE & OLD CHAPULTEPEC.

When managers moved into the specifics of what divided the parties from each other, they also found plenty to discuss. Whigs and Democrats clearly disagreed over policy measures, such as the level of tariff protection and the federal role in promoting economic development, stretching back to the Jacksonian era. In the current election, one editor argued, "the parties, the policies, the measures, and the men opposed to each other were, in general, as different as possible, in nearly all points, whether doctrinal, or practical, or personal. They offer not merely a comparison. but a contrast."

Such differences went back to the original advocacy by John Quincy Adams in his first annual message in 1825, of a vigor-

ous government role in the process of economic development. Democrats continued to be fearful of any manipulation of the natural order of the economy on behalf of private economic interests. Pierce, his supporters claimed, was "a politician of the Virginia school, in favor of an economical administration of the general government, of a strict construction of the constitution, and as a republican of the Jeffersonian cast." To the Whigs, in contrast, the Democrats were "the do-nothing school of politicians, who adjure all the essential powers of the Constitution." But "negatives are not principles." The Whigs, in their turn, expounded their usual notions of vigorous government action. "Protection to American labor," for example, was "a Whig doctrine," as was internal improvements by an activist government. To both sides "the issues of the day" continued to be those that a generation had fought over for almost thirty years. Others in this category included differences over foreign affairs—the Democrats were too aggressive, the Whigs were too pusillanimous.

At the same time, a new agenda was also emerging in 1852. Each party tried to position itself to take advantage of it as best it could. Slavery extension and nativism, which were to be become the main political issues of the mid-1850s, now appeared on the scene. Both parties sought to take advantage of ethnic and religious divisions. Democrats had long enjoyed the support of Irish Catholics in the cities. In 1852, Whigs tried very hard to win them over to "the Irishman's friend," Scott on the ground of General Pierce's alleged hostility to Catholics.

The style of political discourse of the day called for the most lurid, frightening language. Both parties employed the most polarizing, threatening messages they could devise. At the same time, neither tried to disguise their very different world views about matters of economic development and federal power. Some of the language was quite personal—negative campaigning was not the creation of another age. Pierce was, in Whig eyes, a coward in Mexico and a drunk all the time. For Democrats, Scott was silly, befuddled, and inept. Behind character assassination lay still another long standing issue: the qualities and abilities needed to run the country. To Whigs, Pierce was "a fourth-rate lawyer" and "a small [rather] than a great soldier." The Democrats actually issued a pamphlet "Dangers of Electing an Incompetent Man President." Still, the extremism of the language should not blind anyone to the

alternatives offered, the chords touched, and the strategies followed in the slashing give and take of words.

By early fall the campaign was in high gear and unrelenting. Both parties displayed great energy and intensity. To be sure, there were always loose ends, missed opportunities, and uncovered areas. Organization was never quite perfect, communications could always be improved. However, the purpose was clearcut and the coverage extensive.

There were several different polling days starting with a few state elections in October which always signaled the way that the canvass was going, to the presidential polling day in November. Each party compiled local poll books listing the names and partisan identification of every voter. The leaders brought their own partisans to polling stations by wagon and horseback. They supplied voters with ballots to be deposited in the poll boxes. Activists stood by the polls to watch and count and prevent mischief (such as switching ballots) by the other side. Election day was a fitting, well-organized, and energetic finale to all that had gone before.

By nightfall on November 2, the issue was settled. Franklin Pierce's smashing victory (254 to 42 in the electoral college, 51 to 44 percent in the popular vote) was the product of shrewd organizing and campaigning and the ability of Democrats to maximize their normal popular majority. As the last election in the two-party system established in the Jacksonian era, the 1852 contest nicely showed the development and maturing of the structure of American campaigning amid the populist democracy that defined the American political culture at mid-century.

Grand National Banner print for the Democratic candidates.

Carte de visite of Pierce, circa 1861.

Campaign biography of the
Democratic presidential and
vice presidential candidates.

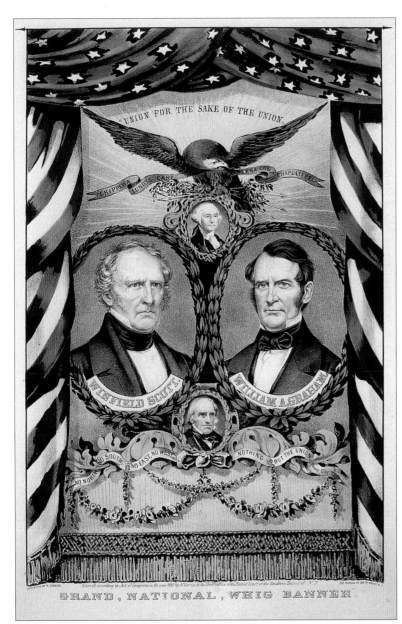

Grand National Banner print for the Whig candidates.

Miniature painting on glass of Scott
is mounted as a brooch.

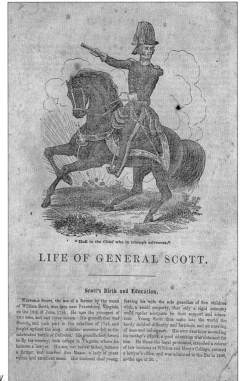

A Scott campaign biography.

Silk ribbon glorifying General Scott's military career. "Lundy's Lane" (July 1814) was the most contested land battle of the War of 1812.

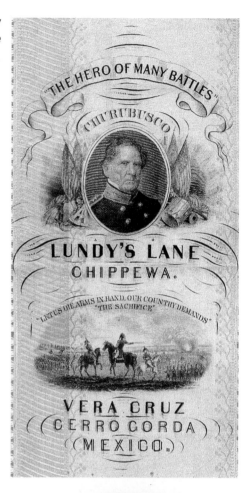

Felt table cover with a portrait of Daniel Webster. It is bordered by elaborate floral patterns and urns in each corner.

Silk ribbon with Pierce and King portraits.

Pair of high-relief metal plaques of Pierce and Scott.

Cigar box labeled "GENERAL FRANKLIN PIERCE."

"GEN. PIERCE'S GRAND MARCH," is one of the few campaign
items showing Pierce in military uniform.

PRESIDENT PIERCE'S
INAUGURAL ADDRESS,
MARCH 4th, 1853.

My Countrymen—

It is a relief to feel that no heart but my own can know the personal regret and bitter sorrow over which I have been borne to a position, so suitable for others, rather than desirable for myself.

The circumstances under which I have been called, for a limited period, to preside over the destinies of the Republic, fill me with a profound sense of responsibility, but with nothing like shrinking apprehension: I repair to the post assigned, not to one sought, but in obedience to the unsolicited expression of your will, answerable only for a faithful, and diligent exercise of my best powers.

I ought to be, and am, truly grateful for the rare manifestation of a nation's confidence, but this, so far from lightening my obligations, only adds to their weight. You have summoned me in my weakness, you must sustain me by your strength. When looking for the fulfilment of reasonable requirements, you will not be unmindful of the great changes which have occurred, even within the last quarter of a century, and the consequent augmentation and complexity of duties imposed, in the administration both of your home and foreign affairs.

Whether the elements of inherent force in the Republic have kept pace with its unparalleled progression in territory, population, and wealth, has been the subject of earnest thought and discussion, on both sides of the ocean. Less than sixty-three years ago, the Father of his country made "the" then "recent accession of the important State of North Carolina to the Constitution of the United States," one of his special congratulations. At that moment, however, when the agitation consequent upon the revolutionary struggle had subsided, when we were just emerging from the weakness and embarrassments of the Confederation, there was an evident consciousness of vigor, equal to the great mission so wisely and bravely fulfilled by our fathers.

It was not a presumptuous assurance, but a calm faith, springing from a clear view of the sources of power, in a government constituted like ours. It is no paradox to say that, although comparatively weak, the new-born nation was intrinsically strong Inconsiderable in population and apparent resources, it was upheld by a broad and intelligent comprehension of rights, and an all-pervading purpose to maintain them, stronger than armaments. It came from the furnace of the revolution, tempered to the times. The thoughts of the men of that day were as practical as their sentiments were patriotic. They wasted no portion of their energies upon idle and delusive speculations, but, with a firm and fearless step, advanced beyond the governmental land-marks, which had hitherto circumscribed the limits of human freedom, and planted their standard where it has stood, against dangers which have threatened from abroad, and internal agitation, which has at times fearfully menaced at home. They proved themselves equal to the solution of the great problem, to understand which their minds had been illuminated by the dawning lights of the revolution. The object sought was not a thing dreamed of—it was a thing realized. They had exhibited not only the power to achieve, but what all history affirms to be so much more unusual, the capacity to maintain. The oppressed throughout the world, from that day to the present, have turned their eyes hitherward, not to find those lights extinguished, or to fear lest they should wane, but to be constantly cheered by their steady and increasing radiance.

In this our country has, in my judgment, thus far fulfilled its highest duty to suffering humanity. It has spoken, and will continue to speak, not only by its words but by its acts, the language of sympathy, encouragement and hope, to those who earnestly listen to tones which pronounce for the largest rational liberty. But, after all, the most animating encouragement and potent appeal for freedom will be its own history, its trials, and its triumphs. Pre-eminently the power of our advocacy reposes in our example; but no example, be it remembered, can be powerful for lasting good, whatever apparent advantages may be gained, which is not based upon eternal principles of right and justice. Our fathers decided for themselves, both upon the hour to declare and the hour to strike. They were their own judges of the circumstances, under which it became them to pledge each other "their lives, their fortunes, and their sacred honor," for the acquisition of the priceless inheritance transmitted to us. The energy with which that great conflict was opened, and, under the guidance of a manifest and beneficent Providence, the uncomplaining endurance with which it was prosecuted to its consummation, were only surpassed by the wisdom and patriotic concession which characterized all the counsels of the early fathers.

One of the most impressive evidences of that wisdom is to be found in the fact, that the actual working of our system has dispelled a degree of solicitude, which, at the outset, disturbed bold hearts and far-reaching intellects. The apprehension of dangers from extended territory, multiplied States, accumulated wealth and augmented population, has proved to be unfounded. The Stars upon your banner have become nearly three-fold their original number, your densely populated possessions skirt the shores of the two great oceans, and yet this vast increase of people and territory has not only shown itself compatible with the harmonious action of the States and the Federal Government in their respective constitutional spheres, but has afforded an additional guarantee of the strength and integrity of both.

With an experience thus suggestive and cheering, the policy of my administration will not be controlled by any timid forebodings of evil from expansion. Indeed, it is not to be disguised that our attitude as a nation, and our position on the globe, render the acquisition of certain possessions, not within our jurisdiction, eminently important for our protection, if not, in the future, essential for the preservation of the rights of commerce and the peace of the world. Should they be obtained, it will be through no grasping spirit, but with a view to obvious national interest and security and in a manner entirely consistent with the strictest observance of national faith. We have nothing in our history or position to invite aggression, we have everything to beckon us to the cultivation of relations of peace and amity with all nations. Purposes, therefore, at once just and pacific, will be significantly marked in the conduct of our foreign affairs.

I intend that my administration shall leave no blot upon our fair record, and trust I may safely give the assurance that no act within the legitimate scope of my constitutional control will be tolerated, on the part of any portion of our citizens, which cannot challenge a ready justification before the tribunal of the civilized world. An administration would be unworthy of confidence at home or respect abroad, should it cease to be influenced by the conviction that no apparent advantage can be purchased at a price so dear as that of national wrong or dishonor. It is not your privilege, as a nation, to speak of a distant past. The striking incidents of your history replete with instruction, and furnishing abundant grounds for hopeful confidence, are comprised in a period comparatively brief. But if your past is limited, your future is boundless. Its obligations throng the unexplored pathway of advancement, and will be limitless as duration. Hence, a sound and comprehensive policy should embrace, not less the distant future, than the urgent present.

The great objects of our pursuit, as a people, are best to be attained by peace, and are entirely consistent with the tranquility and interests of the rest of mankind. With the neighboring nations upon our continent, we should cultivate kindly and fraternal relations. We can desire nothing in regard to them so much as to see them consolidate their strength, and pursue the paths of prosperity and happiness. If, in the course of their growth, we should open new channels of trade, and create additional facilities for friendly intercourse, the benefits realized will be equal and mutual. Of the complicated European systems of national polity we have heretofore been independent. From their wars, their tumults and anxieties, we have been, happily, almost entirely exempt. Whilst these are confined to the nations which gave them existence, and within their legitimate jurisdiction, they cannot affect us, except as they appeal to our sympathies in the cause of human freedom and universal advancement. But the vast interests of commerce are common to all mankind, and the advantages of trade and international intercourse must always present a noble field for the moral influence of a great people.

With these views firmly and honestly carried out, we have a right to expect, and shall under all circumstances require, prompt reciprocity. The rights which belong to us as a nation, are not alone to be regarded, but those which pertain to every citizen in his individual capacity, at home and abroad, must be sacredly maintained. So long as he can discern every star in its place upon that ensign without wealth to purchase for him preferment, or title to secure for him place, it will be his privilege, and must be his acknowledged right, to stand unabashed even in the presence of princes, with a proud consciousness that he is himself one of a nation of sovereigns, and that he cannot, in legitimate pursuit wander so far from home, that the agent, which he shall leave behind in the place which I now occupy, will not see that no rude hand of power or tyrannical passion is laid upon him with impunity. He must realize that upon every sea, and on every soil, where our enterprise may rightfully seek the protection of our flag, American citizenship is an inviolable panoply for the security of American rights. And, in this connexion, it can hardly be necessary to re-affirm a principle which should now be regarded as fundamental. The rights, security, and repose of this Confederacy reject the idea of interference or colonization, on this side of the ocean, by any foreign power, beyond present jurisdiction, as utterly inadmissible.

The opportunities of observation, furnished by my brief experience as a soldier, confirmed in my own mind the opinion, entertained and acted upon by others from the formation of the government, that the maintenance of large standing armies in our country would be not only dangerous, but unnecessary. They also illustrated the importance, I might well say the absolute necessity of the military science and practical skill furnished, in such an eminent degree, by the institution, which has made your army what it is, under the discipline and instruction of officers, not more distinguished for their solid attainments, gallantry, and devotion to the public service, than for unobtrusive bearing and high moral tone. The army, as organized, must be the nucleus, around which in every time of need, the strength of your military power, the sure bulwark of your defence —a national militia—may be readily formed into a well disciplined and efficient organization. And the skill and self-devotion of the navy assure you that you may take the performance of the past as a pledge for the future, and may confidently expect that the flag, which has waved its untarnished folds over every sea, will still float in undiminished honor. But these, like many other subjects, will be appropriately brought, at a future time, to the attention of the co-ordinate branches of the government, to which I shall always look with profound respect and with trustful confidence that they will accord to me the aid and support which I shall so much need, and which their experience and wisdom will readily suggest.

In the administration of domestic affairs, you expect a devoted integrity in the public service, and an observance of rigid economy in all departments, so marked as never justly to be questioned. If this reasonable expectation be not realized, I frankly confess that one of your leading hopes is doomed to disappointment, and that my efforts, in a very important particular, must result in a humiliating failure. Offices can be properly regarded only in the light of aids for the accomplishment of these objects; and as occupancy can confer no prerogative, nor importunate desire for preferment any claim, the public interest imperatively demands that they be considered with sole reference to the duties to be performed. Good citizens may well claim the protection of good laws and the benign influence of good government; but a claim for office is what the people of a Republic should never recognize.

No reasonable man of any party will expect the administration to be so regardless of its responsibility, and of the obvious elements of success, as to retain persons known to be under the influence of political hostility and partizan prejudice, in positions which will require not only severe labor, but cordial co-operation. Having no implied engagements to gratify, no rewards to bestow, no resentments to remember, and no personal wishes to consult, in selections for official station, I shall fulfil this difficult and delicate trust, admitting no motive as worthy either of my character or position, which does not contemplate an efficient discharge of duty, and the best interests of my country. I acknowledge my obligations to the masses of my countrymen, and to them alone.

Higher objects than personal aggrandizement gave direction and energy to their exertions in the late canvass, and they shall not be disappointed. They require at my hands diligence, integrity, and capacity, wherever there are duties to be performed. Without these qualities in their public servants, more stringent laws, for the prevention or punishment of fraud, negligence, and peculation, will be vain. With them, they will be unnecessary.

But these are not the only points to which you look for vigilant watchfulness. The dangers of a concentration of all power in the general government of a confederacy like ours are too obvious to be disregarded. You have a right, therefore, to expect your agents, in every department, to regard strictly the limits imposed upon them by the Constitution of the United States.

The great scheme of our constitutional liberty rests upon a proper distribution of power between the State and Federal authorities; and experience has shown, that the harmony and happiness of our people must depend on a just discrimination between the separate rights and responsibilities of the States, and your common rights and obligations under the general government. And here, in my opinion, are the considerations which should form the true basis of future concord in regard to the questions which have most seriously disturbed public tranquility. If the Federal Government will confine itself to the exercise of powers clearly granted by the Constitution, it can hardly happen that its action upon any question should endanger the institutions of the States, or interfere with their right to manage matters strictly domestic according to the will of their own people.

In expressing my views upon an important subject, which has recently agitated the nation to almost a fearful degree, I am moved by no other impulse than a most earnest desire for the perpetuation of that Union, which has made us what we are—showering upon us blessings, and conferring a power and influence which our fathers could hardly have anticipated, even with their most sanguine hopes, directed to a far off future. The sentiments I now announce were not unknown before the expression of the voice which called me here. My own position upon this subject was clear, unequivocal, upon the record of my words and my acts, and it is only recurred to at this time because silence might, perhaps, be misconstrued. With the Union my best and dearest earthly hopes are entwined. Without it, what are we, individually or collectively? What becomes of the noblest field ever opened for the advancement of our race, in religion, in government, in the arts, and in all that dignifies and adorns mankind?

From that radiant constellation, which both illumines our own way and points out to struggling nations their course, let but a single star be lost, and, if there be not utter darkness, the lustre of the whole is dimmed. Do my countrymen need any assurance that such a catastrophe is not to overtake them while I possess the power to stay it? It is with me an earnest and vital belief, that as the Union has been the source, under Providence, of our prosperity to this time, so it is the surest pledge of a continnance of the blessings we have enjoyed, and which we are sacredly bound to transmit undiminished to our children. The field of calm and free discussion in our country is open, and will always be so, but it never has been, and never can be traversed for good in a spirit of sectionalism and uncharitableness. The founders of the republic dealt with things as they were presented to them, in a spirit of self-sacrificing patriotism, and, as time has proved, with a comprehensive wisdom, which it will always be safe for us to consult. Every measure, tending to strengthen the fraternal feelings of all the members of our Union, has had my heart-felt approbation. To every theory of society or government, whether the offspring of feverish ambition or of morbid enthusiasm, calculated to dissolve the bonds of law and affection which unite us, I shall interpose a ready and stern resistance. I believe that involuntary servitude, as it exists in different States of this confederacy, is recognized by the constitution. I believe that it stands like any other admitted right, and that the States where it exists are entitled to efficient remedies to enforce the constitutional provisions.

I hold that the laws of 1850, commonly called the "compromise measures," are strictly constitutional, and to be unhesitatingly carried into effect. I believe that the constituted authorities of this Republic are bound to regard the rights of the South in this respect, as they would view any other legal and constitutional right, and that the laws to enforce them should be respected and obeyed, not with a reluctance encouraged by abstract opinions as to their propriety in a different state of society, but cheerfully, and according to the decision of the tribunal to which their exposition belongs. Such have been, and are, my convictions, and upon them I shall act. I fervently hope that the question is at rest, and that no sectional, or ambitious, or fanatical excitement may again threaten the durability of our institutions, or obscure the light of our prosperity.

But let not the foundation of our hope rest upon man's wisdom. It will not be sufficient that sectional prejudices find no place in the public deliberations. It will not be sufficient that the rash counsels of human passion are rejected. It must be felt that there is no national security but in the nation's humble, acknowledged dependence upon God and his overruling providence.

We have been carried in safety through a perilous crisis. Wise counsels, like those which gave us the constitution, prevailed to uphold it. Let the period be remembered as an admonition, and not as an encouragement, in any section of the Union, to make experiments where experiments are fraught with such fearful hazard. Let it be impressed upon all hearts, that beautiful as our fabric is, no earthly power of wisdom could ever re-unite its broken fragments.

Standing as I do almost within view of the green slopes of Monticello, and, as it were, within reach of the tomb of Washington, with all the cherished memories of the past gathering around me, like so many eloquent voices of exhortation from Heaven, I can express no better hope for my country, than that the kind Providence which smiled upon our Fathers, may enable their children to preserve the blessings they have inherited.

HOLBROOK, PRINT.

Hand-tinted lithograph by Charles Magnus of New York showing the Presidents of the United States.

*Opposite: Text of Pierce's
inaugural address printed on silk.*

★

1856

31 STATES
IN THE UNION

DEMOCRAT

James Buchanan

ELECTORAL VOTE 174, POPULAR VOTE 45.3%

REPUBLICAN

John C. Frémont

ELECTORAL VOTE 114, POPULAR VOTE 33.1%

AMERICAN (KNOW-NOTHING)

Millard Fillmore

ELECTORAL VOTE 8, POPULAR VOTE 21.6%

MICHAEL F. HOLT
is Langbourne M. Williams Professor of
American History at the University of Virginia.
He is the author of several books and articles on
the politics of the 1850s including *Forging A
Majority: The Formation of the Republican
Party in Pittsburgh, 1848–1860* (1969); and *The
Political Crisis of the 1850s* (1978). He is
currently writing a history of the Whig party.

During the presidential election of 1856, no major innovations in the techniques used by political parties to mobilize voters were introduced, but a major shift in the tactical goals such techniques were intended to achieve was produced. Because custom prohibited presidential candidates in the nineteenth century from personal campaigning, their characters and abilities usually mattered far less to voters than the political party they represented. Since the 1830s the vast majority of voters had enlisted behind one of two major parties—the Whigs or the Democrats—and their devotion to those organizations had been both passionate and steadfast. Hence the goal of both parties had been to reinforce the emotional attachment and arouse the competitive spirit of the party faithful in order to generate the largest possible turnout of the previously committed. First-time voters were wooed, but parties wasted little effort trying to convert the rank-and-file of the opposition.

By 1856 the parties had perfected a variety of techniques to achieve these goals. Multilayered local organizations canvassed potential voters months before the election, identified friends and foes, and made sure that supporters were supplied with party-printed ballots to cast on election day. To instill in voters a sense that they were participants in rather than mere spectators to, the combat between parties, each party entertained supporters with barbecues, stirred enthusiasm with mass rallies (featuring officeholders and—especially—presidential electors as surrogate speakers for presidential candidates), and rekindled organizational loyalties by holding torchlight parades led by bands where party members marched in phalanx and often in distinctive party uniforms and drove wagons carrying posters, banners, and gigantic illuminated transparencies with pictures of the party's candidates. To stir competitive juices still further and personify interparty conflict, the parties also arranged debates between speakers from the rival parties, so that supporters of each had a chance to cheer on its champions and boo its foes.

No campaign consisted solely of hoopla, however. Campaign biographies, pamphlets, congressional speeches, and newspaper editorials were distributed by the hundreds of thousands and were perused in party reading rooms as well as private homes. Even without radio and television, the nineteenth-century electorate may have been better informed about contrasting party positions on issues than their twentieth-century counterpart. Serious printed matter was always supplemented by lighter fare. Glee clubs sang campaign songs. Cartoons mocked opponents and portrayed the party's candidate as a sure winner. Widespread betting on the election's outcome, with the projected size of majorities in individual states used as handicaps, complemented the favorite metaphor of songs and cartoons—a horse race—and gave party loyalists additional incentive to maximize turnout.

Frémont silk ribbon. Explorer, politician, and soldier, Frémont was the first presidential candidate of the Republican party.

All these techniques were utilized in 1856, but the traditional objective of using them to reawaken party identities and reignite reciprocal animosities no longer sufficed. The election of 1856 occurred in the midst of a tumultuous period characterized by a sectional strife over the extension of slavery so rancorous as to threaten to disrupt the Union, by powerful nativist and anti-Catholic hysteria, by widespread disgust with politicians and politics as usual, by an extensive realignment of voters' allegiances, and by the mushrooming of new parties. One of the major contestants in 1852, the Whig party, had almost completely disintegrated by the start of 1856. It had been displaced by two new populistic parties competing to rally the anti-Democratic vote—the exclusively northern Republican party that opposed the extension of slavery and demanded that the North, not the South, control the national government and the anti-immigrant, anti-Catholic American or ("Know-Nothing") party that had emerged from the off-year state and congressional elections of 1854 and 1855 as the fastest-growing political force in the nation. Meanwhile, the Democrats, after winning the presidency in 1852, had suffered massive defections of their northern electorate while their incumbent President Franklin Pierce was widely discredited because of his complicity in the enactment and enforcement of the Kansas-Nebraska Act (which had reignited sectional wrangling over the extension of slavery) and his blatant courting of foreigners and Catholics with his patronage policies.

All this sharply differentiated the election of 1856 from its five predecessors. The three-way race complicated calculations as to how any single party could amass a majority of electoral votes and raised the very real possibility that the election would be thrown into the House of Representatives, where the Know-Nothings might have a decisive advantage. That situation in turn forced all three parties to focus their efforts on particular states and regions and to write off others. The frenzied atmosphere surrounding the election gave issues unusual salience, for the stakes seemed enormously high: whether to break the grip of the South on Washington and thus protect the liberties of northerners from an apparent Slave Power conspiracy against them, to defend southern rights from northern assault, to check a purported papal plot against republican self-government by restoring native-born Protestants to the rule of America, or to save the Union from the disruption that many were sure would follow a Republican triumph. Consequently, the style of campaigns in 1856 cannot be separated from their substance. Vital issues, far more than techniques, generated a higher level of voter turnout that year than any yet reached in a presidential election.

The election of 1856 also challenged the logic of traditional tactics and demanded new approaches. Pre-election canvassing usually required efficient local organizations and had always relied on fixed party identities among the electorate, but by 1856 many local organizations had been shattered and voters' loyalties oscillated from week to week in response to events. Techniques aimed at arousing the previously committed against traditional foes were useless to new parties that lacked long-time supporters and were trying to combine former enemies in new coalitions. Because Democrats needed replacements for the defections they had suffered since 1852, all three parties in 1856 therefore gave priority to winning converts from other parties and mobilizing previous nonvoters,

Silk ribbon for Buchanan and Breckinridge.

Silk ribbin for Buchanan and Breckinridge.

BUCHANAN & BRECKINRIDGE.

rather than simply arousing the faithful. That goal meant exploiting current issues that appealed to voters in terms of demographic (rather than party) identities—voters were courted as northerners or southerners, Protestants or Catholics, native-born Americans or immigrants. All three parties also poached on the remnants of the once powerful Whig party, and in a nineteenth-century version of "Democrats for Nixon," each published endorsements of its candidate by prominent Whig leaders in hopes of swaying undecided Whig voters.

The Know-Nothings were first to name a ticket. Confident they could hold their own party members through their oaths of allegiance to the secret fraternal order from which the party had sprung, they reached for additional support by nominating Millard Fillmore, a former Whig President from New York, with a former Democrat, Andrew Jackson Donelson of Tennessee, as his running mate. A member of the order, Fillmore was not known as a nativist. The men behind Fillmore's nomination believed that his record of evenhandedly enforcing the Compromise of 1850 while President would rally a bipartisan coalition of conservative, pro-Union Whigs and Democrats from both sections who feared that a Republican triumph might provoke southern secession and who blamed Democrats for recklessly inflaming sectional conflict.

Fillmore's nomination gave a schizophrenic tone to the Know-Nothing effort. During 1854 and 1855, Know-Nothing campaigns in cities had been (often quite literally) hard-hitting. Gangs of Know-Nothing toughs had roamed the streets on election day, maiming and murdering immigrants to stop them from voting. In cities such as Baltimore and New Orleans, where Know-Nothing lodges managed Fillmore's campaign, violence against potential Democratic voters was once again the order of the day. In contrast to this working-class rough-and-tumble, Fillmore's campaign team, which Fillmore himself controlled, took the high road by presenting Fillmore as the only candidate who could peacefully resolve sectional conflict and reunite Americans in patriotic devotion to the nation. This theme assured that Know-Nothing rallies were heavily festooned with flags and other patriotic symbols, and that Know-Nothing speeches were larded with patriotic platitudes and encomiums to revolutionary forefathers like Washington. Because the party's leadership, unlike its rank-and-file, sought to calm rather than arouse sectional and partisan animosities, the campaign's tone was staid and sober compared with those of its opponents. In particular, the Know-Nothings eschewed the vitriolic attacks on Democrats that had characterized Whig (and previous Know-Nothing) campaigns.

Again in contrast to the vicious tactics of grassroots Know-Nothing clubs, the party leadership tried to exploit the widespread disgust with politics as corrupt and unresponsive by high-mindedly promising to restore politics to the supposed purity of an earlier age. Thus one pro-Fillmore cartoon, entitled "Fancied Security of the Rats," portrayed Fillmore as a farmer guarding a corn crib labeled the "Government Crib" into which his two opponents, the Republican John C. Frémont and the Democrat James Buchanan (with faces attached to the bodies of rats), were trying to climb. The vigilant

Silk ribbon for Fillmore and Donaldson with picture of Fillmore.

Fillmore tells the rats, "Ah, you rascals. I'll have a rap at you directly that will make you scatter and keep you away from this crib for four years."

From the moment of Fillmore's nomination in February, the Know-Nothing campaign encountered problems that raised new tactical imperatives. Spurning both Fillmore and the Know-Nothing platform as too pro-southern, most northern Know-Nothings rejected the nomination, bolted the party, and called for a North American convention to meet in New York City on June 12, five days before the Republican convention was to meet in Philadelphia. Violence in Kansas and the caning of Massachusetts Senator Charles Sumner by a South Carolinian in May intensified northern anger at the South and thereby increased the probability that northern Know-Nothings would merge with Republicans, an alliance that appeared to materialize when both the North American and Republican conventions nominated Frémont.

That bargain in June, however, hardly guaranteed northern Know-Nothing votes for Frémont in November, and for the remainder of the campaign Know-Nothings and Republicans engaged in a ferocious tug-of-war for this crucial bloc of northern voters. Know-Nothing strategists knew that they could never outbid Republicans in vituperating the South, so instead they exploited the anti-Catholicism of northern Know-Nothings by refurbishing Fillmore's nativist credentials and challenging those of Frémont. Returning from a European tour in June, Fillmore gave a brief speech endorsing all the antiforeign and anti-Catholic tenets of the Know-Nothing creed, a speech which Know-Nothings widely disseminated in pamphlet form. Simultaneously, Know-Nothing newspaper editors across the North published the false charge that Frémont himself was Catholic to deter Know-Nothings and other Protestants from supporting him. Because Democrats were assured of immigrant Catholic support and feared Frémont far more than Fillmore, they too cynically pilloried Frémont as a Catholic to prevent northern Protestants from rallying behind him.

Republicans, whose only hope was amassing the broadest possible coalition of northern voters, fought back. Because the party did not even form in many northern states until the spring of 1856, Republicans lacked well-oiled organizations and established voting habits. Instead, their strategy was to exploit northern resentment at so-called aggressions by a Slave Power conspiracy against the liberties and rights of northern whites, a conspiracy given concrete form by the twin issues of Bleeding Kansas and Bleeding Sumner. Bashing the South and calling on northerners to unite behind their party to defend their rights thus formed the primary themes of Republican speakers.

To outbid Know-Nothings for the votes of northern Know-Nothings, however, Republicans also had to counter the charge of Frémont's Catholicism. They frantically published evidence that Frémont was Episcopalian, secured endorsements from prominent Know-Nothings like James W. Barker (former president of the Know-Nothing national council), deployed former Know-Nothings as speakers for Frémont, and included anti-Catholic appeals in state platforms and local newspaper editorials in places where Know-Nothings had been especially strong. Further to co-opt the Know-Nothing appeal, Republicans organized hundreds of Wide-Awake marching clubs across the North, for Wide-Awakes had been a popular name for Know-Nothing lodges. Republicans also tried to exploit the antipolitician sentiment that had originally helped fuel the Know-Nothing outburst by presenting Frémont, who was considerably younger than Fillmore and Buchanan and who lacked the lengthy political experience of those two old pros, as an outsider, a fresh face, a man of the people. A popular Republican campaign song, sung to the tune of "Camptown Races," portrayed Frémont as a vigorous young mustang easily outdistancing the old and lame Buchanan.

Far more than either the Democrats or the Know-Nothings, Republicans depended upon whipping up enthusiasm among voters, especially younger voters, and they achieved dramatic success. Day and night, day after day, Frémont glee clubs sang, mass rallies drew spectacularly large crowds, and Republican supporters paraded through country hamlets and city streets. "Men, Women & Children all seemed to be out, with a kind of fervor I have never witnessed before in six Pres. Elections," exclaimed a veteran politico from Indiana. "Flags across the streets meet the eye in every direction; music in open carriages, with placards to announce political gatherings; ward meetings and mass meetings and committee meetings every day and every night," reported a stunned Philadelphian. Indeed, although the Republicans never managed completely to defuse the charge of Frémont's Catholicism, it was clear by September, when Republicans swept the state elec-

Small tooled-leather wallet with a painting on glass of Buchanan.

tions in Maine, that Frémont, not Fillmore, would garner the vast majority of the anti-Democratic vote in the North.

Republican success at Fillmore's expense in the North contributed to the unraveling of the other assumption upon which Know-Nothings based their hopes—Fillmore's supposed ability to rally a broad coalition of conservative, pro-Union Whigs and Democrats from both the North and South. The top priority of southerners was to stop Frémont, and as Fillmore's prospects in the North dimmed, Buchanan seemed to many of them the only candidate who could do it. By the fall, indeed, Fillmore's advisers knew that his only chance was to carry enough southern states to throw the election into the House, but that chance in turn depended upon proving that Buchanan could not carry key northern states that the Republicans had not yet sewed up.

To the Know-Nothings' dismay, moreover, many Whigs refused to come out for Fillmore because they spurned the Know-Nothings as a bigoted movement of lower-class rabble, and because they regarded Fillmore as an apostate from Whiggery for accepting their nomination. As Daniel Webster's old Massachusetts ally Rufus Choate, both of Maryland's senators, and even Henry Clay's son came out for Buchanan, Fillmore pathetically sought endorsements from uncommitted Whigs like Thomas Corwin of Ohio and Hamilton Fish of New York. Largely unsuccessful in that attempt, he helped arrange a convention of Whig veterans in September, but the Whig nomination they gave him was by that late date almost worthless.

Most crippling to Fillmore's hopes had been the nomination of Buchanan by the Democrats in May. The Know-Nothings had counted on running against either Pierce or Stephen Douglas, who both bore responsibility for the sectionally divisive Nebraska Act, and Buchanan's candidacy upset their calculations. As minister to England during Pierce's administration, Buchanan escaped the stigma attached to its domestic policies. As an experienced officeholder known as "The Old Functionary," Buchanan seemed a sage statesman who challenged Fillmore's claim to be the only safe pro-Union candidate. Thus virtually all conservative Democrats and many Whigs turned to him rather than Fillmore. Finally, as a Pennsylvanian who had built an efficient personal organization, Buchanan gave the Democrats an edge in what all three parties recognized was the pivotal state in the North.

Far more than the other two parties, the Democrats relied on traditional tactics to reinforce previous party identity and mobilize voters. Pillorying the Know-Nothings as un-American bigots, Democrats painted Republicans as nativist, abolitionist, and pro-black fanatics and called on former Democrats to come home. Songs and cartoons shrewdly mocked their enemies and praised the Democratic ticket of Buchanan and John C. Breckinridge. One cartoon entitled "Buck Taking the Pot," showed Buchanan holding a pot of "Union soup" and promising to share it with every state. Fillmore, blindfolded and holding a dark lantern in a gibe at the secret rituals of the Know-Nothings, gropes wildly for the pot and forlornly admits that Buchanan holds all the aces. Meanwhile Frémont lies prostrate far from the prized pot and complains that he has stumbled over the rock of disunion. Songs boasted that

> The Democrats are in the field,
> And are determined not to yield;
> And certainly they'll have good luck,
> For they have nominated "Buck."

and, to the tune of "Old Dan Tucker," that

> Oh! Buck and Breck are bound to win—
> No power can stop them coming in;
> The Pennsylvania steed is lucky,
> And so's the one from old Kentucky.
>
> Other nags may take the track,
> But never one that's safe to back—
> The woolly horse [Frémont] can't reach
>   the quarter,
> And what is more he hadn't orter.
>
> The thimble rigger's toadies say,
> Know Nothing stock will win the day;
> But thimble riggers are complaining,
> That he was broke down in the training.

Despite delightful ditties and clever cartoons, Democrats never generated as much enthusiasm as did the Republicans in 1856, but they possessed an asset of even greater value than enthusiasm—a well-drilled organization that raised and spent far more money than both their rivals combined, that marched Democratic voters to the polls on election day with machinelike efficiency, and that manufactured new Democratic voters where they were most needed. Ultimately, organization won the election for Buchanan, for in the end the race hinged on who would win October gubernatorial and congressional elections in Indiana and Pennsylvania. Democratic losses in one or both would have driven fearful conservatives, especially in the South, into the Fillmore camp and perhaps paved the way for a Fillmore or Frémont victory. Aware of the stakes, Democrats "piped" or "colonized" enough illegal voters from Kentucky, Ohio, Illinois, and Michigan into Indiana to win the governorship. Their feats in Pennsylvania, where they faced a combined Know-Nothing/Republican Union ticket in October, were even more prodigious. Awash in money, they flooded every home in Philadelphia and other parts of the state with Democratic propaganda. They paid taxes for thousands of Democratic voters who otherwise would not have met the state's suffrage requirements. And they illegally naturalized thousands of alien immigrants who gratefully cast Democratic ballots. Together these tactics allowed Democrats to eke out a narrow victory in the all-important Keystone State.

The October results killed Fillmore's chances, dampened Republican morale, and almost assured Buchanan's victory since now a sweep of the South seemed certain. At that point, only one thing could defeat

Carte de visite of Fillmore by Matthew Brady.

Buchanan—fusion of Fillmore/Frémont electoral tickets in crucial states of the lower North. But Millard Fillmore, who genuinely feared Frémont's victory far more than Buchanan's, intransigently forbade his supporters to enter into any such arrangments. Thus James Buchanan won the election of 1856 even though he garnered only 45 percent of the popular vote, by carrying every slave state except Maryland (Fillmore's lone trophy), and five critical northern states—California, Illinois, Indiana, Pennsylvania, and New Jersey. Frémont swept the rest of the North. Reciprocal resentments and fears between hostile groups, the enthusiasm generated by Republican hurrah techniques, and genuine fear for the safety of the Union evoked an enormous turnout, but it was a splendidly efficient, if occasionally lawless, organization that gave the White House to the Democrats for four more years.

Above: Two local political club silk campaign ribbons.
Right: Both silk ribbons were distributed nationally
and feature campaign slogans. The Buchanan ribbon reads:
"We Po'ked 'em in '44/We Pierced 'em in '52 and we'll Buck 'em in '56."

Metal pinback with a rebus design picturing buck+cannon [Buchanan] and Breckinridge.

Frémont silk ribbons. Known as the "Pathfinder," Frémont had explored and mapped areas west of the Mississippi River. Note this inscription on the ribbon at left.

Grand National Banner print of the Democratic candidates.

JAMES BUCHANAN.

"I most heartily pledge myself, should the nomination by the Convention be ratified by the people, that all the power and influence constitutionally possessed by the executive, shall be exerted in a firm but conciliatory spirit during the single term I shall remain in office, to restore the same harmony among the sister States which prevailed before this apple of discord, in the form of Slavery agitation, had been cast into their midst.

"Should I be placed in the Executive chair, I shall use my best exertions to cultivate peace and friendship with all nations believing this to be our HIGHEST POLICY, as well as our most IMPERATIVE DUTY.

JAMES BUCHANAN."

Buchanan silk ribbon with an excerpt from his July 16, 1856 letter accepting the Democratic nomination.

Campaign locket with ambrotype portraits of Buchanan and Breckinridge.

Metamorphosis mechanical card. Postage was only three cents in 1856.

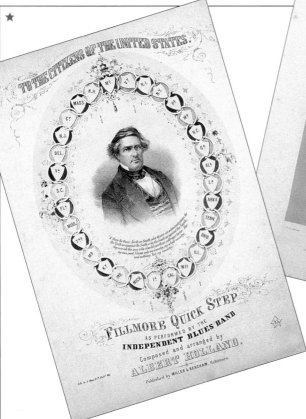

Selection of sheet music from the 1856 campaign. Collectors are attracted to the graphic quality of sheet music.

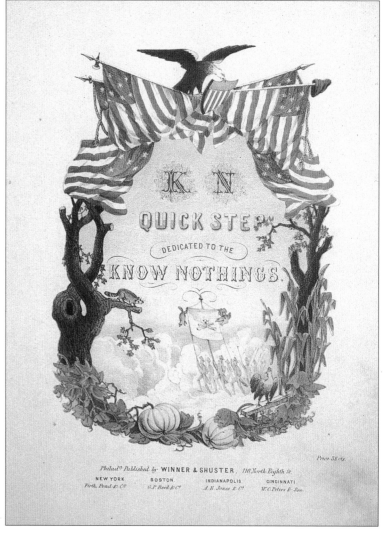

Silk ribbon for Fillmore and Donaldson with typical Know-Nothing quote.

FILLMORE

AND

DONELSON

THE
UNION

FILLMORE & DONELSON

NATIONAL UNION.

"I know nothing but my Country, my whole Country, and nothing but my Country."

Grand National Banner print of the American (Know-Nothing) party candidates.

Silk ribbons for Frémont. A large variety of ribbons were produced for John C. Frémont. The election of 1856 was the first time a candidate's wife appeared on campaign items.

A Frémont campaign biography.

A rare Frémont/Dayton cotton flag banner.

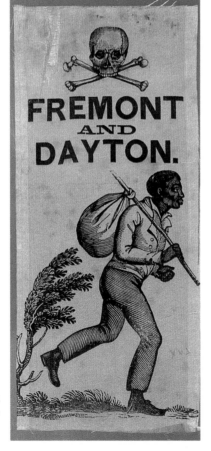

Truly a great satiric political ribbon. Frémont and the Republicans are mocked by the Democrats as radicals who will free the slaves while the American (Know-Nothing) party heads for Salt River, or oblivion.

Right: Ribbon depicting a fleeing slave shows the Democrats' blatant appeal to racism. Freedom, far right, was used generically on this Republican ribbon.

1860

33 STATES
IN THE UNION

REPUBLICAN

Abraham Lincoln

ELECTORAL VOTE 180, POPULAR VOTE 39.8%

DEMOCRAT

Stephen A. Douglas

ELECTORAL VOTE 12, POPULAR VOTE 29.5%

DEMOCRAT

John C. Breckinridge

ELECTORAL VOTE 72, POPULAR VOTE 18.1%

CONSTITUTIONAL UNION

John Bell

ELECTORAL VOTE 39, POPULAR VOTE 12.6%

In terms of its consequences, the 1860 presidential election was the most momentous in American history. The campaign preceding the election in November was, in the words of one historian, "a campaign like none other." Among its most unusual features was the fact that there were four major candidates in the field.

The first party to select a standard bearer was the Constitutional Union party, which was organized expressly for this election. Representing yet another attempt to form a national conservative organization in place of the defunct Whig party, its convention nominated for President John Bell of Tennessee, a southern moderate. He ran on a platform that simply called for the maintenance of the Constitution, the Union, and the laws.

The sectional controversy of the 1850s had taken its toll on the Democratic party, and the division now ran so deep that the northern and southern wings could not agree on a candidate. Eventually northern Democrats nominated Senator Stephen A. Douglas of Illinois on a platform upholding the doctrine of popular sovereignty (this was the idea that the residents of a territory should decide whether they wanted slavery or not). The vast majority of southern delegates bolted and nominated Vice President John C. Breckinridge on a platform calling for adoption of a congressional slave code for the territories. In the South, Breckinridge was considered the regular Democratic candidate.

The Republicans surprised veteran party watchers by selecting Abraham Lincoln of Illinois as their presidential nominee. Lincoln had been out of public office for more than a decade, but he had gained national attention from his debates with Douglas in 1858, was acceptable to all factions of the party, and came from a critical state. The delegates concluded that Lincoln was their strongest candidate, and he was nominated on the third ballot.

With the Democratic party divided, Republicans expected to win and, according to one party leader, "everywhere surpassed their opponents in earnestness and enthusiasm." Neither the Bell nor the Breckinridge parties conducted a particularly vigorous campaign. The Republicans and Douglas Democrats were much more energetic since the election would be decided in the North, and only Lincoln and Douglas had any chance of carrying free states. The only hope of defeating Lincoln was that Douglas would take enough northern states to send the election into the House of Representatives. Popular interest remained high despite the election's seemingly foreordained outcome.

To a large extent, campaign techniques in 1860 carried forward those developed in presidential elections since 1840. Parties relied on countless speeches by party orators to bring their message to the voters. Prominent Republicans such as William H. Seward and Salmon P. Chase stumped for Lincoln. In the North, a majority of Democratic leaders endorsed Douglas, while in the

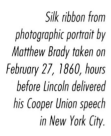

Silk ribbon from photographic portrait by Matthew Brady taken on February 27, 1860, hours before Lincoln delivered his Cooper Union speech in New York City.

of New Hampshire served as secretary and ran the speakers' bureau, and Senator Preston King of New York supervised the distribution of campaign literature from Washington. The key leaders of the Douglas campaign were Augustus Belmont, who was national chairman and took charge of fundraising, and Congressman Moses Taylor of Louisiana, who looked after day-to-day affairs mostly from Washington. The Breckinridge campaign was largely run from Washington by a group of party insiders; it was managed by Isaac Stevens of Oregon. Congressman Alexander Boteler of Virginia headed the Bell campaign apparatus.

The parties produced campaign documents of various kinds, including biographies of the candidates, congressional speeches, and short tracts written specifically for the election. Most pamphlets were distributed either by party newspapers, the state committee, or a congressional franking committee in Washington. With the biggest war chest, Republicans were the most active in circulating printed materials. They sent out copies of the Lincoln-Douglas debates of 1858, and Horace Greeley and John F. Cleveland brought together a number of important campaign documents in a *Political Textbook for 1860*, which went through fourteen editions. The power of the Republican juggernaut was demonstrated by the situation in Madison County, Illinois, a rural locality, where the party had disseminated an astonishing six thousand documents by the middle of June.

Several campaign biographies of Lincoln were produced. An early one by Ichabod Codding, an abolitionist, portrayed Lincoln as an advanced opponent of slavery and was immediately suppressed by ner-

South they mostly supported Breckinridge (although a few, headed by Alexander H. Stephens of Georgia, backed Douglas). Bell had some prominent supporters, but his campaign failed to attract young men, who traditionally supplied much of the energy and performed the bulk of the labor of a national campaign.

Campaign organizations followed the structure perfected in previous national campaigns. Governor Edwin D. Morgan of New York was chairman of the Republican campaign committee with primary responsibility for raising money, George G. Fogg

vous Republicans. William Dean Howells wrote a biography; he was later rewarded by appointment as consul in Venice. A life appeared in German, but the most widely circulated campaign biography in 1860, with estimated sales of 200,000 copies, was written by John Locke Scripps. Jointly sponsored by the Chicago *Tribune* and the *New York Tribune* and based partly on material supplied by the candidate, Scripps's thirty-two-page study sold for as little as two cents a copy in large lots. Republican clubs were urged to purchase multiple copies for distribution. The other parties did not go in for campaign biographies, except for a life of Douglas penned by James W. Sheehan of the Chicago *Times*.

Recognizing that naturalized voters were a key element in many northern states, Republicans made special appeals to Germans and other immigrant groups. Besides newspapers, campaign pamphlets, and documents in foreign languages, the party established a special division, headed by the German-American leader Carl Schurz, to coordinate foreign-born orators stumping for Lincoln.

Newspapers remained the primary means of reaching the voters. Most newspapers of this era were highly partisan, and hewed to the party line rather than objectively reporting the news. Republicans surpassed their opponents, both in the number and the quality of their papers. In the South, the press divided between Bell and Breckinridge, with a few sheets (such as John Forsythe's Mobile *Register*), supporting Douglas. Douglas's campaign was hurt by the absence of a major paper in either New York or Chicago; in the latter city, Cyrus McCorm-

Stephen A. Douglas silk ribbon from photographic portrait by Matthew Brady.

ick bought the financially strapped *Times* and promptly swung it away from Douglas. Special journals created for the campaign also appeared. The most famous was *The Rail Splitter*, a Republican sheet printed in Chicago. Published every Saturday, it included the usual partisan editorials and slanted news, along with cartoons, songs, and jokes designed to lampoon the opposition and bring a touch of humor to the campaign. It circulated widely among Republican clubs.

The other standard campaign practice, perfected earlier, was the mass meeting.

Throughout the contest, the parties held countless rallies, parades, picnics, barbecues, pole raisings, and other events to attract and entertain the masses. Flags, banners, and likenesses of the candidates decorated buildings and were strung across streets in countless communities. The Breckinridge forces, for example, kicked off their campaign with a large rally in Washington, D.C., featuring a speech by President James Buchanan. And Douglas was greeted by demonstrations in various communities he visited, including Chicago, where downtown buildings were illuminated in his honor and the occasion culminated with a spectacular show of fireworks.

Republicans held a well-publicized meeting in Lincoln's hometown of Spring-

field in August to ratify his nomination. Thousands of Republicans, including a number from nearby states, flocked to the Illinois capital on foot, on horseback, in wagons, and by specially chartered trains. The buildings in the center of town were decorated with flags, transparencies, and banners. A huge parade stretching some eight miles kicked off the proceedings at ten in the morning. At its head was an immense ball with mottoes such as "The Republican ball is in motion," and "We link—on to Lincoln—our fathers were for Clay." Then came Republican clubs and bands, couples on gaily decorated horses, floats, county and town delegations, and over a hundred wagons hauling celebrants. Wagons and floats were festively decorated and carried signs and prominently displayed vari-

Lincoln formally accepting the Republican party's nomination, Springfield, Illinois, June 16, 1860. Lincoln gave a ringing endorsement of the Union: "A house divided against itself cannot stand."

ILLINOIS STATE HISTORICAL LIBRARY

ous party symbols. Emblazoned with a banner that read "Protection to American Industries," one float even contained a woolen mill making cloth.

After passing Lincoln's home while the candidate watched from the front porch, the procession wound its way to the fairgrounds, where Republicans had erected five stands for the many speakers to address the assembled throng. Constant cheering and singing rent the air. Evening brought more speeches in town, along with a fireworks display and a torchlight parade past illuminated buildings. "As far as the eye could reach," one newspaper reported, ". . . a seemingly interminable line of flame stretched out its moving length." In all, perhaps fifty thousand people participated in the festivities.

To a much greater degree than in their first national campaign four years earlier, Republicans in 1860 utilized party symbols and exploited campaign pageantry. They emphasized Lincoln's humble origins, portraying the candidate as a self-made man and hence a symbol of democracy. This rail-splitter image began when his cousin John Hanks appeared at the Republican state convention in Decatur, Illinois, with two rails he claimed to have split with Lincoln in 1830. These objects created a sensation on the floor, and under the direction of Richard Oglesby, an Illinois Republican leader, an industry in Lincoln rails soon developed, as Republican clubs eagerly sought to purchase the genuine article or a close substitute. Banners and transparencies pictured Lincoln in rude western garb with an axe; split rails or a log cabin were often also visible.

Republicans routinely referred to their candidate as Honest Abe, Honest Old Abe, or

ILLINOIS STATE HISTORICAL LIBRARY

Detail of opposite photograph. Lincoln is seen somewhat clearer.

just Old Abe in order to enhance his image as a common man. This emphasis on Lincoln's personal integrity stood in sharp contrast to Buchanan's sorry record of corruption, and the nickname "Abe" reinforced the image of Lincoln as a humble man of the people. Ironically, Lincoln hated the name and never used it—its almost universal adoption was strictly for campaign purposes.

Party songs were another standard feature of the campaign. Here again, the Republicans outdid their opponents. Campaign songs were a traditional way of rousing enthusiasm and entertaining the faithful, and glee clubs often led the crowd in singing. Most songs contained little ideological content; a thumping melody and some sharp digs at the opposition were

SHAWNEE WIDE-A-WAKES.

Lincoln and Hamlin!

Wide-Awakers were ardent Lincoln supporters who paraded along military lines. Over their suits, they wore kepis and capes.

what counted. Of all the campaign songs Republicans sang in 1860, none was more popular than "Ain't you glad you joined the Republicans," set to the tune of "The Old Gray Mare." It began:

> Old Abe Lincoln came out of the wilderness,
> Out of the wilderness,
> out of the wilderness,
> Old Abe Lincoln came out of the wilderness,
> Down in Illinois.

The chorus went:

> Ain't you glad you joined the Republicans,
> Joined the Republicans,
> joined the Republicans,
> Ain't you glad you joined the Republicans,
> Down in Illinois?

On election night when Lincoln left the Springfield telegraph office once victory was assured, the crowd of Republicans outside spontaneously broke into this song.

Cartoons were an important feature of all four parties' campaigns, although Re-

publicans were again most active in this regard. Republican cartoons, and some issued by their opponents, incorporated the symbol of the split rail. Pro-Bell cartoons emphasized the Union issue and the extremism of the other candidates; a particularly well-executed drawing showed the other three candidates ripping the country apart while Bell tried to sew it back together. Both wings of the Democratic party aggressively exploited the race issue, and party cartoons frequently contained unfavorable images of blacks and ugly racial references. Opponents also routinely portrayed the Republican party as an extremist organization that threatened the Union. One anti-Lincoln cartoon, issued by Currier and Ives, showed Lincoln sitting on a rail held by Horace Greeley of the *New York Tribune* battering down the door to the lunatic asylum while an assortment of Republicans representing various radical enthusiasms wait to enter.

Vendors sold a wide variety of additional campaign items in 1860, and ardent partisans, including ladies, wore medals, ribbons, and other trinkets to proclaim their preferences. The well-funded Republicans distributed the largest number of such items. The Republican emphasis on symbols and Lincoln's personality accorded trinkets, visuals, and campaign paraphernalia a central role. Campaign tokens and badges referred to Honest Abe, Republican marchers carried axes, and party stationery displayed a split-rail fence as well as the candidate's visage. These objects sometimes contained references to issues, including slavery extension, the homestead law, the tariff, and the Union. Militantly antislavery items seem to have been circulated primarily if not exclusively in rock-ribbed Republican areas. Likewise,

Centerfold wood-block print from Harper's Weekly illustrating a Wide-Awake torchlight parade in New York City, October 3, 1860.

items endorsing a protective tariff were particularly used in Pennsylvania and New Jersey, where tariff sentiment was strong.

The Bell and Douglas campaign items emphasized the Union. One Bell token, for example, proclaimed "The Constitution and the Union/Now and Forever," while a campaign ribbon read, "The Union and the Constitution/One and Inseparable." Douglas items also stressed the Union, but many contained references to Douglas's doctrine of popular sovereignty. One Douglas token, with a rather long inscription, declared, "Popular Sovereignty/Non Intervention by the General Government in Any of the States or Territories of the Union/Let the People of Each Rule." Alone among the candidates, Breckinridge items paid only lip service to the Union, and often coupled references to it with endorsements of southern rights, as for example in the token that said, "Our Rights,

the Constitution and the Union." In New Orleans, an enraged mob nearly lynched a dealer of campaign buttons whose stock mistakenly included a Lincoln medal.

The major innovation of the Douglas campaign was an extensive speaking tour by the candidate. Before the Civil War presidential candidates, respecting the popular belief that it was improper to seek the office, traditionally did not campaign in person. Douglas initially announced his intention to follow this precedent, but facing an uphill battle, he changed his mind. His extensive speaking tour was unprecedented and in many ways foreshadowed modern presidential campaigns. Accompanied by his vivacious wife, who remained at his side throughout the campaign, Douglas left New York City in July under the guise of traveling to see his mother in upstate New York and visit his boyhood home in Vermont. Douglas's trip

Breckinridge-Lane ferrotype set in brass with stickpin on back.

fooled no one. From railroad platforms, hotel balconies, and other locations he delivered a series of political speeches warning that the Union was in peril. Tracing his circuitous route, the Republican press lampooned the candidate's "maternal pilgrimage" and circulated a broadside requesting information on the "lost" son.

Following his swing across New England, Douglas traveled through the upper South, emphasizing the Union issue and attacking the Breckinridge faction as disunionists. After a brief stop in New York City, he was off again, this time heading west. On September 15, two months after he had started, he was finally reunited with his mother. He then pushed across upstate New York and into the western states, delivering another series of political addresses along the way. When the October state elections in Pennsylvania, Indiana, and Ohio unmistakably indicated that Lincoln would be elected in November, the Illinois senator, defying threats to his personal safety, entered the deep South, speaking in Tennessee, Alabama, and Georgia. He continued to attack disunionists in the South, and as he had done earlier, denied that Lincoln's

election would justify secession. The Little Giant finished his strenuous three-and-a-half month campaign, during which he had spoken almost every day, on election eve in Mobile. He had visited twenty-three states in the Northeast, the Northwest, the upper South, and the deep South, and in the process broken his health.

In contrast to Douglas, Lincoln did not campaign in 1860. Adopting the time-honored stance of presidential candidates, Lincoln told one supporter, "By the lesson of the past, and the united voice of all discreet friends, I am neither [to] write or speak a word for the public." Setting up shop in the governor's room in the State House, he greeted visitors but said nothing of consequence. In fact, Lincoln was the least active of the four candidates and the only one who did not make a single speech.

Instead, the major innovation of the Republican party in the 1860 campaign was the Wide-Awake society. Marching clubs had appeared in earlier campaigns, but never on the scale or with such fanfare as the Wide-Awakes. The first Wide-Awake club had been formed in Hartford in February 1860, for the state election. The concept caught on, and in the summer of 1860 similar societies, also taking the name Wide-Awakes, were organized throughout the North. Communities wishing to organize official Wide-Awake societies were instructed to contact the Hartford club for information.

Made up mostly of young men, the Wide-Awakes were a Republican marching organization. Members sang campaign songs, shouted party chants, cheered and marched in Republican parades. Members also did much of the onerous daily work, such as distributing literature, putting up handbills, and compiling voter lists. Their uniform was made up of a military hat, glazed cape (to protect them from the oil drippings), and an oil lamp or torch, usually mounted on a rail and often decorated with a flag emblazoned with Lincoln's name. Enterprising merchants sold complete uniforms for $1.15 or more. It has been estimated that there were 400,000 Wide-Awakes in 1860. In the West, they sometimes took the name "Rail Splitters" or "Rail Maulers."

Members were organized along military lines with officers and privates. At night with their torches blazing they presented a spectacular sight. Officers carried different colored lanterns depicting their rank. They practiced intricate marching steps to entertain spectators, including a zig-zag maneuver that imitated a split-rail fence. Most clubs had a band that played martial music and campaign tunes, and as they marched, members sang campaign tunes and shouted partisan chants in unison.

The popularity of the Wide-Awakes prompted opponents to emulate their example. The Douglas forces organized the "Ever Readys," "Little Giants," and "Douglas Invincibles." The Bell organization followed suit with the "Bell Ringers," "Minute Men," and "Union Sentinels"; these clubs often carried bells as well as torches. Even the Breckinridge forces, though not numerous in the North, marched as "National Democratic Volunteers." None of these rival societies, however, attracted anywhere near the publicity or membership of the Wide-Awakes. Nor could they match the enthusiasm of the confident Republicans. At least one Republican campaign cartoon portrayed Lincoln as a Wide-Awake, alertly

preventing his opponents from breaking into the White House.

A monstrous Wide-Awake parade was held in New York City in October, shortly before the election. Republicans claimed that 100,000 people witnessed what they called a rally of banners of light. Spectators jammed Broadway as an estimated ten thousand Wide-Awakes marched in steady cadence, their lamps blazing, while rockets and roman candles roared from the rooftops across the sky. The martial music, spectacle of light, and rhythmic tread of the marchers mingled with cheers of spectators to produce a powerful impression.

Stimulated by the Republicans' pageantry and Douglas's speaking tour, the turnout was only slightly below that of 1856. Lincoln ran first among the four candidates but with less than 40 percent of the popular vote failed to gain a majority. He easily outdistanced his rivals in the electoral college, however, winning 180 electoral votes. Because of his strength in the heavily populated North, he was elected even though he did not carry a single southern state and had virtually no support in that region outside the border states. Even if the votes for Douglas, Bell, and Breckinridge had been combined behind a single candidate, Lincoln still would have won.

Aided by effective symbols such as the rail-splitter image and the Wide-Awake Society, Republicans had managed to carry their first national election. In response to Lincoln's victory, the states of the deep South seceded from the Union, and in April 1861, six weeks after he was inaugurated the first Republican President in American history, the Civil War began.

CHICAGO HISTORICAL SOCIETY

Above: Oil painting of Lincoln as the "Rail-splitter." The campaign theme was to portray Lincoln as a figure with whom ordinary Americans could identify.

THE GREAT UNION TORCHLIGHT PROCESSION IN NEW YORK, ON THE 23RD OF OCTOBER, 1860.—NO. 1. CAPTAIN RYNDERS' POCKET-PIECE.—NO. 2. FULL RIGGED SHIP, DRAWN BY TEN HORSES.—HORACE GREELEY AND A DARK-COLORED YOUNG LADY.—NO. 4 KNIGHTS OF THE UNION AND TEMPLE OF LIBERTY.—SEE PAGE 368.

GREAT UNION TORCHLIGHT PROCESSION IN NEW YORK— EMBLEMS IN THE FIRST DIVISION—NO. 1. WAGON WITH INSCRIPTIONS OF YOUNG MEN'S INDEPENDENT CLUB.—NO. 2. A FAST SPECIMEN AMERICA.—NO. 3. TRUCK BEARING INSCRIPTION AND SHIELDS OF THE THIRTEEN STATES.—SEE PAGE 368.

The great Union torchlight parade, New York City, October 23, 1860.

Multicolored political chart illustrating the 1860 candidates and the principal issues.

This fine silk ribbon features Brady portraits of Lincoln and Hamlin.

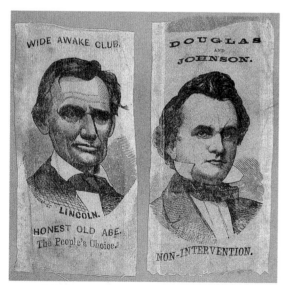

Pair of silk ribbons with engraved portraits of Lincoln and Douglas.

Above: There are many styles of Lincoln cotton flag banners from this campaign. The Douglas portrait flag banner, however, is an extremely rare item.
Below: Campaign imagery began to appear on cachets, or commemorative envelopes, circa 1856. These 1860 engraved envelopes have slogans and pictures of the candidates.

Foldout brass book-locket with photographs of Lincoln and Union generals.

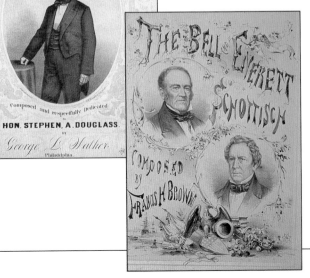

A variety of campaign sheet music.

The obverse and reverse of 1860 "donut" ferrotypes showing the four presidential and the four vice presidential candidates.

A Bell and Everett silk ribbon from photographic portraits by Matthew Brady.

Grand National Banner for Bell and Everett.

During the 1860 campaign, mass-produced photographs were sold to the public. In 1859 a process was developed for reproducing inexpensive sheets of tintypes (in smaller forms known as ferrotypes)—hence a new campaign item, photographs of the candidates. There are more than 120 different photographs of Lincloln.

Above: Ferrotype pin of Douglas and his wife. Left: Carte de visite of Stephen Douglas.

Silk ribbons from photographic portraits by Matthew Brady. John Bell (left) and John Breckinridge.

A. Lincoln.
President.

Plaster figurine of Douglas, circa 1860.

Left: Woven silk ribbon imported from Switzerland for Lincoln's 1861 inauguration. The image was taken from a Currier & Ives print after a Brady photo. Below: Lincoln shaving mug, circa 1862.

Milkglass plaque of Lincoln.

Tintype portraits of Lincoln and his wife Mary.

Portrait of President-elect Lincoln from
Frank Leslie's Illustrated Newspaper.

Staffordshire figurine of Lincoln.
British potters used an earlier mold
of Prince Albert to make this piece.

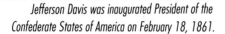

Jefferson Davis was inaugurated President of the
Confederate States of America on February 18, 1861.

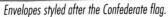

Envelopes styled after the Confederate flag.

Ferrotype portraits 1 1⁄2" in size, set in ornamental brass frames. Abraham Lincoln and Hannibal Hamlin, top row. Jefferson Davis and Alexander Stephens, below.

Jefferson Davis sheet music.

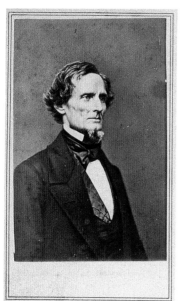

Jefferson Davis and Alexander Stephens cartes de visite. Stephens was vice president of the Confederacy.

Davis ferrotype medallion.

★

1864

36 STATES
IN THE UNION

REPUBLICAN

Abraham Lincoln

ELECTORAL VOTE 212, POPULAR VOTE 55%

DEMOCRAT

George B. McClellan

ELECTORAL VOTE 21, POPULAR VOTE 45%

HAROLD M. HYMAN
is William P. Hobby Professor of History and
director of the Center for the History of
Leadership Institutions at Rice University. The
winner of numerous awards for his work in
constitutional history, legal history, and the
history of the Civil War era, he has lectured and
served on the faculties of several universities in
the United States and abroad. Among his most
prominent publications are *A More Perfect
Union: Constitutional Impacts of the Civil War
and Reconstruction* (1973); *Equal Justice Under
Law* (1982); and *Quiet Past and Stormy Present?
War Powers in American History* (1986).

We shall not cease from exploration
And the end of our exploring
Will be to arrive where we started
And know the place for the first time.
—T.S. ELIOT, FOUR QUARTETS

Lincoln said it best. In December 1864, soon after winning the first presidential reelection since Jackson, he surveyed, as custom required, the state of the Union. He ranked "our popular elections" as the nation's "most reliable indication of public purpose," and saluted "the extraordinary calmness and good order with which the millions of voters met and mingled at the polls." From nominating conventions to balloting, the 1864 elections gave "strong assurance . . . [that] the purpose of the people within the loyal States to maintain the integrity of the Union was never more firm nor more nearly unanimous than now."

But it was a changed Union from the one that had muddled into war in 1861. In late 1864, bluecoats (including black bluecoats) were battering the Confederacy toward extinction. Voters, both white and black soldiers, Lincoln continued, were "the voice of the people now for the first time heard" in favor of a constitutional amendment abolishing slavery throughout a future re-United States. It was "only a question of *time* as to when the proposed amendment will go to the States for their action," he predicted. "And as it is to so go at all events, may we not agree the sooner the better?"

But suppose Lincoln had lost? Defeat could have meant a permanent slaveholding Confederacy within or without the American Union. Looks backward are in order at the political institutions and procedures that bore this heavy responsibility.

Hardly reshaped in terms of organization by three years of civil war, two major state-based national parties still dominated the 1864 scene. In 1860 the Republicans were a restless, dynamic, diverse coalition of former Whigs, disillusioned Democrats, and ardent antislavery exponents. That year, although the Democrats had fractured four ways, its candidates won 44 percent of the popular vote. Then, early in the war, Democratic party chiefs repaired alliances of staple agriculturalists, bankers, and urban workers, primarily by rediscovering the Bill of Rights, but only on behalf of whites, especially those who ran afoul of wartime internal security and conscription improvisations.

By 1862 Democrats were again a resourceful conservative minority, denouncing Union war policies, especially Lincoln's Emancipation Proclamation. Party networks distributed newspaper editorials, pamphlets, and lampoons highlighting all homefront disaffections. Cartoonists caricatured Lincoln as Napoleonic dictator "King Linkum I" and as a sexually fixated mulatto gorilla. Bigotry veiled behind states' rights won rewards. Antiwar and antiemancipation Democrats took thirty-two seats in the House of Representatives, governorships in New York and New Jersey, and control of half of the Union states' legislatures. In 1863's off-year elections, conservative "Peace Democrats" and "copperhead" factions benefited from discontents about military casualties, infla-

Lincoln ferrotype in an ornate brass shell.

tion, taxes, conscription, internal security excesses, and (most especially) emancipation.

Meanwhile, as incumbents, Republicans were accountable for administration policies. What held Lincoln's coalition of small farmers, moneyed interests, industrial workers, recent immigrants, and antislavery activists together?

Patriotism provided one powerful adhesive. A second derived from moral imperatives that the Republicans discerned in a wholly free-labor society, and a third from their welcoming stance toward changes. The war itself was a "dynamometer," wrote Ralph Waldo Emerson, a "new glass to see all our old things through, how they look, . . . a realist, shattering everything flimsy and shifty, . . . [including] party walls that have stood fifty or sixty years as if they were solid." Emerson advised "anxious" conservatives that the war would not obey those wishing "to keep it well in hand."

Commander-in-chief Lincoln displayed similar insights in his 1861-63 orders suspending enforcements of the prewar fugitive slave law, emancipating slaves, and reconstructing governments in occupied rebel states. Mainstream Republicans like Lincoln accepted as war aims such policies as the abolition of slavery, which had been advanced earlier only by the party's "radicals."

In 1862-63 Congress, with Lincoln's warm support, enacted "nonwar" laws. Actually war aims, they promised settlers in the nation's territories—future states—inexpensive homesteads and tax-supported higher education, both without formal race or gender restrictions, and subsidized railroad construction across those immense tracts, if and when the Union won the war. Land, livelihoods, and literacy were core goals of antislavery activists. Combined with the Union's military progress and Lincoln's decision for emancipation, these future-looking laws infused Republican campaign strategy and countered the Democrats' negativism with a positive vision of postwar society.

To communicate this vision, Republicans in 1863 organized two state-based organizations, the Union League and the Loyal League, the latter embracing also coalitionist War Democrats. The Leagues synchronized speakers' schedules and reprinted favorable editorials, speeches, judicial decisions, and sermons. Enjoying War Department cooperation unavailable to Democrats, Republican managers obtained army contracts for local businessmen. Military parades and bemedalled combat heroes inspired audiences. The army furloughed units from critical New England and Ohio River states, less to overawe opposition than to enable "thinking bayonets" (Lincoln's phrase) to vote.

Republicans enlisted women's associations such as teachers' societies and Protestant charitable and missionary auxiliaries in party operations, tapping new reservoirs of talent, energy, and social sensitivity.

A second tactic that Lincoln encouraged party officials to employ aimed at immigrant groups, especially Germans. Predisposed toward national union, antislavery, and other Republican causes, large numbers of German-speaking Americans lived in strategic military and voting areas like Missouri and Pennsylvania. Ethnic politics now expanded beyond the Irish.

Last among the 1863's lessons for Lincoln and other Republicans was the absolute essentiality of the military vote. The enlistments of whole regiments would be expiring in 1864. Would balloting troopers opt to continue the war or to end it? Might the antidraft riots of 1863 be echoed a year later in mass violence at the polls? Auguries seemed dour as elections impended in 1864. Many Republicans, including Lincoln, feared defeat on election day.

All party operations, including election activities, cost money. In the 1850s both parties had created national committees to raise funds, to coordinate nominating conventions and election campaigns, and to prevent or heal schisms. But the parties remained statewide associations of volunteers, many of whom held an elective or appointive public office. Politicians subsisted on patronage. Lincoln's Cabinet activists, War Secretary Edwin M. Stanton, Treasury Secretary Salmon P. Chase, and Postmaster-General Montgomery P. Blair had enormous favors to trade. These included military supply contracts and commissions, draft deferments, and postmasterships and tax collectorships, the last being by far the most numerous federal presence in the thousands of small communities in which most Americans then lived. Party regulars

determined who received local public works contracts and won staff jobs in state jails, county asylums, and city schools. Rich men yearned for diplomatic appointments, lawyers for judgeships, parents for military educations, or commissions for sons.

The Republican National Committee made itself an effective middleman in this political commerce. Every career politician understood and utilized this Byzantine patronage system, but few more zealously and effectively than Lincoln. Tradition barred him from direct roles in the nominating convention and in the campaign. But incumbent Presidents, even those not seeking reelection, influenced party choices. An intense political activist, Lincoln, by personality and purposes, was incapable of aloofness. Democratic speakers, lampoonists, and cartoonists were correct to center their major attacks on him. By 1864 he had returned the presidency to the vital center of political life, making it again America's only truly national office.

In theory, all elected officials were states' men, a few, fortunately, becoming statesmen. Though national nominating conventions selected candidates and platforms, parties in the 1860s remained locality- and state-oriented.

Large ethical imperatives like patriotism or antislavery had to compete against both entrenched bigotry and local pocketbook concerns (a later truism was that all American politics are local). Party politics encouraged presidential personality cults and mercenary favor-tradings at nominating conventions and during election campaigns. These techniques identified winnable nominees. Party regulars trumpeted candidates' virtues, recorded adversaries' vices, and devised platforms to attract voters and inspire future policies. Presidential nominating conventions and elections registered Americans' profoundest hopes and fears, and were the occasions for their advancement or frustration. The hoopla at conventions and during campaigns also filled social needs. Only spasmodic religious revivals, agricultural or industrial fairs, vaudeville troupes, and court sessions competed for popular attention.

And in 1864 the conventions and elections received and deserved special respect. Few nations then practiced democracy. No previous American presidential election had occurred during wartime. But proposals to suspend elections received no serious consideration during the Civil War, although no other warring nation behaved similarly. The 1864 nominations and elections proved, moreover, to be untainted by verifiable corruptions. Two vigorous national parties prepared to offer voters unambiguously differing alternatives.

In mid-nineteenth century America, platforms were serious commitments. By 1864 both Republican and Democratic national committees possessed unprecedentedly effective networks for ascertaining constituent sentiment, incorporating it into the platform, and receiving feedback from the grass roots. Energized by its Union and Loyal Leagues, the Republican apparatus worked better. Exploiting telegraph and rail communication and cooperative journalists as never before, Republican national and state committeemen at Lincoln's urging tested opinion in numerous communities and army camps. The resulting information gave Lincoln levers with which to pry Re-

publican senators and representatives, many of whom were delegates to the nominating convention, to his positions and support.

Convening in Baltimore in June, Republican delegates took comfort from recent Union military successes. Like the Democrats, Republicans had avoided serious factional splits since 1860. And in 1864 there were no antiwar, racist riots like those that a year earlier had blighted the very city in which they were assembled, as well as New York and Chicago, where soon the Democrats would convene. While the platform committee labored, speakers differentiated between constitutional authority as employed by Lincoln and Napoleonic abuse. Defenders stressed Lincoln's argument that the threat of disloyalty was real not theoretical, that democratic procedures remained unimpaired, and that legislation and judicial decisions had increased official accountability.

Overcoming boomlets for other candidates, Lincoln's backers won him easy renomination, and contrived the vice presidential nomination for a coalitionist War Democrat, Andrew Johnson of Tennessee. Lincoln enthusiastically approved the Republican platform. It looked forward to a still state-centered but adaptable, better democratized, more liberal Union. Republican strategists—the best one was in the White House—understood clearly that the platform's forthright war-to-final-victory and antislavery planks were the pivots on which the election would turn. The platform made mainstream politics the judgment long advanced by abolitionists that slavery had destabilized prewar political and constitutional processes, caused the war, and fueled the white South's resistance. The "platform's implied warning was that wrong choices by voters would end the war prematurely, allow a slaveholding Confederacy to outlast a negotiated peace, and thus negate the soldiers' sacrifices while fatally undercutting free labor.

The platform represented change indeed. Federal protection for slaveholders was as old as the Constitution. Racism was deeply rooted in American law and custom. Slaves still constituted the single most valuable form of private property in the nation. The idea of the nation destroying property rights, even those of disloyal slaveowners, offended many persons in this intensely capitalist society. Earlier in 1864, Senate Republicans had passed a proposed Thirteenth Amendment to the Constitution abolishing slavery nationwide (as always, an unspecified conditional phrase was: if and when the Union won the war), but the measure failed in the House. With Lincoln's agents busy on the floor and behind scenes at Baltimore, the platform emphatically endorsed the amendment proposal, to "terminate and forever prohibit" slavery everywhere in the totally re-United States, a commitment the delegates cheered.

The platform also touched tangentially on the issue of blacks' equality before state laws. Party makeweights such as Ohio Senator Benjamin Wade and Maryland Representative Henry Winter Davis had raised disturbing questions in Congress about the racial exclusions blacks suffered in the "reconstructed" southern governments Lincoln was encouraging with Union army help. The platform avoided the divisive subject of national authority intruding, on behalf of blacks, in states' internal legal procedures.

McClellan ferrotype in an ornate brass shell.

Instead it opted for a more easily defended though related concern about black Union soldiers (most of whom were recent slaves) captured by Confederates. Slaveholding states made felons of blacks armed against whites. Republican platform-writers demanded prisoner-of-war status for captives "without regard to distinction of color, [and] the full protection of the laws of war." A sense was brewing of equality before law as a minimum recognition of an American's status as a person.

Homeward-bound delegates knew that they had to persuade voters that the future of free labor itself hinged on the election's outcome. Some depicted the argument pictorially. They reproduced a pro-Confederate map that predicted the permanent division of the once-United States and of the rest of North and Central America, plus the Caribbean islands, as a consequence of Democratic victory. Republican pamphlets reinforced arguments that federalism, as redefined by extreme state rights advocates since 1820, had become a "Chinese shoe" protecting bigotry and illiteracy, blunting the nation's conscience, and frustrating the access of free labor to the vast western territories.

1864 Frémont ferrotype in an ornate brass shell. Frémont had opposed Lincoln's renomination and toyed with a third-party candidacy.

Democratic delegates to the convention in Chicago in August had papered over their 1860 schisms. The platform called the war a failure, denounced emancipation, condemned Republican fiscal policies, and exploited every popular uneasiness and distress. Convention speakers and later campaigners targeted Lincoln particularly. His 1862-63 orders emancipating the rebels' slaves, the recruitment of black bluecoats, and the reconstruction of state governments in the militarily-occupied areas of the contracting but still survivable Confederacy, made it clear, Democrats insisted, that he had joined the race-mixing Republican radicals.

Declaring the Constitution crippled if not dead, the platform insisted that the Lincoln administration was prolonging the conflict in order to foist emancipation on the nation, in the process trampling on the rights both of whites and states, especially by imposing test oaths on voters and office-holders and by censoring newspapers and the mails. The platform called for peace without victory and a return to the prewar Union. The platform ignored the plight of black Union troops held in Confederate prison camps, as it did all wartime changes in race relationships. The platform's omissions and vague "Union as it was" language could be made to imply a great deal. Even the continuation of slavery as the price of an armistice leading to a negotiated peace with a permanent Confederacy was evokable from its text and from the party's historical context. It seemed—and Republicans helped it seem—that the most reactionary Democratic "Copperhead" and peace-at-any-price factions dominated the party's proceedings.

The candidate was ex-U.S. army General George B. McClellan. He was eternally bitter at Lincoln for having removed him from command, both for lack of vigor in combat and for disagreements on returning fugitive slaves, emancipation, and other war aims. Though not specifically seconding the party's defeatist platform, McClellan agreed that the preservation of the Union was the sole avowed object for which the war was commenced, and that it should have been conducted only for that object.

During the campaign Democratic speakers invoked their party's platform endlessly, especially in the most Negrophobic northern cities and border states. Party spokesmen and journalists condemned the war as a bloody masquerade aimed at making Lincoln military dictator over a centralized, racially mongrelizing despotism. Cooperative academics, artists, and ministers circulated Democratic propaganda, including pseudoscientific suggestions about the inherent inferiority of blacks, and barbs like these:

> Honest Old Abe, when the war first began,
> Denied abolition was part of his plan;
> Honest old Abe has since made a decree,
> The war must go on till the slaves all are free,
> As both can't be honest, will some one tell how,
> If Honest Abe then, he is Honest Abe now?

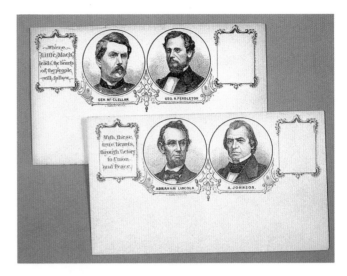

Conventioners became campaigners. As autumn advanced, both parties arranged for speakers, choirs, athletic events, fireworks, torchlit assemblies, barbecues, and liquid refreshments to bring in the citizenry. Copies of party platforms circulated along with "potted" biographies of candidates, the latter often supplemented by stylized, flattering etchings and lithographs. Posters, lampoons, graffiti, and pamphlets celebrated candidates and platforms, while denouncing the opposition, often in coarse imagery.

Republican campaigners risked the election on the premise that enough white Americans had become willing, from patriotism, reactions against race bigotries, and economic self-interest, to elevate sights about war aims. So risking defeat, spokesmen raised the level of their campaign discourse to encompass the nation's ethical and moral duty to protect those giving it allegiance, whites and blacks alike. Republicans transformed the ambiguities and omissions in the Democratic platform into advantages to themselves, especially the lack of concern about the fate of the nation's blacks, slaves and free, and of the black Union soldiers, should the war end (as some Democrats wished) in a negotiated return of the Confederacy to a chastened Union.

Republicans raised frightening but plausible questions about the consequences of Democratic victory. Would the 1850 fugitive slave law be reenacted? The Emancipation Proclamation repudiated? The principles of the infamous 1857 *Dred Scott* decision or the 1861 *Lemmon* case (the latter sanctioned the sale of slaves even in a state that forbade slavery) reborn in legislation or judicial appointments by a reac-

tionary President and Congress? Were the nation's promised aids to homesteaders, education, and communications to be abandoned like the blacks?

Republican organizers built on their experiences with "Wide-Awake" volunteer groups in 1856 and 1860, and with Union and Loyal Leagues in 1862 and 1863. Banners carried by militia, home guard, and army paraders extolled "Honest Abe" and other Republican-Union candidates. Newspaper editors received copies of speeches by Lincoln, Republican congressmen, and supportive generals—especially those of Grant's battlefield reputation and antislavery inclinations. War Department advertising was unlikely to follow if editors buried these speeches.

Democrats also twisted all available patronage screws. But they lacked control over federal departments, support of the most successful generals, and excitement from dynamic visions of the future. Theirs was only the critic's role. In addition to denouncing emancipation, they derided the administration's military record, homefront policies, and reconstruction plans.

Lincoln's party benefited from the Union's improved military situation (what contrasts to previous years!), the free states'

1864 campaign envelopes.

McClellan cardboard badge.

political realignments, and the increasing acceptance of abolitionist arguments. By seceding and triggering civil war, Republicans contended, defenders of slavery had provoked the nation's major woes. Abolition was essential both to Union military victory and post-reunion stability. It could occur, Republican campaigners insisted, without centralizing the federal system.

Emphasizing slavery's dark history and free labor's bright future, Republicans exploited their effective information network to carry their messages. This network now embraced interlocking medical, moral, and missionary societies concerned with the welfare of soldiers and freedmen, as well as professional and student groups, veterans associations, and significant women's auxiliaries.

Editors of foreign language newspapers and chairmen of fraternal societies for the foreign-born served large immigrant concentrations, especially in German-American areas.

Republican spokesmen savaged opponents and mounted their own candidates and purposes. For example, the double-page centerfold etching, "The Chicago Platform," by extraordinarily talented artist Thomas Nast, appeared originally in *Harper's Weekly*, a relatively highbrow New York periodical. But, copied endlessly throughout the unseceded states and in regimental publications, it contributed shorthand ideas about election issues to pro-Union ministers, school debaters, and newspaper editorialists. The Republicans got to the voters more systematically, thoroughly, and imaginatively than their Democratic analogs.

Some states still did not provide for soldiers to vote absentee. The War Department again furloughed home whole regiments to states not providing this opportunity. Many soldiers voted Democratic, but most favored Republican candidates and policies. The presence in their home communities of these uniformed citizens amidst their families, mocked Democratic allegations about Lincoln as a dictator.

Everywhere the Republicans exploited the "Lincoln image." It was exploitable because Lincoln had proved himself respectful of the nation's past, sensitive to its present needs, yet willing to risk his reelection by envisaging a less racially-bigoted, more perfect Union. In the unique American political culture that the wartime context made the more intense, families in big cities and in isolated hamlets hung on their walls sentimental prints of Lincoln as rail-splitter, father, and overseer of the Cabinet, along

Lincoln cardboard badge.

with pictures of successful Union generals and local heroes. Popular sculptor John Rogers cast and sold many thousands of copies of bronze mantelpiece statuettes depicting Lincoln as emancipator and, as the military's incurably civilian overlord, the distributor of rations to distressed people, whites and blacks. In short, a Republican message of 1864 was that democracy and federalism have nothing to fear from the Union's vast military forces.

The election deeply disappointed most northern Democrats and whites in Confederate states. Lincoln won 55 percent of the popular vote (as against only 39 percent in 1860). His electoral college triumph, 212 votes to 21, made it impossible to dispute the results. McClellan carried only Delaware, Kentucky, and New Jersey, the last being the only non-slave state to choose a Democratic governor. Republican candidates regained majorities in all state legislatures lost two years earlier, gloried in a 42 to 10 majority in the United States Senate, and celebrated command of 145 of the 185 seats in the House of Representatives. Yet in every state the Democrats remained a strong second force. The two-party system was sound.

In postelection weeks, Lincoln reflected on the meaning of the voting. He assumed that he would hold office until March 1869. If visibly aged, Lincoln was still only fifty-five years old in 1864 and apparently healthy. No President had ever been murdered. He anticipated the passage of the proposed constitutional amendment abolishing slavery. His educability on diverse matters, especially the need for emancipation, his capacity to lead and to learn, to grow as the

people grew, impressed the generation. The reformer Robert Dale Owen expressed a common assessment:

> Some men stand still, amazed, when the tempest darkens around them; others grow and rise to the height of the occasion; but few have ever grown and risen as did this man; his mind maturing and his views expanding under the stirring influences of the times. . . . [Lincoln's] was an old familiar name for which the majority voted . . . in 1864; yet it was scarcely a reelection. It was not the same man that the people had elected President four years before.

Nor the same country. A majority of Americans had placed their faith in Lincoln's vision for the Union. And though fate banished him to the grave before he could do more than show the way, Lincoln set a clear course in his second inaugural, in which he pleaded that the re-united nation "strive on to finish the work we are in."

Broadside for a Lincoln-Johnson rally.

Multicolored 1861 song sheet.

Metal-framed lantern with glass inserts holding paper portraits and patriotic images. Similar items were used in parades between 1860 and 1900.

Tintype of Mary Todd Lincoln.

Lincoln and Johnson ornate cartes de visite.

Lincoln-Johnson print with Union army and navy commanders.

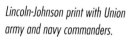

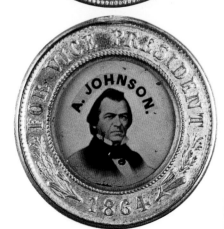

Two-sided Lincoln-Johnson ferrotype.

Rare 1864 cotton flag banner.
"FREE" is composed of 35 stars.

1864 paper broadside. Note "Union" Republican ticket.

Union Republican Ticket.

ABRAHAM LINCOLN,
OF ILLINOIS, FOR PRESIDENT.

ANDREW JOHNSON,
OF TENNESSEE, FOR VICE-PRESIDENT.

The end is not far distant, if we will only be true to ourselves. Their only hope is in a divided North. —*Gen. Grant.*

I hope peace will come soon, and come to stay, and so come as to be worth the keeping in all future time.—*Abraham Lincoln.*

Differences of opinion only encourage the enemy, prolong the war, and waste the country. If the rebellion triumphs, Free Government, North and South, fails.—*Andrew Johnson.*

For Electors of President and Vice-President of the United States.

William H. Y. Hackett,
Daniel M. Christie,
Archibald H. Dunlap,
Allen Giffin,
Henry O. Kent.

1864 campaign ribbon with designation of Lincoln's generals as "PEACE COMMISSIONERS."

PEQUEA, PROVIDENCE
AND
MARTIC DELEGATION.

FOR PRESIDENT,
Abraham Lincoln.

VICE PRESIDENT,
Andrew Johnson.

PEACE COMMISSIONERS,
ULYSSES S. GRANT,
D. G. FARRAGUT,
WM. T. SHERMAN,
PHILIP H. SHERIDAN.

Lincoln tintype in leather case.

Currier & Ives cartoon showing Lincoln and McClellan's opposing views on the treatment of white southerners and northern black soldiers.

Right: Silk ribbon promising voters "PEACE, AMNESTY, EMANCIPATION."
Far right: Newspaper announcement of the New York State election results.

Brass pipe with a
McClellan bowl.

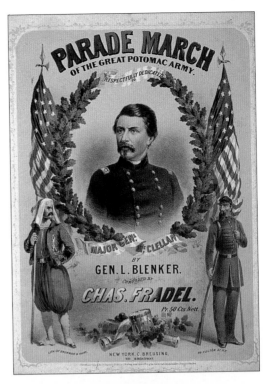

Examples of colorful McClellan sheet music.

McClellan
ferrotype
affixed to
an ornate
ribbon rosette.

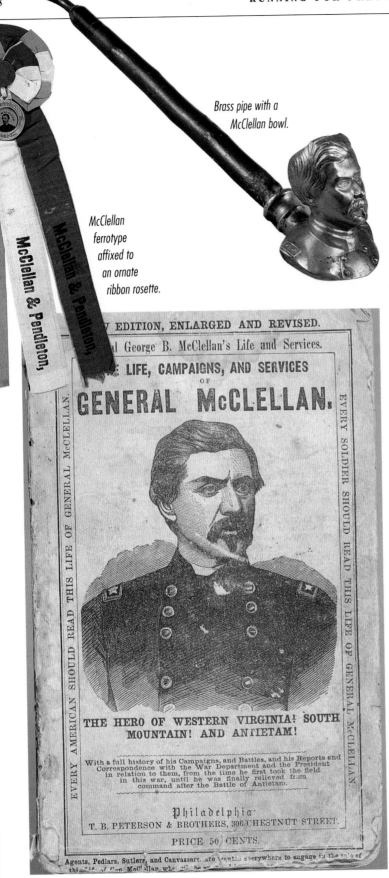

A McClellan campaign biography.

Harper's Weekly *centerfold illustrating the 1864 Democratic platform.*

Frémont-Cochrane ferrotype token for the aborted 1864 third-party.

Print of McClellan and Pendleton protecting Lady Liberty from the ravages of war.

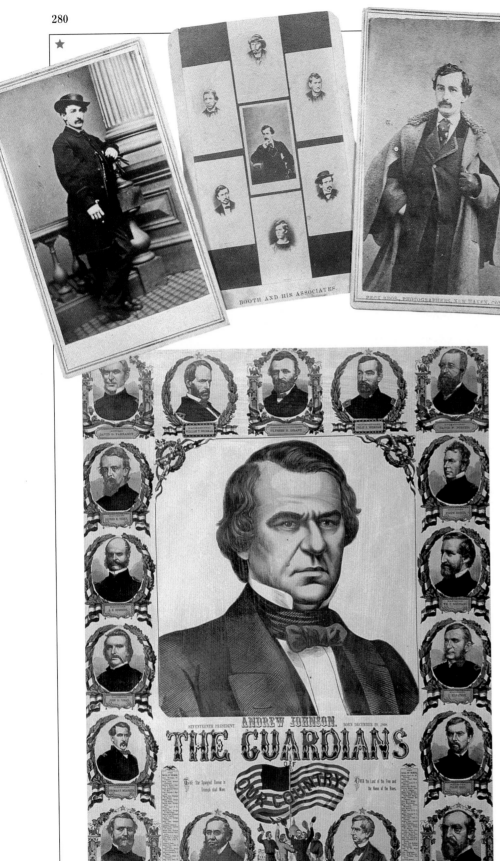

Cartes de visite of Lincoln's assassin, John Wilkes Booth, and the alleged conspirators.

BOOTH AND HIS ASSOCIATES.

PECK BROS., PHOTOGRAPHERS, NEW HAVEN, CONN.

Playbill from a John WIlkes Booth performance in Boston, March 6, 1863.

MRS. JNO. DREW'S

ARCH STREET THEATRE

Acting and Stage Manager, - MR. WM. S. FREDERICKS
Business Agent and Treasurer, - MR. JOS. D. MURPHY

FIRST BENEFIT OF MR.

JOHN WILKES BOOTH

This Evening, Friday, March 6th, 1863,

Will be presented, First Time in Three Years, Shakspere's Play of the

MERCHANT of VENICE

Terminating with the Celebrated TRIAL SCENE.

And with the following Excellent Cast :

SHYLOCK,	-	-	JOHN WILKES BOOTH
Mrs John Drew		as	Portia
Mrs Chas. Henri		as	Nerissa
Miss E. Price		as	Jessica
Mr Barton Hill		as	Basanio
Mr Frank Drew		as	Gratiano
Mr Albaugh		as	Antonio
Mr Ringgold		as	Lorenzo
Mr Seymour		as	Launcelot Gobbo
Mr Fisher		as	Old Gobbo
Mr Craig		as	Salarino
Mr Little		as	Salanio
Mr Chas. Henri		as	Tubal
Mr Rogers		as	Balthazar
Mr Wilson		as	Stephano

Magnificos, Officers of Justice, &c.

Scene—Partly at Venice, and partly at Belmonte, the Seat of Portia.

The Orchestra, led by Mr. CHARLES R. DODWORTH, will perform a Popular Overture, and other Musical Selections.

The performances to conclude with, 1st time in three years, Shakspere's Comedy of

CATHARINE AND PETRUCHIO

PETRUCHIO,	-	-	JOHN WILKES BOOTH
Baptista,			Mr Wallis
Grumio,			Mr Frank Drew
Biondello,			Mr Ringgold
Hortensio,			Mr Craig
Music Master,			Mr Chas. Henri
Tailor,			Mr Seymour
Cook,			Mr Fisher
Gregory,			Mr Rogers
Ralph,			Mr Wilson
Walter,			Mr Worth
Pedro,			Mr Little
Catharine,			Mrs John Drew
Bianca,			Miss Gardiner
Curtis,			Mrs Jones

To-Morrow, Mr. Booth in the Play of The Robbers.

Doors open at 7 o'clock.   To commence at half-past 7.

U. S. Job Print, Ledger Buildings, Phila'a

Multicolored poster of Andrew Johnson after he became President.

Andrew Johnson medal from the 1866 Philadelphia National Union Convention held to rally support for Republicans in the forthcoming congressional elections.

Right: Ticket to the Senate impeachment trial of President Andrew Johnson. In violation of the 1867 Tenure of Office Act, President Johnson dismissed Secretary of War Edwin M. Stanton. The House of Representatives impeached Johnson on February 24, 1868, but the Senate acquitted him (May 16, 1868).

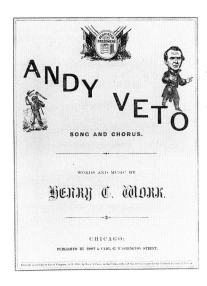

Sheet music satirizing Johnson's 1866 veto of the Freedmen's Bureau, an agency designed to aid the freedmen.

★

1868

37 STATES
IN THE UNION

REPUBLICAN

Ulysses S. Grant

ELECTORAL VOTE 214, POPULAR VOTE 52.7%

DEMOCRAT

Horatio Seymour

ELECTORAL VOTE 80, POPULAR VOTE 47.3%

Hans L. Trefousse

is a Distinguished Professor at Brooklyn
College and the Graduate Center of the City
University of New York. He is the author of
books on the Civil War and Reconstruction,
including *The Radical Republicans* and
biographies of Andrew Johnson, Carl Schurz,
Benjamin E. Butler, and Benjamin Franklin.

The 1868 presidential election can only be understood against the background of Reconstruction. How quickly and under what conditions the southern states were to be restored to the Union had long been the chief issue between the Republican Congress and the Democrats and President Andrew Johnson. While the Republicans insisted on safeguards for the freedmen—particularly on the extension of suffrage to southern blacks—the Democrats and Johnson denied the right of Congress to dictate to the states. Waxing ever more bitter, this controversy culminated in February 1868, in the impeachment of President Johnson. The subsequent trial lasted well into May, by which time the quadrennial presidential race was already well under way.

This contest had provided the Republicans with a perfect candidate. When the President dismissed Secretary of War Edwin M. Stanton because of his support of the radical Republicans, the Senate, invoking the Tenure of Office Act, ordered his reinstatement. But General Ulysses S. Grant, the Civil War hero now serving as Secretary of War ad interim, refused to cooperate with Johnson in trying to prevent Stanton from reoccupying the War Department. The result, to the great benefit of the Republican party, was a complete break between the President and the general.

The Republican National Convention opened on May 20 at Crosby's Opera House in Chicago, four days after the first vote ac-

quitting the President, and six days prior to the conclusion of the trial. It was called to order by Governor Marcus Ward of New Jersey, the chairman of the national committee, who nominated Carl Schurz, the famous German-American journalist and reformer as temporary chairman. Schurz's brief keynote address set the tone for the ensuing campaign. "I spurn the idea," he said, "that the American people could ever so forget themselves as to throw their destinies into the hands of men who, but yesterday, strove to destroy the Republic, and who, today, stand ready to dishonor it." The usual committees on credentials and resolutions were appointed, General Joseph P. Hawley became permanent chairman, and the delegates welcomed a deputation from a soldiers and sailors convention which enthusiastically endorsed Grant. A premature effort to nominate the general miscarried; the convention listened to a patriotic speech by Governor Joseph Brown of Georgia, formerly a secessionist but now a Republican, and adjourned for the day.

On the next morning the delegates received resolutions from the National Council of Union Leagues, which demanded protection for blacks in the South and advocated the nomination of General Grant. After the Ohio newspaperman and politician Friedrich Hassaurek, and the Illinois General (later Governor) John M. Palmer addressed the convention, a band played

Elaborate ferrotype of Horatio Seymour and Francis Blair.

patriotic songs, and the committee on resolutions brought in the proposed platform. Expressing pride in the success of Reconstruction, the platform asserted that the guarantee of equal suffrage in the South was the undoubted duty of Congress but that in the loyal states, the question of the suffrage was up to the people. It denounced repudiation and corruption, condemned Andrew Johnson, and upheld the rights of immigrants. Amended to include a reaffirmation of the principles of the Declaration of Independence, the platform was adopted. Then General John A. Logan proposed the nomination of General Grant; the band played "Hail to the Chief," and the motion carried unanimously. The strains of the "Battle Cry of Freedom" reverberated through the hall, and a special song written for the occasion, "We'll Fight It Out There, on the Old Union Line," ended the proceedings.

The vice presidential nomination was more controversial. Benjamin F. Wade, the President Pro Tem of the Senate and acting vice president, had been considered frontrunner, at least as long as it was likely that he would soon occupy the White House. But Johnson's acquittal on the first vote had diminished the radical senator's chances; the party was no longer as ideologically committed as before, and it was looking toward others to balance the ticket. Reuben E. Fenton of New York, Henry Wilson of Massachusetts, and Schuyler Colfax of Indiana were nominated as well as Wade, who lost to Colfax on the sixth ballot.

It was Grant's letter of acceptance that was to serve the party as a rallying cry throughout the campaign. "Let us have peace," he wrote, and the expression was to be endlessly repeated by his supporters.

The Democrats met on July 4, at newly inaugurated Tammany Hall in New York. The President's trial had ended in acquittal, and he was now an active candidate for the nomination. Had he not defied the radical Congress to uphold the rights of the southern states, precisely as demanded by the Democrats? He thought the party was in his debt, and he was sanguine of success. In addition, Chief Justice Salmon P. Chase, who had broken with the radicals during the impeachment trial (over which he presided with great circumspection) also had presidential ambitions. While he refused to give up his advocacy of black suffrage, in the end he agreed that its bestowal was up to the states themselves, and his supporters argued that he alone could garner enough black votes to defeat Grant.

But neither of these candidacies was realistic. Johnson had never developed an organized following among the Democrats, who resented his retention of Secretary of State William H. Seward and his efforts to form a third party, while they found Chase's racial views too liberal. When the convention was called to order by August Belmont, no ground swell developed for either of the two outsiders.

After the keynote speaker, Henry L. Palmer of Wisconsin, expressed great pride in the fact that delegates from all sections of the country were present, the convention appointed the usual committees, listened to a reading of the Declaration of Independence, and adjourned until July 6, the following Monday. On that day, Governor Horatio Seymour of New York, the permanent chairman, delivered a speech attacking the Republicans for violating the Declaration of Independence. Resolutions from the National Labor Union called for equal taxation and an eight-hour day; the delegates received a memorial from the Women's Suffrage Association, and welcomed Generals William B. Franklin and Henry W. Slocum who headed a deputation from a conservative soldiers and sailors convention. The platform, adopted on July 7, called for the immediate restoration of all states to their privileges within the Union and amnesty for all past political offenses, insisted upon the rights of the states to regulate the suffrage and the payment of bonds in greenbacks unless otherwise stated, and contained an endorsement of Andrew Johnson's stewardship as well as a long attack on Reconstruction. Amended to include praise for the workingmen as well as for the Chief Justice, it clearly defined the party's appeal for a reversal of national policies.

The nominations for President revealed considerable disunity. George H. Pendleton was the candidate of the soft-money advocates, but others with different ideas—including Andrew Johnson, Winfield S. Hancock, Sanford E. Church, James E. English, and Thomas A. Hendricks—were also nominated. Chase's supporters withheld his name until the twelfth ballot, and the struggle between soft- and hard-money forces continued. In the end, on the twenty-second ballot, Seymour, a foe of inflation, became (over his protests) the party's choice. General Francis P. Blair, Jr., the son of the famous member of Andrew Jackson's kitchen cabinet, won unanimous support for second place.

This result did not bridge the rift between hard- and soft-money advocates and alienated the President as well as the Chief Justice. Believing he had been treated shabbi-ly, Johnson refused for many weeks to endorse Seymour, while Chase's supporters (particularly the New York *Herald*) made no secret of their disappointment. It was not a good beginning.

These two tickets foreshadowed the direction of the campaign. It was to be fought over Reconstruction and freedmen's rights, especially suffrage. The Republicans proceeded to "wave the bloody shirt" (as the lurid dredging-up of wartime issues was called) and the Democrats used the racial question for all it was worth.

The controversy was heightened by the fact that during the New York draft riots in 1863 Seymour had addressed the perpetrators as "my friends," and that Blair had written a letter to the Missouri Unionist James O. Broadhead in which he proposed that the new President declare the Reconstruction acts null and void, disperse the Republican governments in the South, and call for new elections. Both actions were splendid targets for Republican campaigners who used them for all they were worth.

The contest began almost immediately. Ratification meetings were held with great fanfare, and both parties staged mass meetings—the most popular form of campaigning at the time. Bands played, torch parades enlivened the proceedings, and distinguished speakers (often former generals) entertained the public. Thus on July 16, in South Bend, Indiana, the Grant and Colfax Club raised a pole 150 feet in height, nailed thirty-foot-long streamers to the top, and watched while one hundred "True Lights" marched to the Court House Square. Torchlights and martial music delighted the

Multicolored Seymour-Blair woven silk ribbon. Seymour campaign items are scarcer than those of Ulysses S. Grant.

a hundred thousand spectators in New York. Like their adversaries, they were able to feature former generals as speakers, and, if some were ex-Confederates, most were conservative Unionists.

Naturally, cartoonists were fully involved. The Republicans had the edge on their opponents, with Thomas Nast of *Harper's Weekly* lending his considerable talents to the vilification of the Democrats. On September 5, a full-page illustration, entitled "This Is a White Man's Government," appeared in the magazine. Three conspirators—a nativist stereotype of an Irish denizen of the Five Points, a Confederate veteran, and August Belmont (all with their feet on the flag and a prostrate freedman)—were shown endorsing the Democratic platform's assertion that "we regard the Reconstruction Acts (so-called) as usurpations, and unconstitutional, revolutionary, and void." A smaller cartoon pictured Seymour as Lady Macbeth trying to rid herself of the Draft Riot speech by exclaiming, "Out, Damned Spot!" Another illustration summed up the contest by depicting what it called "Both Sides of the Question, The Boys in Blue v. the Boys in Gray," a rendering of the veterans of the two hostile armies.

A different campaign document was a pamphlet by the famous humorist "Petroleum V. Nasby" (David R. Locke). Entitled "IMPENDIN CRISIS UV THE DIMOCRACY," it was "Dedicated to Horashio Seemore, the Troo Dimokrat, to whom My Sole Hez Alluz Gone out Sence the Riots in Noo York, in 1863." Written in the style of the notorious Copperhead from Confederate Crossroads,

crowd, and General Jasper Packard, who was to be Colfax's successor in Congress, delivered a stirring address. On August 12, a crowd of sixty thousand attended a ratification meeting at the Court House Square in Chicago, and the newspapers reported tremendous numbers of spectators elsewhere: thirty thousand in Bangor, fifty thousand in Indianapolis, and similar figures in other cities. These estimates may have been exaggerated, but there is no question that large turnouts were common; the entertainment provided by the bands, the festivities, and the speakers constituted prime diversions. In addition, the Grant and Colfax forces were supported by special organizations called the Tanners and the Boys in Blue, the latter reminding spectators of the solidarity of the Republicans with the defenders of the Union.

The Democrats were no less active. They too held mass meetings in major cities, and on October 4, allegedly attracted

it was facetiously directed to "All the fol-
lowin in the North:"

1. All them which dont want ther daw-
ters to marry niggers, and which demand
a law to protect em agin em.

2. All them which stand on the street
corners perpetooally, shakin for fear
the niggers will be elevatid to an ekali-
ty with them.

The Democrats were not far behind
with their cartoons and pamphlets. In one
of the latter, called "The Lively Life of U. S.
G., H. U. G., and U. H. G., the Political Trip-
lets," they sought to belittle the general's
career—his name changes, his alleged
drunkenness, his ignorance of politics, and
other shortcomings. Cartoons of Grant riding on a bottle as if it were a horse, of rag-
ged blacks, and of a Negro woman spanking
his behind circulated, and the New York
World published separate editions of a
Campaign World, containing speeches and
letters from leaders supporting Seymour
and Blair.

Throughout the campaign, the Republicans' main effort was to implicate their
opponents with supporters of the "Lost
Cause." That Wade Hampton and Nathan
Bedford Forrest were active in the Democratic camp was an excellent excuse for the
other side to wave the bloody shirt. Had not
both been Confederate generals, and had
not Forrest been the perpetrator of the
atrocious Fort Pillow massacre—the wan-
ton torture and murder of captured black
soldiers? Had not the opposition candidate
himself betrayed his southern sympathies
during the draft riots? As for Blair, Grant's
partisans labeled his letter to Broadhead a
call for insurrection and an extralegal

disregard of Congress. Reminding the electorate of Grant's slogan, "Let us have
peace," they contrasted it vividly with his
antagonists' invitation to further strife.
"Republicans," the Chicago *Tribune* exhorted on July 27,

the campaign is now fully opened.
Shall Grant and Colfax be elected, the
Southern States reconstructed, peace
be preserved and the Union saved, or
will you have Seymour and Blair, repudiation, and another terrible, desolat-
ing war? The New York convention,
composed mainly of peace sneaks, Cop-
perheads, and rebel Generals, made a
platform, which in connection with
Blair's letter, make their treasonable
designs transparent and unmistakable.

Grant's alleged virtues, his victories,
his heroism, and his unassuming nature
became the staples of the Republican press.
Constantly harping on his great achievements, it did not permit anyone to forget
that he was the victor of Appomattox, and
as such fully deserving of the presidency.
But there were certain difficulties to be

*Satirical card with Grant
riding the back of a freedman
to the White House while
Seymour tumbles from his
Confederate mount.*

RADICAL DESTRUCTION.   A MATCH   DEMOCRATIC CONSTRUCTION.

Dedicated to Horatio Seymour
& FRANK P. BLAIR

Allegorical print. Peace and prosperity under Democratic Seymour compared to "RADICAL DESTRUCTION" under Republican Grant.

his family, and his dubious record during the war provided endless material for the Republicans. By October, when because of defeats in Indiana, Ohio, and Pennsylvania, Democratic prospects looked dim, suggestions were made that Seymour withdraw in favor of some other candidate, a development the Republicans published with pleasure.

The Democrats were equally aggressive. Racism was their stock in trade, and as early as May 23, the New York *World* carried a headline, "SUBLIME SAMBO," in describing the Republican platform. "Suffrage for Everybody Except Southern White Men," it complained, while continuing to stress the alleged injustice of imposing black suffrage upon the South but not upon the North. As the New York *Herald* succinctly stated,

> Universal Nigger Suffrage is the Great Issue of the Campaign. There is no other issue but this, and the whole campaign turns purely and simply upon this point of the political status of the nigger in the Southern States, and the right of the States themselves to regulate that status. Universal nigger suffrage and the correlative oppression of the white man are the points that divide the parties and the people.

As time went on, the Democrats printed frequent reports of outrages supposedly perpetrated by blacks, and extending their attack to include the entire Reconstruction program, asserted that what mattered was the restoration of government by law. Naturally, they denied the insanity charges against the Seymour family, which, they maintained, had rendered distinguished-public service for generations.

overcome. In December 1862, Grant had issued Order Number 11, which expelled all Jews from the Department of the Tennessee, and although Abraham Lincoln (upon the protest of leading Jewish citizens) had reversed the edict, it became in 1868 a matter of deep embarrassment for the Republican party. In article after article Grant newspapers assured their readers that patriotic "Hebrews" supported the ticket. Let Israelites remember Confederate intolerance and vote for the general, urged the Chicago *Tribune*, while the *New York Times* insisted that Democratic efforts to alienate Republican Jews were unsuccessful. A "wealthy Israelite" in Indiana had even bet $10,000 at three-to-one odds that Grant would win. Jewish Grant and Colfax Clubs were organized, and by September it was reported that three out of four Jews were supporting the general.

In the meantime, attacks on Seymour mounted. His actions during the draft riots, Blair's incendiary letter, alleged insanity in

Grant presented a target also. Had he not butchered thousands during his campaign against Richmond? Cotton speculator, butcher, heartless leader who refused to exchange prisoners—these were some of the charges brought against the general. Democratic newspapers reprinted Order Number II with gleeful accounts of meetings of Jewish organizations denouncing it and demanding revenge. Charging that the slogan, "Let us have peace," was a sham, the Democrats compared the peace that Grant brought with that which the Russians imposed upon Poland. In this manner, they played up the alleged horrors of "radical Reconstruction," which they promised to end forthwith.

The two parties used poetry to further their interests. Thus Miles O'Reilley in the New York *Tribune*:

> So boys! A final bumper
> While we all in chorus chant —
> For next President we nominate
> Our own Ulysses Grant!

> And if asked what state he hails from
> This our sole reply shall be
> "From near Appomattox Court House
> With its famous apple tree"

During the course of the campaign, it became more and more obvious that Seymour and Blair would lose. The party was split from the start by the rift between inflationists and their opponents, and the New York *Herald*, chagrined at Chase's defeat, predicted disaster the moment Seymour was nominated. Then, when the results of September and October state elections came in, few could doubt the final outcome in November. To be sure, Seymour did not withdraw; on the contrary, he became more active and went on a campaign trip to a number of cities in New

Multicolored cloth banner with Grant's conclusion to his letter accepting the Republican nomination.

York and the West, and Blair, who had also been urged to give way to a less controversial candidate, likewise stayed in the race. But all that Seymour's canvassing accomplished was to enable the Republicans to point with pride to their candidate's refusal to do likewise. The riot at Camilla, Georgia, on September 19, where several black Republicans were wantonly killed by a Democratic mob, did not help Seymour; nor did a joint resolution excluding all unreconstructed states from the electoral college. When the count was complete. Grant had carried all but two northern and five southern and border states. The electoral vote was 214 to 80, and the popular vote was 3,012,833 to 2,703,249. While the Democrats had done well to garner 47 percent of the electorate, they had not been able fully to recover from their wartime misfortunes. The memories of the Civil War and the presence of a black electorate in the South kept them from recapturing the White House.

Pinback badge with paper photo of
Seymour and Blair.

Price 10 Cents—A Liberal Discount to the Trade.

THE

Impendin Crisis uv the Dimocracy,

BEIN

A BREEF AND CONCISE STATEMENT UV THE
PAST EXPERIENCE, PRESENT CONDISH-
UN AND FUCHER HOPES UV THE
DIMOKRATIC PARTY:

INCLOODIN

THE MOST PROMINENT REESONS WHY EVRY DIMO-
KRAT WHO LOVES HIS PARTY SHOOD VOTE FOR

SEEMORE and BLARE, and agin GRANT and COLFAX.

By PETROLEUM V. NASBY,

Formerly Paster in charge of the Church of the Noo Dispensashun, late Perfesser uv
Biblikle Politics in the Southern Military and Classicle Institoot, and now
Postmaster at Confedrit X Roads, wich is in the State uv Kentucky.

AMERICAN NEWS CO.,
119 & 121 NASSAU STREET,
NEW YORK.

Satirical booklet suggesting that the Democrats were nothing but illiterate boors.

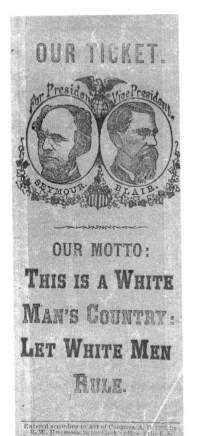

OUR TICKET.

For President   Vice President

SEYMOUR.   BLAIR.

OUR MOTTO:

THIS IS A WHITE
MAN'S COUNTRY:
LET WHITE MEN
RULE.

Entered according to Act of Congress, A. D. 1868, by
B. W. Hitchcock, in the Clerk's office of the U. S.
District Court for the Southern Dist. of New York.

Seymour-Blair silk ribbon with
an obviously racial appeal.

Anti-Seymour broadside satirizing how the Democrats would treat the freedman. The cartoons were drawn by Thomas Nast.

HORATIO SEYMOUR AND HIS FRIENDS!

HOW DEMOCRATS TREAT THE COLORED MAN!

"**Remember this: that the bloody, and treasonable, and revolutionary doctrine of public necessity can be proclaimed by a MOB as well as by a Government.**"

These were the words of Horatio Seymour, Presidential candidate of the Rebel Democracy, delivered on the Fourth of July, 1863, in the city of New York.

On the thirteenth day of July, 1863, the Democratic MOB, thus appealed to, attacked the office of an Assistant Provost Marshal, charged in part with the execution of a conscription ordered by President Lincoln. Gettysburg, Vicksburg, Port Hudson, and other fields, had rendered necessary the refilling of the Union armies.

The MOB by whom the Provost Marshal's office was destroyed held the city for several days, growing in numbers, brutality, licentiousness, and treason with each hour's sway. This seditious riot was the reserve of Lee's army, and had evidently been organized to act in concert as he advanced on Philadelphia. His early defeat, however, prevented the consummation of the conspiracy, of which Horatio Seymour's words, quoted above, are the key-note. Rebel agents were leading the mob, and actively inciting it to greater atrocities. Just before it broke out, Clement L. Vallandigham, the leader of the Northern Rebels, who had been sent South beyond the Union lines on account of seditious speeches and acts, ran the blockade at Wilmington, N. C., reached the British port of Nassau, and sailed immediately, with a party of Confederate agents, for Halifax, Nova Scotia, avowing on the voyage that his object was the direction of riots to be fomented in Northern cities, and designed to aid projected military movements of the Confederacy. He arrived about the twenty-eighth of June, 1863. At that date the Rebel army, under Lee, was occupying the Cumberland Valley, in Pennsylvania. The Copperhead, Vallandigham, left Halifax for Boston. Attempts to incite riots were made there immediately after his arrival. They failed. In New York Horatio Seymour, acting in concert with Lee in Pennsylvania, and Vallandigham in Boston and Canada, advised the MOB that it was lawful for them to resist the Government. The MOB bettered the bloody instructions, and, during the time in which they held sway, burned, destroyed, and plundered private property to the amount of ONE MILLION THREE HUNDRED AND SIXTY-SIX THOUSAND THREE HUNDRED AND SEVENTY-NINE DOLLARS, ($1,366,379,) besides destroying public property to a large extent. The fury of the Democratic rioters was chiefly turned upon prominent Republicans, and especially upon the unoffending colored people of the city. The buildings of the COLORED ORPHAN ASYLUM were burned to the ground, and its inmates brutally outraged. A majority were only saved from murder by the exertions of the Metropolitan Police, under the command of a Republican Superintendent, Mr. Kennedy. The publication office of the *Tribune* was gutted; the house of Mayor Opdyke, a Republican, was plundered. All leading Union men's lives were threatened, their residences attacked, robbed, and in many instances burned. Everywhere the NEGROES were assailed, hung on trees—in one instance burned alive—beaten to death, without regard to sex or age. It was only by the greatest exertions of the military and police that the lives of any of these unoffending citizens were saved. During the prevalence of this reign of terror, FIFTEEN HUNDRED (1,500) PERSONS were murdered and maltreated; only ONE HUNDRED AND SIXTY-SIX (166) of whom were white persons. Fifteen soldiers were killed, and seventy-two wounded. Seventy-six white civilians (males) and three females were also killed. About one-half of these were known to be rioters. The balance of those known to be killed and wounded were colored persons; many of them being women and children.

In the midst of this carnage, Governor Seymour arrived. On the fourteenth of July, the second day of the riot, he addressed the congregated assassins and Democrats in front of the City Hall. They stopped in their bloody and seditious brutalities to listen to the following speech:

"**MY FRIENDS:** I have come down here from the quiet of the country to see what was the difficulty; to learn what all this trouble was concerning the draft. Let me assure you that I am YOUR FRIEND. [Uproarious cheering.] YOU HAVE BEEN MY FRIENDS—[Cries of 'Yes, yes!' 'That's so!' 'We are, and will be again!']—and now I assure you, my fellow-citizens, that I am here to show you a test of my FRIENDSHIP. [Cheers.] I wish to inform you that I have sent my Adjutant General to Washington to confer with the authorities there, AND TO HAVE THIS DRAFT SUSPENDED AND STOPPED! [Vociferous cheers.] I ask you, as good citizens, to wait for his return; and I assure you that I will do all that I can to see that there is no inequality and no wrong done to any one. I WISH YOU TO TAKE GOOD CARE OF ALL PROPERTY, AS GOOD CITIZENS, AND SEE THAT EVERY PERSON IS SAFE. The safe keeping of property and persons rests with you, and I charge you to disturb neither. It is your duty to maintain the good order of the city, and I know you will do it. I wish you now to separate as good citizens, and YOU CAN ASSEMBLE AGAIN WHENEVER YOU WISH TO DO SO. I ask you to leave it all to me now, and I WILL SEE TO YOUR RIGHTS. Wait until my Adjutant returns from Washington, AND YOU SHALL BE SATISFIED. Listen to me, and see that there is no harm done to persons or property, but retire peaceably."

Major General JOHN A. DIX, then commanding in New York, knew his man, and, when SEYMOUR made an enquiry about troops, replied: "I BEG TO LET YOU KNOW THAT I HAVE TROOPS ENOUGH AT MY COMMAND TO TAKE CARE, NOT ONLY OF THE RIOTERS, BUT OF YOU."

Let it be remembered that Horatio Seymour, Democratic candidate for President, encouraged the New York rioters by recognizing them, while their hands were red with loyal blood, as "HIS FRIENDS!"

Let it be remembered that no leading Democrat was injured by them!

Let it be remembered that Vallandigham, who was charged by Jeff. Davis to incite riots in the North, nominated Horatio Seymour in the recent Democratic Convention!

Let it be remembered that this same Vallandigham is a candidate for Congress, in the interest of the new Rebellion, threatened by Seymour, Blair, Wade Hampton, Fort Pillow-Forrest & Co.!

Let it be remembered that all the New York rioters, now living, will vote for SEYMOUR and BLAIR, and against GRANT and COLFAX!

Let it be remembered that the rebels who deserted their country's flag, and tried to destroy, through bloody rebellion, this FREE REPUBLIC, will vote for SEYMOUR AND BLAIR, in the hope of winning at the ballot-box what they lost on the field—the continued enslavement of the colored man, and the triumph of those who claim that this Government was not established for ALL MEN, but for the WHITE MAN's benefit only.

Let it be remembered that every colored voter who acts with the Democracy sustains the party that sustained slavery, desires caste to be established by his own disfranchisement, and upholds the New York Democratic murderers and rioters, who killed so many members of his own race!!

Grant silk ribbon with a patriotic appeal.

OUR CHOICE.

**For President,
ULYSSES S. GRANT.**

For Vice-President,
SCHUYLER COLFAX.

We Saved the Union in the Field—Let us Preserve it at the Ballot-Box.

1868 stylized Grand National Banner. Several versions were done for this campaign.

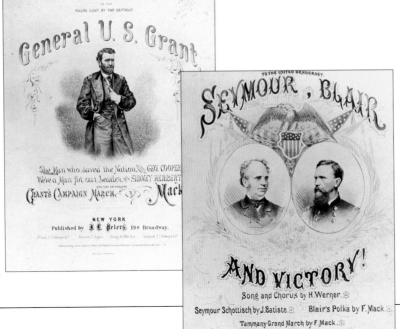

Campaign sheet music for both candidates.

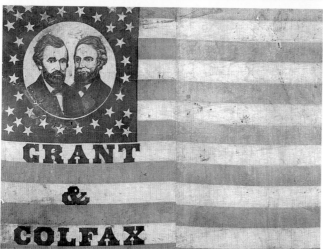

Three cotton flag banners. All flag banners are variations of the national flag. Congress outlawed this "desecration" in 1905.

A rectangular papermâché snuffbox with a hinged lid.

Grant brass pinback.

An exceptional Grant ferrotype.

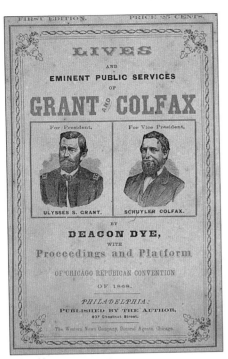

A Republican party campaign
biography of Grant and Colfax.

Examples of elaborate campaign cartes de visite.

Seymour badge with
a paper portrait inset.

1868 campaign letterhead. Political stationery had been in use since 1840.

Stained glass window almost elevating Grant and General Sherman to sainthood. This unusual item was used as a sample to show the excellent workmanship of the manufacturer.

GRANT ✦SHERMAN✦

Grant badge with a paper portrait inset.

Cotton banners. The Seymour is hand-painted and signed "CHARLES & JULIA COLTON."

Metal and glass lantern with colored paper inserts. Affixed to poles, these items were carried in torchlight parades.

Silk ribbon with portraits of Grant and Colfax.

Pair of Grand National Banner prints.

Elaborately woven silk necktie with portraits of the Republican candidates.

★

1872

37 STATES
IN THE UNION

REPUBLICAN

Ulysses S. Grant

ELECTORAL VOTE 286, POPULAR VOTE 55.6%

LIBERAL REPUBLICAN & DEMOCRAT

Horace Greeley

ELECTORAL VOTE,* POPULAR VOTE 43.9%

* Because Greeley died before the electoral college met, Democratic electors scattered their vote.

WILLIAM S. McFEELY
is a graduate of Amherst College and holds a
Ph.D from Yale. Presently the Richard B.
Russell Professor at the University of Georgia,
he is the author of *Yankee Stepfather: General
O.O. Howard and the Freedmen* (1968); *Grant:
A Biography* (1981); and most recently,
Frederick Douglass (1990).

The campaign of 1872 was rich in paradox. The Republican renomination of an incumbent President was not surprising, but Ulysses S. Grant's opponent did not come from the Democratic party. Instead an old foe of the Democrats, Horace Greeley, was chosen by the "best men" within the President's own party, men who had turned against the Republican administration. The leader of their Liberal Republican party, Senator Carl Schurz, was unable to lead; he could not be the presidential candidate because he had not been born in the United States. The Democratic party, fiercely partisan enough to field a candidate in the middle of a civil war, named no candidate of its own. The most telling campaigners were not the candidates, but two cartoonists. And the most interesting ballot cast was one that resulted in the arrest of the voter, which sparked a campaign for votes that took four decades to win.

President Grant was immensely popular as a military hero, but his four years in the White House had produced a mixed record. On the negative side, the President seemed inattentive to his job. Cabinet members had come and gone and indecision seemed the rule. In the Black Friday debacle of 1869 (caused by James Fisk and Jay Gould's attempt to corner the gold market), frantic speculators who had driven up the gold market tried desperately to sell as the market collapsed. Grant and Secretary of the Treasury George Boutwell had moved, in the end, to steady the market, but in the ensuing investigation, charges of personal involvement in the speculations by members of Grant's own family had tarnished his record. So too had well-founded rumors of widespread corruption in the Interior, Navy, and War departments. Grant was also on a collision course with Congress over his insistence that the United States annex the Dominican Republic.

On the other hand, Grant's record had its positive side. Secretary of State Hamilton Fish was making progress toward settling, for a relatively modest sum, the American claims against Great Britain for the damage done American ships by boats built in Britain for the Confederacy. The secretary's cautious negotiating, however, did not satisfy expansionists, who, with their eye on Canada, demanded that "indirect" damages done by the privateers be compensated by larger payments.

Most controversial were actions taken by the administration in behalf of the freed people of the South. Grant had endorsed the Fifteenth Amendment to the Constitution, designed to ensure that black citizens could vote, and he had signed the Ku Klux Klan Bill, as it was known, that Congress had deemed necessary to prevent the violent intimidation of black voters. The Klan had been particularly virulent in South Carolina where blacks (a majority in that state as they were in Mississippi) were making the greatest gains politically. Grant's Attorney General, Amos T. Akerman, a former Confederate soldier from Georgia, finding his attempts to prosecute Klan members under the law frustrated by the intimidation of witnesses, persuaded Grant to lift the writ of *habeas corpus* in nine South Carolina counties. Then Akerman conducted vigorous prosecutions and, in federal court, won convictions. The lifting of the writ raised the ire of civil libertarians and white supremacists alike. Despite the fact that Akerman had then been fired, Grant was accused of militarism.

The civil libertarians in this instance were forerunners of a movement growing within the Republican party. Uneasy about the vulgar wrangling and graft of the post-Civil War years, "an aristocracy of brains, education, and talent" (in John G. Sproat's phrase) sought to reform American politics. These "best men" were, by 1872, ready to bolt the regular Republican party, call themselves Liberal Republicans, and run their own candidate for President.

Before the new group met in convention, the labor movement took action. In February 1872, the National Labor Union, founded in 1866 to work for an eight-hour day and other reforms, converted itself into the National Labor Reform party. They nominated for the presidency Associate Justice of the Supreme Court David Davis. Davis, eager for the White House, hoped that this nomination would be endorsed by the Liberal Republicans when they met in the spring. When Davis's candidacy failed there, he declined to run on the Labor ticket as well. His action seriously undercut this entry of labor into presidential politics as an independent party.

The Liberal Republicans met in May, long the month for reform groups to assemble. Inside Cincinnati's Exposition Hall, they brought to the platform the chair John Adams was said to have sat in when he signed the Declaration of Independence. "There had never been a better class of men gathered on such an occasion," concluded the *New York Tribune*. These gentlemen had had enough of vulgarity. They had in mind a path to the White House well clear of corruption (and the very real problems of Reconstruction), a path that would lead straight back to republican virtue. At the birth of the republic, good men had led the nation; now, contended reform-minded intellectuals like Senator Schurz, Edwin L. Godkin (editor of *The Nation*), Charles Francis Adams (son and grandson of Presidents) and Adams's sons Charles Francis and Henry (both of whom wrote for the *North American Review*) the people would once again choose a man of superior character and wisdom.

The self-appointed delegates, nineteenth-century liberals to the core, had a common purpose of cleansing the body politic. They were determined to cure the nation of a corrupting patronage system by civil service reform and to end special favors to entrepreneurs not always above using bribes to gain tariff protection by imposing free trade. To achieve these goals, Grant must go. The question was who could beat him.

The convention's intelligent, eloquent chairman was Senator Carl Schurz of Missouri. He led the delegation in the drafting of an idealistic platform, but his German birth put the presidency outside his reach. His choice was Charles Francis Adams, whose distinctions were, first, as American minister, having kept Great Britain out of our Civil War and, second, being an Adams. On the first ballot he had a plurality, but was short of a majority. Adams was anything but charismatic and not a few delegates hoped for someone more exciting. The person who provided that excitement, in eccentric form, was Horace Greeley, the editor of the *New York Tribune*, one of the nation's most popular and powerful newspapers. Governor B. Gratz Brown of Missouri, long a foe of Schurz's, began the move to Greeley by withdrawing his own name in the editor's favor. (Brown's reward was his nomination for the vice presidency.)

Despite slight slippage on the fourth ballot, Greeley steadily gained strength. Schurz, too scrupulously fair to use a parliamentary ploy and call for an adjournment vote to stop the landslide, allowed the voting to go to a sixth ballot. When the Illinois delegation switched from its two favorite sons, David Davis and Lyman Trumbull, to the candidate from New York, the "stampede" began; Horace Greeley became the Liberal torch bearer.

Greeley favored tariff protection and had never staunchly supported civil service reform (which Grant had diminished as an issue by instituting some reforms himself). These positions, combined with his quirky personality, alarmed many of the founders of the movement and drove some intellectuals from it. Greeley, though he had been campaigning for the post, was an unlikely man to run for President. Gawky, wispy-whiskered, and famous for his squashed down white hat, he possessed unorthodox enthusiasms—vegetarianism, Fourierism, and human-manure scientific farming, for example. These made him scarcely the classical leader the original Liberals might have dreamed of. As Henry Adams put it: "If the Gods insist on making Mr. Greeley our President, I give up."

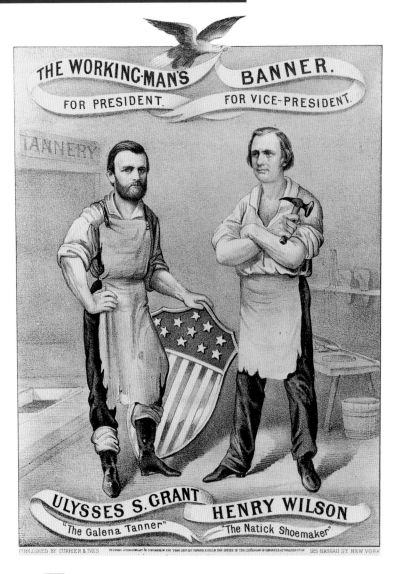

The Republican convention that opened on June 5, in Philadelphia's Academy of Music had no problem about its candidate. The 734 delegates were in town to renominate the President whom everyone referred to as General Grant. On the eve of the convention, "a large meeting of Grant men made their first parade with torches, banners and music, turning out very strong." The parade began with the firing of a cannon; the signal for the opening of the convention the next day was a barrage of artillery fire. It was a war hero that they were determined to reelect. The "bloody shirt," a constant reminder by Republican candidates of the valor and sacrifice of the Civil War, was already being waved.

Grand National Banner print of the Republican candidates.

Greeley campaign items featuring his characteristic hat.

With a bow to the Thirteenth, Fourteenth, and Fifteenth amendments recently added to the Constitution, former Governor William Claflin of Massachusetts declared, "The promises made four years since of progress and reform have been faithfully fulfilled in the guarantee by the nation of equal rights to all . . . and in securing peace and order throughout the entire republic." Recalling the firm enforcement of federal laws designed to halt the violent outrages against the freed people, the dedicated old abolitionist, Gerrit Smith, more in hope than in assurance, told the assembly that "Grant had blessed the country, and now we want to give him time to finish his work by crushing the Ku Klux Klan and saving the negro."

William H. Grey of Arkansas tried to remind his fellow delegates that "the great problem in the South was not yet solved"; the colored people "demanded their civil rights and proper respect." Other black delegates from the South indicated that they knew "where our interests lie." As Frederick Douglass had put it a month earlier (as he failed to follow Charles Sumner, the senator most committed to racial equality, into the Liberal camp): "If the Republican party goes down, freedom goes down with it."

Greeley's hope on this issue was that the spirit of reform would touch the "thinking people" of the South—gentlemen like his fellow Liberal Republicans. A spirit of reconciliation would result in fair treatment of all Southerners, including the freed black citizens. Southern Republicans, acutely aware of the violent intimidation of the freed people, considered this naive at the very least. Like their counterparts a century later, students from Howard University in Washington went South to urge black voters to vote not only to exercise their rights, but to ensure the election of Republicans who, in what proved a forlorn hope, would ensure their physical safety.

Greeley was adamant. He was convinced that goodwill would lead to acceptance of the laws passed to protect the freed peoples' rights; he assumed that the laws would be obeyed. Greeley had been a leader in the successful effort to pardon Confederate President Jefferson Davis, and throughout his campaign his promise was "Full Amnesty" for all former Confederates; reconciliation was his strongest theme.

There has never been so bleak a Democratic convention as the meeting in furnace-hot Baltimore on July 5, 1872. Posters mocking the easily-caricatured Greeley filled windows near Ford's Opera House, but party leaders had already decided that the Liberal

Republican candidate was to be the Democrats' choice as well. One careful student of the election, Michael Perman, denies that the Democrats were asleep. He sees the union with the Liberals as "the culmination of convergence." The slavery issue had disrupted old alliances; now, in "broad-based coalition" the Democrats could escape the "animus and exclusiveness of its identification with the South." The only problem was that if Greeley had alienated many Liberals, he was even more of an anathema to white southerners. The coalition was not going to work.

To match the Liberal Republican's use of John Adams's chair, the Democrats produced another relic of the Declaration of Independence, Jefferson Randolph, the grandson of a signer, to open the meeting. When in the alphabetical polling, the Alabama votes went to Greeley, the subtext of the coalition against the Republicans was revealed. The goal of the Democrats was not to achieve the reforms that the "best men" espoused, but the return to order in the South—based on letting the "thinking people" (the white establishment, which was now largely Democratic) take charge. The Alabamians had given the signal that southern Democrats, openly committed to ending racially integrated government in their region, felt secure with the New York editor, despite the fact that he had been a strong opponent of slavery. The presence in the Georgia delegation of four Confederate generals led by General John B. Gordon reinforced the view that the Democrats determined to restore white supremacy would prevail no matter how much any candidate talked about equality. Greeley was nominated for President as was Gratz Brown for vice president.

HORACE GREELEY.   B. GRATZ BROWN.

Cartes de visite for Greeley and Democratic vice presidential nominee B. Gratz Brown.

But Greeley was a sick man. Despite his vegetarianism and careful attention to his health, his chronic insomnia suggested that he suffered from a neurological ailment. Publicly, however, he owned up to none of this and plunged into an exhausting round of campaign trips. During one stretch of eleven days, he made two hundred speeches. His call for national reconciliation moved many audiences. He knew how to reach the people. To the dismay of the intelligentsia, he used slang and the simple, clear language he had long championed in his newspaper.

Republican strategists began to worry. Knowing that Grant was no orator, they had been, for the most part, content with his decision to spend the summer sitting on the filigreed porch of his Long Branch, New Jersey, cottage, smoking cigars and watching the sea. There seemed to him nothing pressing to do in Washington; when summoned Cabinet members returned to the city early in August, they found that their President had decided not to bother to make the trip.

Greeley ferrotype badge.

The Republicans had one ally who was unequivocal in his determination to depict Horace Greeley as a fool and a knave. Thomas Nast, the famous cartoonist for *Harper's Weekly*, was merciless in his full-page drawings: Greeley shaking hands with John Wilkes Booth across the grave of Abraham Lincoln, with Confederate flag bearers cheering them on, was one scathing example. When the Liberal Republican and Democratic standardbearer was not depicted as evil, Nast turned him into a Humpty Dumpty clown. The counterattack came from Matthew S. Morgan in *Frank Leslie's Illustrated Newspaper*. For

yet another time, Grant had to face the ancient charge that he was a drunk, but some of Morgan's wit may have backfired. He depicted Grant, for example, as a reeling idiot, driving a wagon of split logs into town (which he had done) to vote for James Buchanan in 1856 (which he also had done). A good many veterans, not above a drink themselves, may have identified with their old commander as they sought to make a peacetime living as Grant had once had to do.

These magazines reached few readers except an affluent minority of Americans, but their brilliantly vicious pictures were often torn out and tacked on prominent walls for public display.

As Susan B. Anthony would tell anyone who would listen (and many who would not), half of American adults could not vote. The Fifteenth Amendment, ratified in 1870, specifically prohibited using race as a disqualifier, but, theoretically at least, it left open the question of gender. Anthony had worked determinedly (and unsuccessfully) to have the woman's vote explicitly included. Now two years later she and her fearless allies took the matter straight into the conventions and a polling place.

Early in the Liberal Republican's Cincinnati convention, "the Chairman began reading a communication that was listened to gravely until the words 'claim her rights' was reached, when the whole assembly broke into a tumult of laughter and applause." Laura De Force Gordon's plea to address the meeting was referred to the Committee on Credentials—to die. As Chairman Schurz was presiding, Anthony, undaunted, appeared at his side determined to speak. "A titter passed through the assembly, mingled with hisses," wrote the amused reporter for the *New York Tribune,* a paper that prided itself on being a friend of reform.

The cofounder of the National Woman Suffrage Association "stood her ground," but Schurz studiously refused to recognize her and she left unheard. In June, Anthony and her allies also attended the Republican convention and "were disgusted with the equivocal reception they met." In July, on the final night of the convention, as the Democratic convention's chairman, Senator James R. Doolittle, was leaving the platform, Isabella Beecher Hooker appealed to him to "use his influence with the convention to give them a hearing, but he appeared to be utterly incredulous of his persuasive ability in that direction." Then he made a remark to the effect that women should be married. At that point, unmarried Susan B. Anthony, who had allowed Mrs. Hooker to try a conciliatory approach, stepped forward; hastily excusing himself, the senator fled.

Back home in Rochester, Anthony appeared at her local polling place and registered to vote; on election day she (and fifteen other women) voted. Anthony and three registrars were arrested. At her trial, Associate Justice of the Supreme Court Ward Hunt, on circuit, directed that she be found guilty and fined $100. Refusing to pay, she argued with Hunt, with irrefutable logic clearly stated, that the denial of her vote was a complete denial of her rights as a citizen. He would not relent, but the fine was not enforced; this prevented her from appealing to the full Supreme Court as she had hoped to do. Published as a pamphlet, the transcript of the trial is a classic of feminist literature.

Grant ferrotype badge.

Two minor parties campaigned and appeared on the final tally of votes. A small band of Democratic loyalists, calling themselves the Straight-Out Democratic party, bolted from Greeley. To swell their slim numbers they joined forces with the men trying to take labor into presidential politics and made Charles O'Conor, a respected but little-known New York lawyer, their standard-bearer.

Pressure from this alliance forced both major candidates to make a concentrated effort to win labor votes. Greeley gave speech after speech stressing working-class issues and claimed to be the workers' champion. To counter this (and with no mention of the Republican party at all), posters appeared showing "The Workingman's Banner" waving

Thomas Nast cartoon. Greeley, as Mr. Pickwick, is addressing a convention of disaffected Republicans and a number of his former political enemies.

THE CINCINNATI CONVENTION, IN A PICKWICKIAN SENSE.

Horace Pickwick. "Men and Brethren! A new leaf must be turned over, or there are breakers ahead. The Cincinnati Convention may prove a fiasco, or it may name the next President."

over the heads of Grant, in a tanner's apron, and Wilson, holding a cobbler's mallet. In a Whitmanesque pose, the hand of Grant's burly right arm, with sleeves rolled up, rests insouciantly on his hip. Wilson's arms are linked across a massive chest. Workers were enjoined to vote for "The Galena Tanner" and "The Natick Shoemaker." (Grant had hated his father's tannery; and it had been a long time since Wilson, once apprenticed to a shoemaker, had made any shoes.) Nearly thirty thousand voters heeded neither the speeches nor the poster, but these votes for O'Conor amounted to less than one percent of the total vote.

The other party with a national tally was the single issue Prohibition party. James Black of Pennsylvania, the founder of the party, was its candidate in this their first presidential campaign. He won only 5,608 votes nationwide.

The October elections in Indiana, Ohio, and Pennsylvania were watched with keen interest. Not since Andrew Jackson's day had an elected President failed to carry at least two of those three states. Republican candidates won in both Ohio and Pennsylvania and popular Democratic Senator Thomas A. Hendricks won the governor's seat in Indiana by a slim margin. Republicans breathed easier.

Ulysses Grant, as myth has it, was the valiant and victorious general who, having saved the Union and brought it peace, entered politics only when called from the plough to aid his country in time of need. Grateful countrymen turned to him after Andrew Johnson failed to keep the faith of the martyred Abraham Lincoln. Above the fray, Grant, during his presidential campaigns, stood aside from ordinary politics and politicians.

None of this was true. In 1872, Grant (and even more sharply his wife, Julia Dent Grant, who was determined to hold onto the house she was to live in longer than any other she and her husband shared) kept an eagle eye on every aspect of the campaign. And they had been careful to be ready for it. Grant had not taken an active role in the complex matter of settling the Alabama. claims, pending with Great Britain since the Civil War, but he instructed Secretary of State Hamilton Fish to complete the agreement before the election. Fish came close; the matter was before an international board of arbitration and the President's campaign workers could point proudly to the peaceful process of settling a quarrel with a nation which had been our foe in two wars.

The President did not, however, rest comfortably on such laurels. When George William Child, the editor of the Philadelphia *Public Ledger*, and Henry Wilson and others fell into despair about the campaign, Child visited Grant and complained that, while Greeley was making effective speeches, the President (seemingly incapable of a good speech) made none. Child feared the President did not have the campaign on his mind. Grant

> said nothing, but sent for a map of the United States. He laid the map on the table, went over it with a pencil, and said, "We will carry this State, that State, and that State." . . . When the election came, the result was that Grant carried every State that he said he would.

At the height of the campaign, Grant told Congressman James A. Garfield confidently that the fine rhetoric of the Liberal Republicans was only "the deceptive noise made in the West by prairie wolves; it sounded like hundreds of voices, but turned

out to be only two." On election night, a group of Grant loyalists (including former Confederate General John S. Mosby) sat with the President in the White House as telegraphic returns came in. When the returns, overwhelmingly in his favor, came in from New York, Grant knew he had won—and went to bed.

The final tally was 3,597,132 votes for Grant; 2,834,125 for Greeley. The President had received a greater percentage of the vote than had Abraham Lincoln in the midst of the Civil War. The Democrats, as part of a coalition, had their worst showing of the nineteenth century, if the divided election of 1860 be excepted. Greeley won only five former slave states—Kentucky, Maryland, Missouri, Tennessee, and Texas. Elsewhere in the South, Republicans (both black and white, although increasingly the former) were still able to stave off the white supremacists. Loyalty to Grant and to Lincoln's Republican party held.

For Horace Greeley, the campaign came to the saddest end of any in our history. A week before the election, his wife, long in precarious health, died. Three weeks later, Greeley himself was dead; the exact nature of his illness is still not clear, but the exertions of the campaign certainly contributed to his weakening. President Grant rode in an open carriage, surrounded by fifty policemen, to the funeral at the Church of the Divine Paternity in New York; crowds along the street muffled the instinct to cheer. The black-bordered columns of the *New York Tribune* carried the long list of names of the many printers and other workers who attended the great editor's funeral. The story omitted mention of the presence of the President of the United States.

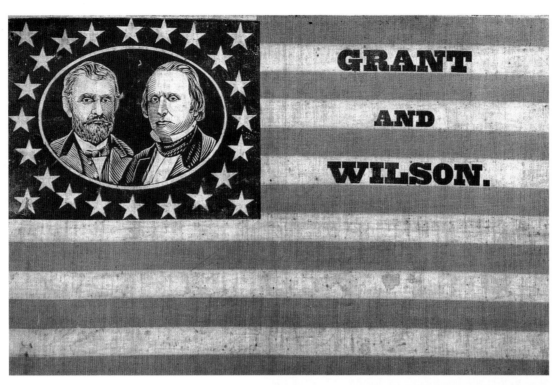

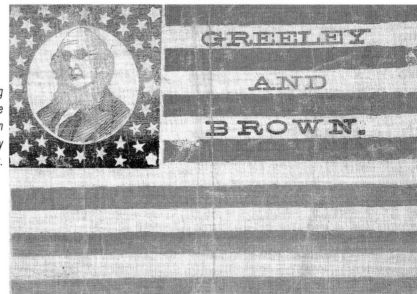

Three rare flag banners. There are very few known examples of Greeley portrait flags.

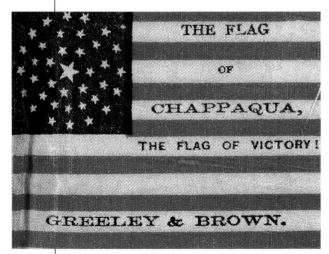

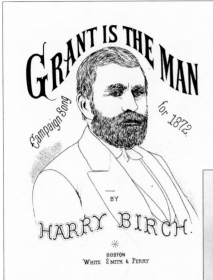

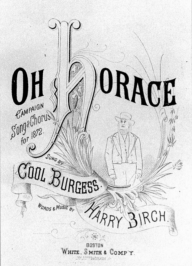

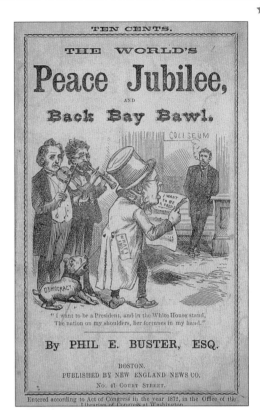

Anti-Greeley satirical pamphlet.

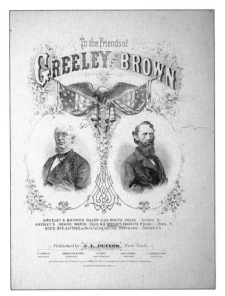

Campaign sheet music.

Greeley was known as the "Sage of Chappaqua,"
referring to his home north of New York City.

HORACE GREELEY.   B. GRATZ BROWN.

Glass goblets commemorating
the 1872 candidates.

Silver-plated serving tray engraved with a portrait of Grant.

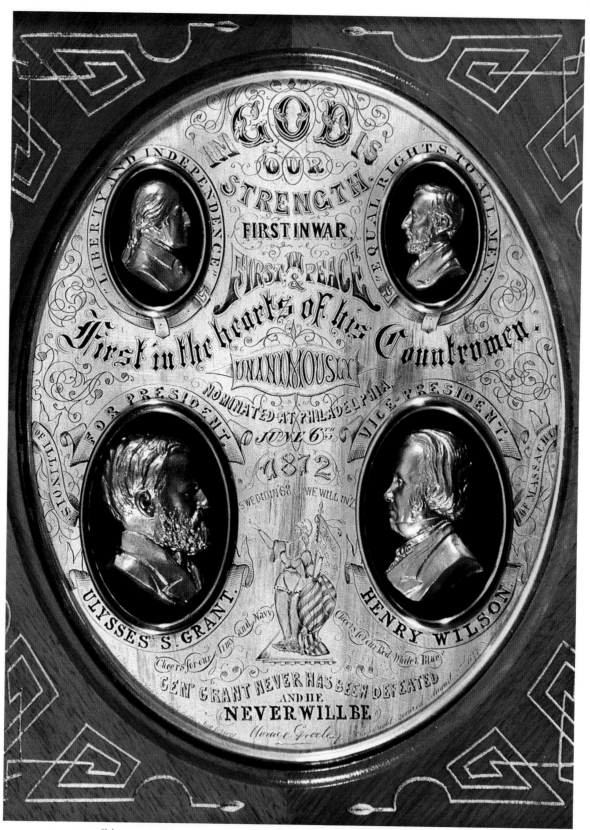

Elaborate engraved steel plaque with high-relief brass portraits of Washington, Lincoln, Grant, and Wilson.

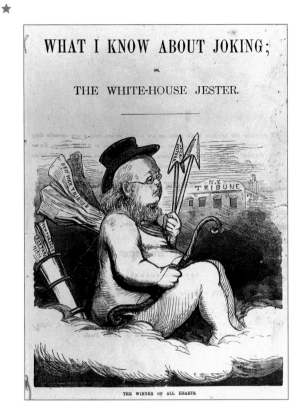

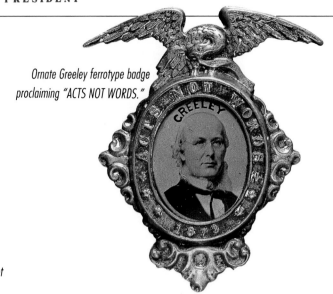

Ornate Greeley ferrotype badge proclaiming "ACTS NOT WORDS."

Anti-Greeley satirical pamphlet with cover illustration by Thomas Nast.

Carte de visite for Grant and Wilson.

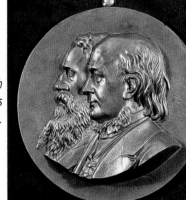

Brass plaque which hung in Greeley's Tribune office.

Grant-Wilson embossed leather medallion.

Ornate portrait badges in stamped brass shells.

Grant castiron match holder.

*Embossed brass
shell medallions of
Grant and Greeley.*

Grand National Banner print
of the Democratic candidates.

Brass campaign clothing
button comparing Greeley
to Benjamin Franklin.
Both were publishers and
wore similar eyeglasses.

Greeley autographed chromolithograph.

Unusual photo badge of Greeley and Brown
in the shape of Greeley's characteristic hat.

Whimsical anti-Greeley portrait fan festooned with feathers to imitate Greeley's lavish beard. The reverse has an assortment of satirical cartoons.

WEIGHED IN THE BALANCE AND FOUND WANTING

U. S. G.: "Well, who'd have thought that the old white hat, boots and axe would have more weight than all these hangers-on of mine?"

THE WHITED SEPULCHRE. COVERING THE MONUMENT OF INFAMY WITH HIS WHITE HAT AND COAT

"WHAT ARE YOU GOING TO DO ABOUT IT," IF "OLD HONESTY" LETS HIM LOOSE AGAIN?

MIXING DAY AT HARPERS'—MAKING MUD TO FLING AT GREELEY.

Editor Curtis.—"Don't spit in it, Thomas; it is not gentlemanly."

CLASPING HANDS OVER THE BLOODLESS (SAR)C(H)ASM

★

1876

33 STATES
IN THE UNION

REPUBLICAN

Rutherford B. Hayes

ELECTORAL VOTE 185, POPULAR VOTE 48%

DEMOCRAT

Samuel J. Tilden

ELECTORAL VOTE 184, POPULAR VOTE 51%

DONALD A. RITCHIE
is associate historian in the Senate Historical
Office and an adjunct faculty member of the
Cornell in Washington program. His books
include *James M. Landis: Dean of the Regulators*
(1980); *Press Gallery: Congress and the
Washington Correspondents* (1991); and a high
school textbook, *History of a Free Nation* (1991).

W

hen the crowds gathered to commemorate the hundredth anniversary of the Battle of Bunker Hill in June 1875, they especially cheered those troops representing the southern states. "Nearly all of these had served in the Confederate army," noted *The Centennial History of the United States,* "and their presence in the metropolis of New England was an emphatic proof that the Union has indeed been restored." But while the centennial of the American Revolution raised hopes for an era of national reunion, the presidential election of 1876 reopened the old wounds and threatened renewed division.

The United States had suffered economic turmoil since its last presidential election. A postwar railroad boom had collapsed in the Panic of 1873, throwing the stock exchanges into chaos, closing banks, causing five thousand businesses to fail, and triggering strikes, unemployment, and homelessness. Falling crop prices hurt farmers, as did the government's deflationary policies, which the farmers claimed had doubled the cost of repaying their debts. In the White House, Ulysses S. Grant, the hero of Appomattox, proved unequal to the challenge of a national economic crisis. Repeated scandals in his administration further undermined Grant's national standing. Although he had made a muddle of the presidency, Grant would have accepted a third term if it came to him as "an imperative duty." The House of Representatives squelched that conceit in December 1875, by voting 233 to 18 to denounce a third term as "unwise, unpatriotic, and fraught with peril to our free institutions."

Benefiting from the hard times, Democrats in 1874 had won their first majority in the House since the Civil War, increasing from 30 percent to 62 percent of the House membership. Anticipating the upcoming presidential election, congressional Democrats investigated every agency of the administration, and had little trouble finding irregularities. One probe caused Secretary of War W.W. Belknap to resign for selling lucrative trading posts at western military forts. Grant's own treasury secretary, Benjamin Bristow, revealed that whiskey distillers had bribed government officials to avoid paying federal taxes. Republican journalist Benjamin Perley Poore despaired that his once noble party "had sunk under the combined effects of political money making, inflated currency, whiskey rings, revenue frauds, Indian supply steals, and pension swindles."

Anti-third-term sentiments opened the Republican nomination to a host of ambitious politicians. The clear front-runner was former Speaker of the House James G. Blaine of Maine, whose early training as a newspaper editor had given him a professional knack for generating publicity. Blaine faced intense rivalry from New York Senator Roscoe Conkling, a vainglorious man who had never forgiven Blaine for cutting remarks about his "turkey gobbler strut" and Hyperion curl, which had spawned countless editorial cartoons. Indiana Senator Oliver P.

Morton drew his support from the Reconstruction governments in the southern states. Reformers in the party rallied behind Secretary Bristow. Trailing the pack were the favorite-son governors—John F. Hartranft of Pennsylvania and Rutherford B. Hayes of Ohio.

Blaine jumped into the lead by uncharacteristically "waving the bloody shirt." When House Democrats proposed amnesty for former Confederates, he demanded that Congress exclude Confederate President Jefferson Davis for his complicity in the mistreatment and death of Union soldiers at Andersonville prison. Sputtering Democrats who rose to Davis's defense simply reinforced their image as the party of rebellion. Having made himself the man to beat, Blaine immediately became mired in scandal when newspapers published charges that he had improperly accepted railroad stocks. Blaine defended himself vigorously, but public doubts about his integrity tormented the rest of his political career. Still, at the convention Robert G. Ingersoll shook the rafters when he nominated Blaine as the party's "plumed knight." Blaine might have secured the nomination that evening if local officials had not announced their inability to light the hall's gas lamps. Adjournment gave anti-Blaine forces time to coalesce, and the variety of opposition, from spoilsmen to reformers, eventually settled upon Rutherford B. Hayes. Cynics noted that the gas burned brightly in the convention hall after Hayes won the nomination.

Noncontroversial Rutherford B. Hayes had been everyone's first choice for vice president ("Conkling and Hayes is the ticket that pays," ran one slogan), and sec-

ond choice for President. An upright family man and Harvard-trained lawyer, Hayes had a creditable military record as a Union army general. In the House he had supported Reconstruction, and he campaigned for giving blacks the right to vote in Ohio as well as in the South. The three-term governor managed to preserve a dual image as party loyalist and reformer. Hayes's letter accepting the nomination appealed broadly to his party by endorsing civil service reform, hard currency, public schools against sectarian (Catholic) interference, and peace in the southern states through "a hearty and generous recognition of the rights of all by all."

Meeting in St. Louis, the Democrats had little trouble choosing as their nominee New York Governor Samuel J. Tilden, who had prosecuted the "Tweed Ring" in New York City and fought the "Canal Ring" in Albany. Also a hard-money man, Tilden overwhelmed Indiana Governor Thomas A. Hendricks, an inflationist, but accepted Hendricks for vice president to balance the ticket. Austere, methodical, and secretive, Tilden had amassed a fortune as a corporate lawyer, railroad reorganizer, and land and stock speculator, earning a reputation as "the Great Forecloser." A bachelor, Tilden lived in a "fine old mansion" on Manhattan's Gramercy Park. As the Democratic candidate, he called for "a revival of Jeffersonian democracy," with its decentralization of government and "high standards of official morality."

Tilden represented the conservative business and financial wing of the Democratic party, which promised retrenchment and reform, and offered little to depressed farmers or discontented workers. Since both parties were divided on the currency issue, neither the Republicans nor the Democrats made it a prominent theme during the campaign. Inflationists turned to the Greenback party for currency reform, but their candidate, eighty-five-year-old inventor and philanthropist Peter Cooper, seemed unlikely to rally many voters.

As tradition dictated, the candidates did not campaign. Tilden, in frail health and naturally reclusive, remained in New York. Hayes similarly believed that "silence is the only safety." The *Nation* noted that Hayes would not discuss current issues except to agree that "ours was a republican form of government and this was the hundredth year of the national existence." Hayes left Ohio only to visit the Centennial Exhibition in Philadelphia—where he went unrecognized until he signed the register at a pavilion. Hayes did encourage his vice presidential candidate, New York Representative William A. Wheeler, to speak in a few critical states, but Wheeler declined due to insomnia. "Speaking, and the presence of crowds, excite me and intensify my wakefulness," he apologized. In the absence of their candidates, both parties rallied the faithful with torchlight parades, barbecues, fireworks, songfests, and endless hours of political speeches.

Behind the scenes, the two national party organizations operated very differently. Republican National Committee chairman Zachariah Chandler relied on the various state party organizations to conduct their own campaigns, expecting that Republican patronage men would work hard to keep their jobs. The national committee devoted its attentions to assessing Republican officeholders 2 percent of their salaries to

Cabinet card photograph of Rutherford B. Hayes and his wife. Cabinet cards first appeared in the 1860s as larger versions of the carte de visite.

underwrite the party's campaign literature. Chandler had been the choice of Grant, not Hayes, for national chairman, and he rarely communicated with the nominee. By contrast, Tilden worked closely with Democratic national chairman Abram S. Hewitt, a New York congressman and industrialist (and Peter Cooper's son-in-law). In a pioneering application of business methods to politics, Hewitt introduced new techniques of promotion and salesmanship, organizing a Literary Bureau that produced pamphlets and a hefty campaign textbook and a Speakers' Bureau that both scheduled speakers and provided them material geared to each locality. *New York Tribune* editor Whitelaw Reid warned Hayes that Tilden felt confident of victory, adding, "my experience with him has led me to regard him as the most sagacious political calculator I have ever seen."

Democrats largely ignored Hayes and focused on Grant era scandals and on corruption in the southern "carpetbagger" governments. They acted as if they were prose-

Stereoscopic cards picturing large street banners for Michigan rallies supporting Hayes & Wheeler and Tilden & Hendricks. These cards, placed in special viewers, give the appearance of a three-dimensional scene.

these emotions with such songs as "O Stand Fast, Dear Native Land," "The Boys in Blue," and "The National Veterans' Song." "Attention, Ye Freeman!" warned black Republicans that:

> Traitors are lurking, and craftily working
> In secret to gain what was hopeless in fight;
> O Freedom! to cripple thy motions by fetters,
> *White Liners* still plot with their northern
>   abettors:
> Now flout them with scorn!
>   A glorious morn,
> Shall send them back slinking to shadows
>   of night.

Candidate Hayes wanted Republican speakers to emphasize "the danger of giving the Rebels the Government," believing that northern fears of the South put the Republicans on the safest road. "It leads people away from hard times, which is our deadliest foe." Republican stump speakers warned that Tilden's election would nullify the constitutional amendments that gave the freedmen their political and civil rights, and denounced the atrocities of the Ku Klux Klan. The fiery Robert Ingersoll reached the apex of "bloody shirt" rhetoric when he told a Grand Army of Republic convention:

> Every man that tried to destroy this nation was a Democrat. Every man that loved slavery better than liberty was a Democrat. The man that assassinated Abraham Lincoln was a Democrat. . . . Soldiers, every scar you have on your heroic bodies was given to you by a Democrat.

The two parties stood most starkly opposed on the issue of Reconstruction. Democrats had committed their party to removing federal troops, and counted on the votes of the already "redeemed" southern states. Republicans continued to embrace Re-

cuting the entire Republican party. Democratic speakers extolled "Honest Sam Tilden," and one party song promised:

> The night of gloom is gliding out,
> Forth breaks the rosy day,
> And Tilden is the sun of hope,
> That lights the nation's way.

Republicans responded by fighting the election of 1876 as if it were the last campaign of the Civil War. Union men had been offended by the large numbers of ex-Confederates elected to Congress in 1874, and saw the gains of the war about to evaporate with a Democratic presidential victory. The "Hayes & Wheeler Song Book" played to construction, but privately candidate Hayes doubted "the ultra measures relating to the South." He favored reconciliation between the sections, assuming that if treated fairly, the South would protect the rights of the freemen. Unaware of the candidate's uncertainty, John M. Langston exhorted an audience of blacks that in view of Tilden's plan to leave suffrage to the states, "if you still wish to stay in politics, to preserve your citizenship, and use your franchise, and be *men*, you will vote for Hayes and Wheeler."

On election night, a headline in the Republican *New York Tribune* conceded: "Tilden Elected." Tilden polled 250,000 more popular votes than Hayes, winning the southern states, New York, Connecticut, New Jersey, and Indiana (the same combination of electoral votes that later put Democrat Grover Cleveland in the White House). But federal troops still occupied Louisiana, Florida, and South Carolina. Republican politicians immediately concentrated on winning their electoral votes. With these, and a single disputed elector in Oregon, Hayes could be President.

Republicans attributed Democratic victories in the South to intimidation of the freedmen. Groups like South Carolina's "Red Shirts" had invaded Republican meetings, harassed speakers, and threatened audiences. Hayes did not doubt that the majority of voters in the disputed southern states had been Republicans. "But the Democrats have endeavored to defeat the will of the lawful voters by the perpetration of crimes whose magnitude and atrocity has no parallel in our history," he wrote in his diary. Anxious not to appear ambitious for office, Hayes had acted so coolly indifferent in the weeks leading up to the election that he surprised even himself. He had steeled himself for defeat.

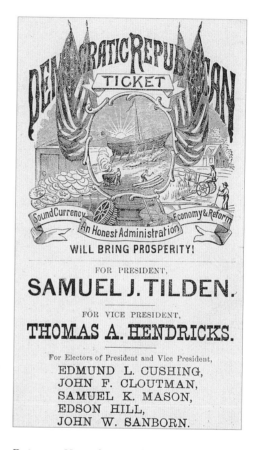

Campaign ballot with promises of honesty and prosperity contained in the Democratic platform.

But once Hayes became honestly convinced that he had won the election he fought tenaciously to claim the office. It was Tilden, not Hayes, whose nerves failed and let the presidency slip away.

The three disputed southern states each submitted two conflicting certificates of election. Tilden needed only one of these states to win; Hayes needed them all. The Constitution empowered the House to choose a President if no candidate won a majority of the electoral college, and the Democratic majority there would have elected Tilden. But the Constitution also assigned the President of the Senate to count the electoral ballots. The Senate's Republican majority want-

Campaign ribbons on salesman's sample card used to solicit merchants' orders.

ed President Pro Tempore Thomas Ferry (in place of the deceased vice president) to make the choice. Assuming that Ferry would count the Republican ballots, Democrats objected. Finally, on January 18, 1877, a joint committee proposed creation of a special electoral commission to determine which ballots were valid. To this commission the House would appoint three Democrats and two Republicans; the Senate three Republicans and two Democrats; and the Supreme Court two Democrats, two Republicans, and one independent.

Neither side initially liked the plan. Democratic Speaker Samuel Randall thought it "positively disgraceful to talk about raffling off the Presidency!" Tilden, too, deplored the commission, but vacillated and finally agreed to support it. Randall then went along, feeling pressure also from businessmen who wanted a peaceful solution to the political crisis. "We will be strengthened in business circles all over the U.S. by assuming the attitude of the party that are for peace and harmony," one Philadelphia merchant advised the Speaker. The *Cincinnati Gazette* correspondent Henry Van Ness Boynton similarly observed that "the business interests of New York (Democrats and Republicans) made themselves felt." For his part, Hayes considered the commission "a surrender," and suspected the motives of its principal author, Senator Roscoe Conkling, who despised Hayes's plans for civil service reform. But the Senate approved the bill by a comfortable margin of 47 to 17. In the House, five-sixths of all votes for the commission came from Democrats.

Democrats expected Supreme Court Justice David Davis to hold the swing vote on the commission, and hoped for his support on at least some of the disputed ballots. Then, unexpectedly, Democrats and Green-backers in the Illinois legislature elected Davis to the Senate. Davis resigned from the court and declined to join the commission, where his place was taken by Justice Joseph Bradley. On February 2, the electoral commission convened in the Supreme Court chamber at the Capitol. Sitting like a court, the commission heard Democratic counsel David Dudley Field question "whether or not the American people stand powerless before a gigantic fraud," and entreat them to investigate voting irregularities behind the Republican certificates. For the Republicans, William M. Evarts insisted that the commission lacked authority to conduct an investigation of the state election boards. Justice Bradley accepted Evarts's argument and sided with the Republican members of the commission. By repeated votes of 8 to 7, the commission declared that Hayes had won all the disputed electors.

A joint session of Congress still had to count the ballots. Benjamin Perley Poore recalled that "disappointed politicians and place-hunters among the Democrats talked wildly about inaugurating Mr. Tilden by force." Democratic Representative Henry Watterson summoned a hundred thousand Tilden supporters to march on Washington. "Irreconcilable" Democrats in the House planned to filibuster to prevent the counting of the ballots.

Behind-the-scenes negotiations prevented the centennial election from ending in violence. "Authorized friends" of the Republican candidate had approached southern Democrats in Congress to reach a compromise. Republicans dangled promises of railroad construction in the war-ravaged South.

Elaborately woven silk ribbons from the Philadelphia Centennial Exhibition of 1876.

Grand National Banner print for the Republican candidates.

ize southern Democrats. Tilden refused to speak out against this "intrigue," warning his party's firebrands that another civil war would "end in the destruction of free government." Henry Watterson dolefully concluded that the missing ingredient in Tilden's character was "the touch of the dramatic." Lacking Blaine's audacity or Hayes's determination, Tilden "was a philosopher and took the world as he found it."

Angry House Democrats could yet have stalled the counting of the ballots. When the electoral commission voted consistently for Hayes, Speaker Randall had been ready to propose legislation to make the secretary of state acting President until a new election could be held. However, Randall again deferred to Tilden's wishes and backed away from confrontation. Some House members publicly talked of the need of shedding blood. But after Louisiana Representative William Levy, one of the Wormley Hotel negotiators, announced that he had "solemn, earnest, and, I believe, truthful assurance" that Hayes would withdraw troops from the South, Democratic resistance waned.

At 4 A.M. on March 2, pages awakened sleeping senators, who marched in procession to the House chamber, carrying two mahogany boxes filled with electoral ballots. Despite the late hour, the House galleries were overcrowded with "excited citizens." Senator Ferry read the ballots and declared Hayes and Wheeler elected. On a train bound for Washington, an aide rapped on the door of Hayes's sleeping compartment to read a telegraph confirming his election.

Elected President on the strength of the disputed electoral ballots, Hayes deserted the southern Republicans who had certi-

southerners were more interested in the removal of all federal troops from their states. Meeting at the Wormley Hotel in Washington, on the evening of February 26, Hayes's men agreed that he would withdraw federal troops, appoint a southerner to the Cabinet, and assist in the economic rebuilding of the South, promises that helped neutral-

Matching pair of woven silk ribbons. Identical designs were, and still are, used by manufacturers for opposing parties.

fied them. South Carolina's embattled governor, Daniel H. Chamberlain, pointed out that his state had "94,000 colored voters and 68,000 white voters," and that the Democrats claimed to have polled "23,000 *more* than their entire voting strength." Their surplus must have come from fraud and intimidation of black voters. Yet Hayes held up his end of the bargain and removed federal troops from the South Carolina statehouse. The departing governor issued a statement to South Carolina Republicans: "Today—April 10, 1877—by the order of the

President whom your votes alone rescued from overwhelming defeat, the Government of the United States abandons you."

Months later, journalist John Russell Young discussed the election with Senator Conkling. The verdict of the electoral commission, Conkling reflected, was not that of the people. "He commended the patience and submission of the Democracy, and especially of Mr. Tilden, in accepting it peacefully, and said with feeling that the Republicans would never have endured what had been imposed by them upon the Democrats."

Below and opposite: Stone-lithographs, identical in design, utilizing the Centennial theme.

Matched sheet music. Intricate hand-cut type is the main graphic motif.

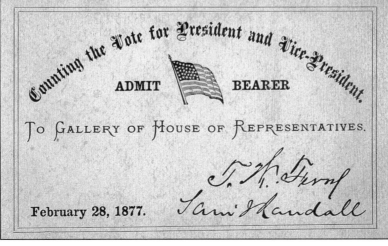

Admission ticket to the electoral vote-counting held in the House of Representatives. The joint session of Congress actually counted the presidential electoral vote on March 2, but tickets bearing several dates had been prepared in advance.

Rutherford B. Hayes.

William A. Wheeler.

Samuel J. Tilden.

Thomas A. Hendricks.

Cabinet card photographs of the 1876 candidates and their running mates. Perhaps no more than a hundred varieties of campaign items — mainly badges, tokens, and ribbons — survive from this spirited but poorly financed campaign.

Embossed tin-shell medallion of Hayes.

Silvered brass badge of Hayes and Wheeler.

Ferrotype badge of Tilden and Hendricks with a Victorian filigree border.

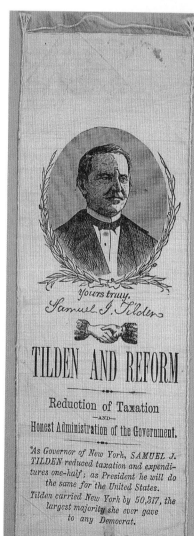

Printed ribbon with Tilden's tax reduction promise.

Pair of cotton bandannas
for party's Centennial
candidates. Note George
Washington's image
above them.

Graphic cotton pennant.

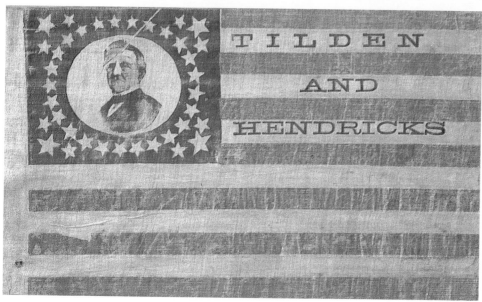

Above: An outstanding example of perhaps the most graphic cotton flag banner ever designed.
Left: Tilden portrait cotton flag banner.

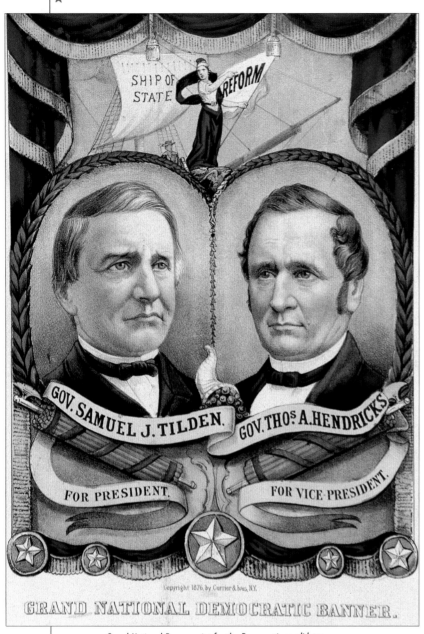

Grand National Banner print for the Democratic candidates.

Broadside announcing a rally for the Democratic candidates.

Pair of silk ribbons with paper photographs applied
to the cloth. Delicate even when first issued this
set has survived the years in excellent condition.

Simulated bank note. Peter Cooper, who received 1 percent of the 1876 vote as the presidential candidate of the Greenback party, was a harbinger of the currency debates of the 1880s and 1890s.

BE STRONG!
BE COURAGEOUS!
For President,

PETER COOPER, the FRIEND of the Working Man, the PROTECTOR of the Poor and Distressed

THE LORD IS
WITH THE RIGHT.
For V. President,

1776   THE BANK OF BREAD.   1876

PAY TO THE ORDER OF
OWN LABOR, FOR AN
YOURSELF, BY YOUR
HONEST DAYS WORK,

PETER COOPER.

THREE DOLLARS

SAM'L F. CARY.

National Prosperity
cannot be restored by
enforcing idleness on a
large portion of people.
PETER COOPER.

By Voting for Cooper & Cary, and against National Banks, Untaxed Bondholders and Monopolists.

No. ☐   Independent Greenback Party.

No Nation can exist
with an untaxed mo-
nopoly in its midst.
SAM'L F. CARY.

Hayes lantern with paper transparencies to allow light to shine through stars and portrait.

Paper ballots for the 1876 election.

Lithographed tin collar-box dated March 4, 1877, commemorating the inauguration of Hayes and Wheeler. These tins held replaceable shirt collars.

Colored lithograph under glass, mounted as a brooch. Picturing a torchlight campaign marcher and the legend "Our Boys in Blue/ we go for Hayes."

Portrait badge with paper photographs of Tilden and Hendricks.

Medallic badges for Hayes and Tilden. The rooster was the Democratic party symbol.

Tilden ferrotype.

Color lithograph poster glorifying the Republican candidates while explaining the party's platform.

1880
38 STATES
IN THE UNION

REPUBLICAN
James A. Garfield
ELECTORAL VOTE 214, POPULAR VOTE 48.5%

DEMOCRAT
Winfield S. Hancock
ELECTORAL VOTE 155, POPULAR VOTE 48.1%

GREENBACK-LABOR
James B. Weaver
ELECTORAL VOTE 0, POPULAR VOTE 3.4%

LEONARD DINNERSTEIN
is a professor of history at the University
of Arizona. His published works include the
Leo Frank Case (1968); *America and the
Survivors of the Holocaust* (1982); and
*Uneasy at Home: Antisemitism and
the American Jewish Experience* (1987).
At present, he is completing a study
of American antisemitism.

Graphic cotton pennant. The hand-cut wood type in a floral design was typical of the period.

In the campaign of 1880 we find what may be the most forgotten election in American history. Few can remember the major party candidates—Winfield Scott Hancock for the Democrats and James A. Garfield for the Republicans—and hardly anyone can name the candidates of the minor parties: James B. Weaver of the Greenback-Labor party and Neil Dow of the Prohibitionists. Nonetheless, the 1880 campaign dramatized the contrast between the traditional way of conducting presidential elections and modern campaign methods. Hancock sat back in the old style and waited for events to occur; he made no effort to direct them. Garfield made decisions that others followed and guided his party to a narrow victory in November.

After the nominating conventions, pundits assumed that General Hancock, a Union veteran who hailed from Pennsylvania and had distinguished himself at Gettysburg, and his running-mate, William H. English of Indiana, would emerge victorious. There had been relatively little opposition to the nominations, the Democrats appeared unified, and the Republicans looked anguished and divided. Garfield, also a former Union general and later a congressman from Ohio, emerged as the party's standard-bearer after thirty-five fruitless ballots. To placate those whose assistance he needed but whose confidence he lacked, the nominee chose Chester Alan Arthur of New York as his running-mate.

Election custom dictated that presidential and vice presidential nominees acknowledge their nominations and enunciate their views in letters of acceptance. These letters embodied and repeated the platform planks adopted by their party's convention. In 1880 none of the four major nominees made memorable statements, and only Arthur strongly committed himself to civil service reform. Opposition to further Chinese immigration, a burning issue in California and the West, the continuation of the tariff to help American industry (although the Democrats supported a tariff for revenue only), and separation of church and state were among those items included in the party platforms. Garfield, in particular, not wishing to divide his party any further, gave only perfunctory endorsement to civil service reform, spoke vaguely on the currency, and evaded the tariff. Hancock's letter abounded with platitudes. *Harper's Weekly* thought it possessed "a certain child-like innocence" while the other national weekly, *The Nation,* wrote that "no one but a scoundrel or a person of defective understanding would dispute a single proposition contained in it."

Two minor parties, the Prohibition and the Greenback-Labor, thought they knew how to solve the nation's ills. The former nominated a temperance crusader, Neal Dow of Maine, while the latter picked former Union General, James B. Weaver of Iowa. The Prohibitionists believed that corking the liquor flow would produce prosperity and happiness for the nation. The Greenback-Labor party favored larger policies that future candidates would embrace—a national currency, an eight-hour workday, sanitary codes in industry, curtailment of child labor, congressional regulation of interstate commerce, votes for women and equal voting rights for African-Americans.

The Republicans and Democrats campaigned along familiar lines. Both parties muddied issues or, more frequently, ignored them. The Republicans reminded voters that they had fought and died to save the Union and continually "waved the bloody shirt" until a Democratic-Fusion candidate won the Maine gubernatorial election in September. Then Republican orators put away the "bloody shirt" and emphasized the protective tariff. They warned voters that "a tariff for revenue only," which the Democratic platform called for, would increase unemployment and reduce protection for American manufacturers. The Democrats recalled the "fraud of '76," and charged Republicans with corruption in Washington.

On the major problems of the day—the industrial transformation of America and its polarizing consequences of enormous wealth and acute poverty—the major parties said nothing. On the other issues—resumption of specie payment for greenbacks, silver coinage, and civil service—both Republicans and Democrats equivocated. Recognizing that the election would be extremely close, neither party cared to alienate any voting bloc by taking a strong stand on controversial matters. Only the minor parties expressed themselves vigorously; but national prosperity diminished their appeals.

From his home in Ohio Garfield meticulously planned Republican strategy. He directed even minor details and personally wrote to county committee chairmen all over the country. During the campaign what often appeared careless, untoward, and bizarre had in reality been well thought out in advance. By remaining at home for most of the period between nomination and election, he conformed to the prescribed pattern of political behavior.

Garfield also inaugurated the "front porch" campaign whereby voters came to him and he received an amazing mixture of admiring throngs. No presidential candidate had ever before welcomed the variety of visitors that Garfield handled with perfect aplomb. An endless stream of politicians, Union veterans, businessmen, suffragists, prohibitionists, and children made the pilgrimage to his farm in Mentor, Ohio. They came singly and in groups. They carried banners, presented petitions, offered gifts, recited speeches, sang songs, and declaimed poetry. They climbed fences, trampled grass, shouted, whistled, and cheered. Some wore linen dusters and tricornered hats, others made speeches in German. They ranged from the lordly Senator Roscoe Conkling of New York to the earnest Young Men's First Voters' Garfield and Arthur Club of Cleveland. Some ate sandwiches; others munched cookies; all quenched their thirst with whatever liquid refreshment the candidate's wife provided.

Aside from entertaining patricians and plebeians, and placating curiosity-seekers and well-wishers, the Republican nominee organized a talented campaign staff who solicited assistance from the financially powerful and politically potent. To obtain financial aid from men like Jay Gould, Chauncey Depew, and John D. Rockefeller, Garfield pledged to appoint to the Supreme Court only men who respected the "vested rights" of capitalists.

The Republicans also exploited Hancock's record to their advantage. His lack of political experience, his staunch southern support, and his careless statements exposed him to telling charges. A biting Republican campaign pamphlet, "A Record of the Statesmanship and Political Achievements of General Winfield Scott Hancock . . . compiled from the Records," summarized his "achievements." Upon opening it, one found seven blank pages and at the bottom of the eighth page one word: "finis." Hancock's popularity in the South gave Republicans the opportunity to portray the general with a parody of the then popular Gilbert and Sullivan tune, "When I Was a Lad" (from *H.M.S. Pinafore*):

> In the Union War I fought so well
> That my name is greeted with the "rebel yell"

Hancock also committed what Garfield characterized as a "fatal error" with his ill-considered remarks about the tariff. Hancock stated that regardless of whether a Republican or a Democrat were elected, a certain amount of money had to be raised by a tariff, and that the manufacturing interests of the country would have "just as much protection under a Democratic Administration as under a Republican Administration." He concluded with the opinion: "The tariff question is a local question." *Harper's Weekly* called the statement "loose, aimless, unintelligent, absurd." *The Nation* declared, "The General's talk about the tariff is that of a man who knows nothing about it, and who apparently, until he began to talk, had never thought about it."

Thomas Nast titillated millions and supplied the coup de grace with a scathing cartoon of a perplexed Hancock asking New Jersey's Senator Theodore F. Randolph,

Unique rebus ferrotype badge for Winfield Hancock — hand+cock.

"WHO IS TARIFF, AND WHY IS HE FOR REVENUE ONLY?" Although unfair to the Democratic nominee, whose words had been twisted out of context, the cartoon expressed exactly Hancock's difficulties by portraying him as a befuddled campaigner.

In contrast to the empty but shrewd Republican campaign the Democrats offered little. They made slurs against Garfield and dug up some incriminating material about his past involvement with the Crédit Mobilier scandal. They also accused Garfield of having left a tailor's bill unpaid many years earlier and of stealing furniture from a southern widow during the Civil War. And they too produced a pamphlet comparing the "Bright Record of the Patriot Hancock" with the "Black Record of the Politician Garfield."

Stereoscopic cards of Garfield and Hancock.

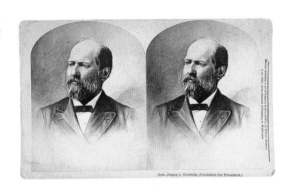

Stereoscopic cards of Garfield and Hancock.

None of these limp efforts had much impact. Indeed, there is no indication that either the Republican or Democratic platforms, candidates, or "issues" affected enough voters to alter the eventual outcome.

What proved decisive were the activities in Indiana and New York. Indiana, which held its state elections in October, had gone Democratic in every one of them since 1870. In 1880, however, the Republicans eked out a victory. It is impossible to isolate the determining factor in an election where the majority won by only 6,953 votes out of nearly half-a-million cast. Nevertheless, certain points stand out: poor management, dissension among the Democrats plus a weak nominee for governor, astute Republican planning, local issues, and much skulduggery. Both parties threw their most powerful resources into the Hoosier state,

and there were nightly barnfires, parades, and rabble-rousing speeches. But the Republicans campaigned more effectively. They wisely ignored the issues of silver coinage and greenbacks—two volatile topics in debtor Indiana—but exploited Hancock's comment about the tariff as "a local issue," and warned that under the Democratic administration manufacturers would be unprotected and workers unemployed.

Each party accused the other, and not without justification, of using violence, thieves, desperadoes, gangsters, and ruffians. The Democrats added that "southern Negroes" had been herded into Indiana to pad the Republican vote, or, as the Democratic Executive Committee put it, the Republicans had a "scheme to Africanize our state for political purposes. . . ." The charge sounds accurate because in a state with 498,437 eligible voters, 470,699 votes were cast. Not to be outdone, however, the Republicans countered with a stinging rebuke of the South's (hence the Democratic party's) treatment of African-Americans:

> Sing a song of shotguns,
> Pocket full of knives
> Four-and-twenty black men,
> Running for their lives;
> When the polls are open,
> Shut the nigger's mouth.
> Isn't that a bully way
> To make a solid South?

> Northern sympathizers
> Making speeches chaffy!
> Major-General Hancock
> Eating rebel taffy;
> English in a quandary
> How to save his dollars!
> Along comes a solid South
> And fits them all with collars.

Of all the corrupt practices in the Indiana campaign, purchased votes probably did most to tip the scale for the Republicans. After the election the *Evansville Courier* wrote, "The crisp, new two-dollar Treasury notes with which the First District is flooded tells a tale of party shame that every Republican, be he never so unprincipled, should blush at." As the historian James Ford Rhodes later wrote, in Indiana "money was used to an extent hitherto unknown in American politics."

With Indiana safely Republican, the nation focused its attention on New York. Both parties suffered from internal dissension in New York in 1880; but the Republicans overcame their differences before November. The Democrats were ostensibly united, but the antics of Tammany Hall chief John Kelly caused many to question his commitment. Perhaps in no other state were the comparable skills of the respective presidential candidates tested as in New York. Garfield made personal contact with the leaders, soothed their hurt feelings, and indicated that he would be responsive to their needs as President. Hancock, on the other hand, left the management of affairs to Kelly and former Governor Samuel Tilden, who had no use for one another, and this resulted in his undoing.

The Kelly-Tilden feud affected the party's activities in the state, and especially in New York City. Kelly had promised the Democratic National Convention in June that he would work for Hancock's election. Yet he chose William Grace, a Catholic, to run for mayor of the city. Grace's selection angered Tilden's followers and complicated Democratic problems. If elected, Grace would have been the first non-Protestant mayor of New York in two hundred years. Kelly chose him

Mechanical advertising card that can be rotated to change portrait from Hancock to Garfield.

because the Tammany leader wanted a pliable figurehead in City Hall. But Grace's appearance on the ticket not only intensified the party split but unnecessarily alienated Democrats who would not support a Catholic candidate. The New York *Herald* succinctly summarized the prevalent anxiety: "This is a Protestant country and the American people are a Protestant people." For that reason, many of Tilden's supporters rejected Grace and combined with the Republicans to nominate William Dowd. A large number of Democrats supported him, and some voted a straight Republican ticket as well. Nevertheless Dowd lost the mayor's contest to Grace by three thousand votes: 98,715 to 101,760.

Had Kelly really backed Hancock, he never would have chosen a controversial nominee for mayor. An astute politician, he should have picked an individual who would have united the party and attracted independent (and perhaps Republican) voters. Kelly, however, cared only about his own welfare.

Toward the end of a dull national campaign the publication in Kelly's newspaper, *The Truth*, of "The Morey Letter" creat-

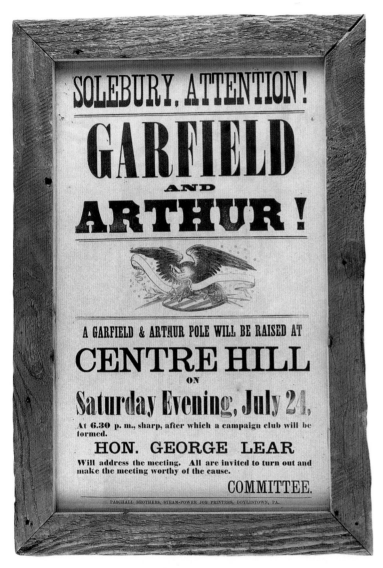

Broadside from eastern Pennsylvania calling for involvement in the local Republican club.

comment, for he had "hoped to answer all of my accusers by silence" but advisers urged him to allay public fears and deny its authenticity. Therefore, five days after its publication, Garfield announced that he had not penned the letter. Nevertheless, his denial sounded contrived, and many westerners, who wanted Chinese immigration curbed, did not believe him. Although the forgery did not affect the outcome of the election, the suspicion that Garfield favored cheap Chinese labor cost him California (which the Republicans had counted on) and probably Nevada (which went Democratic in a presidential contest for the first time).

The final election results, however, confirmed Garfield's campaign judgments and reflected, as well, Kelly's undermining of the Democratic ticket. New York proved decisive. Garfield carried it and won the race with 214 electoral votes to Hancock's 155. Had New York's 35 votes gone to Hancock, the Democrats would have elected their first President since 1856. Preliminary estimates had given Hancock a minimum of 65,000 votes over any Republican in New York City. He carried the city, however, by only 41,000 votes. The Republican carried the state by only 21,000. Had John Kelly supported a less divisive mayoral candidate and delivered the expected votes, the Democrats would have organized the next administration in Washington.

In the final tally, Garfield nosed out Hancock by a razor-thin margin of less than 10,000 votes: 4,454,416 to 4,444,952. James B. Weaver, the Greenback-Labor candidate, came in third with 308,578 votes, and Prohibitionist Neal Dow received just over 10,000 votes. The Republicans won the entire North and West (with the exception of

ed political ripples. The letter, purportedly written by Garfield the previous January to indicate his support for continued Chinese immigration, turned out to be one of the most notorious campaign forgeries in American history. Garfield never wrote the letter; indeed, the man to whom it allegedly had been sent, Henry L. Morey, never existed. The Republican nominee at first refused to

New Jersey, Nevada, and five of California's six electors). Hancock carried the South and the border states. Seventy-eight percent of all eligible voters cast ballots, a still-unsurpassed record.

The Greenback party influenced the outcome in California, Indiana, and New Jersey. In California, Greenbackers polled 3,392 votes, while Hancock edged out Garfield by the slender margin of seventy-eight votes: 80,426 to 80,348. In Indiana Weaver garnered 12,986 votes while fewer than 7,000 separated Hancock from Garfield. And in New Jersey, where the party won 2,617 votes, the Republicans emerged victors by only 2,010 votes. Neal Dow and his Prohibitionists did not affect the final outcome.

The Republicans had a superior candidate, better organization, and the advantage of general prosperity. The Democrats had a bumbling nominee, no program, and serious local divisions. Most northern businessmen, farmers, and laborers supported Garfield. Aside from the Solid South there were no significant blocs or pressure groups working for either of the major candidates. And despite the guffaws and apprehensions that greeted Hancock's remarks on the tariff, issues had little effect on the outcome. The Morey Letter lost some votes for the Republicans, and money purchased Indiana; but the election hinged on New York where a united Democratic party might have elected Hancock President.

Democrats and Republicans alike acknowledged Kelly's responsibility for Garfield's victory. Epithets and indignant commentary flooded newspapers and personal correspondence. Politicos castigated "the notorious and treacherous Kelly" whose "pigheadedness" brought the party down.

Mobile's *Daily Register* scored the Tammany chieftain and other New York City leaders who had "as certainly and as effectively sold General Hancock to the enemy as the brothers of Joseph sold him to the Egyptians." *The Chattanooga Times* reflected: "New York would have elected Hancock. Mr. Kelly threw it away to gratify his evil temper."

Those who knew best, in New York City, denounced Kelly even more vigorously. The *Herald* accused the Tammany leader of wantonly sacrificing "the Hancock ticket to his unscrupulous quest of local power." Both Republican and Democratic party workers admitted that Kelly had swapped votes with the Republicans, thereby helping both Garfield and Grace, and one informant claimed that five thousand Hancock ballots had been thrown into the Hudson River and never counted.

A cohesive Democratic party might have elected Hancock. The election thus pointed up the decentralized nature of the party. The Republicans were better organized, hence more effective. But the Democrats, while strong in local enclaves, showed no ability to unite for the quadrennial election or to subordinate local concerns to national needs.

Another conclusion one might draw from the election is how little the major parties differed from one another in political outlook and popular favor. No analyst of this election could possibly attribute the result to disagreements on issues. Campaign strategies and tactics, politicians, management, propaganda, ignorance, and underhandedness combined to put Garfield in the White House.

Colored printed yard goods cut from cotton bunting
with a repeating Hancock and English pattern.

Pair of cotton campaign banners.

*Matching pairs of campaign cotton bandannas. Bandannas were used for
political purposes as early as the first quarter of the nineteenth century.
Note the excellent graphic designs.*

Cigar box labels promoting both parties.
The cigars were identical but one chose
from the box which suited his political views.

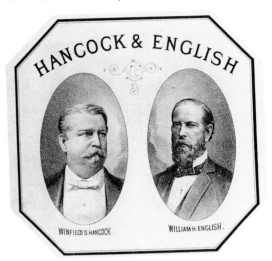

Advertising trade cards printed with messages from local merchants.

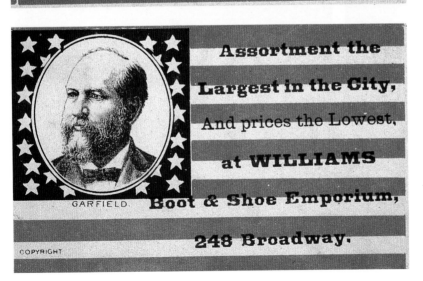

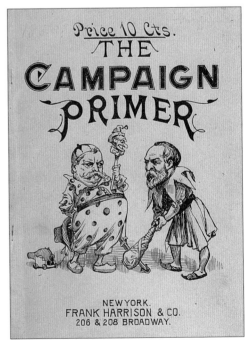

Satirical campaign booklet poking fun at both candidates.

Advertisment cards which were inserted into cigarette packages.

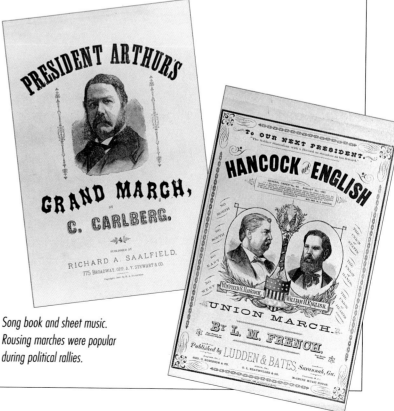

*Song book and sheet music.
Rousing marches were popular
during political rallies.*

★

Small campaign die-cut.

Brass badge
with portrait
of Garfield
reminding
voters of his
Civil War
record.

Carved-shell
cameo of Garfield.

Pair of inlaid enamel brass
badges. Clover was the
insignia of the corps
Hancock commanded
during the Civil War.

Mechanical nose-thumbers of Garfield and
Hancock. By depressing a lever, the candidate
would thumb his nose at his opponent.

A vigilant eagle perched atop the
candidate was a prevalent design motif.
Ferrotype badge of Garfield and Arthur.

Matched pair of cardboard portrait badges.

360

Lithographed tobacco tin with rotating mechanical disc which shows both presidential candidates and their running mates.

This Wedgwood Eturia pitcher commemorates either Garfield's inauguration or his death as both events occurred in 1881.

Wooden lid of a small trunk lined with a print of the Democratic candidates.

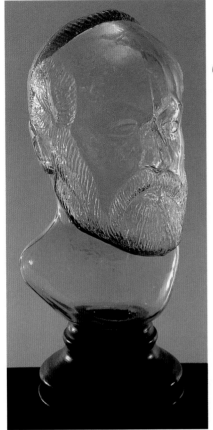

Garfield clear glass bottle.

Pair of Garfield shaving mugs. Note separate
holder for the shaving brush.

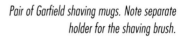

Nickel-plated suspender clasp
with portraits of Hancock
and English.

Chester A. Arthur is pictured
on an 1880 ironstone plate.

Program for the 1881 inaugural ball.

Ornate stained glass window glorifying Garfield. This item was used as a sample to show the workmanship of the manufacturer.

Garfield memorial items.

★

1884
38 STATES
IN THE UNION

DEMOCRAT
Grover Cleveland
ELECTORAL VOTE 219, POPULAR VOTE 48.5%

REPUBLICAN
James G. Blaine
ELECTORAL VOTE 182, POPULAR VOTE 48.2%

GREENBACK-LABOR
Benjamin F. Butler
ELECTORAL VOTE 0, POPULAR VOTE 1.8%

PROHIBITION
John P. St. John
ELECTORAL VOTE 0, POPULAR VOTE 1.5%

LEWIS L. GOULD
is Eugene C. Barker Centennial Professor
in American History at the University of Texas
at Austin. He is the author of *The Presidency of
William McKinley* (1980) and *The Presidency
of Theodore Roosevelt* (1991).

Of all American presidential elections, 1884 is correctly regarded as one of the dirtiest. Two evenly divided parties fought a bitter race that turned on the personal character of the two candidates—the Democrat Grover Cleveland and the Republican James G. Blaine—rather than on substantive issues. Both parties used the techniques of communal public spectacles, the resources of the press and the machinery of their campaign organizations to dramatize the differences between Cleveland and Blaine as individuals. Scandal and controversy marked the election from its opening stages through the final counting of votes. The election produced a razor-thin victory for Cleveland and added such memorable phrases to national political folklore as "Tell the truth," "Burn this letter," and "Rum, Romanism, and Rebellion."

The most popular figure in the Republican party and a compelling orator, Blaine had been Speaker of the House of Representatives and senator from Maine and had served President James A. Garfield as secretary of state. He was particularly identified with the protective tariff, the central doctrine of Republican economic policy. So enthusiastic were his supporters that they were called "Blainiacs."

Unfortunately Blaine had notable weaknesses as a candidate. Many critics believed that he had used office for personal gain. His financial connections with an Arkansas railroad while he was Speaker had become public knowledge in 1876 and had denied him the Republican nomination that year. The alleged proof of Blaine's guilt was contained in letters of his that later fell into the hands of a man named Mulligan. The "Mulligan Letters" dogged Blaine throughout 1884. He had written on some "Burn this Letter when you have read it," and the phrase "Burn this letter" became a staple at Democratic rallies.

Once Blaine had been nominated, many high-minded Republicans in the Northeast bolted the Republican ticket. Known as Mugwumps (an Indian word meaning "big chief"), these Republican reformers pursued Blaine relentlessly. They uncovered additional Mulligan letters and raised the question of Blaine's moral fitness for the nation's highest office. One of them, the German-American reformer Carl Schurz, wrote of the evil effect which the mere fact of his election would inevitably produce. The Mugwumps looked to the Democrats to provide them with an alternative to Blaine.

The Democrats cooperated by nominating Grover Cleveland, the governor of New York. A lawyer in Buffalo, Cleveland had risen from mayor of that city in 1881 to the state house in Albany in 1882 and now to the leadership of his party two years later. He had won a reputation for personal honesty and opposition to government activism in Albany where enemies spoke of him as "The Veto Governor." A large man whom his relatives called "Uncle Jumbo," Cleveland was convinced of his own rectitude. "It is no credit to do right," he said privately, "I

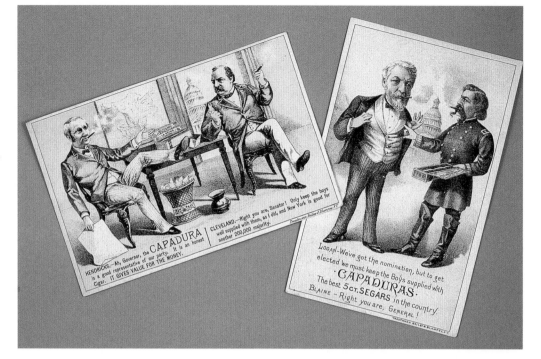

am never under any temptation to do wrong."
He did not campaign actively for the nomination, but, several friends, including William
C. Whitney, a wealthy New Yorker, and an influential Democrat named Daniel Manning
pushed his candidacy. There were few other
credible candidates for the fractious Democrats in 1884, and Cleveland won on the second ballot on July 11, 1884. His running-mate
was Thomas A. Hendricks of Indiana. It was a
victory, said the Mugwumps, for "Grover the
Good" who was their choice "not because of
his party but despite of it."

Then came the bombshell. On July 21 a
Buffalo newspaper broke the story about
what Cleveland called "my woman scrape."
A decade earlier Cleveland had been involved with Maria Halpin, a Buffalo woman who
was friendly with several men in Cleveland's
circle. She had become pregnant and called
her son, born in September 1874, Oscar Folsom Cleveland. She named Grover Cleveland as the father. Cleveland accepted responsibility and paid for the child while he
was in an orphanage. Maria Halpin later became an alcoholic. The initial impact on

the Cleveland supporters, especially the
Mugwumps, was profound. There were further charges that Cleveland was still im-
moral and that his "debaucheries continue
to this hour." Republicans exploited the incident in their rallies: marchers walked
behind baby carriages and sang "Ma! Ma!
Where's My Pa!"

The Democratic candidate responded
effectively, wiring his supporters in Buffalo
a three-word telegram: "Tell the Truth."
Cleveland admitted that he had slept with
Maria Halpin once, and urged his friends to
emphasize that he had been honorable in
accepting responsibility for the child. Coming early in the campaign, the attack did
not have a lasting effect on his race for the
presidency. For many supporters, his conduct in this episode came to seem symbolic
of his honesty and integrity. Since Cleveland's public life was spotless and his private life in question, while Blaine's private
life was pure and his public affairs under a
cloud, said one Cleveland man, "we should
elect Mr. Cleveland to the public office he is
so admirably qualified to fill, and remand

Mr. Blaine to the private life which he is so eminently fitted to adorn."

The Democrats tried to find equally damaging information about Blaine. For family and employment reasons, Blaine and his wife had married secretly and then had remarried publicly. Newspaper stories alleged that Mrs. Blaine had been pregnant at the time of the first wedding. When Cleveland received letters damaging to Blaine, he tore them up. "The other side can have a monopoly of all the dirt in this campaign." Neither candidate, however, condemned in public the personal character of the campaign.

The customs of the time did not call on presidential candidates to campaign actively. Such a strategy suited Cleveland, who was not a good public speaker. He accepted the nomination officially on July 29, and issued the letter of acceptance that became the keynote of his campaign. Until October he remained at his duties in Albany where he corresponded about the progress of the canvass. He made a few appearances toward the end of the campaign in New York City, New Jersey, and Connecticut. For the most part, he allowed Democratic state organizations to carry the burden of the fight.

The Democrats had a better organized campaign than did their rivals. Arthur Pue Gorman, a United States senator from Maryland, was in general charge of the Democratic effort as chairman of the party's executive committee, while William C. Whitney raised money and directed activities in New York and the Northeast. The Republican campaign directors, B.F. Jones and Stephen B. Elkins, were not so effective as their Democratic counterparts.

Twenty years after the Civil War, the militarized style of campaigning was still in vogue. Torchlight parades, marching ranks of supporters, bands and transparencies—all filled the cities of the nation. Men marched with their campaign organizations—the Buffalo Democratic Legion, the Niagara Falls Cleveland Club, Blaine and Logan clubs, and many others. Revelations in September of additional Mulligan Letters fortified the chants of the Democrats as they walked along:

> Blaine, Blaine, James G. Blaine
> The continental liar from the State of Maine
> *Burn this letter!*

Electoral calculations favored the Democrats. The Republicans had been in power since 1860, and the country seemed ready for a change. A mild recession added to voter uneasiness. With the South solidly Democratic, the party had more than 140 electoral votes toward the 201 needed for an election. If Cleveland could win New York, New Jersey, Connecticut, and a midwestern state, he would be the next President. A campaign centered on personalities minimized

Tin parade helmet with an oil-burning torch on top. Marchers protected themselves with heavy oilcloth capes often decorated in patriotic patterns.

Cartoon print vividly showing the evils of the Democratic tariff for revenue policy while praising the Republican protective tariff.

The effects of a Tariff exclusively for Revenue as laid down in the Democratic Platform and which the Democratic Congressmen tried to enact last winter at Washington.

The effects of Protection to American Industries as guaranteed by the Republican Party and Platform.

Democratic Free-Trade Means low wages, children in rags and ignorance

Republican Protection Means good wages, happy homes and education for your children.

If you are satisfied with this picture vote for Cleveland and Hendricks.

If you prefer this picture vote for Blaine and Logan.

divisions among the Democrats and prevented mistakes that might cost them victory.

To counter the Democratic approach, the Republicans relied on their candidate, the tariff issue, and probes at the opposition's weak spots. One perceived area of Democratic vulnerability was with the labor vote. To that end the Republicans subsidized the Greenback-Labor party and its candidate, Benjamin F. Butler, as a way of siphoning labor support from Cleveland. Despite vigorous campaigning, Butler did not prove to be much of a factor at the polls. The Prohibition party, and its candidate, John P. St. John, posed trouble for the GOP since dry voters tended to be former Republicans. St. John's strength in upstate New York proved important on election day.

The major focus of the Republican campaign was Blaine. He wanted to make the protective tariff the central theme of the election, and stressed economic issues in his letter of acceptance. Emphasize *wages*, especially *wages*, he told Republican editors when they wrote tariff editorials. Blaine also had appeal to Irish-American voters who applauded his attacks on Great Britain when he was secretary of state in the Garfield administration.

Republican disunity worried Blaine. A particular source of apprehension was Roscoe Conkling, a former senator from New York whose hatred of Blaine extended back to their quarrels on the House floor during the 1860s. They had battled through the 1870s until Conkling left public life after the death of President James A. Garfield. Now a lawyer with a corporate practice, "Lord Roscoe" still had influence in upstate New York, and Blaine wanted his support. Republicans went to see Conkling to ask for his endorsement of Blaine. Conkling gave them a contemptuous reply: "Gentlemen you have been misinformed. I have given up criminal law."

As problems mounted Blaine decided to make a personal campaign tour. He was not the first to do so. Stephen A. Douglas had campaigned in 1860, as did Horace Greeley in 1872, and James B. Weaver (the candidate of the Greenback-Labor party) in 1880. Despite Democratic charges that he was lowering the dignity of the process, Blaine set out on a tour of the East and Midwest.

The crowds that he encountered were enthusiastic. "Hosts of one hundred thousand people were not unusual," wrote one journalist. Emphasizing the tariff issue, Blaine warned of the dangers of Democratic victory. "It would be," he said, "as if the dead Stuarts were recalled to the throne of England." On the road for six weeks, he delivered more than four hundred speeches. At a time when states voted on different dates, the tour seemed to be working. He received large majorities when Maine and Vermont voted in September, and Ohio went Republican during the middle of October.

These were states, however, that Blaine was expected to carry. The great prize was New York. Reports indicated an extremely close contest. Could Blaine make the difference with his personal appeal? "Your presence will greatly help and we should have it for a week," the candidate was told. There were predictions of a Democratic victory in the state.

Portrait badge with Cleveland and Hendricks flanking the Statue of Liberty. France officially presented the statue to the United States in 1884.

Blaine was tired after weeks of campaigning. He thought about returning to Maine for the remainder of the canvass, and then decided to make the tour of New York that the managers were advising. He crossed the state from October 20 through October 28, and then arrived exhausted at his New York City hotel. On October 29 he was scheduled to meet with several hundred Protestant ministers in the hotel lobby. The person who had been designated to speak on behalf of the clergymen was delayed. They called on a Presbyterian minister named Samuel D. Burchard as a last-minute replacement. "We are Republicans," Burchard said in his speech, "and don't propose to leave our party and identify ourselves with the party whose antecedents have been rum, Romanism, and rebellion." Blaine made a response that did not refer to Burchard's remark.

Map print showing Blaine's solutions to regional economic problems. California: "NO COMPETITION WITH COOLIE LABOR." The Northeast: "NO TRIBUTE TO ENGLAND FOR AMERICAN FISH." The Utah Territory: "DEATH TO POLYGAMY."

Distracted by events, he had missed the significance of the statement. Burchard had attacked American Catholics at a time when Blaine was courting the Irish-American vote.

The Democratic campaign had assigned a stenographer to follow Blaine around. When Arthur Pue Gorman saw Burchard's phrase in the stenographic report, he asked: "Surely, Blaine met this remark?" Told that the candidate had ignored the phrase, Gorman gave his orders. "This sentence must be in every daily newspaper in the country tomorrow, no matter what it costs." Election day was Tuesday, November 4. During the weekend before the Democrats saw to it that handbills and leaflets showered the country with "The Three R's." By the time Blaine disavowed the Burchard remark as an "unfortunate and ill-considered expression" and said he was "the last man in the United States who would make a disrespectful allusion to another man's religion," the damage had been done.

October 29 had been a bad day for Blaine. It became worse when he attended a dinner at Delmonico's restaurant given in his honor by the richest Republicans. Jay Gould was there and other millionaires such as Russell Sage, Cornelius Bliss, and D.O. Mills. Blaine spoke about foreign trade and the record of the Republican party in achieving prosperity. For the Democrats, however, the occasion became "The Boodle Banquet" and "Belshazzar's Feast," and their cartoons contrasted Republican wealth with Democratic poverty and frugality. It was another public relations disaster for Blaine.

His ill-fortune continued on election day. Heavy rains in upstate New York held down the vote in an area where the Republicans hoped to do well. The election was very close. Cleveland had swept the South as expected, and Blaine was running well in the Midwest as the early returns came in. New York would obviously be crucial, and the result was in doubt for several days. A recount was ordered, and the final tally showed that Cleveland had carried New York by 1,149 votes. St. John and the prohibitionists had won 25,000 votes, most of which might otherwise have gone for Blaine.

The 36 electoral votes for New York gave Cleveland 219 in all, and the election. Blaine received 182 electoral votes. The Democrat had carried Connecticut, Indiana, New Jersey, Delaware, and the South for 183 electoral votes, and New York put him over the top. Blaine won 48.2 percent of the popular vote; Cleveland garnered 48.5 percent. The popular vote totals were equally close. Cleveland won 4,875,971 votes to Blaine's tally of 4,852,234. After the initial count Republicans contended that vote frauds in New York had deprived Blaine of victory in that state, but others conceded that the result was fair. "It was a lack of votes, not a theft of votes, that lost the State to Blaine," said one after the results were officially recorded.

Ecstatic Democrats held rallied to endorse Cleveland's victory. Now crowds sang:

> Hurrah for Maria! Hurrah for the kid
> I voted for Cleveland,
> And damned glad I did!

Post-mortems assigned credit for the Democratic victory in New York to Burchard's remark, the defection of prohibitionist voters, and the opposition of Conkling. These transitory events were less important than long term trends. Since Blaine won 400,000 more votes than James A. Garfield had received in 1880, it was clear that the Republican candidate had done better than any other possible nominee of his party. In a Democratic year, when economic conditions hurt the party in power, Cleveland kept his party together and used its electoral advantages to secure a narrow triumph.

After the election of 1884, the major parties moved away from the campaigns of personalities and the style of spectacular politics that had characterized the Cleveland-Blaine contest. Their emphasis shifted to issues such as the tariff and to educating the electorate through pamphlets and newspaper stories. The race between Cleveland and Blaine displayed the politics of the Gilded Age in all their flamboyance, color, and controversy. For James G. Blaine, it meant the end of his hopes for the White House. For Grover Cleveland, there lay ahead the two non-consecutive terms as President that gave him a special place in the history of the nation's highest office.

Posters (above and opposite) with patriotic motif,
candidates' biographies, and each party's platform.

The party platform was designed to be read. They were concise
statements of the party's principles and proposed program for the nation.

Top: Advertisement card. This thread manufacturer did not want to show favoritism!

Above: A poster for Scribner's Magazine. A facsimile street banner is used to promote the November 1884 issue.

Advertisement card featuring both parties.

Sampling of textiles produced for the 1884 campaign. The study of American textiles as both social history and as an art form has benefited enormously since the publication of Herbert R. Collins's *Threads of History* (Smithsonian Institution Press, 1979).

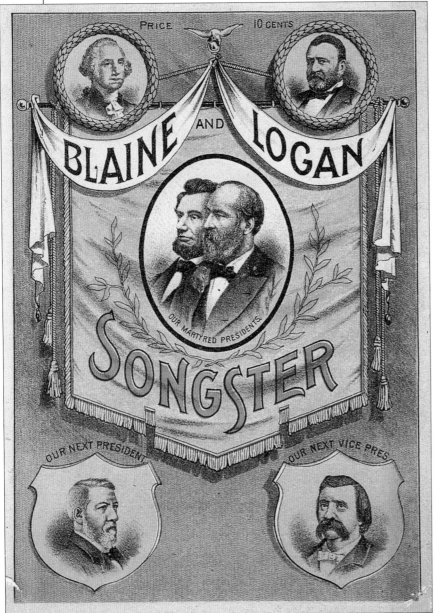

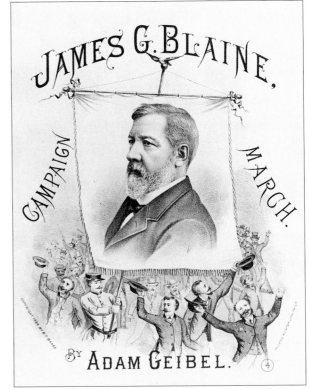

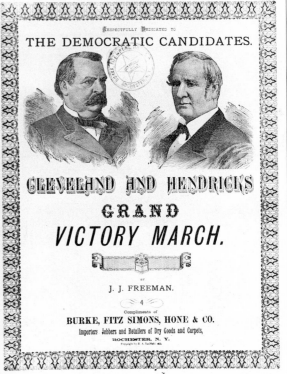

Examples of 1884 campaign sheet music
and songsters. The wedding march
commemorates Cleveland's marriage to
Frances Folsom in June 1886.

Fan portraying Cleveland and his Cabinet, circa 1885.

Lithographed print of the 1884 Republican nominees.

Silk campaign ribbons.

Cleveland-Hendricks print recalling previous Democratic luminaries: Jefferson, Jackson, McClellan, and Tilden.

These graphic portrait badges are among the myriad produced for the campaigns of the late nineteenth century.

Repeating pattern cotton bunting for both parties. These fabrics, sold by the bolt, were used to decorate stages and halls.

General Benjamin Butler was the Greenback-Labor party candidate. This spoon badge proclaims him the "WORKINGMEN'S FRIEND."

1884.

PEOPLE'S PARTY

FOR

PRESIDENT.

Benj. F. Butler.

VICE-PRESIDENT,

A. M. West.

1884 Butler portrait ribbon.

Porcelain match holder with Civil War cap lid which proclaims Butler is "A MATCH FOR ANYONE."

Nonmechanical castiron bank shows a squatting figure of Butler with frog's legs holding a wad of useless greenbacks inscribed: "For the masses, this is $100,000."

38 STATES
IN THE UNION

REPUBLICAN

Benjamin Harrison

ELECTORAL VOTE 233, POPULAR VOTE 47.9%

DEMOCRAT

Grover Cleveland

ELECTORAL VOTE 168, POPULAR VOTE 48.6%

PROHIBITION

Clinton B. Fisk

ELECTORAL VOTE 0, POPULAR VOTE 2.2%

UNION LABOR

Anson J. Streeter

ELECTORAL VOTE 0, POPULAR VOTE 1.3%

J.F. WATTS

is professor of history and head of the World
Civilizations Program at The City College of New
York, where he has taught since 1965. He has
served as chairman of the history department and
won the college's Outstanding Teacher Award. He
has published essays and texts on American
legal, social, and ethnic history.

Every four years the great popular referendum of the presidential election measures that moment's reflection of the thoughts and desires of voting Americans. Just as time obscures the passions around which distant political battles raged, history reveals them. The 1888 campaign between the Democratic incumbent Grover Cleveland and his Republican challenger Benjamin Harrison surely qualifies now as an obscure event. Just as certainly, to that long-gone American electorate the importance of the bitter Cleveland-Harrison struggle justified its gaudy display of campaign excesses. Old traditions of corruption and vituperation melded with new organizational techniques and the emerging technology of an industrializing society to produce a campaign that reached deeply down into the population, inspiring visceral responses scarcely attuned to two colorless if well-mannered candidates.

The ensuing process created national icons out of a pair of somber politicians. High-speed printing presses expelled massive doses of propaganda. Millions of decorative political objects poured from American factories, for wearing, waving, flaunting, saving. Countless specimens still exist, with collectors, in museums, in neglected attics. Badges, banners, lanterns, torches, lapel ornaments, studs, ribbons, glass and ceramic bric-a-brac—hundreds of specimens suggesting Cleveland as Caesar or Harrison as Lincoln. That the projections but dimly represented either the men or their programs mattered then not at all. They just seemed to, even though both candidates were unsociable men of modest aims.

Heavy and stolid, Grover Cleveland in his three decades upon the public stage had displayed a narrow range of admirable characteristics: rectitude, objectivity, self-sacrifice, responsibility. Left destitute as a teenager in upstate New York when his father died leaving nine children, Cleveland doggedly found success and respect as a lawyer in booming mid-century Buffalo.

Personal honesty distinguished itself in a tawdry age, to the extent that Cleveland's reputation survived two incidents either of which might have sunk most political careers. In 1859, he fathered an illegitimate child, an event then usually considered a permanent badge of shame. Four years later, his family decided that his two brothers would join the Union armies and Grover would remain in Buffalo to support his mother and sisters. A substitute was contracted, itself not then especially noteworthy unless later political passions arose, as they did with vengeance.

Buffalo elected Cleveland mayor in 1881, and the Democrats sent him to Albany as governor a year later. Here he stood most vividly against the Tammany Hall machine of his own party, intoning the appealing catchphrase "A Public Office Is a Public Trust." Young Governor Cleveland immediately became for the Democratic party a symbol of honesty in a national politics polluted with corruption. In 1884, at the age of forty-

Bye, free trade baby!
Rock it, Grover, tenderly?
Bye, free trade baby,
We've smashed the cradle!
Good-by!

Ma, Ma, Where's My Pa.
Fired from the White House.
——HA, HA, HA!

Anti-Cleveland card. Cleveland is shown rocking a cradle which represents the contested tariff issue. The bottom lines parody the famous 1884 campaign ditty.

sharecropper South, Civil Service Mug-wumps, free traders and protectionists, advocates of the gold standard, and those of unlimited coinage of silver. They all rose in support of the man in the White House.

The President received the news as a mixed blessing. The job often overwhelmed him. "I am almost crazy over the things that crowd upon me," he confided to a friend. Yet his life had achieved a happy balance in June 1886, when Cleveland, 49, finally abandoned bachelorhood to marry the winsome 22-year-old Frances Folsom. He soon developed a revealing perspective on politics. "My wife sits by me," he wrote to a friend during the 1888 campaign,

> . . . I am sure of one thing. I have in her something better than the Presidency for life—though the Republican party and papers do say that I beat and abused her. I absolutely long to be able to live with her as other people do with their wives. Well! Perhaps I can after the 4th of next March.

The President's doubts about the election reflected his risky strategy for the campaign. Should the Democrats choose to fight on all battlefronts they might well dissolve into antagonistic factions. Already Cleveland faced unceasing pension demands from Civil War veterans, to many of whom, irrespective of party, he already represented an anathema because he had dodged the war. Another bitter debate that transcended party concerned the struggle over gold and silver coinage between creditors and debtors, and their loud supporters in Congress. Again, the sometimes violent war between labor and corporate capital impended, even after the excesses of the infamous 1886 Haymarket Square affair in Chicago. Cleve-

seven, Grover Cleveland went to the White House as the first Democrat elected since James Buchanan in 1856.

Four years later, President Cleveland remained in Washington throughout the first week of June 1888, while the Democratic party's national convention met in St. Louis. Belying their deserved reputation as an occasionally-collected confederation of feuding clans, the Democrats routinely renominated the incumbent. The modest accomplishments of his first term papered over simmering internecine feuds and aspirations of a party which seemed to include utterly incompatible elements. To St. Louis went Tammany, its cousins from the other big cities, the segregationist cotton-and-land faced endless patronage requests from job-starved Democrats, countered by claims of virtuous long-standing Republican officeholders and the high-minded preachings of Mugwump Civil Service advocates. The President managed to subordinate all of these issues by choosing to attack head-on the sacred cow of the American economic and political system, the protective tariff.

Tariff, protective tariff, customs duties, protectionism, the American Plan—whatever the terms, this emotional banner spread across the political landscape. Few Americans understood the abstruse detail, yet most had an opinion, often loudly expressed. In boardrooms and saloons, protection claimed to be synonymous with the American Way of Life, a shield for "infant industries" against the "international capitalists" and "pauper labor" of Europe. It promised a full lunch pail, the expansion of jobs in an industrialized America now swelling with immigrants, its frontier towns linked by rail, its economy transformed by inventions and technological wonders. So went the litany of obvious success, or the propaganda of big business, depending on one's perspective. Whatever the reasons, what the protective tariff meant to the electorate cannot be underestimated.

As configured dispassionately, a tariff imposes customs duties on imports, thus raising revenues while shielding products from foreign competition. Cheaper goods held off the American market forced their users to pay higher prices, however, while artificially supporting the prices of American goods. By 1887, rates set twenty-five years earlier protected some four thousand items, and produced a major surplus in the

United States Treasury. The 1886-87 Treasury revenue of $371 million, driven by $217 million in customs duties, generated a surplus of $103 million. Even aside from such negative macroeconomic implications as a constricted money supply and credit deflation, Cleveland found unconscionable excess. Monopoly-inspired high prices across the industrial board resulted in unearned extravagant wealth, and a surplus of money in Washington that could only continue to tempt the array of venal politicians long accustomed to the spoils Mark Twain dubbed the Gilded Age.

Cleveland had announced his intentions in his state of the union message of December 1887. In April, the bill to revise tariffs, the Mills Bill, went to the House. Far from a radical attempt to do away with tariff protection, this legislation advocated serious study of the entire question and contained suggestions for reductions so modest that many businessmen remarked in private that they could live with it easily. Nonetheless,

Ceramic novelty with Cleveland and Harrison on a scale. Figures can be moved to tip the balance in either's favor.

Photograph showing a Republican headquarters. The numbers on the roof are approximate state winning differences of Harrison over Cleveland in 1888.

the Republicans (and some Democratic protectionists) immediately twisted Cleveland's arguable reforms into marvelous political burlesque which would be played out through the fall campaign. Anticipating the battle with glee, Republican leaders fought each other for the chance to run against Grover Cleveland.

The Republican party that gathered in Chicago had about finished with the politics of Civil War vengeance. The Bloody Shirt was unfurled now and then at the convention and in the campaign, but increasingly emphasis went to national concerns and the future. To sober GOP politicians, industrial and corporate concerns, the labor and farm questions, the quality and quantity of the money supply, immigration, even foreign policy transcended former habits.

The man who more than anyone else had shaped this party spent the summer, with characteristic drama, in a castle in Scotland. James Gillespie Blaine had lost the 1884 election to Grover Cleveland by a

whisper and a roar. A handful of votes kept him from the White House. A fusillade of partisan charges against his character and integrity both confirmed Blaine's detractors and strengthened his idolizers. The matinee idol of the late nineteenth-century American political stage, Blaine, though absent from the convention, suffused its proceedings. He remained, projecting power, at the Scottish castle of his friend Andrew Carnegie. Even in the gloaming, at any moment Blaine and Carnegie could use in the study a private telegraph line to Chicago.

Senator John Sherman of Ohio led the first roll call. But he fell far short of a majority, and the nomination finally went on the eighth ballot and with Blaine's long-distance support to a respected and comfortable figure with a famous name, Benjamin Harrison of Indiana. Like his 1888 rival for the presidency, Benjamin Harrison conveys to his historical imagery the sense of stiff formality. His contemporaries describe him as a "human iceberg." On one occasion, a close friend told Harrison bluntly: "For God's sake be a human being down there. Mix around a little with the boys after the meeting." Later, the taciturn candidate reported, "John, I tried it, but I failed. I'll never try it again. I must be myself." Which prompted an aside to a third party: "Don't think he *means* to insult you, it's his way." Despite the frosty exterior, Harrison had captured the respect and deference automatically conferred by that generation to men of accomplishment and reputation.

His great-grandfather and namesake signed the Declaration of Independence, his grandfather was President William Henry Harrison, his father a member of Congress. Benjamin Harrison the younger became an early Republican in the 1850s, fought with William Tecumseh Sherman around Atlanta, and earned brigadier general's rank, the citation signed by Abraham Lincoln mentioning "ability . . . manifest energy and gallantry." By the 1870s he had become one of Indiana's prominent political leaders. He lost the 1876 gubernatorial race, won a Senate seat in 1881, and lost his bid for re-election. Throughout these years, Harrison steadfastly supported such staple nationalizing policies of the GOP as the gold standard, business expansion, veterans' benefits and, naturally, a high protective tariff.

Eight weeks of hard campaigning presented the electorate with a mixture of the old political devices and the new fillips made possible by technology. Pamphlets, tablets, and broadsides poured from print shops onto the nation-girdling railroad network. Telegraph communication had become increasingly sophisticated, newspaper wire services linked the vast rural expanses to the cities. Political operatives, especially the Republicans, understood the advantages of national symbolism, of projecting candidates as larger-than-life.

From the mundane precincts of machine shops, potteries, lithographers, drill presses, textile mills, foundries, and all the garment trades came an avalanche of political gimmicks emblazoned with caricatures of Cleveland and Harrison. Children's toys, trading cards, embroideries, hat torches, clay pipes, lapel pins, plates, bandannas, bowls, belt buckles. Homes, shops, meeting halls, and people were proudly decorated. The robust response to such emotional appeal reflected the importance of the event. While later generations would find little to distinguish between these parties of a cen-

tury ago, contemporaries had no such problem. "We" were the true Americans, "They" were crooks and cowards, and worse.

Receptivity to this partisan fervor characterized the political map. In the Solid Democratic South, Republicans were anathema and would remain so for another seventy-five years. Race and segregation underlay Democratic party sovereignty, safely in old Confederate hands. New England, located on the opposite emotional side, remained staunch and solidly Republican. Republicans also enjoyed majority support in the vast trans-Mississippi west, and Democrats became competitive elsewhere, particularly in the burgeoning cities. As the rivals organized the campaign their respective leaders concluded that the election depended on a few swing states (New York, New Jersey, Connecticut and Indiana in particular), on money, and on the ability to raise grass-roots emotions. To this organizational challenge the Republicans responded brilliantly by putting their campaign into Matt Quay's hands.

Parade torch in the form of Harrison's high hat.

Mechanical folding paper puzzle. Cleveland turns into a pig being pursued by Harrison and Morton.

Matthew Stanley Quay ran Pennsylvania politics through an organization as modern as it was efficient. Combining the resources of federal patronage with munificent corporate support, Quay sat atop a massive dispensary of economic and political power, connecting local interests throughout the state with commercial and industrial might. Smart and tough, Quay enjoyed the hard work of politics, valuing its power and prestige more than the conventional vulgarities of graft. Against him, the Democrats chose poorly. The nominal co-chairman of the Democratic National Committee, aging party loyalist Senator William H. Barnum of Connecticut, quickly and comfortably assumed figurehead status. His peer, a vinegary Ohio railroad baron named Calvin Brice, accepted the trying task of raising corporate money for a balkanized campaign organization. Senator Arthur Pue Gorman, a gifted Maryland politico, tried to fit together a national scheme. Democratic credibility did not gain from the common knowledge that all three figures were longtime supporters of the pro-

tective tariff. More significantly, each geographical area answered to a different local political grandee, and no one could impose a consensus on where time and resources would be concentrated. Further complicating the Democrats' efforts, President Cleveland refused to participate in his own re-election campaign.

The incumbent, faithful to the responsibilities of the office as he saw them, hated politics, at least that version practiced in public view. While odd by today's standards, Cleveland's presidential isolation did fit a now-bygone tradition. Indeed until the twentieth century but a scant few Americans ever heard a presidential voice. The reticence reflected the concern of the Founding Fathers that presidential demagogy constituted an omnipresent danger as an incitement of class conflict. Consequently, nineteenth-century Presidents adopted carefully circumscribed modes of communication. All messages to Congress were delivered in writing. Public speeches, if any, reflected generalized themes of constitutional propriety and republican virtue. Jefferson hardly ever spoke in public,

Madison never. Jackson averaged one public appearance per year, Grant three. Cleveland, in his few public remarks, did not discuss in invidious fashion patriotism, his own policies or political opponents by name. For the 1888 campaign, he merely released a letter to the Democratic national committee accepting the nomination and stating his positions in the ponderous prose style then favored. He then retreated into the splendid isolation of the White House, claiming to be "too busy" for campaign appearances. To one national committee suggestion that he visit a large and politically-significant national farmers' meeting came the reply that it would conflict with the President's vacation. In his stead, the Democrats tried to send onto the hustings, their vice presidential nominee, Allen Granberry Thurman.

"The Old Roman" defined the meaning of Political Warhorse. Seventy-five and debilitated when, oddly, selected as running-mate by Cleveland, Thurman could scarcely campaign. At one important mass rally, in New York City's Madison Square Garden, the ancient warrior wobbled on the stage to announce that he felt too ill to speak. Fearing the worst, Thurman's own family resisted national committee entreaties for appearances. Ironically, the decrepit vice presidential nominee soon became a symbol for virile tradition. For years Thurman had cultivated the image of the common man, friend of workers and tillers of the soil. On hundreds of public occasions the verbose politician's omnipresent red bandanna had mopped his brow and absorbed the excrescences of his snuff. In the fall of 1888, totems of "The Knight of the Red Bandanna" spread across America just as the old man himself no longer could.

Uncountable red bandannas poured out of textile mills. Most were about 22" square and bore likenesses of the Democratic candidates, or such slogans as "Tariff Reform," "Red Hot Democrat," or "Rights of Working-men." One retailer catalogued a hundred different styles, on linen (at $1) or cotton (at 10¢). The party faithful waved them by hand, attached them to sticks, flew them from buggy whips or, in "The Old Roman's" own grand tradition, used one to manage snuff. A popular musical accompaniment, "for sale at all music stores," embellished the legend:

THE RED BANDANNA

Yes let the Red Bandanna wave on high!
  They will have to wash their blood red
    shirt:
'Tis their banner that is all befouled!
  'Tis an object of disgust and dirt!
We have got a little uncrowned Queen,
  She's a woman who is fit to reign;
With the help of solid men,
  We will put her there again,
At the finish of the big campaign.
Wave the Red Bandanna, boys!
  All along the line!
The Red Bandanna, Bandanna,
  That's the countersign!
The Red Bandanna will elect two honest
  men I know:
The noblest Roman of them all and the
  Man from Buffalo.

Away from the gusto of torchlight hyperbole, the serious business of presidential politics unfolded. In New York City, Quay installed a cohort of trusted Pennsylvanians and quickly raised a fortune to spend on vote production. Businessmen's committees produced about $4 million, an unprecedented sum, and Quay and his industrious national organization spent it with efficiency and imagination, as propaganda and oratory largely replaced bribery and coercion. Perhaps ten thousand local GOP clubs mushroomed, replete with the full array of banners and bandannas and inscribed bric-a-brac so welcomed in Victorian-American homes. Tons of literature printed in Chicago and Pittsburgh flooded westward. Private polls revealed trends and soft spots. Salaried stump speakers and local politicos worked designated territories. Senator Sherman loyally toured the swing states of Connecticut, New Jersey, New York, and Indiana. The redoubtable Blaine lent his aura and rhetoric in New York and Indiana. For every Democratic speech, ten Republicans appeared.

Quay believed the election hung on New York. Certainly, its Democratic wars presented tempting vistas. The Democratic governor, David B. Hill, Cleveland's successor, state-party rival and 1888 candidate for reelection, courted Tammany Hall and alienated the city's good-government reformers. The President steadfastly refused to endorse the governor. Wholesale voting irregularities, so rich in New York tradition and inventiveness, presented Quay with healthy challenge. "I do not propose that the Democrats shall steal New York from Harrison," he declared. "The false registration must be stopped." The Republican National Committee put up $25,000 in reward money for fraud catchers, and quickly paid a well-publicized bounty to a police department detective, a Democrat, who uncovered a GOP aberration! Moreover, a Quay-subsidized city directory succeeded in removing illegal voters and making difficult last-minute registrations. The city's eighty-thousand-odd Irish-American voters especially enjoyed Quay's attention. Ward organizers received about $80,000, much of it seen in mass rallies, parades and special mailings—all conveying Republican steadfastness a-

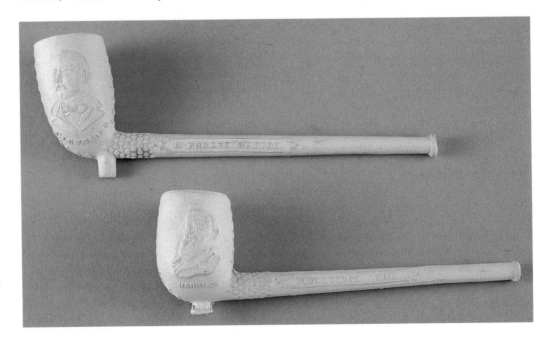

Clay pipes with molded busts of Cleveland (top) and Harrison.

gainst the British. According to their political weight, German, Italian, and Swedish neighborhoods were similarly favored. Valuable ballast came too from the GOP vice presidential candidate, Levi P. Morton, Wall Street insider and prominent national political figure.

The Democrats were, of course, assured a sweep of the old Confederate states, as well as the strenuous exertions of big-city machines. But the sectional and local nature of the party *per se* produced a national organization underfinanced and strategically confused. Money remained in short supply, as did campaign literature and artifacts. Some lobby support materialized, particularly from the American Free Trade Association, and from such influential publications as the *New York Times, New York Evening Post, Springfield Republican, Harper's Weekly* and the *Nation*. On the stump, old Thurman delivered a few roars, but the President remained, resolutely, silent.

Cleveland bore personal integrity as a political badge, which helped some. The party produced a variegated flood of objects, as did many enterprising advertisers. One Cleveland trading card had the President touting a "favorite ale," and another depicted Mrs. Cleveland selling for a textile outfit. An inventive yarn goods shop in Jamestown, New York, issued a fanciful card with the presidential couple intently staring into its display window. An embroidered silk ribbon had the Clevelands endorsing "Richmond Straight Cut Cigarettes." The official Democratic materials tended to present a more sober presidential image with suitable suggestions, "A PUBLIC OFFICE IS A PUBLIC TRUST," "TARIFF REFORM," "LOW TAXES." Such vision might appear on a parade torch or a pink ceramic pitcher.

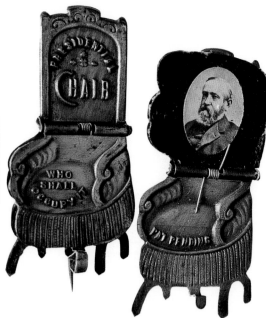

Mechanical pin-back brooch which flips open showing Harrison in the presidential chair.

Through the summer months Frances Cleveland by herself became a brief campaign highlight. "Frankie Clubs" sprouted, and her face dotted the nation on posters, dinner plates, handkerchiefs, playing cards and song sheets. "Frankie—The Nation's Favorite Belle," suggested table napkins. Or, as an embroidered silk ribbon had it, "Mrs. Cleveland/Queen of 60 Millions of Free People." A presidential rumble went out to still the craze as "undignified."

Republican efforts dwarfed the Democratic output. Of the seven hundred varieties of campaign paraphernalia identified, such as clay pipes, razors, toys, pocket watches, umbrellas, and wide varieties of glass and ceramic products, about two-thirds were Republican. While GOP abuse remained a minor key in political materials, Cleveland proved particularly vulnerable to Civil War bitterness.

Unlike his Republican predecessors, President Cleveland frequently vetoed the continually-mounting appeals for veterans' pensions. Moreover, his innocuously-intended attempt to return captured Confederate battle flags to their states caused a commotion nasty enough to force him to rescind it. Palpable hostility prevented Cleveland from taking a scheduled trip to the 1887 Grand Army of the Republic National Convention. Campaign songs suggested the enmity:

A SUBSTITUTE HE FOUND

Boss Grover when he's jolly
 Knows naught of melancholy,
And stamps out pension folly
 For those who saved the flag.

(chorus)

For when the strife was raging,
For when the strife was raging,
For when the strife was raging,
 A substitute he found,
 A substitute he found,
 A substitute he found.
If all had done as Grover
 Sent substitutes moreover,
They all could live in clover
 And none want pensions now.

(chorus)

Perchance the land in trouble
 Might nevermore be double,
But bursted like a bubble
 Still what did Grover care.

(chorus)

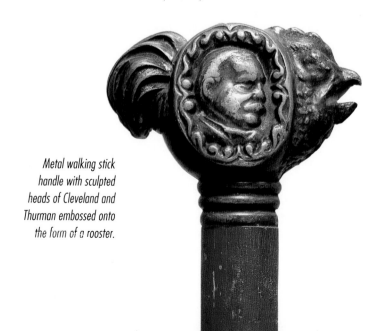

Metal walking stick handle with sculpted heads of Cleveland and Thurman embossed onto the form of a rooster.

WE ARE COMING, GROVER CLEVELAND

We are coming, Grover Cleveland,
 eight hundred thousand strong,
As vet'rans of the Union
 to right our comrades' wrong,
Some now leave beds and crutches,
 stout-hearted as of yore,
Your vetoes are behind us,
 your insults are before,
Where Harrison is leading,
 with shout and cheer and song,
We are coming, Grover Cleveland,
 eight hundred thousand strong . . .

We've seen at comrades stricken
 sarcastic vetoes hurled,
We rise from farms and workshops,
 from factory and mill,
With hearts that burn and souls on fire,
 eight hundred thousand still,
And sons and daughters joining
 to help the cause along,
We're coming, Grover Cleveland,
 about four million strong.

We are coming, Grover Cleveland,
 loyal host and true,
Beneath the Union banner,
 we form our ranks anew,
With ballots as the weapons,
 we'll sweep the land amain,
For all the loyal freemen
 will catch the glad refrain,
And rally on the colors,
 a grand majestic throng,
We are coming, Grover Cleveland,
 some forty million strong.

In one form of Democratic retaliation, songs and orators lampooned the Harrison campaign's ubiquitous recollection of his grandfather's then-well-remembered "Tippecanoe and Tyler Too" 1840 election. Many local Republican clubs actually erected log cabins, some with hard cider facilities. The orgy of nostalgia spawned "Tippecanoe and

The classic Republican portrait badge for the 1888 campaign.

Morton Too, 1840-1888" logos on textiles and crockery; and upon a steel-ribbed "parade ball" fourteen feet in diameter which traveled from Maryland to Harrison's front lawn in Indianapolis, and then throughout the Midwest. Democratic choruses learned the words to "His Grandfather's Hat—It's Too Big for Ben." Republican tunesmith's responded with "The Same Old Hat—It Fits Ben Just Right." Soon, three-inch novelty beaver hats appeared, usually emblazoned "The Same Old Hat," less often, "His Grandfather's Hat." Amidst all the glorious foolishness, and to the surprise of both parties, the Republican candidate himself came forward to earn critical acclaim, and critical votes as well.

The traffic on North Delaware Street in Indianapolis began in June when news of Harrison's nomination arrived from Chicago. Friends and townspeople, with congratulations and good wishes were greeted at the door by the candidate, who took to delivering brief comments on the issues facing the American people. Every day, crowds arrived from the surrounding country towns, and Harrison spoke to them of patriotism and the protective tariff and the philosophical and political differences at stake in November. In far-off New York City an alarmed Quay reflected conventional wisdom: "Shut up General Harrison," he told associates. Yet GOP locals could not resist, and sent trainloads of delegations often numbering in the thousands. From Chicago, Kentucky, Ohio, Iowa, Minnesota, Missouri, eventually from Pennsylvania and New York. Indianapolis became a one hundred-day political circus.

The candidate addressed about ninety groups of astonishing diversity—a claque of costumed children, a howling crowd of workingmen six thousand strong, several all-black delegations, a daily ration of veterans garbed in blue, an endless string of loyal Republicans, "drummers" (i.e., traveling salesmen), ladies' associations, tin plate manufacturers, and the "Carrie Harrison Club, of Oxford, Ohio." Estimates suggest that over three hundred thousand people heard his voice. He spoke clearly, without bombast, never patronizing, conveying a commanding presence, a dignified bearing. A secretary's shorthand transcription, as reviewed and corrected every evening by the candidate, went onto the Associated Press wire before bedtime for morning newspapers coast to coast. The aloof "iceberg" of individual encounters could control and satisfy any crowd. By August, Quay remarked that "if Harrison has the strength to [keep talking], we could safely close these headquarters and he would elect himself."

Virtually every speech pounded on the theme of the protective tariff. The tariff issue connected political and economic power with the burlesquery of the campaign. By itself, the American Iron and

Harrison-Morton victory celebration ribbon.

Steel Association issued over one million pamphlets. The American Protective Tariff League vetted the reliability of congressional candidates. The more daring Democrats equated the status quo with excessive profits, without advantage to wage earners.

But the labor movement feared the predicted flood of cheap foreign goods and remained carefully protectionist. Republicans attacked "Grover Cleveland's formal declaration of war against the industrial system of America." Their operatives churned out the message on materials for street and home:

PROTECT HOME INDUSTRY
TIPPECANOE AND TARIFF TOO
PROTECTION TO AMERICAN HOMES
NO BRITISH PAUPER WAGES FOR
    AMERICANS
THE STARS AND STRIPES WILL
    ALWAYS WAVE FOR PROTECTION

With a nod to Stephen Foster's "Camptown Races," they sang

Ben Harrison is a thoroughbred,
    du da, du da
There are no flies upon his head,
    du da, du da,
No clogs or heavy weights he wears,
    du da, du da
Protection is the flag he bears,
    oh, du da day !

Also present on the political landscape, somewhere between secret strategy and public buffoonery, lay dirty politics. In the latter stages of the campaign the Republicans accentuated their staple charge that the Cleveland administration bowed before Queen Victoria. The ancient anglophobe prejudice still resonated, particularly among the politically-potent Irish-Americans, whose Home Rule dreams were just then collapsing in

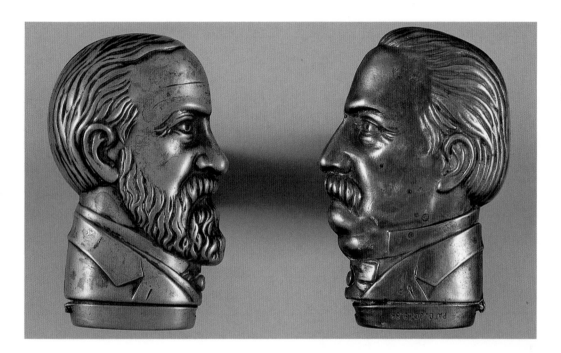

Brass matchsafes of Harrison and Cleveland. These pocket items were used prior to the invention of safety matches.

London. Cleveland thus chose a most un-propitious time to ask the Senate to ratify a treaty on the long-vexatious question of fishing rights in Canadian waters.

In late August the Republican-controlled Senate defeated the treaty. Cleveland quickly responded by demanding Senate approval of retaliatory measures against the Canadians, and the Democrats blared out their own pro-Irish virtue.

Reading of this stratagem infuriated a Republican in California named George Osgoodby, who quickly produced a classic of American politics. Writing as "Charles F. Murchison," ostensibly British-born and American naturalized, Osgoodby asked British Ambassador Sir Lionel Sackville-West for political guidance. The answer, in effect: vote for Cleveland! This "Murchison-Sackville-West" exchange surfaced in the newspapers in late October. Quay released "millions" of copies.

Blaine's oratory soared. Editorials pulsated. The furious and embarrassed Cleveland, claiming "a Republican plot," sent the hapless Englishman home. And Democratic organs circulated scurrilous tales of Harrison's disdain for Irishmen.

Scattered Democratic newspapers quoted the Republican candidate as saying:

> A dollar a day is enough for any workingman. . . . I would force you to work by the bayonet, or I would shoot you down like dogs. . . . If it were not for [the Irish] we would not need half of our penitentiaries. . . . They are only good to shovel dirt and grade railroads, for which they receive more than they are worth.

Harrison, naturally, replied. On October 25 in Indianapolis a carefully organized rally, with Congressman William McKinley and three United States senators on the plat-

Right and opposite: An attractive pair of matching ribbons for the 1888 campaign.

form, several prominent Irish-American trade unionists extolled Harrison to a crowd of over ten thousand workingmen. The candidate, for once visibly upset, denounced liars and Democrats without making fine distinctions. He paid fulsome rhetorical tribute to "my fellow citizens of Irish nativity or descent."

Vituperation remained active to the very end, propelled by a serious last-minute Indiana Republican scandal. On October 31, the Democratic Indianapolis *Sentinel* published a facsimile of a letter signed by Republican National Committee treasurer W.W. Dudley, a close Harrison associate. Directed from New York headquarters at Indiana campaign leaders, it carried instructions for the organization and payment of "floaters," that is, votes for hire. Firestorms continued, the news filling the nation along the wire services. "FRAUD." "PLOT." "FORGERY." "DEBAUCHERY." The *Sentinel* went after its own townsman in language indicative of existing political emotions:

> Harrison has for years consorted with the worst gang of political prostitutes that ever disgraced an American state. . . . He has never disavowed, repudiated, denounced, or even mildly criticized a Republican rascal or a Republican fraud. . . . This talk of Benjamin Harrison's spotlessness and purity is disgusting in the extreme.

The Republican counter-offensive, led by the shaken Quay, relied on the shortness of time and the fullness of defensive bombast. Time ran out, and the emotionally drained electorate went to the polls.

Harrison lost the popular vote by about 91,000 (0.75 percent), won the electoral vote, 233 to 168, and went to the White House. Only New York and Indiana switched party preferences from 1884. In Indianapolis, the general's front porch exertions outweighed the Dudley "floater" letter. Quay's prescience regarding New York intrigue played out fully, as Hill kept the governorship for the Democrats but Harrison defeated Cleveland for the determining 36 vote electoral prize. The narrowness of the result is actually deceiving, since Democratic numbers were inflated by increased voting in the one-party South, and Republicans showed clear advances elsewhere. Yet even the victory itself is less significant than the means through which it was achieved. In this respect, the forces surrounding the 1888 Harrison-Cleveland struggle presaged major American political change in its merchandizing of the candidates.

Perhaps never before (but certainly ever since) had the images of political candidates been divorced so effectively from the colorless men themselves and their modest ideas and objectives. The late nineteenth-century marriage of industrial technology to advertising symbolism began the process of mass emotional political retailing. The hinterlands opened to political salesmanship.

The Republicans understood nationalism, industrialization, technology, and marketing, however imperfectly. Harrison himself claimed that "providence has given us the victory." Supposedly Quay retorted privately that Harrison "would never know how close a number of men were compelled to approach the penitentiary to make him President." Both misjudged their own efforts. Run from New York, the 1888 Republican campaign sent its message, in print and artifact, everywhere. In its exaggerated and gaudy packaging, it sold well.

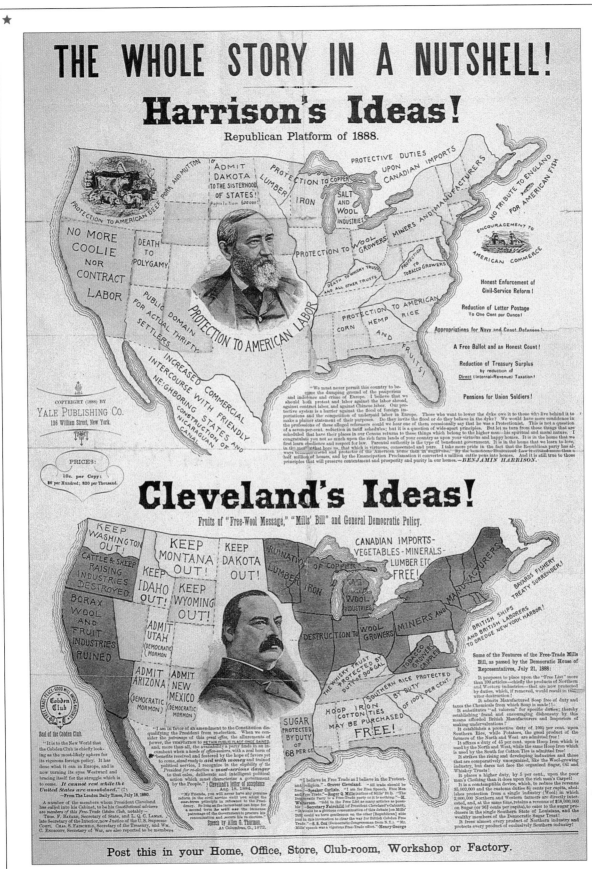

Comparative map print showing the Republican party's contemptuous view of Cleveland's tariff policies.

Sampling of badges from the 1888 campaign. Design variation was limited only by the manufacturer's imagination.

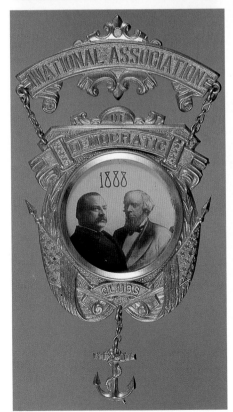

Bridle decorations featuring Harrison and Morton. Partisan equestrians could proclaim their support while riding.

Sampling of the many textiles available during the 1888 campaign. The Cleveland and Harrison cotton bandannas are perhaps the finest textile portraits ever manufactured.

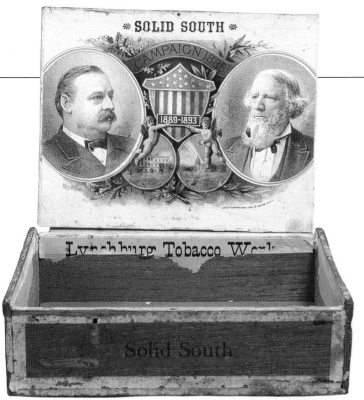

Cigar box from the 1888 campaign.

Campaign songster.

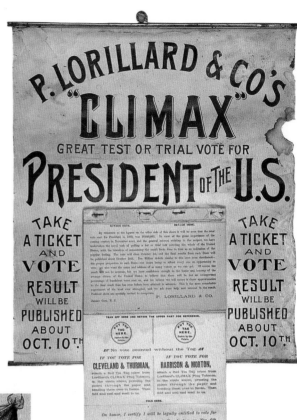

Pre-election poll. Participants had
to attach a proof of purchase from
Lorillard's Climax plug tobacco.

Tobacco cards from the 1888 campaign.

Hexagonal paper lantern from the 1888 campaign. The paneled paper designs were supported by an interior thin spring-wire frame.

Cotton apron commemorating the Centennial inauguration of Harrison.

Cloth-covered Harrison-Morton parade helmet.

Harrison paper-covered wooden whistle from the 1888 campaign.

Celluloid bookmark, circa 1892. Cleveland is pictured with Vice President Adlai Stevenson.

Below: Glass chimney detailed with acid-etched portraits of Harrison and Morton. Right: 1888 lithograph issued by an Ohio cigar manufacturer.

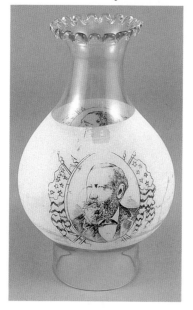

1888 advertisement card using a patented flag banner design.

Advertisement fan with portraits of Cleveland and Thurman.

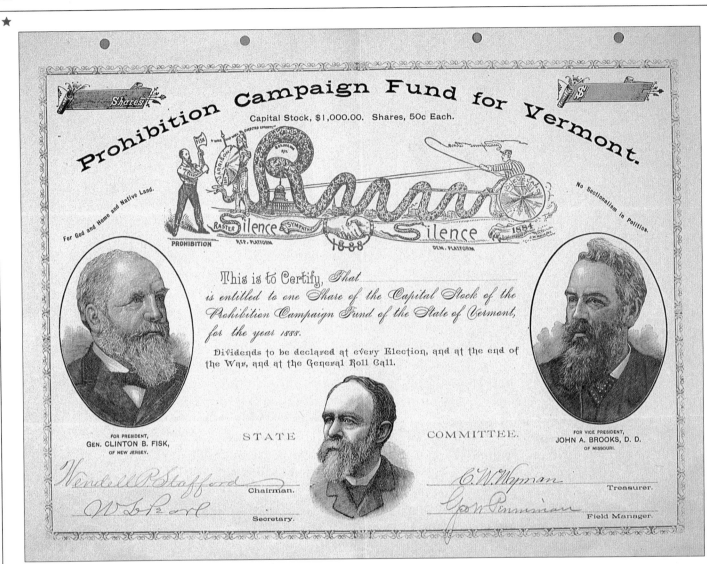

Stock certificate issued by the Vermont Prohibition party to raise $1,000 in fifty-cent shares. Clinton B. Fisk received 2.2 percent of the national vote in the 1888 election.

Pair of 1888 advertisement cards using patented designs.

Rare poster for the 1888 Union Labor candidates, Andrew J. Streeter and Charles Cunningham. They received 1.3 percent of the vote.

★

1892
44 STATES
IN THE UNION

DEMOCRAT
Grover Cleveland
ELECTORAL VOTE 277, POPULAR VOTE 46.1%

REPUBLICAN
Benjamin Harrison
ELECTORAL VOTE 145, POPULAR VOTE 43%

PEOPLE S PARTY
James Weaver
ELECTORAL VOTE 22, POPULAR VOTE 8.5%

PROHIBITION
John Bidwell
ELECTORAL VOTE 0, POPULAR VOTE 2.2%

ROBERT A. FRATKIN

is the author of *An Examination of Executive Privilege* (1965) and numerous articles on campaign history. He has been managing editor of the "APIC Keynoter," a journal of American political history since 1979, and has served as president of the American Political Items Collectors (1978–83).

In 1888 an honest Republican lawyer with a strong belief in Civil Service reform defeated the incumbent President, an honest Democratic lawyer with a strong belief in Civil Service reform. During their terms in office, both had ignored demands for patronage appointments and antagonized important politicians in their parties—men who actively sought to deny them renomination. In 1892, the President and the ex-President were to meet again, reargue the tariff and monetary issues, and face the challenge of a new political movement that appealed to elements in both the traditional parties.

Grover Cleveland left the White House in 1889 with a sense of relief, and returned to the practice of law. He then watched the Harrison administration commit what he considered to be one blunder after another. Chief among his disappointments was passage of the McKinley Tariff Bill in 1890, and the subsequent 12 percent rise in American tariffs. There was a large federal surplus when Cleveland left office; in three years, the Harrison administration had spent the surplus and was operating at a deficit.

With Cleveland apparently withdrawn from active politics, his successor as governor of New York, now U.S. senator, David B. Hill actively sought the Democratic nomination. But when the first ballot was taken at the Democratic convention in Chicago on June 21, Hill could not stop Cleveland from achieving the necessary two-thirds majority. After two ballots, Adlai Stevenson of Illinois,

a free silver advocate, received the vice presidential nomination. An unreconciled Hill left the convention convinced that Cleveland would eventually have to make peace on Hill's terms, and acknowledge his power to deliver the New York vote in November.

In the Republican party, Benjamin Harrison, the incumbent President, also faced a challenge to renomination. Though he had won enactment of the 1888 Republican platform's major goals, the McKinley Tariff Act, the Sherman Anti-Trust Act, and the Sherman Silver Purchase Act, voters in the midterm elections of 1890 returned Congress to the Democrats.

National and state Republican leaders were also keenly unhappy with Harrison as an individual. Thomas Collier Platt, a New York Republican leader, commented that the President was "as glacial as a Siberian stripped of his furs." Harrison particularly antagonized party professionals with his unexpected independence in patronage appointments, alienating House Speaker Thomas B. Reed, Mark Hanna (treasurer of the Republican National Committee), Matthew S. Quay (U.S. senator from Pennsylvania and chairman of the Republican National Committee during Harrison's first campaign), Platt and others. These men believed that Harrison would not be reelected, but that James G. Blaine could win.

Blaine never declared his candidacy, however, and the convention quickly nominated Harrison for a second term. Vice president Levi P. Morton, a more popular figure than the President, hoped for renomination. However, Morton's unwillingness to seek support, and a tradition of not renominating vice presidential candidates, resulted in the selection of longtime Platt opponent Whitelaw Reid, publisher of the *New York Tribune*, and, at that moment, minister to France.

The Republican platform supported the protective tariff, bimetallic coinage, and paper of equal debt-paying value. Its thorniest plank was the pledge to guarantee and protect "the integrity of the ballot and the purity of elections . . . in every state." Republican political strength in the South rested heavily on the black vote. After federal troops had been withdrawn, Democrats regained state and local control. In most southern states, new literacy and poll tax requirements effectively limited Negro voting. The Republican-sponsored Federal Elections Bill, introduced by Congressman Henry Cabot Lodge of Massachusetts, would have provided federal supervision for national elections, but was defeated in the Senate in 1890. The "force" bill was, however, an issue of great importance to the national Republican party, and became a major source of contention during the campaign.

Besides the Democrats and Republicans, "third parties" put forward candidates in 1892. These parties were encouraged by the recent adoption of the "Australian" secret ballot in thirty-five of the forty-four states. The newest, largest party was an outgrowth of the Grange movement.

The agricultural South, Midwest, and West had experienced great economic hardship. By 1892, crop prices had decreased dramatically and farm foreclosures were widespread. In the South, tenant farming and merchant credit arrangements gave economic control to local businessmen. In the West, farming, livestock, mineral development, and lumber industries were routinely victimized by predatory railroad rates and central business-owned facilities for processing, storage, and distribution.

In the 1890 congressional elections, the farmer's plight in the Midwest and South gave rise to a popular revolt against high tariffs, high interest rates, and low prices. Colonel L.L. Polk, president of the National Farmers Alliance, Mary Elizabeth Lease, William A. Peffer (who became senator from Kansas following the 1890 landslide), and other populist orators of the day had supported the Democrats in 1890. Mrs. Lease, "the Kansas Pythoness," incited Grange groups to political action, saying during one of 160 speeches she made in the congressional campaign of 1890, "What you farmers need to do is raise less corn and more Hell."

Populist leaders now contemplated a national political party. The organizing convention of the People's party met in Omaha, Nebraska, on July 4. No third-party convention ever had a broader representation of "the plain people who made America." Along with farm and labor groups, the convention included the Nationalist followers of Edward Bellamy, Henry George's Single Taxers, and Susan B. Anthony's feminists. In a stirring speech, Ignatius Donnelly contended that the republic had begun without millionaires or paupers, and now, after 116 years of major party government, there were over 8,000 millionaires and 1.5 million tramps; "the whole land is blistered with mortgages and the whole people are steeped . . . in poverty."

For many of the 1,300 delegates, this was more a religious experience than a political convention. After many speeches, and later during the reading of the platform, "Amens" could be heard throughout the hall. Union army General James B. Weaver, who had run for President on the Greenback party ticket in 1880, was overwhelmingly nominated as the People's party candidate in 1892. A former Confederate general, James G. Field of Virginia, became the vice presidential candidate in the closest vote of the convention.

The platform demanded free coinage of silver, the nationalization of railroads, telegraphs, and telephones, a national currency, and a graduated income tax. It also sought to void land grants to non-American citizens, railroads, and corporations.

Populists saw a conspiracy among the wealthy, the banks, the railroads, and the British to demonetarize silver in order to make European-held gold bonds more valuable and benefit the sinister "international gold ring." Both major parties, they charged, represented the same monetary interests, and would do nothing to help the plight of the "plain people."

The issues of the protective tariff versus free trade and bimetallism versus free coinage separated the three "national" parties. But other issues had more practical importance for state and local politicians and voters. For both Democrats and Republicans, the "force" bill and Negro voting rights dominated their approach to the South. Populists in the South faced a different dilemma. Although the national People's party sought southern electoral votes, many of its local supporters feared that the party might take enough votes from the Democrats to produce Republican victories and restore black voting strength.

Labor strife during the summer of 1892 was particularly violent. On June 29, ten died during a bloody confrontation between striking union workers and Pinkerton Agency "guards" at the Carnegie steel mills in Homestead, Pennsylvania. More blood was shed between striking silver miners and federal troops in Idaho, between coal miners and state militia in Tennessee, and between railway switchmen and state troops in Buffalo, New York. These events, cited repeatedly by Democrats and Populists for the rest of the campaign, dealt a stunning blow to Republican arguments that protectionist policies benefited labor, and cost Harrison needed votes in the industrial states.

Political frosted-glass figural bottles seldom contain such detail as this one of Cleveland.

1892 milkglass tumblers. Transfer portraits are of Harrison with Whitelaw Reid and Cleveland with Adlai Stevenson.

With Iowa, Wisconsin, and Illinois safely Republican in previous elections but now in doubt, both parties opened adjunct national headquarters in Chicago. Democrats discussed fusion slates with the Populists, whereby each party would nominate certain candidates for local offices and share presidential electors as a way to defeat the Republican candidates. The Chicago Democratic Headquarters Committee approved fusion wherever it met the needs of the local state committees.

Most campaign activities outside the largest cities were generated on the local level. Local units were responsible for rallies, parades, picnics, mass meetings, welcoming visiting dignitaries, and circulating campaign literature. Large open-mesh street banners with pictures of the candidates hung across Main Streets. Local political headquarters and businesses placed orders for colorful silk and cotton lapel ribbons imprinted with their names, candidate likenesses, and party slogans. Many ribbons bore dates, and were used for picnics, parades, and other specific events. Local headquarters displayed large portrait banners

and distributed brass shell badges, ribbons, posters, sheet music, and other campaign paraphernalia. The musical hit of the campaign was "Baby Ruth and Baby McKee," a song about Cleveland's popular young daughter and Harrison's grandson.

Both Democrats and Republicans established ethnic committees. In New York, the Democratic party organized the Irish-American Democratic Union and the German-American Cleveland Union. The Harrison campaign, through the Irish-American Republican Clubs, emphasized the President's warm reception for the papal delegate sent from Rome to the Chicago World's Fair. The Democrats countered with a letter from Mrs. Delia Parnell, mother of the Irish patriot, recommending that true Irishmen vote for Cleveland.

In both parties, however, campaign organization in New York, a key state, was delayed by rancor left over from the pre-convention period. Efforts to heal these rifts continued well into the campaign.

Reconciliation in New York, with thirty-six electoral votes, was particularly difficult for Cleveland. With a large "Cleveland and Stevenson" electric sign outside the hall, the Democratic party held its notification ceremony in front of eighteen thousand Cleveland supporters at Madison Square Garden on July 20. This was a break from traditional notification ceremonies, small gatherings at which a committee from the national convention officially informed the candidate that he had been nominated.

This public event did not solve the party's problems. Not only did Cleveland have to mollify David B. Hill and Tammany, he also had to satisfy his own most enthusiastic followers, who would be alienated by concessions to the regular Democrats. William C. Whitney, his campaign manager, believed that Cleveland would certainly retain his original supporters; they had few alternatives. To succeed, Whitney insisted, the candidate had to make peace with those who had opposed him for the nomination. "It's no use to say not to trust any of them," Whitney warned. "We have got to trust them; they have an organization and the power . . . (and are indispensable to victory)." His strategy was to co-opt people around Hill so that Hill would either join the campaign or break with his allies. Whitney had succeeded in making peace with Tammany Hall's Richard Croker, and persuaded Cleveland to accept Lieutenant Governor William Sheehan, an old enemy, as chairman of the state campaign committee.

Cleveland met with Croker and Sheehan on September 8 over dinner. Cleveland asked how the campaign was going. Sheehan, very unpleasantly, said it was not going well. He complained that the pro-Cleveland newspapers were attacking him and the Tammany leaders in intolerable terms. He demanded that Cleveland put an end to these attacks, and agree, if elected, to give the New York organization more patronage than he had in his previous administration. Cleveland swore that he would give no such pledge. When asked what he would do instead, Cleveland said,

> I will appeal from the machine to the people. This very night I will issue a declaration to the electors of the state telling them the proposition you have made to me and the reasons why I am not able to accept it. I will ask them to choose between us. Such is my confidence in the people that before the week ends I believe that your machine will be in revolution against you.

The confrontation worked, forcing the regular Democratic organization to look at its alternatives and realize that joining the campaign was its only viable choice. Bowing to Cleveland's resolve, Hill made his first public appearance in support of the Democratic ticket in Brooklyn on September 19.

Tammany showed its unity with the ticket by distributing thousands of "pasters," a printed list of electors and candidates to be pasted on ballots in order to assure a straight party vote. Tammany's best orator, William Bourke Cockran, who had asked the convention in Chicago not to "invade New York" by nominating Cleveland, offered his services and was immediately dispatched to states as far west as Indiana. On October 25, Tammany held the largest public gathering of the campaign, with Hill appearing in support of the ticket.

Republicans too faced the nettlesome problem of party unity. After the convention, Blaine had issued a brief statement in favor of Harrison's reelection. Party leaders considered this insufficient, and finally, on October 13, Blaine assured them of his commitment to Harrison's reelection. The next night, in his only public speech of the campaign, he called on Irish-Americans to support Harrison as a way to advance the cause of Irish independence.

The People's party nominee, General Weaver, opened his campaign in Des Moines, Iowa. His appearances drew increasingly enthusiastic responses in the western silver states, where Democrats sought to form fusion tickets. Unofficial fusion was agreed upon in Oregon, Nevada, Minnesota, and Nebraska; Kansas and North Dakota fielded sanctioned fusion tickets. In Colorado and

Idaho, free-silverites dominated the Democratic party and offered full support to the Populists, putting up no candidates of their own. Meanwhile, Republicans were busy in the South forming secret alliances with the Populists in most states; only in Louisiana was there a formal fusion ticket.

To counteract the popularity of Weaver and the Populists, southern Democrats emphasized the dangers of the "force" bill and of black dominance should the Republicans win. "Just to think—a Negro to be armed; whites and blacks to mix in the same schools by compulsion and to be brought into close and equal relations . . . and abolition of the laws against inter-marriage of whites and blacks. Let our misguided brethren who are following Weaver . . . and others of that ilk look this squarely in the face. Vote for the South and for liberty."

In September, victories in five early southern state elections calmed the Democratic fears. The Republicans, seeing their potential for success in the South fade, were also troubled by the fusion tickets in the western states. Worse still, mid-month presidential elections in Maine and Vermont showed a lower than expected Republican vote. By month end, both parties realized that New York, New Jersey, Connecticut, and Indiana were critical. During the fall registration drives, each side accused the other of fraud; evidence suggests that both were right.

In October, the American Protective Tariff League distributed more than one million "poetical patty-pans" bearing the inscription "Harrison-Reid and Protection," supposedly made from American tinplate. The Democratic Campaign Committee responded by distributing rectangular pieces of metal in the shape of a small sardine-can lid, with portraits of Stevenson and Cleveland on one side, and on the other, statements claiming that the Republican tinplate pan had been made from imported British steel and coated with Australian tinplate using machinery imported from Britain.

Indiana was the most ardently contested state outside of New York. Yet a *New York Herald* reporter noted the almost complete absence of the usual campaign hoopla, "the old time big wagons with red, white and blue trimmings, and girls all in white." Indiana was becoming an increasingly industrial state, and the pivotal issue was the tariff. Both Whitelaw Reid and Adlai Stevenson entered the state in the last weeks of the campaign. Stevenson, with his strong voice and commanding presence, was considered the best Democratic orator. On one occasion, he addressed a crowd of sixty thousand in Shelbyville. In Illinois, Republicans countered native-son Stevenson with Robert Todd Lincoln, the son of the martyred Republican President.

Cleveland restricted his public appearances, making only four speeches to large audiences. Unable to use President Harrison because of his wife's prolonged illness and death in October, the Republican campaign relied on Whitelaw Reid, Chauncey Depew, Thomas B. Reed, Senator John Sherman, Governor McKinley, and Senator Quay to appear on his behalf. McKinley, the best known noncandidate speaker for Harrison, made several lengthy trips, speaking from Iowa to Maine.

On the Saturday night before the election, Cleveland reviewed a parade of over 40,000 enthusiastic marchers, arranged by the New York Businessmen's Cleveland and

Stevenson Club. Over 300,000 spectators were said to have viewed the event.

In summing up the political season, the *New York Herald* commented on "an unprecedented absence of noisy demonstrations, popular excitement, and that high pressure enthusiasm which used to find vent in brass bands, drum and trumpet fanfaronade, boisterous parades by day and torchlight processions by night, vociferous hurrahs, campaign songs, barbecues and what not."

It was estimated that the national Democratic party spent $2.35 million in the 1892 campaign, $800,000 more than the Republicans, and probably the largest expenditure up to that time to elect a President. Both Harrison and Cleveland were well known to voters as men of integrity who disagreed on complex issues. Most of the money was spent on books, pamphlets, leaflets, and other efforts to educate the electorate about the differences. The People's party campaign, lacking industry or banking support, was almost entirely financed by "passing the hat" at public meetings.

The campaign closed on a quiet note. This had not been a time of high excitement, candidate vilification, or critical turning points. The only real fervor was generated by the Populists. Voters would now answer the remaining questions—the effect of fusion tickets in the western and southern states, the impact of the "force" bill in the southern states, and economic concerns over Republican tariffs in the industrial states.

Election day, November 8, 1892, found good weather across the nation. Voting was noticeably less disorderly than in previous elections, credited by many to the use of the secret ballot in most states.

Lithographed Harrison 1892 tin shell button.

Party officials on all sides found less evidence of bribery, voter coercion, and partisan fistfights. In Wyoming, women voted for the first time in a presidential election, while in the South, newly enacted poll tax and literacy requirements took over 30 percent of the white voters and over 90 percent of the Negro voters off the rolls. In Lockport, New Yorkers used the first mechanical voting machines.

When the votes were counted, the Democrats, for the first time since 1858, controlled the presidency, the Senate and the House of Representatives. Cleveland had won New York, the South, the "doubtful" states of Wisconsin and Illinois, five other states, and five of 14 electoral votes in Michigan—for a total of 277 out of 444 votes in the electoral college. Harrison received 145, and Weaver, who polled over one million votes, only 22. Grover Cleveland gained the distinction of being both the 22nd and 24th U.S. President, and Benjamin Harrison, to his embarrassment, not only lost Indiana, his home state, but also his home county of Marion.

An 1892 election day medal portraying Mr. and Mrs. Cleveland with their daughter. The candy bar, Baby Ruth, was named for her.

Tobacco advertisment card with woven silk ribbons of President and Mrs. Cleveland.

1892 anti-Cleveland satirical paper currency.

Salesmen's paper cigar box label.

Advertisement cards portraying the Clevelands and domestic themes.

Centerfold from Judge magazine, a Republican weekly. This and its Democratic counterpart, Puck, featured superb satirical cartoons on almost every issue of the day.

Metal plaque with reverse-painted glass portraits of Harrison and Reid.

Glass paperweight with Republican slogans and portraits of Harrison and Reid.

An 1892 pocket game.

An 1892 advertisement card asking the crucial question.

Glass whiskey flask with portraits and slogan "OUR CHOICE CLEVE & STEVE."

Cedar cigar boxes with bold lettering.

Selection of ribbons and bandannas from the 1892 campaign. The slogans are a wonderful example of how each party attempted to convey its message to the electorate. The People's party ribbon is rare.

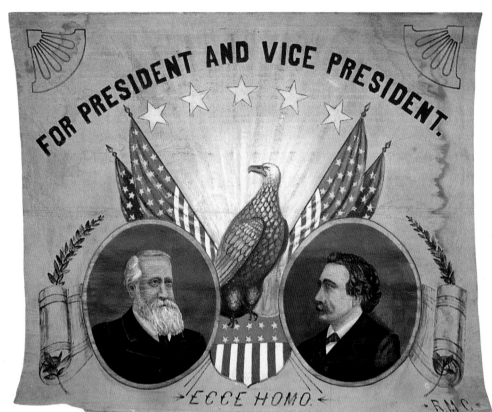

Large hand-painted banner. An example of American folk art, banners of this type were made by local artists for rallies.

Campaign poster.

Metallic lapel studs. The "force" bill, which passed the House in June 1890, provided for federal supervision of elections to protect black voters in the South.

Inaugural program, March 4, 1893.

Silk inaugural ribbon.
Thomas Nast created
the Tammany tiger.

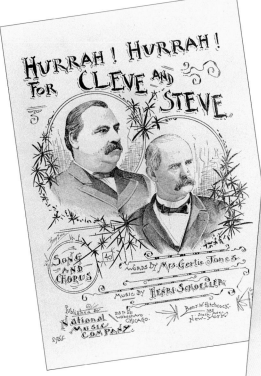

Campaign sheet music.
Example on right
features Cleveland's
daughter and Harrison's
grandson, Baby McKee.

★

1896

45 STATES
IN THE UNION

REPUBLICAN

William McKinley

ELECTORAL VOTE 271, POPULAR VOTE 51.1%

DEMOCRAT

William J. Bryan

ELECTORAL VOTE 176, POPULAR VOTE 47.7%

DONALD A. RITCHIE
is associate historian in the Senate Historical
Office and an adjunct faculty member of the
Cornell in Washington program. His books
include *James M. Landis: Dean of the Regulators*
(1980); *Press Gallery: Congress and the
Washington Correspondents* (1991); and a high
school textbook, *History of a Free Nation* (1991).

Silver and gold dazzled the depression-weary voters of 1896. Both the Democratic and Republican candidates promoted currency reform as a solution to the nation's economic crisis, reversing their parties' historic positions. While the incumbent Democratic President Grover Cleveland clung to the gold standard for stability and fairness to creditors, his party rushed to embrace the coinage of silver to stimulate inflation and ease the burden of debtors. On the Republican side, the front-running contender William McKinley preferred to straddle the currency issue by continuing his support of bimetallism, but conceded to the demands of his party's gold standard advocates. When easterners hammered a strong gold-standard plank into the Republican platform, western silverites marched out of the convention in protest. Above in the press box, a tall, young former congressman, now reporting for the Omaha *World-Herald*, climbed upon a desk for a better view of their departure. None of the Republican delegates could have suspected that within three weeks this "interested spectator," William Jennings Bryan, would become the Democratic presidential candidate, under the banner of free silver.

For parades, passions, and the percentage of eligible voters that it attracted to the polls, the campaign of 1896 outdid all others. Its opposing candidates stood in sharp contrast. McKinley was a son of Ohio, the "mother of presidents," and at fifty-three a conventionally conservative politician. A generation younger at thirty-six, Bryan represented the frontier state of Nebraska and dynamic new forces in politics. McKinley, however, had the additional asset of a brilliant campaign manager, Marcus Alonzo Hanna. A coal and iron industrialist from Cleveland, Hanna had raised funds and campaigned for local Republican candidates for decades without earning much notice within his party—until he determined to make McKinley President.

Civil War veteran William McKinley chaired the powerful House Ways and Means Committee and gave his name to the Protective Tariff of 1890. Blaming the McKinley tariff for higher prices, voters that year swept the Republicans out of their congressional majorities and McKinley out of his House seat. Then the economic depression of 1893 shifted voter anger onto the Democrats, resurrecting the status of both the tariff and its namesake. McKinley was a pragmatic politician, highly skilled in the arts of accommodation. One newspaper reporter observed that McKinley's pronounced eyebrows gave his photographs a sternness that this "gentle, kindly disposed man" lacked. Gregarious but "no glad-hander," he had a calm demeanor and subdued sense of humor, attributes that helped him defeat his rival for the nomination, the powerful Speaker of the House Thomas B. Reed, whose wit and biting sarcasm made people uncomfortable, even as they laughed.

With eastern gold standard Republicans favoring Speaker Reed, and "favorite son" candidates holding other delegate blocs, Hanna looked to the southern delegations as the key to the nomination. During the winter of 1895, Hanna rented a house in Georgia, where he and his candidate wooed southern Republicans with promises of future federal patronage. Having secured a majority on the Republican National Committee, which would decide contested seats at the convention, Hanna advised southern party leaders to act as arbitrarily as necessary to elect McKinley delegates. When their opponents bolted and formed separate delegations, the National Committee by wide margins rejected the "bolters" in favor of McKinley's "regulars." This southern strategy netted almost two hundred delegates, a third of McKinley's total, and caused Speaker Reed's unnerved campaign manager to admit to the press that McKinley would be nominated on the first ballot—as he was.

After the convention, Hanna planned a vacation cruise before he returned to run an educational, business-like campaign as chairman of the Republican National Committee. McKinley and Hanna anticipated that their Democratic opponent would be Richard Bland, author of the Bland-Allison Act for limited coinage of silver, and a man as bland as his name. This scenario evaporated when William Jennings Bryan rose to speak in favor of a free silver plank at the Democratic convention. Silver was "a cause as holy as the cause of liberty—the cause of humanity," Bryan declared in a magnificent baritone voice that filled the convention hall without amplification. He called for another Andrew Jackson to speak for "the common people" against organized wealth. Employing the rhetoric of the populist farm movement, he warned urban America: "destroy our farms and the grass will grow in the streets of every city in the country." And he concluded by hurling a powerful metaphor against the opponents of silver: "You shall not press down upon the brow of labor this crown of thorns, you shall not crucify mankind upon a cross of gold."

Bryan stood before the convention with his head hung down and arms outstretched in the image of a crucifixion. For a moment the huge hall remained silent, then "bedlam broke loose, delirium reigned supreme." The *Washington Post*'s correspondent described the yells as "so deafening that only at irregular intervals could the music of the noisy band be heard, the stamping of the feet was as the roll of thunder." The next day, on the fifth ballot, the Democratic presidential nomination went to Bryan.

Bryan's triumph disrupted all the other parties. Taken by surprise, Hanna canceled his vacation plans to revamp Republican strategy. The Prohibitionist party split over free silver, and the Populist party fell reluctantly into ranks behind Bryan. Populist delegates hated to tie their party to Bryan's kite, but the professional politicians among them steered the convention toward fusion. In a futile gesture to preserve what was left of their separate identity, the Populists nominated their own vice presidential candidate, Tom Watson of Georgia. The breakaway silver Republicans nominated Bryan; while gold-standard Cleveland Democrats formed a national Democratic party and ran their own candidate.

Few prominent Democrats would campaign for Bryan, nor did many large newspapers endorse him. Such traditionally Democratic papers as the *New York World, Boston Globe*, and *Louisville Courier-Journal* sided with the financial markets against the Democratic candidate. One notable exception was the *New York Journal,* whose publisher, William Randolph Hearst, opposed free silver but endorsed Bryan as a man of the people. Hearst's editorial cartoonist, Homer Davenport, gave the campaign the unforgettable image of "Dollar Mark Hanna," dressed in a checkered suit covered with dollar signs, manipulating a pygmy McKinley. The Dollar Mark cartoons propelled Davenport to fame, diminished McKinley's public image, and wounded Hanna's feelings. Mrs. Hanna hated Davenport "worse than snakes."

Lacking an outlet in the major metropolitan press, and without funds to carry on extensive advertising, an undaunted Bryan took his campaign to the people through a vigorous speaking schedule across the nation. Reporters described Bryan's rear platform oratorical style as "intimate, easy, and colloquial." He spoke in short sentences, using plain words of few syllables. He made his points briefly and drove them home effectively. Biblical quotations and parables scattered throughout his remarks always brought cheers from his audiences. The tremendous crowds convinced Bryan he was going to win.

Bryan's success on the stump made Mark Hanna talk fretfully of sending McKinley out as well, but his candidate rejected the idea. "I might just as well put up a trampoline on my front lawn and compete with some professional athlete as go out speaking against Bryan," McKinley protest-

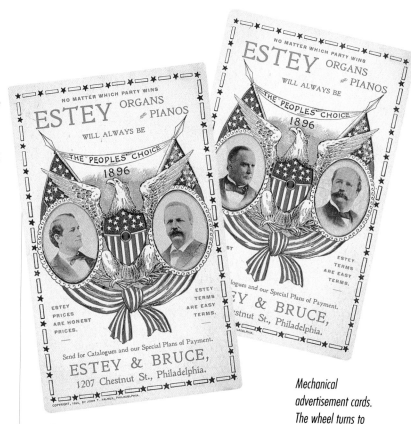

Mechanical advertisement cards. The wheel turns to show "THE PEOPLE'S CHOICE."

ed. "I have to *think* when I speak." He preferred to read his speeches and even edited the remarks of the leaders of visiting delegations, to avoid indiscreet or divisive references. While he lacked Bryan's dynamism, McKinley possessed a "mesmeric quality" that captured audiences. As celebrated an orator as Wisconsin's Robert La Follette, Sr., rated McKinley "a magnetic speaker" with a "clear, bell-like voice."

McKinley opened his official campaign exactly where he would remain until election day, on his bunting-covered front porch in Canton, Ohio. From that fixed point, McKinley awaited the hundreds of delegations that traveled to Canton by train (at inexpensive excursion rates), and paraded to his home, all carefully scheduled. The candidate delivered set speeches interspersed with personal references to each of the delegations of farmers, laborers, merchants, and church members that crowded onto his lawn. They totaled an estimated 750,000— more than a tenth of all McKinley voters in the election.

McKinley felt more comfortable talking about tariffs than currency, where his position was less than clear. In Congress, he had voted with bimetallists to override Rutherford B. Hayes's veto of the Bland-Allison bill. While he accepted a gold plank in the platform, he balanced it with a pledge to seek an international agreement on silver, highly unlikely as that was. Friendly reporters counseled McKinley that Bryan had made free silver "practically the only issue of the campaign," and urged him to declare unequivocally against silver. At the end of July, while addressing a Pennsylvania delegation, McKinley proclaimed: "Our currency today is good—all of it as good as gold— and it is the unfaltering determination of the Republican Party to so keep and maintain it forever." Republicans drew a collective sigh of relief, for their candidate at last had said "gold."

Although bowing to gold, McKinley tied it to the themes of protection, prosperity, and patriotism. "I am glad to know that this year is going to be a year of patriotism and devotion to country," McKinley told visiting delegations; "that the people of the country this year mean to maintain the financial honor of the country as sacredly as they maintain the honor of the flag." Delegates wore gold bug lapel pins, and women carried red, white, and blue umbrellas. Hanna also called for all Americans to participate in a national "Flag Day" just before the election, causing Illinois's radical Governor John Peter Altgeld to denounce the McKinley campaign for having "prostituted the American flag to the level of an advertising medium."

Since the Northeast stood solidly Republican, and the South and West were Bryan's territory, both parties looked to the Midwest. Hanna opened an office in Chicago to coordinate publicity and speakers. While McKinley stayed in Canton, the Republican speakers bureau paid 1,400 speakers to stump the nation, and to follow Bryan's campaign train from stop to stop. Republican publicity agents distributed some 200 million pamphlets, many in German, Swedish, French, Spanish, Italian, Norwegian, Finnish, Dutch, and Hebrew. Speeches, booklets, posters, and slogans poured out of the Republican headquarters, boosting McKinley as "The Advance Agent of Prosperity" and promising "A Full Dinner Pail" after his election.

Mark Hanna had paid for McKinley's preconvention expenses, $100,000 out of pocket, and took personal charge of raising funds for the campaign. Contributions came from Democratic as well as Republicans bankers and businessmen, appalled by Bryan's free silver platform and rabble-rousing campaign. Reports surfaced through-

Celluloid campaign button with a Bryan caricature. The celluloid pinback button was patented prior to the 1896 campaign.

Metal pins with gold and silver coin motifs.

out the campaign that employers were threatening to reduce wages or cut jobs if Bryan won. To counter charges of intimidation, Republicans organized enormous working-class parades under McKinley's banner. The overwhelming labor vote for McKinley suggested that workers saw his victory in their self interest. As Senator Henry Teller, leader of the silver Republicans, regretfully concluded, "If I were a working man and had nothing but my job, I am afraid when I came to vote I would think of Mollie and the babies."

Bryan's single theme of free silver offered little to labor, but it was the only issue that held together disparate followers from three parties, and inflamed their passions. Occasionally he addressed other issues in the Democratic platform, notably his opposition to federal intervention in labor strikes. The danger came not from small lawbreakers, he asserted, but from "men who think that they are greater than the Government." He promised to enforce antitrust laws and to appoint Supreme Court justices opposed to trusts. Bryan also took pains to explain why some of his agrarian supporters blamed their economic woes on international Jewish bankers. By denouncing the Rothschilds, he assured Jewish Democrats: "We are not attacking a race; we are attacking greed and avarice, which know neither race nor religion."

Mark Hanna's counterpart, Democratic National Committee chairman James K. Jones, also set up offices in Chicago. But Jones lacked Hanna's tactical genius and cooperative candidate. Bryan, he later reminisced, "was a law unto himself." Senator Jones needed to rebuild the Democratic committee after the departure of the gold Democrats and their campaign contributions. Tight finances especially restricted the production of campaign literature. Bryan's organizational support stemmed less from the party apparatus than from a network of free silver clubs, particularly in rural districts. Since Bryan was running on the Democratic, Populist, and Silver Republican tickets, the clubs attracted a multipartisan membership. Club members paraded enthusiastically and provided eager audiences for free silver speakers. The clubs also raised money by selling free silver pamphlets, notably William Hope Harvey's *Coin's Financial School*, an immensely popular booklet featuring a young savant who lectured leading financiers on the wisdom of bimetallism.

The 16:1 ratio of silver to gold provided Bryan's supporters the symbolism for their pageantry. At one stop the candidate rode in a carriage drawn by sixteen white horses and one yellow horse. At others he would be greeted by sixteen young women dressed in white, and one in yellow, or presented with similar mixes in chrysanthemums. Well wishers pressed on Bryan lucky coins, gold-headed canes, a silver watch, and an inkstand shaped like a stack of sixteen silver dollars, with a gold coin as its lid handle.

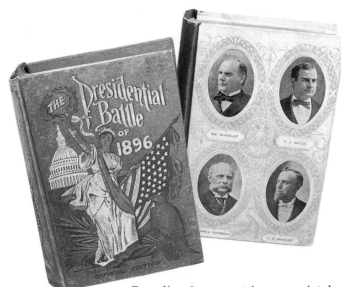

Political campaign books. This type of book was hastily written and padded with speeches and campaign proceedings.

Traveling in a most inappropriately named railroad car, the "Idler," Bryan conducted a punishing campaign. On a single day in Michigan, he spoke—without benefit of the public address systems of a later age—in Muskegon, Holland, Fennville, Bangor, Hartford, Watervliet, Benton Harbor, Niles, Dowagiac, Decatur, Lawrence, Kalamazoo, Battle Creek, Marshall, Albion, Jackson, Leslie, Mason, and Lansing, delivering a total of twenty-five speeches, and finishing near midnight. Desperately afraid of losing his voice, he employed various remedies to soothe his throat after speaking, and catnapped whenever possible between stops. Bryan ended his national tour on election day in Lincoln, Nebraska, where the "Bryan Home Guards" escorted him to vote. For one hundred days he had traveled sixteen thousand miles and given six hundred speeches to an estimated five million listeners. Yet these prodigious personal efforts could not overcome the machine that McKinley and Hanna had constructed.

Although Bryan concentrated on the Midwest, he did not carry such critical states as Wisconsin, Illinois, and Indiana, which Cleveland had won four years earlier. The *New York World* offered a plausible explanation for his failure in the midwestern farm states, noting that the price of wheat had risen from sixty-four to eighty-two cents a bushel the month before the election. Midwestern wheat farmers could see the end of the depression—which they blamed less on eastern industrialists than on farmers farther west who were flooding the markets and depressing prices.

Nevertheless, currency and economics remained the dominant issues of the campaign. When the *Chicago Record* polled voters it found similar breakdowns in both parties. In their sample, 41 percent of Bryan's voters cited free silver as the most important issue, while 40 percent of McKinley's supporters listed sound money. Smaller percentages of Bryanites cited the income tax, the restoration of prosperity, and opposition to the government's antilabor policies. Only one percent supported Bryan out of traditional Democratic loyalties. Among other Republicans the protective tariff, the needs of farmers and workers, a demand to suppress disorders in the states, and a dislike of Bryan's class-oriented campaigning spurred voters. Only 2 percent said they voted for McKinley because they always leaned Republican.

William Allen White, the Kansas editor, believed that the election had divided the nation between creditors and debtors. "McKinley won because the Republicans had persuaded the middle class, almost to a man, that a threat to the gold standard was a threat to their property." If McKinley appealed to the middle class, Bryan failed to attract the labor vote on his appeal of haves versus have-nots. Labor feared that Bryan's election would shut down the factories, and the Democrats could not overcome their image as the party of the "empty dinner pail." Even farmers, Bryan's core constituency, divided between the needier westerners and more prosperous midwesterners. Moreover, Bryan's rural America was dwindling; only two decades later the census would show a majority of the population living in urban areas.

The election marked the end of one political era and the beginning of another. After a generation of partisan stalemate, the Republicans now claimed a solid electoral majority. The currency issue became irrelevant when new discoveries of gold in South Africa and the Yukon brought about through gold the inflated currency that the silver movement had promised. New demands for agricultural products from Europe and America's growing cities stimulated a generation of farm prosperity. The middle and upper classes, frightened by Bryan and the Populists, began to move toward a new progressive reform movement that expropriated and enacted into law much of Bryan's platform. At the same time, partisan display diminished. After 1896, marching clubs and torchlight parades became less common, along with the use of floats, banners, glee clubs, brass bands, all-day rallies, and other nineteenth-century devices to stimulate voter enthusiasm.

When the cheering stopped, McKinley went to the White House to become a beloved and martyred President. Bryan, in losing his election, won a higher total and a higher percentage of the votes cast in 1896 than would elect Woodrow Wilson in 1912. He lost two more campaigns for the presi-

Brass stickpin. The Republican party, both in 1896 and 1900, appealed to laborers with the "Full Dinner Pail" slogan. Reference is to benefits derived from the protective tariff.

dency and spent the rest of his life as a troubadour in search of a crowd and an issue as congenial as free silver. Still, his first battle won widespread admiration even from such unlikely sources as Nannie Lodge, wife of Senator Henry Cabot Lodge, the author of the Republican gold standard plank. "The great fight is won," she wrote to a British friend after the election:

> . . . a fight conducted by trained and experienced and organized forces, with both hands full of money, with the power of the press—and of prestige—on one side: on the other, a disorganized mob at first, out of which burst into sight, hearing, and force—one man, but such a man! Alone, penniless, without backing, without money, with scarce a paper, without speakers, that man fought such a fight that even those in the East can call him a Crusader, an inspired fanatic—a prophet! It has been marvelous. . . . We had during the last week of the campaign 18,000 speakers on the stump. He alone spoke for his party, but speeches which spoke to the intelligence and hearts of the people, and with a capital P. It is over now, but the vote is 7 millions to 6 millions and a half.

Campaign sheet music.

Cotton bandannas with
major slogans of each party.

Metal matchsafes with
McKinley and Bryan.

Castiron McKinley bootjack.

Desktop metal match holder. The wings, originally silver, lift.

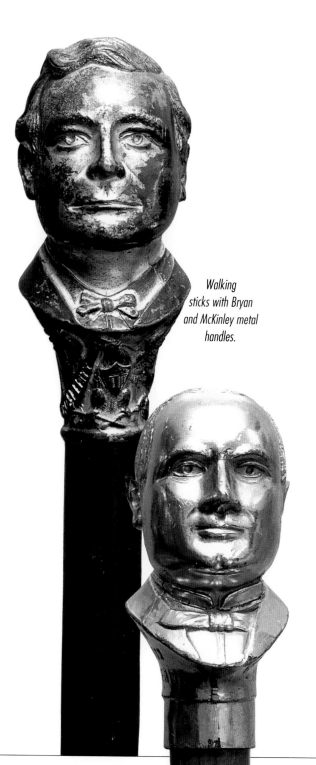

Walking sticks with Bryan and McKinley metal handles.

Porcelain campaign lapel studs.

Mechanical badges which open to reveal the candidates' portraits. Note that McKinley items are gold and the Bryan items are silver.

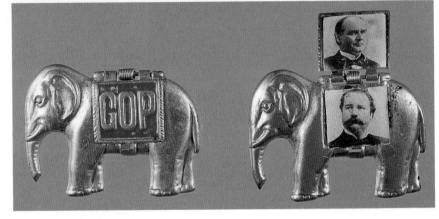

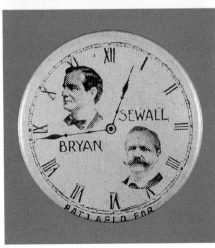

Bryan celluloid buttons. The currency issue dominated this campaign and is so reflected in the artifacts.

Paper hat issued by a Boston newspaper. Folded another way, it displays McKinley.

Cotton bandanna with slogan "THE POOR MAN'S CANDIDATES."

Campaign button with paraphrase of the concluding sentence in Bryan's speech of July 8, 1896, "The Cross of Gold."

Glass whiskey flask with Republican "Sound Money" slogan. Far right: Glass candle lantern with acid-etched portraits of Bryan and Sewall.

THE LOCKOUT IS ENDED; HE HOLDS THE KEY.

McKinley poster stressing the 1896 economic themes. The gold key will unlock prosperity.

Silk flag banner of McKinley and Hobart.

Silk ribbon with Republican slogans.

Mechanical campaign card predicting Republican prosperity as opposed to Democratic economic ruin.

Wooden gold key. An inaugural souvenir sold in Washington, D.C.

Satirical mechanical "broken dollar" comparing the prosperity of sound money with the economic ruin of free silver. Front and back views.

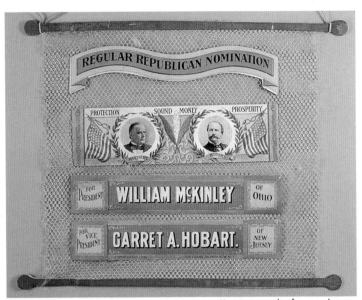

Miniature sample of a street banner.

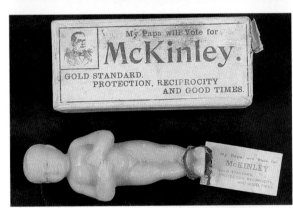

Soap baby proclaiming "My papa will vote for McKinley."

McKinley campaign umbrella.

McKinley cane with a gold handle.

Ceramic
plate and
milkglass pitcher
with photographic images.

Gold-painted metal mantel clock
with shipping and industry themes.

Republican ribbon badge from McKinley's
hometown, Canton, Ohio.
Picture is of Mrs. Ida McKinley.